PETER IN THE GOSPEL OF JOHN

Society of Biblical Literature

Academia Biblica

Steven L. McKenzie,
Hebrew Bible/Old Testament Editor

Sharon H. Ringe,
New Testament Editor

Number 27

PETER IN THE GOSPEL OF JOHN
The Making of an Authentic Disciple

PETER IN THE GOSPEL OF JOHN
The Making of an Authentic Disciple

Bradford B. Blaine, Jr.

Society of Biblical Literature
Atlanta

PETER IN THE GOSPEL OF JOHN
The Making of an Authentic Disciple

Copyright © 2007 by the Society of Biblical Literature

All rights reserved. No part of this work may be reproduced or transmitted in any form or by any means, electronic or mechanical, including photocopying and recording, or by means of any information storage or retrieval system, except as may be expressly permitted by the 1976 Copyright Act or in writing from the publisher. Requests for permission should be addressed in writing to the Rights and Permissions Office, Society of Biblical Literature, 825 Houston Mill Road, Atlanta, GA 30329, USA.

Library of Congress Cataloging-in-Publication Data

Blaine, Brad, 1960–
  Peter in the Gospel of John / Brad Blaine, Jr.
     p. cm. — (Society of Biblical Literature Academia Biblica ; no. 27)
  Includes bibliographical references.
  ISBN 978-1-58983-272-5 (paper binding)
  1. Peter, the Apostle, Saint. 2 Bible. N.T. John—Criticism, interpretation, etc. I. Title.

BS2615.52.B53 2007
226.5'092—dc22
[B]   2007008568

Printed in the United States of America
on acid-free paper

TABLE OF CONTENTS

Acknowledgements	ix
Abbreviations	xi
Chapter 1. Introduction	1
Peter in the Gospel of John: Why Ask the Question?	1
Methodology	4
Survey of Scholarship	7
Peter as the Beloved Disciple's Subordinate	8
Peter as the Beloved Disciple's Equal	18
Summary	22
Peter and the Twelve	23
John and the Synoptics	25
Identity of the Beloved Disciple	26
Chapter 2. Peter's Call, Naming, and Confession	29
Introduction: Peter in John 1–6	29
The Call of the First Disciples: 1:35–40	30
Peter Meets Jesus: 1:40–42	33
Peter's Confession: 6:66–71	39
Conclusion	50
Excursus: Johannine-Matthean Parallels in Peter's Call, Naming, and Confession	52
Chapter 3. The Footwashing, The Prediction of the Denials, and Peter's Promise to Follow Jesus	57
Introduction: Peter in John 13	57
Jesus Prepares to Wash the Disciples' Feet: 13:1–5	59
Peter's Reaction to the Footwashing: 13:6–11	62
Curiosity About the Traitor: 13:21–26	69
Peter's Promise to Follow Jesus: 13:33–38	74
Conclusion	78
Chapter 4. Swordplay and Denials	81
Introduction: Peter in John 18	81
Jesus and the Disciples in the Garden: 18:1–9	82
Swordplay: 18:10–11	84
The Three Denials: 18:15–27	90

Arrival at the Courtyard and the First Denial: 18:15–17	91
The Second and Third Denials: 18:25–27	98
Conclusion	101

Chapter 5. The Race to the Empty Tomb — 105
    Introduction: Peter in John 20 — 105
    Mary Magdalene Reports to Peter and the Beloved
        Disciple: 20:1–2 — 107
    The Footrace: 20:3–5 — 110
    Entry into the Tomb: 20:6–10 — 115
    Conclusion — 122

Chapter 6. John 21 as Gospel Supplement — 127
    Introduction: The Place of John 21 in the Fourth Gospel — 127
    Reasons for Ascribing John 21 to a Redactor — 129
        The Double Ending: 21:1–25 // 20:28–31 — 129
        Changes in Structure and Language — 132
        New Images and Themes — 135
    Conclusion — 141

Chapter 7. The Fishing Expedition and the Miraculous Catch Of Fish — 143
    Introduction: Peter in John 21:1–11 — 143
    Disaster at Sea: 21:1–3 — 143
    A Change in Fortune: 21:4–6 — 147
    Peter and the Beloved Disciple Take
        Center Stage: 21:7–8 — 149
    Missionary Work: 21:9–11 — 154
    Conclusion — 158

Chapter 8. Shepherd and Martyr — 161
    Introduction: Peter in John 21:15–25 — 161
    Questions and Answers: 21:15–17 — 161
    Peter's Fate Foretold: 21:18–19 — 172
    An Alternate Form of Witness: 21:20–25 — 175
    Conclusion — 179

Chapter 9. Conclusion — 183
    Introduction: How to View Peter? — 183
    Peter's Christology — 184
    Peter and the Beloved Disciple — 186
    Peter and the Apostolic Church — 190

CONTENTS

Concluding Thoughts 193

Bibliography 197

Index of Scripture 213

ACKNOWLEDGEMENTS

More people than I could possibly name have assisted me in the writing of this dissertation, whether providing broad academic insight, inspiration for the project itself, or encouragement in general—a commodity I have come to rely on greatly. One person who will probably be surprised to find his name listed here is Dr. John Seidensticker, not a biblical scholar but a scientist and expert in tiger conservation at Washington's National Zoological Park. Dr. Seidensticker created what I am sure is the most flexible work schedule ever afforded an animal keeper in allowing me to care for the zoo's prized collection of tigers while pursuing my master's degree at Wesley Theological Seminary.

While studying at Wesley, I was fortunate to have as co-supervisors Professors Sharon H. Ringe and Craig C. Hill, who introduced me to the most vibrant aspects of biblical exegesis and encouraged me to continue my studies of Peter at the doctoral level. Since that time I am glad to say that they have become my colleagues at Wesley, and I continue to seek their counsel and value their friendship.

In the four years pursuing my DPhil at Oxford University, my supervisor, Dr. Christopher M. Tuckett, proved a tremendous academic resource and reliable conversation partner, always finding the spare hour (or two) to meet with me, and responding to each and every phone call and email—an amazing feat considering how ill-timed and desperate so many of them were. I am also indebted to Dr. Christopher Rowland, whose weekly NT graduate seminar at Queen's College in Oxford provided me with an opportunity to read aloud excerpts from my dissertation and raise questions concerning all things Petrine. My DPhil examiners, Dr. John Muddiman of Oxford and Dr. Ron Piper of St. Andrews, were extremely gracious in their treatment of my dissertation, and I shall always be grateful that they chose to use my *viva voce* as an occasion to suggest ways to strengthen it rather than as an opportunity to dissect its shortcomings, which would have made for a very long afternoon.

Most of all I would like to thank my wife, Belinda, who has read every word of this dissertation a hundred times over, scrutinizing every jot and tittle when her own job dictated that she be elsewhere. Her constant love and support have made this project possible.

ABBREVIATIONS

AB	Anchor Bible
ACNT	Augsburg Commentaries on the New Testament
AnBib	Analecta biblica
ANTC	Abingdon New Testament Commentaries
AThR	*Anglican Theological Review*
BETL	Bibliotheca ephemeridum theologicarum lovaniensium
Bib	*Biblica*
BR	*Biblical Research*
BRev	*Bible Review*
BTB	*Biblical Theology Bulletin*
CBC	Cambridge Bible Commentary
CBET	Contributions to Biblical Exegesis and Theology
CBQ	*Catholic Bible Quarterly*
ETL	*Ephemerides theologicae lovanienses*
ET	*Expository Times*
FFNT	Friendship First New Testament
HeyJ	*Heythrop Journal*
HNTC	Harper's New Testament Commentaries
HTR	*Harvard Theological Review*
HTS	Harvard Theological Studies
IBT	Interpreting Biblical Texts
ICC	International Critical Commentary
INT	*Interpretation*
JBL	*Journal of Biblical Literature*
JSNT	*Journal for the Study of the New Testament*
JSNTSup	Journal for the Study of the New Testament: Supplement Series
JSOT	*Journal for the Study of the Old Testament*
JSOTSup	Journal for the Study of the Old Testament: Supplement Series
JTS	*Journal of Theological Studies*
KBANT	Kommentare und Beiträge zum Alten und Neuen Testament
LTP	*Laval Théologique et Philosophique*
MNTC	Moffatt New Testament Commentary
NCB	New Century Bible
NEchtB	Neue Echter Bibel
NIBCNT	New International Biblical Commentary on the New Testament
NICNT	New International Commentary on the New Testament

NJBC	*New Jerome Biblical Commentary*
NovT	*Novum Testamentum*
NTD	Das Neue Testament Deutsch
NTL	New Testament Library
NTS	*New Testament Studies*
NovTSup	Supplements to Novum Testamentum
RevExp	*Review and Expositor*
RHR	*Revue de l'histoire ecclésiastique*
SANT	Studien zum Alten und Neuen Testaments
SBL	Society of Biblical Literature
SBLDS	Society of Biblical Literature Dissertation Series
SKKNT	Stuttgarter kleiner Kommentar. Neues Testament
SNTSMS	Society for New Testament Studies Monograph Series
SPCK	Society for the Propagation of Christian Knowledge
ST	*Studia theologica*
SVTQ	*St. Vladimir's Theological Quarterly*
TS	*Theological Studies*
TynBul	*Tyndale Bulletin*
WBC	Word Biblical Commentary
ZNW	*Zeitschrift für die neutestamentliche Wissenschaft und die Kunde der älteren Kirche*
ZTK	*Zeitschrift für Theologie und Kirche*

CHAPTER 1

INTRODUCTION

PETER IN THE GOSPEL OF JOHN: WHY ASK THE QUESTION?

The purpose of this study is to examine the characterization of Peter in the Gospel of John. As far as most scholars are concerned, Peter does not fare particularly well in John's Gospel. Three of the most common observations made about him are that he has a "low" Christology, which prevents him from recognizing certain truths about Jesus and causes him to be rather reckless in his devotion, that he is the subordinate of the Beloved Disciple (BD), who is the only true exemplar of sustainable faith in the Gospel, and that he is the representative of the Apostolic church, a less enlightened ecclesial entity than the Johannine church.[1]

Peter's refusal to allow Jesus to wash his feet (13:4–10), his inability at the Last Supper to submit a question to Jesus about the identity of the traitor (Judas)

---

[1] Pervasive patterns of what might be called "Petrine denigration"—many of which focus on his Christology and his relationship to BD—are briefly summarized in the third part of this introduction. For especially negative appraisals of Peter in the Gospel of John, however, see A. J. Droge, "The Status of Peter in the Fourth Gospel: A Note on John 18:10–11," *JBL* 109 (1990): 307–11; D. H. Gee, "Why Did Peter Spring into the Sea? [John 21:7]," *JTS* 40 (1989): 481–89; A. H. Maynard, "The Role of Peter in the Fourth Gospel," *NTS* 30 (1984): 531–48; E. L. Titus, *The Message of the Fourth Gospel* (New York: Abingdon, 1957) 220; G. F. Snyder, "John 13:16 and the Anti-Petrinism of the Johannine Tradition," *BR* 16 (1971): 5–15; M. Goulder, *St. Paul vs. St. Peter: A Tale of Two Visions* (Louisville: WJK, 1994) *passim*; P. S. Minear, "The Beloved Disciple in the Gospel of John: Some Clues and Conjectures," in *The Composition of John's Gospel: Selected Studies from Novum Testamentum* (ed. D. A. Orton; Leiden: Brill, 1999), 186–204; and M. W. G. Stibbe, *John* (London: T & T Clark, 1996), 144–50; 180–84; 210–15. In addition to these studies, many recent monographs and commentaries boldly identify Peter as the subordinate of the Beloved Disciple, including M. H. Crosby, *"Do You Love Me?": Jesus Questions the Church* (Maryknoll: Orbis, 2000), 161; J. F. O'Grady, *According to John: The Witness of the Beloved Disciple* (New York: Paulist, 1999), 35; and A. G. Brock, *Mary Magdalene, the First Apostle: The Struggle for Authority* (HTS 51; Cambridge, Mass.: Harvard University Press, 2003), 40–60.

without going through BD (13:23–25), his attack on the servant of the high priest (18:10), his failure to enter the courtyard of the high priest on his first try (18:15–16), his denials of Jesus—which, unlike in the Synoptic Gospels, do not include a "cathartic" weeping scene (18:17, 15–27)—and his "second-place finish" in the race to the empty tomb (20:2–10) are often seen to reflect his low standing.

When, in chapter 21, he is seen by the scholarly majority to perform well, three times professing his love for Jesus and earning a commission to tend and feed Jesus' lambs and sheep, the explanation (or disclaimer!) is often provided that this material comes from a later period, perhaps a period of intense persecution or internal turmoil. During this period, it is suggested, the Johannine community—acting through a scribe other than the Evangelist—decided to "rehabilitate" Peter in order to garner the support of the Apostolic church or acknowledge Peter's growing popularity.[2] But even in John 21 Peter is rarely if ever described as getting out completely from under the shadow of BD. J. H. Charlesworth speaks for many when he says that "[t]he editor who added chapter 21 intends to elevate Peter, but also to continue the portrayal of the Beloved Disciple as exalted above him."[3]

In my opinion, there is room in the Johannine literature for a more positive evaluation of Peter, one that does not depend on a few "rehabilitative" verses in chapter 21. The aim of this study is to show that Peter is portrayed very positively in the Gospel, appearing as an exemplary disciple and hero of the Johannine community. His positive traits, which include courage, zeal, loyalty, love, resourcefulness, and determination, are meant to be emulated. His few lapses in faith—although considerable in scope—owe less to inadequate Christology than to misdirected zeal. On the two occasions that Jesus rebukes him (13:8; 18:11), his purpose is to counsel him toward moderation rather than repentance. Peter does not represent Apostolic Christianity or any other rival or competing Christian faction, as most commentaries and monographs suggest, but is presented as an inspirational founding member of the Johannine church, equal in importance to BD.[4] While I agree with the majority of scholars that John 21 is the work of someone other than the Evangelist (called in this study

---

[2] See especially J. L. Martyn, *Gospel of John in Christian History: Essays for Interpreters* (New York: Paulist, 1978), 120; and P. Perkins, "John," *NJBC*, 945.

[3] J. H. Charlesworth, *The Beloved Disciple: Whose Witness Validates the Gospel of John?* (Valley Forge: Trinity Press International, 1984), 42.

[4] Peter is one of only two disciples who appear in the opening call narrative *and* the final resurrection scene (the other being Nathanael), and is therefore a prominent witness to the entire career of Jesus. Peter may be *the* most prominent witness to Jesus' career, for, as is shown by M. Pamment in "The Fourth Gospel's Beloved Disciple," *ET* 94 (1983): 365, John's Gospel shows "no biographical interest" in Nathanael. Although BD is a witness of the highest order, he does not appear until the night before the crucifixion (13:23ff.).

the "Johannine Redactor" or simply the "Redactor"), I do not think the positive portrayal of Peter here marks an abrupt departure from the portrayal given by the Evangelist. As John 21 opens, Peter is not in need of "rehabilitation." He has denied Jesus, but he has also spent more energy and faced more adversity in serving him than any other character in the Gospel. Although there is no need for the Redactor to upgrade Peter's image, he does provide the reader with an update on his post-Easter accomplishments. Invested with pastoral authority by the risen Jesus, Peter appears as the *new shepherd* who assists the Good Shepherd in caring for the flock. Whereas the Fourth Evangelist alludes to Peter's martyrdom in 13:36, the Redactor spells out the specifics of his martyrdom in graphic detail. Peter is arrested and crucified, and in this manner of death "glorifies God" (21:18–19).

I will endeavor to show that Peter and BD do not interact as competitors but as colleagues, specializing in *following, believing* and *testifying* (BD in 18:15–16; 19:26–27; 20:3–10; 21:7 and 24; Peter in 1:42; 6:68–69; 13:37; 18:15–16; 20:3–10; 21:7, 11, 18–19, and 20–23), the three activities fundamental to Johannine discipleship.[5] When they appear to be pursuing different goals, it is because their faith manifests itself in very different ways. Peter's discipleship is noisy and provocative. BD is a more mysterious and ethereal character, subsisting quietly on his faith *in* Jesus and the love *of* Jesus.

Although BD is proudly hailed as the authenticator of material in the Gospel (19:35; 21:24), in the storyworld "he"[6] keeps a fairly low profile, speaking a total of only six words (κύριε, τίς ἐστιν in 13:25; ὁ κύριός ἐστιν in 21:7). While it is not a goal of this study to downplay his unique strengths, I will emphasize that these strengths are not obtained without cost. Subsisting on faith, he is in many respects one-dimensional. Previous studies on Johannine discipleship err, I believe, in failing to point out that BD is conspicuously absent from scenes in which Jesus faces adversity, where the natural response of his other disciples (especially Peter) is to react emotionally, either expressing concern for Jesus' safety or questioning the wisdom of his plans.[7] To say that BD is missing from these scenes because he is paralyzed by piety or terrified of conflict would be to argue more from silence than substance and thus go too far, but the evidence suggests that he does not represent all that it means to be a Johannine Christian. Much of the praxis that goes into Johannine discipleship— for example, serving the church in a courageous leadership capacity (21:11, 15–

---

[5] For more on the Johannine virtues of believing, following, and testifying, see 1:7, 37–40; 2:11; 3:16, 18; 4:39–42; 5:38; 6:2, 40; 8:24; 10:4, 27, 38; 11:16; 12:26; 20:6; 21:20–22.

[6] See below for my argument that BD is male.

[7] In addition to the scenes in which Peter challenges Jesus in an effort to protect him from what he considers to be danger or degradation (13:6–10; 18:10–11), Thomas (14:5), Philip (14:8), and Judas (not the traitor; 14:22) all express concern or uncertainty about some aspect of Jesus' itinerary.

17) and confessing Jesus in the face of a hostile opposition (6:68–69)—is modeled in the acts of Peter. Only together do Peter and BD represent the paradigmatic Johannine Christian.[8]

Although Peter and BD appear together in five scenes (13:23–25; 18:15–16; 20:3–10; 21:7, 20–23), Peter is not portrayed primarily as BD's associate. On only one occasion is he his dialogue partner (21:7).[9] More often than not, Peter appears without BD (1:41; 6:68–69; 13:4–10, 36–38; 18:17–27; 21:11, 15–19). His zeal to follow Jesus does not wilt when he is outside BD's company. By subscribing to the idea that BD is the hero of the Johannine church and Peter is the representative of the Apostolic Christianity, most scholars fail to explore the many positive aspects of Peter's character. Because attempts to reconstruct the Johannine community often depend on the idea that Peter and BD represent different branches of the early Church (or competitive elements *within* the Johannine church), and that Peter's group holds a shakier grasp on certain Christological truths about Jesus, it may be the case that scholars are not terribly motivated to burden Peter with positive traits! While it is beyond the scope of this study to challenge well-entrenched theories about the development of the Johannine community, I hope at least to discredit the idea that Peter represents a non-Johannine branch of Christianity.

Methodology

The primary purpose of this study is to show how Peter functions in the Johannine text, how his faith grows and, occasionally, ebbs in response to crises, how he relates to and interacts with other characters in the storyworld, how he fits into the overall plot of the story, and how, through the direction of the author(s), he teaches about discipleship. Narrative criticism will therefore be the exegetical tool employed most frequently.[10] But this is not a narrative-critical study in the strictest sense, which might analyze the Gospel as a literary and

---

[8] R. H. Lightfoot, *St. John's Gospel: A Commentary* (Oxford: Oxford University Press, 1966), 341, puts it this way: "The beloved disciple understands his Lord better, and is granted greater insight, than St. Peter; the latter is the man of action."

[9] The Greek of 13:24 (νεύει οὖν τούτῳ Σίμων Πέτρος πυθέσθαι τίς ἂν εἴη περὶ οὗ λέγει) suggests that Peter motions rather than speaks to BD, but the interchange still has the characteristics of a dialog.

[10] Among the narrative-critical studies of the Gospel of John that I find particularly insightful are R. A. Culpepper, *Anatomy of the Fourth Gospel: A Study in Literary Design* (FFNT 1; Philadelphia: Fortress, 1983); F. F. Segovia, "The Journey(s) of the Word of God: A Reading of the Plot of the Fourth Gospel," *Semeia* 53 (1991): 23–54; R. G. Maccini, *Her Testimony is True: Women as Witnesses according to John* (JSNTSup 125; Sheffield: Sheffield Academic Press, 1996); and D. Lee, *The Symbolic Narratives of the Fourth Gospel: The Interplay of Form and Meaning* (JSNTSup 95; Sheffield: JSOTP, 1994).

INTRODUCTION 5

artistic whole and ask readers to examine Peter's portrayal without raising questions about the historical situation of the earliest readers. Because I believe that John 21 was not part of the original plan of the Gospel but was added at a later date by a new scribe to address the crisis in faith precipitated by the death of BD, the latter part of this study is occupied to a large extent with historical-critical questions. I will argue that the Redactor plays the role of crisis counselor as much as scribe as he attempts to allay fears in the community that BD's death will delay or otherwise negatively impact the Parousia.[11]

Source criticism, too, is employed in this study, most significantly in chapter two, which looks at Peter's call, naming, and confession (John 1:40–42 and 6:68–69) and shows many thematic parallels to Matt 16:16–19, and in chapter seven, which looks at the miraculous catch of fish (John 21:1–11), an event that demonstrates many parallels to Luke 5:1–11. There is not enough linguistic overlap between John's Gospel and the Synoptic Gospels to make an airtight case that the Fourth Evangelist writes with those entire Gospels laid out before him—blueprints to tinker with where appropriate, as it were—but John *does* seem to be quite familiar with several Synoptic pericopae dealing

---

[11] Chapter six of this study is devoted exclusively to analyzing the place of John 21 in the overall Gospel, and it is there that I present my argument that a redactor (hence *the Redactor*) and not the Evangelist appended it to the Gospel. Although I do not doubt that people other than the Evangelist contributed material to chapters 1–20 (7:53–8:11, for example, missing from important early manuscripts such as P^{66} P^{75} ℵ and B, is an undeniably late addition), and that the Redactor *may* have tinkered with various passages, these do not bear his imprimatur to the extent that they are easily detectable. Other scholars, however—many of whom agree that John 21 is the work of someone other than the Fourth Evangelist—cannot imagine how such a person could append an entire chapter to the Gospel without taking the opportunity to tinker with internal sections that no longer reflect community praxis or belief. Bultmann, for instance, identifies a great many interpolations made by an "Ecclesiastical Redactor" (*kirchliche Red.*). The interpolations are most evident, he says, in passages that (1) echo the Synoptics (1:22–24, 27, 32; 3:24; 4:2; 11:2; 16:5b; 18:9, 13b–14, 24; 32), (2) ply a future eschatology (5:28ff.; 6:39ff., 44b, 54; 12:48), or (3) have Eucharistic overtones (3:5; 6:51b–58; 19:34b). See Bultmann, *The Gospel of John: A Commentary* (trans. G. R. Beasley-Murray; Oxford: Blackwell, 1971) *passim*. Many scholars agree with Bultmann, even if they differ over the nature and location of these glosses (see the discussion in chapter six). On the other hand, many of these disputed verses have, at one time or another, been proffered by scholars as paradigmatic examples of the Evangelist's work. For example, Neirynck, Dauer, and Goulder all argue that passages appearing to assimilate the Synoptics were not crafted in a late redactional stage but demonstrate the Evangelist's familiarity with the Synoptics. See F. Neirynck, "John 21," *NTS* 36 (1990): 321–36; A. Dauer, *Die Passiongeschichte im Johannesevangelium: Eine Traditionsgeschichtliche und theologische Untersuchung zu Joh 18, 1–19, 30* (SANT 30; Munich: Kösel-Verlag, 1972) *passim*; and M. D. Goulder, *Luke—A New Paradigm*, 323–28. Many other scholars who argue for the literary unity of John 1–21 are listed in the third part of this introduction.

specifically with Peter. Whether John knows these pericopae directly, or is familiar with Matthean and Lukan traditions about Peter from afar (perhaps via orality), or borrows from a "pool" of primitive Petrine traditions also known to the Synoptists, is difficult to say.[12] In the call/naming/confession parallel between John and Matthew, however, where John seems to know not just Matthean tradition but Matthew's redaction of Mark, the evidence certainly points toward John's direct knowledge of Matthew's version of events.

Narrative-critical "purists" may argue that these forays into historical-critical and source-critical investigation represent something of an exegetical copout, for lack of a better term. D. M. Gunn, for example, offers a rather withering observation about narrative-critical trends in NT scholarship:

> Narrative criticism of the Gospels and Acts has tended to be relatively conservative in its methodology, concerned with observing the mechanics or artistry of literary construction and often still haunted by historical criticism's need to know the author's 'intention' and the text's 'original' readership if it is to speak legitimately of the text's meaning. While centering interest on the story, especially its plot and characters as elements of an artistic whole, Gospel critics have been reluctant to take a literary approach that unravels unity and/or places the reader in an ideologically exposed position in relation to the text.[13]

In response I can only say that I do not feel so much "haunted" by the need to incorporate historical-critical work in this essentially narrative-critical study of Peter as *confronted* by it. For example, whatever sort of text-critical work one is engaged in when one comes to John 21, the death of BD (implicit in vv. 20–22) appears suddenly as a profoundly important sociological and historical event in the life of the Johannine community, and must be examined as such. The modern reader senses a gap between him- or herself and an early generation of Johannine readers who clearly struggled to make sense of BD's death in light of the "rumor" that he would survive until the Parousia. If there is wisdom in the statement of J. Ashton that the "message of the Gospel is conditioned by the environment in which it was composed," it is particularly true in the case of John 21.[14]

The easiest way to see how Peter fits into the overall plot of the Gospel is to examine his story chronologically. Therefore, after conducting a survey of the

---

[12] The parallels between John's and Matthew's versions of Peter's naming, call, and confession are pursued in the next chapter.

[13] D. M. Gunn, "Narrative Criticism," in *To Each Its Own Meaning: An Introduction to Biblical Criticisms and Their Application* (ed. S. L. McKenzie and S. R. Haynes; Louisville: WJK, 1993), 172.

[14] J. Ashton, *Understanding the Fourth Gospel* (Oxford: Clarendon, 1991), 382.

literature and becoming familiar with certain key concepts in the Gospel, our study of Peter's specific actions begins in earnest in chapter two, where exegesis of the original Greek is designed to lay bare the significance of his naming, call and confession. Chapter three analyzes his activities in John 13, including his refusal to let Jesus wash his feet (vv. 6–10), his inquiry into the identity of the traitorous disciple (vv. 23–25), and his conversation with Jesus about his willingness or capacity to "follow" him (vv. 36–38). Chapter four looks at Peter's actions in John 18, including his attack on Malchus (vv. 10–11), his attempt to enter the courtyard of the high priest (vv. 15–16), and his threefold denial of Jesus (vv. 17–27). Chapter five is concerned solely with the race to the empty tomb (vv. 2–10), an event which—more than any other in the Gospel—elicits complex theories from other scholars as to the nature of Peter's "subordinate" relationship to BD.

At the risk of losing momentum—or, to put it more informally, of allowing Peter's trail to run cold—chapter six examines the place of John 21 in the overall Gospel. The questions of authorship, date, purpose, and circumstances of composition are so weighty here as to defy coherent analysis in a subsection of this introduction or even a lengthy excursus. Chapter seven looks at John 21:1–14, the first "half" of what I will term the "Gospel supplement," which details Peter's decision to lead the disciples on a fishing expedition (vv. 1–4), his spontaneous swim to the risen Jesus (v. 7), and his feat of single-handedly towing ashore the miraculous catch of fish (v. 11). Chapter eight is concerned with the second "half" of John 21, in which Peter makes a threefold profession of love for Jesus, is invested with both missionary and pastoral responsibilities (vv. 15–17), and follows Jesus to martyrdom, treading literally in his footsteps (vv. 18–22). In chapter nine I summarize my findings, making a final case that Peter cuts a very good figure in the Gospel of John.

SURVEY OF SCHOLARSHIP

Very little work has been done on the characterization of Peter in the Gospel of John that is not derivative of work done on BD. With rare exceptions, studies that *do* focus on Peter reach negative conclusions about him, usually identifying him as a subordinate of BD or a well-meaning but impetuous bumbler who misinterprets Jesus' wishes with such consistency that he teaches more negative lessons about discipleship than positive ones.[15] The scholars who have mostly positive things to say about the Johannine Peter can be counted on

---

[15] Rather than detailing in the following literature survey the most fiercely-held anti-Petrine opinions—which will require looking closely at the Greek text of individual pericopae and is accomplished in subsequent chapters—this survey focuses on the basic ways in which Peter has come to be seen as a subordinate of BD and a representative of non-Johannine Christianity.

one hand, and even they are able to proceed essentially by extolling his achievements in John 21 and steering away from the other 95% of the Gospel. Their work claims such a small nook in the literature that it is addressed in what is essentially the coda to the literature survey.

PETER AS THE BELOVED DISCIPLE'S SUBORDINATE

Perhaps more than any other scholar, R. Bultmann is responsible for portraying Peter and BD as competitors and representatives of different strains of Christianity. According to Bultmann, Peter and the Twelve represent Jewish Christianity while BD represents Hellenistic or Gentile Christianity.[16] The race to the tomb pericope, in which BD finishes ahead of Peter and becomes the first disciple in the Gospel to experience a glimmer of post-resurrectional belief, is thought by Bultmann to reveal the proclivities of Johannine faith and tell readers something about the development of the primitive church:

> If Peter and the beloved disciple are the representatives of Jewish and Gentile Christianity, the meaning manifestly is this: the first community of believers arises out of Jewish Christianity, and the Gentile Christians attain to faith only after them. But that does not signify any precedence of the former over the latter; in fact both stand equally near the Risen Jesus, and indeed readiness for faith is even greater with the Gentiles than it is with the Jews: the beloved disciple ran faster than Peter to the grave![17]

Bultmann does not charge the Evangelist with disparaging Peter, as has become an increasingly common practice in recent years. In fact, he believes the Evangelist portrays Peter as having a "healthy, human mind" (*gesunde Menschenverstand*).[18] Unfortunately, a human mind that is merely healthy cannot grasp important truths about Jesus, and Bultmann contends that Peter is easily baffled by revelatory events and misses the symbolism in many of Jesus'

---

[16] Bultmann, *Gospel of John*, esp. 466–73 and 681–715. See also A Kragerud, *Der Lieblingsjünger im Johannesevangelium: Ein exegetischer Versuch* (Hamburg: Grosshaus Wegner, 1959), 49; and L Simon, *Petrus und der Lieblingsjünger im Johannesevangelium: Amt und Autorität* (Frankfurt: Peter Lang, 1994), 21. Bultmann also considers the mother of Jesus a symbol of Jewish Christianity, and thus is able to describe representatives of both Jewish and Gentile Christianity staying with Jesus through the agony of his execution (19:24–26). Centuries before Bultmann, Gregory the Great hypothesized that Peter and BD represent two Christ-faith communities, Peter the Christian church and BD the Synagogue. See the discussion in R. E. Brown, *The Gospel According to John* (2 vols.; London: Doubleday, 1966, 1970), 1.94–110.

[17] Bultmann, *Gospel of John*, 685.

[18] Ibid., 467.

actions. Bultmann devotes a sizeable portion of his commentary to the footwashing scene (13:4–11), describing after much discussion the manner in which Peter balks at the "apparently absurd" image of the incarnate Son of God engaging in a menial chore. According to Bultmann, Peter's weakness is that he "does not understand that Jesus humbles himself to serve his own."[19]

In my opinion, Bultmann errs in arguing that Peter functions primarily in the footwashing scene as "Repräsentant und Sprecher" for the Twelve. Insofar as the other disciples consent with exception to the ritual (implied in 13:5–6), how can this be? Bultmann is, I think, overly devoted to the idea that the Evangelist strives to characterize Jewish Christians as unequipped to conceive of certain truths about Jesus *immediately prior* to introducing BD, whom Bultmann characterizes as the hero of Gentile Christianity and the sole disciple with an intimate sensitivity to Jesus. Bultmann emphasizes that it is BD "and not Peter who reclines in Jesus' bosom, and can mediate Jesus' thought."[20]

Bultmann is, as far as I can tell, unique among scholars in that he believes the primary function of 21:18–23 is to describe the manner in which the full complement of Peter's ecclesial responsibilities passes to BD upon Peter's death. The author of the chapter (Bultmann's "ecclesiastical redactor") "does not have a special interest in the office of Peter; for him the authority of the office is important only because he claims it for the beloved disciple, for through Peter's death it has, as it were, become bereft of a holder."[21] In Bultmann's opinion, death frees Peter from subordination to BD insofar as his ecclesial responsibilities are dispensed to him.[22]

After detailing Peter's prominent role and generally positive characterization in the Synoptic Gospels, O. Cullmann notes that a "somewhat different picture emerges when we turn to the Gospel of John. Here the outstanding role of Peter, which is unchallenged in the Synoptic Gospels, becomes a problem, since for this Evangelist the mysterious unnamed 'Beloved Disciple' of Jesus enters into a certain competition with Peter."[23] Cullmann maintains that the Fourth Evangelist does not "deny directly the special role of Peter within the group of disciples" but agrees with Bultmann that he drastically

---

[19] Ibid., 468.

[20] Ibid., 484.

[21] Ibid., 713. Bultmann assigns to this ecclesial redactor other sections of the Gospel as well, particularly those he construes to have "sacramental" overtones (e.g., 6:51b-58; 19:34b).

[22] Contra R. E. Brown, J. L. Martyn, J. H. Charlesworth, P. Perkins, and many other scholars whose opinions we will shortly explore. Bultmann does not see in 21:15–17 "any tendencies in the direction of ecclesiastical politics—for example the buttressing of the authority of the Roman community" (p. 713).

[23] O. Cullmann, *Peter: Disciple, Apostle, Martyr* (trans. F. V. Filson; London: SCM, 1953), 27.

reduces Peter's (Synoptic) role.[24] By minimizing Peter's achievements and ignoring almost completely the contributions of the Twelve, the group for which Peter speaks in the Synoptic Gospels, John creates space for BD to develop an intimate relationship with Jesus. In stressing that Peter is minimized but never attacked in the Fourth Gospel, Cullmann lets it be known that his interpretation differs from that of E. Käsemann, who believes the Evangelist employs Peter and BD as ciphers in a polemic against the Apostolic church.[25] Yet Cullmann is close enough to Käsemann in his opinion of Peter that he confidently places Peter outside the *Johannine Circle*, the name both scholars give to the community responsible for the Gospel of John and the Johannine Epistles.[26] Building on the work of Käsemann, Cullmann identifies two groups of disciples going back to the historical Jesus. One group, represented by Peter, is "important by virtue of its number and the continuity of its common life." The other, smaller group is represented by BD and rests "on a more inward relationship" with Jesus.[27]

R. E. Brown puts only a mild spin on the "competition" theory of Bultmann and Cullmann when he finds in the text of the Fourth Gospel evidence that Peter represents Apostolic Christianity and BD represents Johannine Christianity.[28] As the only disciples who stand with Jesus during the mass defection of disciples in 6:66–70, Peter and the Twelve represent the new community of faith, or, as Brown terms it, the new Israel. In terms of their overall faith, courage, and insight into Christological truths about Jesus, however, Peter and the Apostolic Christians rank well below the Johannine Christians. Brown points to five specific episodes in the Gospel in which Peter's faith is compared negatively to BD's, and, by extension, Apostolic Christianity is exposed as a lesser strain of the developing Christ faith than Johannine Christianity. These are: 13:23–26 (the discussion about the traitor), 18:15–16 (the entrance into the courtyard of the high priest), 20:2–10 (the race to the tomb), 21:7 (BD's sighting of Jesus and

---

[24] Both scholars hold that John is familiar with certain traditions that appear in the Synoptics but not with the Synoptic Gospels themselves.

[25] See E. Käsemann, "Zum johanneischen Verfasserproblem," *ZTK* 48 (1951): 292–311. In a later work, *The Testament of Jesus* (trans. G. Krodel; Philadelphia: Fortress, 1968), 29, Käsemann boldly claims that "it is obvious that he (BD) obscures the significance for the Church of the Prince of the Apostles."

[26] Cullmann, *The Johannine Circle: Its Place in Judaism, among the Disciples of Jesus and in early Christianity* (trans. J. Bowden; NTL; London: SCM, 1976), 94, adopts the language of Käsemann in describing the Johannine community as the "*ecclesiola in ecclesia*" (p. 25).

[27] Ibid., 94. See also E. C. Hoskyns and F. N. Davey, *The Riddle of the New Testament* (London: Faber & Faber, 1958), 282.

[28] See R. E. Brown, *The Community of the Beloved Disciple: The Life, Loves, and Hates of an Individual Church in New Testament Times* (New York: Paulist, 1979), 71–85.

Peter's leap into the sea), and 21:20–23 (the successful "following" [ἀκολουθέω] of Jesus by both Peter and BD). Brown maintains that in "counterposing their hero over against the most famous member of the Twelve, the Johannine community is symbolically counterposing itself over against the kinds of churches that venerate Peter and the Twelve."[29] He adds that "implicit" in 19:25 is the idea that "Peter is one of those who have scattered, abandoning Jesus," whereas BD stands beneath the cross in bold solidarity with Jesus' mother.[30]

Brown is more adventurous than most scholars in proposing to understand the mechanism by which Johannine Christians distinguish themselves from their Apostolic cousins:

> The one-upmanship of the Johannine Christians is centered on Christology; for while the named disciples (Peter, Andrew, Philip, and Nathanael), representing the Apostolic Christians, have a reasonably high Christology, they do not reach the heights of the Johannine understanding of Jesus... [w]e may make an informed guess that the precise aspect of Christology missing in the faith of the Apostolic Christians is the perception of the pre-existence of Jesus and of his origins from above.[31]

Just how Brown knows that the Twelve do not embrace the doctrine of Jesus' pre-existence is not clear. In my opinion, he radically overplays the extent to which the Twelve *as John portrays them* represent an early Christian community distinct from the Johannine community. For example, he notes that the "presence of the Twelve at the Last Supper (13:6; 14:5, 8, 22) means that the Apostolic Christians are included in Jesus' 'own' whom he loves to the very end (13:1)."[32] Yet no mention of the Twelve is made in these verses. Brown also appears to err in assuming that individual references to Peter, Andrew, Thomas, or Nathanael should be understood as shorthand for "the Twelve."[33] When he says that 6:68–69 is the "prime indicator" of John's effort to make the Twelve representative of a "special group of Christians" distinct from Johannine Christians, should he not be saying that it is the *only* indicator of such an effort?

---

[29] Ibid., 83. In terms of their allegiance to Jesus, he does rank Apostolic Christians ahead of two other first-century Christian groups: Jewish Christians of inadequate faith (cf. 6:60–66; 7:3–5) and Jewish Christians attracted to Jesus but afraid to confess him publicly for fear of expulsion from the synagogue (cf. 9:22–38; 12:42–43).

[30] Ibid.

[31] Ibid.

[32] Ibid., 84.

[33] It is particularly problematic to associate Nathanael with Apostolic Christianity since he is a figure unique to John's Gospel.

Apart from this passage, John shows almost no interest in the activities of the Twelve.[34]

Like Bultmann and Brown, J. L. Martyn endeavors to reconstruct the history of the Johannine community by uncovering layers of redaction in the Gospel and, to a lesser extent, discovers in the characterization of Peter hints about the development of that early community. Still very influential is Martyn's theory that the expulsion of Johannine Christians from the synagogue was the primary formative experience in the history of the community. But Martyn contends that the Johannine church formed its theology not only "vis-à-vis the parent synagogue but in relation to other Christian groups in its setting."[35] The positive characterization of Peter in John 21 marks an abrupt departure from Peter's earlier characterization and provides a window into a "late" phase in the development of the Johannine church (c. 100 C.E.).[36] Only in John 21, according to Martyn, does the reader see the community pursuing a "relationship with the emerging 'great Church' which lives on the frontier of the Gentile mission."[37]

Although I am persuaded by many of Martyn's theories that seek to correlate the development of Johannine theology with the hostile attitude of the synagogue,[38] I disagree that Peter's activities in John 21 symbolize an overture to the "great Church." The viability of this theory depends on 21:15–19 being a full-scale "rehabilitation" of Peter and/or a political maneuver designed to curry favor with the Apostolic church. The text supports neither of these ideas. John 21 *does* seem to acknowledge Peter's ascendancy in the broader church—hence his ability to single-handedly catch such a large variety of fish / novitiates in 21:11—but it also adopts a proprietary attitude toward him, regarding him as an

---

[34] 20:24 describes the Twelve as a collective to which Thomas belongs, but it is not clear if the Evangelist imagines this group assembling in Jerusalem in any sort of purposeful or proactive manner.

[35] J. L. Martyn, *History and Theology in the Fourth Gospel* (3rd ed.; Nashville: Abingdon, 2003), 157.

[36] I agree with Martyn—and many other Johannine commentators—in supposing that John's Gospel was written sometime around 100 C.E. I believe that the supplemental chapter, John 21, was written no more than a decade after the rest of the Gospel since no comment is made about BD's health in John 1–20 and yet his (apparently recent) death is the event that drives the action in John 21. A gap of more than a decade between the writing of the two sections is problematic, however, because there is no extant copy of John's Gospel that lacks chapter 21, and one finds it difficult to envision a scenario in which more than ten years passed without a copy of the non-appended Gospel making its way into circulation.

[37] Martyn, *Gospel of John in Christian History*, 120.

[38] I am open to the possibility that the Johannine Church's own feelings of rejection from the synagogue was the source of much of the early friction, and that it conceived of the synagogue as "hostile" years before true, mutual animosity overwhelmed and then characterized their relationship. See the discussion in S. Ringe, *Wisdom's Friends* (Louisville: Westminster John Knox, 1999), 55.

inspirational founder of the *Johannine* church and authentic Johannine "Christian."[39] For example, in John 21 Peter commands a fishing boat whose crew is one-third "Johannine" (BD and Nathanael). He is the first to reach the risen Jesus on the shore and the only disciple to follow Jesus' directive that the net of fish be dragged to shore. He is the *new shepherd* who assists the Good Shepherd (cf. 10:1–18), guiding and nurturing the community in the absence of the earthly Jesus. And he is one of two disciples who model complete commitment to Christ, the other being the uniquely Johannine BD (see 21:18–23). If there is an implication in John 21 that Peter represents a group of Christians other than Johannine Christians, as many scholars continue to claim, it is subtle indeed.

E. Haenchen offers a blunt condemnation of Peter when he says that he "does not cut a good figure in the Gospel of John. He is not the protagonist among the disciples in the good sense, but indicates their lack of understanding."[40] In his analysis of the footwashing scene (13:6–10), Haenchen, borrowing from Bultmann, notes that Peter demonstrates above all else his "absurd lack of understanding" of the nature of Jesus' salvific work.[41] As for the denial scene (18:17–27), Haenchen argues that the Fourth Evangelist purposely narrates events in a way that prevents the reader from developing genuine sympathy for Peter: "The whole is narrated laconically and unsentimentally. One seeks for a sentence like, 'and he wept bitterly,' here in vain."[42] Haenchen asserts that Peter is portrayed positively by the author of John 21 (not the Evangelist) partly to record his commissioning as pastor of the post-Easter Johannine community but also to counterbalance the very negative portrayal given by the Evangelist in chapters 1 –20: "In view of the way in which Peter is depicted in the Fourth Gospel, it really became necessary that he should be appreciated at least once."[43]

R. A. Culpepper is another renowned Johannine scholar who believes "the Beloved Disciple regularly appears in scenes where he is given some priority or advantage over Peter."[44] For Culpepper, BD is the hero of the Johannine

---

[39] I use this term as a synonym for "early adherent to the Christ faith," recognizing that it was probably not used in the Johannine Church.

[40] E. Haenchen, *John 2: A Commentary on the Gospel of John Chapters 7–21* (trans. R. W. Funk; Philadelphia: Fortress, 1984), 107.

[41] Ibid.

[42] Ibid., 169.

[43] Ibid., 234.

[44] R. A. Culpepper, *John the Son of Zebedee: The Life of a Legend* (Columbia: University of South Carolina Press, 1994), 62. See also B. W. Bacon, *The Fourth Gospel in Research and Debate* (New Haven: Yale University Press, 1918), 198–99, who detects in the Gospel "a marked subordination" of Peter to BD. (Quotation taken from K. Quast, *Peter and the Beloved Disciple: Figures for a Community in Crisis* [JSNTSup 32; Sheffield: JSOTP, 1989], 171 n. 6.)

community because his testimony, unlike Peter's, is inspired by the spirit. As is the case with the scholars we have already mentioned, Culpepper is able to extract aspects of community history from Peter's portrayal:

> The relationship between the Beloved Disciple and Peter suggests further that the former was the Johannine community's apostolic authority, the one from whom the community had received its teachings. He was their link with the earthly Jesus and their witness to the risen Lord. The community recognized the role of Peter, but nevertheless maintained that the Beloved Disciple had been given a unique role... The Beloved Disciple serves, therefore, as an important figure, legitimizing and authorizing the distinctive teaching of the Johannine community in the face of the rising authority of Peter in other traditions.[45]

Again, I believe one has to read much into the text to reach the conclusion that Peter represents a strain of Christianity distinct from Johannine Christianity. It is also not at all clear that Peter's testimony is not inspired by the spirit—or by the Father! (See 2.4)[46]

P. Perkins, who has written extensively on Peter and also the Johannine community, is another who feels that John's Gospel maintains a cooler attitude toward Peter than do the Synoptic Gospels. As she puts it, "the tragedy of Peter's flawed character is highlighted by the Fourth Evangelist. The presence of the Beloved Disciple in the Gospel highlights Peter's failures by demonstrating what is possible for a disciple of Jesus."[47] Although Perkins notes that the Evangelist never casts doubt on Peter's love for Jesus, she spends a great deal of time detailing the inappropriate ways Peter finds to express this love in John 1–20. For Perkins, the Evangelist's dissatisfaction with Peter is most evident in 18:36, a scene in which Peter does not even appear: "My kingdom is not from this world. If my kingdom were from this world, my followers would be fighting to keep me from being handed over to the Jews." Because Peter earlier in the evening lopped off the ear of the servant of the high priest in a botched attempt

---

[45] Ibid., 84.

[46] Prior to narrating Peter's confession in 6:68–69 (which includes a promise to follow Jesus), the Evangelist relays these words of Jesus: "For this reason I have told you that no one can come to me unless it is granted by the Father" (6:65). Considering that Peter eventually makes good on his promise to follow Jesus (21:18–22), can we deny the possibility that his confession—including the testimony that Jesus is the "Holy One of God"—is divinely inspired? The question is pursued in the next chapter.

[47] P. Perkins, *Peter: Apostle for the Whole Church* (Columbia: University of South Carolina Press, 1994), 99.

to prevent Jesus from being handed over to the "the Jews" (18:10–11), Perkins sees 18:36 as a negative critique of his discipleship.[48]

Like Brown and Culpepper, Perkins is able to find positive attributes in Peter essentially by appealing to John 21, the chapter in which he is installed as the shepherd / pastor of Jesus' flock / church.[49] Like most commentators (myself included), Perkins sees John 21 as an editorial addition to the Gospel, probably written by a "final editor."[50] But she differs with me in describing this chapter as the main repository of good will toward Peter. Like Brown and Martyn, Perkins suggests that the desire for inter-church fence-mending motivated the composition of John 21, and that the "acknowledgement of Petrine authority in John 21 may have made it possible for some Johannine churches to amalgamate with Christians from other churches."[51] In her commentary on the Gospel of

---

[48] See Perkins, *Peter*, 98–99.

[49] Ibid., 98–100. Although Perkins concludes her discussion of Peter in the Gospel of John in this monograph by saying that "there is no reason to treat Petrine material (in John 21) as an effort to moderate an anti-Peter tradition in the earlier edition of the Gospel, as is sometimes suggested," her analysis of John 1–20 focuses almost exclusively on Peter's failures. The effect is that she paints a picture of two very different disciples. D. M. Smith, *John* (ANTC; Nashville: Abingdon, 1999), 374, also notes that Peter consistently comes in "a clear second" to BD as a tragic result of being "placed in a rivalry" with him. Like many scholars, Smith points out that Peter "is restored to Jesus' good graces" in John 21 (p. 261). P. Dschulnigg, *Petrus im Neuen Testament* (Stuttgart: Verlag Katholisches Bibelwerk, 1996), 205, is another who notes the impressive turnaround in Peter's fortunes and characterization in John 21. After refusing the footwashing, relying on BD to get a question to Jesus, and denying Jesus (chapters 13 and 18), Dschulnigg argues in John 21 that "erhält Petrus den pastoralen Leitungsdienst über die Schafe Christi in Sorge um das Leben und die Einheit der Kirche in Christus, den Leben und dem Hirten schlechthin."

[50] Perkins, *Peter*, 100. According to C. Conway, "Gender Matters in John," in *A Feminist Companion to John* (ed. A. Levine; 2 vols.; Cleveland: Pilgrim, 2003), 2.99, "the addition of ch. 21 points to the fact that Peter's role in the gospel proper is diminished and demanded attention from early redactors of the gospel."

[51] Perkins, "John," 945. See also A. J. Nau, *Peter in Matthew: Discipleship, Diplomacy, and Dispraise* (Collegeville, Minn.: Liturgical Press, 1992), 9. Charlesworth, *Beloved Disciple*, 388, departs from this theory only slightly in arguing that the competitive struggles between Peter and BD represent the "early rivalry between Rome and Jerusalem." BD (aka Thomas) is "portrayed in a dramatic way as superior to Peter" to counterbalance the image being promulgated by the Roman church of Peter as dynamic leader of the Twelve (p. 431). Charlesworth, 431, theorizes that Peter's portrayal in chapters 1–20 was at some point judged to be overly negative by an editor in the Johannine school, and that "reinstatement was necessary and was achieved partially in the Appendix (chapter 21)."

John, she observes that "[t]he sheep Peter is sent to feed are probably the 'other sheep' of John 10:16 – they must be called by the apostolic mission."[52]

In *The Gospel of the Beloved Disciple*, H. C. Waetjen argues that Peter's "reinstatement" in John 21 "stands in contrast to the perplexing role that he plays in the earlier chapters of the Fourth Gospel. However his function as a character within this narrative world may be evaluated, the historical priority that is attributed to him in the Synoptics, the Acts of the Apostles, 1 Corinthians 15:5, and Galatians 1:18 is displaced by the Beloved Disciple."[53] Waetjen offers his own assessment of Peter's performance in the "narrative world," and it is indeed bleak. He finds an "anti-Petrine bias" permeating the Gospel, and

---

[52] Perkins, *The Gospel according to John* (Chicago: Franciscan Herald Press, 1978), 243. J. F. O'Grady, *According to John: The Witness of the Beloved Disciple* (New York: Paulist, 1999), 36, argues forcefully for this same idea that Peter "functions in a subordinate position to the Beloved Disciple" in John 1–20. So strong is the rivalry between the two in these chapters, O'Grady says, that BD, upon learning the identity of the traitor from Jesus at the Last Supper, deliberately decides not to pass it along to Peter! (In reality we are never told whether BD passes along or withholds information; Jesus begins to speak as soon as BD voices Peter's question.) Only in chapter 21, an epilogue that "focuses on the pastoral office of Peter," does Peter nudge BD out of the limelight long enough to profess his love for Jesus and develop the credentials to feed Jesus' sheep (p. 36). But, O'Grady says, it is a case of too little too late: in the reader's mind a lasting and somewhat negative impression of Peter has already been made. Even as Peter follows Jesus to martyrdom, the reader is acutely aware that "Peter did not come to faith in the risen Lord because of the empty tomb but only through an experience of Jesus as risen. The Beloved Disciple saw and believed" (p. 36). R. F. Collins, "From John to the Beloved Disciple: An Essay on Johannine Characters," in *Gospel Interpretation: Narrative-Critical and Social-Scientific Approaches* (ed. J. D. Kingsbury; Harrisburg, Penn.: Trinity Press International, 1997), 208, also maintains that "the bumbling and impetuous Peter shows himself to be a disciple who really does not comprehend what Jesus is about." A similarly gloomy appraisal of Peter vis-à-vis BD is given by R. Pesch in "The Position and Significance of Peter in the Church of the New Testament: A Survey of Current Research," *Concilium* 4 (1971), 31. Although T. L. Brodie, *Gospel according to John: A Literary and Theological Commentary* (Oxford: Oxford University Press, 1993), 563, does not believe the figures of Peter and BD "correspond accurately to Jewish and Gentile Christianity," he does not dispense with the idea that they are representative figures in some capacity. His own suggestion is that they symbolize "two faces of the church, the contemplative and the official" (p. 564). In stating this, he sounds much like D. J. Hawkin in "The Function of the Beloved Disciple Motif in the Johannine Redaction," *LTP* 33 (1977): 136, who sees Peter as the representative of the *Gesamtkirche* and the Beloved Disciple as the representative of the *Einzelkirche*.

[53] H. C. Waetjen, *The Gospel of the Beloved Disciple: A Work in Two Editions* (London: T & T Clark, 2005), 15.

concludes that Peter is "deliberately being assigned a secondary role among the disciples of Jesus."[54]

Some scholars who subscribe to the rivalry theory do not see Peter and BD as representatives of different communities but of different programs of faith. Not surprisingly, Peter's program is usually thought to be inferior. P. S. Minear deserves to be heard from first because he delivers the most scathing opinion of the Johannine Peter vis-à-vis BD. In analyzing the denial scene (18:15–27), for example, Minear points out that BD, unlike Peter, is "quite willing to accept the charge of guilt by association" and enter the courtyard of the high priest *with* Jesus.[55] In acting so boldly BD shows "no trace of the Galilean reticence or Petrine fear. *Persona grata* bravely takes his stand beside *persona non grata*."[56] (Unfortunately, Minear offers no explanation as to why BD disappears at the precise moment Peter's accusers close in.) According to Minear, Peter is a caricature of helplessness in the denial scene: First, he is refused entry to the courtyard by a *female* gatekeeper—considered by Minear to be particularly humiliating. Second, he is helped across the threshold by BD. Minear concludes his observations by noting that Peter's denials are particularly "shameful in view of the testimony of both the beloved Son and his beloved disciple."[57]

W.W. Watty echoes Minear in observing bluntly that Peter "stands for a negative strain in the gospel."[58] He maintains that Peter's very name "focuses and highlights precisely what the evangelist wishes to correct. He goes out of his way to present a 'Peter of History' with warts and all, because, presumably, the name bestowed by Jesus was assuming an inordinate importance."[59]

---

[54] Ibid., 18. Not only does Waetjen believe the "dissimilarity between Simon Peter and the Beloved Disciple becomes more pronounced" as the Passion nears (p. 19), he believes that the "one who was renamed 'Cephas' never reaches mature discipleship" (p. 23). Waetjen's interpretation of Peter's role in the Gospel concurs with that of B. W. Bacon, *Gospel of the Hellenists* (ed. C. H. Kraeling; New York: Holt & Co., 1933), 483, who claims that, apart from John 21, "the Gospel would leave Peter under the unlifted cloud of disgrace." Quotation taken from Waetjen, *Gospel of the Beloved Disciple*, 23–24.

[55] Minear, "Beloved Disciple," 199.

[56] Ibid.

[57] Ibid.

[58] W. W. Watty, "The Significance of Anonymity in the Fourth Gospel," *ET* 90 (1979): 211.

[59] Ibid. Although B. Byrne, "The Faith of the Beloved Disciple and the Community in John 20," in *The Johannine Writings* (ed. S. E. Porter and C. A. Evans; Sheffield: Sheffield Academic Press, 1995), 43, sets out to show that "anti-Petrine interpretations have no place" in the text of John 20:3–10, his analysis of the scene strongly supports the opposite contention. He says that "Peter serves as something of a foil for the faith of that 'other disciple' upon whom in John's design the central focus falls" (p. 43). Only by having BD outperform Jesus' other close associate, Peter, is the Evangelist able to highlight BD's greater love for Jesus and his "greater readiness to see the 'sign' presented by the empty clothes." Byrne characterizes Peter as the "odd-man-out" in the pericope,

As has been pointed out, many scholars impugn Peter and catalog his failures without bothering to track closely the activities of BD. Typically, they fault Peter for (1) his failure to converse with Jesus during their initial meeting; (2) his refusal to let Jesus wash his feet; (3) his swordplay in the garden on the night of the arrest; (4) his failure to weep after the denials; (5) his decision to dress before swimming to the risen Jesus; and (6) his low Christology—laid bare in his confession of Jesus as the "Holy One of God."[60] BD is not present in any of these scenes. For these scholars (Hoskyns, Droge, Gee, Maynard, Snyder, Titus, Goulder, Stibbe, and Brock to name a very few), Peter is not so much the representative of Apostolic Christianity as he is the representative of *defective* Christianity.[61] He gets it wrong more often than he gets it right. Because their evaluations of Peter hinge on their exegesis of specific pericopae, with much attention paid to the original Greek, their analyses will not be summarized here but are examined closely in subsequent chapters.

PETER AS THE BELOVED DISCIPLE'S EQUAL

As noted, only a very few scholars have mostly positive things to say about Peter in the Gospel of John, and in these studies an inordinate amount of weight is given to the "rehabilitative" material in John 21.[62] C. K. Barrett, for example,

---

and suggests that the Gospel's original audience would have understood the "tongue-in-cheek approach to Peter in this chapter" (p. 42). Byrne assumes, as do many, that Jesus' love for BD is reciprocal. This idea is at best implied in the text (e.g. 13:23). To assume that BD wins the race because he harbors greater love for Jesus than Peter does is to read between the lines. Dschulnigg, *Petrus im Neuen Testament*, 142–45, finds as many negative things to say about Peter as positive, although he believes readers of the Gospel are meant to learn from Peter's mistakes. On the positive side, he considers that Peter "repräsentiert das Leitungsamt in der Kirche und wird so wohl als Typos für das Amt und dessen Funktion im Volk Gottes überhaupt gewertet" (p. 142). Negatively, Peter is "in seinem Versagen primär typischer Jünger zu Mahnung und Trost für alle Glaubendbenden" (p. 145).

[60] As we will see in the next chapter, the title Peter applies to Jesus during his confession in 6:68–69, "Holy One of God," is thought by many scholars to reflect a "low" Christology, for it fails to underscore Jesus' divinity or pre-existence. See especially Maynard, "Role of Peter," 543; Goulder, *St. Paul vs. Saint Peter*, 21; and Gee, "Why Did Peter Spring into the Sea?" 484.

[61] See note 1 for a more complete list of scholars who consistently describe Peter as incapable of recognizing profound Christological truths about Jesus.

[62] Many "biographies" of Peter from the nineteenth century and the early part of the twentieth century present a positive picture of the Johannine Peter that is not altogether accurate, for it combines elements of John's Gospel with material from the Synoptics to put a positive spin on Peter's career. These include: T. W. Allies, *St. Peter: His Name and Office* (London: Richardson and Son, 1852); T. Livius, *St. Peter, Bishop of Rome: The Roman Episcopate of the Prince of the Apostles* (London: Burns & Oates, 1888); F.

in conducting his exegesis of John 21, declares that Peter and BD "are represented as partners, of whom neither can take precedence of the other. Peter is the head of the evangelistic and pastoral work of the church, and it is possible that the evangelist intended to make this positive point rather than polemical allusion to Mark, the gospel guaranteed by, according to tradition, Peter...."[63]

R. Schnackenburg, although he declares that Peter "is surpassed in loyalty and faith in the Passion (19:26) and the empty tomb (20:8) by 'the disciple whom Jesus loved,'" maintains that Peter is the representative of Jesus' most "intimate circle of disciples" (esp. 6:68; 13:6–10; and 20:2).[64] He notes that "[t]he 'competition' between the two disciples never hardens into conflict, and it is not exploited polemically against Peter."[65] R. Bauckham is another who warns against seeing Peter and BD as competitors, noting that each has a positive role to play. He observes that "whereas in Peter's case the Gospel emphasizes his love for Jesus, in the beloved disciple's case it emphasizes Jesus' love for him."[66] Bauckham is convinced that the "point of the double story of the two disciples is to show how each, through his own, different way of following Jesus, relates to the church after the resurrection."[67] Because Bauckham conceives of BD as the author of the Gospel, he is able to assign the positive portrayal of Peter to an eyewitness account.

K. Quast also worries that the "rivalry theory" has been overdone of late, and that scholars focus too closely on the activities of Peter and BD in attempting to "reconstruct the community history and the origins of the

---

Underhill, *Saint Peter* (London: Centenary Press, 1937); and J. Lowe, *Saint Peter* (Oxford: OUP, 1956). While the scholarship of J. H. Bernard, *The Gospel According to John* (2 vols; ICC; Edinburgh: T&T Clark, 1928), is of the highest standard, he introduces into an essentially historical-critical analysis of the Gospel a host of subjective opinions about Peter. In looking for an explanation as to why Peter plunges into the tomb while BD waits outside, for example, Bernard says: "Peter was a man of coarser fibre, more hasty, and more ready to put himself forward. That may be the whole explanation" (p. 660).

[63] C. K. Barrett, *The Gospel according to St. John: An Introduction with Commentary and Notes on the Greek Text* (2nd ed. Cambridge: SPCK, 1978), 577. So H. Thyen, *Entwicklungen innerhalb des johanneischen Theologie und Kirche im Spiegel von Joh 21 und der lieblingsjüngertexte des Evangeliums* (BETL 44; Leuven: Leuven University Press, 1977), 259–99.

[64] R. Schnackenburg, *The Gospel according to St. John* (3 vols.; New York: Crossroad, 1990), 2.75.

[65] Ibid., 1.312. The opposite view is held by Kragerud, *Lieblingsjünger*, 19ff.

[66] R. Bauckham, "The Beloved Disciple as Ideal Author," in *The Johannine Writings* (ed. S. E. Porter and C. A. Evans; Sheffield: Sheffield Academic Press, 1998), 63. A similar argument is made by R. Schnackenburg, "Der Jünger, den Jesus liebte," *Evangelisch-Katholischer Kommentar zum Neuen Testament: Vorarbeiten* (2 vols.; Zürich-Neukirchen: Benziger Verlag Zürich, 1970), 2.105–106.

[67] Ibid.

Christian church."[68] Taking careful note not only of the work of Bultmann and Brown but the prolific research these scholars have inspired in others, Quast expresses concern that commentators' "understanding of the relationship between the Beloved Disciple and Peter has, of course, influenced their understanding of Johannine theology, particularly in the areas of ecclesiology and revelation."[69]

Generally speaking, Quast is more complimentary to the Johannine Peter than most scholars. He is one of the few who focuses less on the Christology of Peter's confession than on its superb timing (the mass exodus of disciples from the ministry), and says that "[o]nly in John's Gospel is Peter's confession juxtaposed to this falling away, which heightens its effect."[70] Although Peter is prone to misunderstanding Jesus, Quast observes astutely that Peter receives too little credit from scholars for managing to reveal "his attachment to Jesus" at almost every point in the Gospel.[71] Quast distinguishes himself from the commentators thus far mentioned in arguing that Peter "does not stand on a pedestal above the other disciples, but, at the same time, there are no aspersions cast on his character, faith, or status."[72]

On these points I agree with Quast. On two other points I disagree with him, and these are worth explicating at this point since his work is so frequently cited in this study. First, I disagree with his contention that only BD represents the "true disciple of Jesus."[73] At regular points in his analysis of John 13-20, Quast turns up evidence that BD is the true and unique paradigm of discipleship for the Johannine community and that his achievements appear most distinct when viewed in comparison with Peter's.[74] In my opinion, it is only *together* that Peter

---

[68] K. Quast, *Peter and the Beloved Disciple*, 12. Quast is so determined to avoid placing Peter and BD in a "rivalry" that he counsels against seeing the race to the tomb as a race at all. He sees it as more of an *event*, in which BD's speed is a product of his "loving relationship with Jesus" (p. 123). This may be going too far. The Evangelist does everything but supply a stopwatch and starting gun to make it clear this is a race. My own quarrel with the majority of Johannine exegetes is not that they see the journey as a race but that they see the race as a metaphor for a Gospel-long competition between Peter and BD.

[69] Ibid., 12. See also L. Hartman, "An Attempt at a Text-Centered Exegesis of John 21," *ST* (1984), 38.

[70] Ibid., 163.

[71] Ibid.

[72] Ibid.

[73] Ibid., 123.

[74] In the race to the tomb, for example, Quast judges that "the two are put into a complementary relationship for the purposes of eliciting faith in the resurrection of Jesus based upon the empirical evidence testified to by the best-known of the Twelve" (p. 123). But this "complementary relationship" is wholly lacking in symmetry. The empirical evidence about the resurrection is gathered exclusively by BD, whose faith makes clear that the discarded garments are signs of the resurrection. According to Quast, Peter serves

and BD represent the paradigmatic Johannine Christian, modeling praxis and faith. Second, and most importantly, I disagree with Quast that Peter and BD should be "understood as representatives of their respective communities."[75] Although Quast says that "each community has its own understanding of the person, work and words of Christ, and these varying perspectives can peacefully co-exist," he also says that "the Johannine community appears to have a condescending attitude toward the circle of Christians represented by Peter. The Apostolic Christians do not have the intimacy with Jesus and the accompanying spiritual insight which the Johannine Christians experience."[76] It is difficult if not impossible to reconcile these statements. Due to his belief that Johannine Christians look down upon the Apostolic Christians, Quast must often work against the grain to show that Peter and BD are not rivals.[77]

After extolling Peter's achievements in the Gospel, T. Wiarda argues that "a corrective is needed to many of the current perspectives on the role of Peter in the Gospel of John. The elements of misunderstanding and inadequacy stressed by scholars who perceive anti-Petrine polemic are indeed present; equally strong, however, are qualities of personal devotion."[78] Wiarda lists eight positive qualities possessed by the Johannine Peter: outspokenness, quick initiative,

---

the scene merely to testify to BD's *process* of discovery. He cannot corroborate BD's actual findings for he does not immediately believe. Is Peter a valuable forensic witness as far as Quast is concerned or a well-placed bystander? Readers are left to wonder.

[75] Ibid., 166.

[76] Ibid.

[77] L. Simon, *Petrus und der Lieblingsjünger im Johannesevangelium: Amt und Autorität* (Frankfurt: Peter Lang, 1994), *passim*, comes fairly close to Quast in many of his opinions about Peter. On the one hand, he sees Peter playing the positive function of witness; along with BD, Peter testifies to Jesus' actions, although he represents the Petrine as opposed to the Johannine "congregation" (*Gemeinde*). On the other hand, Peter suffers from "rashness" (*Besonenheit*) and a general "lack of control" (*Unbeherrschtheit*), which are not emulative traits (p. 16). Simon argues that the author of John 21 (not the Evangelist) works to integrate the Johannine and Petrine communities, removing docetic tendencies from the original edition of the Gospel. Relying heavily on material in John 21, A. Reinhartz, *Befriending the Beloved Disciple* (New York: Continuum, 2001), 127, also crafts a fairly positive portrayal of Peter. Rather than endorsing or opposing Brown's theory that Apostolic Christians, represented by Peter, have a less refined Christology than Johannine Christians, she focuses on the positive contributions each disciple makes within the historical and ecclesiological tale: "On the one hand, the Beloved Disciple does no wrong; he makes no false moves, offers no occasion for rebuke, and is placed in the most intimate relationship with Jesus. On the other hand, Peter, while flawed, is entrusted with the care of Jesus' sheep, speaks for the disciples as a group, and does his best to remain faithful."

[78] T. Wiarda, *Peter in the Gospels: Pattern, Personality and Relationship* (Tübingen: Mohr Siebeck, 2000), 178. It is hoped that this study will be received as the sort of "corrective" for which Wiarda calls.

ability to lead other disciples and influence their opinions, resistance in the name of loyalty, enthusiasm for Jesus, desire to honor/serve Jesus, desire to be loyal to Jesus, and courage.[79] Wiarda departs from scholarly convention in seeing the footwashing incident as evidence that Peter is a disciple defined by "initiative and loyalty to Jesus."[80] He also insists that the race to the tomb does not show Peter losing to BD so much as it shows him "back in action again," recovered or recovering from the horror of the threefold denial and eager to investigate the report from Mary Magdalene about suspicious activity at the tomb.[81] Wiarda says that the hard lessons Peter learns about discipleship, most specifically that love for Jesus is superficial if tinged with zeal or self-interest, serve primarily to illustrate "the dynamics of discipleship, with special relevance perhaps to those in pastoral roles."[82] Although Wiarda examines patterns of behavior in Peter across all four Gospels, and so seeks to understand the *canonical Peter*, his opinions about the Johannine Peter are frequently in line with my own.

SUMMARY

While a few scholars have mostly positive things to say about Peter, they rely largely on material in John 21, a chapter widely considered to be a "late" addition to the Gospel penned by someone other than the Evangelist. The vast majority of scholars contends that Peter is portrayed in a negative light. Almost as a matter of routine, they describe him as being slower of foot (20:2–4) and slower on the uptake than BD (20:6–8; 21:7), noting further that he relies on BD to talk to Jesus (13:23–25), to identify and approach Jesus (21:7), and to negotiate doors that separate him from Jesus (18:15–16). For most commentators, Peter is, in a word, BD's *subordinate*. As he lumbers his way through the Gospel, determined to safeguard Jesus from danger and degradation—and thus keep him available for earthly fellowship—he overlooks the signs pointing to Jesus' divinity and, ultimately, his resurrection. As one who lives in BD's shadow, Peter is often thought to represent a group of Christians other than Johannine Christians. This group is usually assigned the title "Apostolic Christians," but we have seen a variety of ethnic and sociological modifiers applied, such as "Judean," "Roman," "Petrine," and "fleshly" Christians.

---

[79] Ibid., 117–118. The positive traits Wiarda discovers in Peter provide an interesting contrast to the mostly negative traits listed by Simon, *Petrus und Lieblingsjünger*, 16: "rashness, ardent zeal, [and] lack of control" (*Unbesonnenheit, glühender Eifer, Unbeherrschtheit*).

[80] Ibid., 116.
[81] Ibid.
[82] Ibid., 176.

By examining each pericope in the Gospel in which Peter appears, I hope to dispel the idea that Peter is a habitual under-performer who, in his few successful endeavors, relies on BD's sensitivity to Jesus to guide him and who, when left to his own devices, teaches negatively about discipleship as an imposing yet dysfunctional follower of Jesus. My hope is that the reader will discover that Peter's attributes and those of BD are complementary, and that the two characters are depicted by both Evangelist and Redactor as composite halves of the ideal Johannine Christian as well as inspirational co-founders of the Johannine church.

PETER AND THE TWELVE

Compared to the Synoptic Gospels, John's Gospel does not pay much attention to "the Twelve" (οἱ δώδεκα). The Fourth Evangelist refers to them in only two passages, 6:67–71 and 20:24, and only on the first occasion do they play an active role, professing faith in Jesus through Peter, their spokesman. The Redactor shows no interest in them at all, but describes a group of *seven* disciples, also led by Peter, setting out to fish and eventually witnessing the final resurrection appearance (21:1–25).[83] Only *five* disciples (Peter, Andrew, Andrew's anonymous companion, Philip, and Nathanael) are called by Jesus in the opening narrative (1:35–51). Peter associates with the Twelve only on the occasion of his confession.

In the Synoptic Gospels, on the other hand, "the Twelve" are much more prominent. They are Jesus' closest supporters. Although Peter is their spokesman, they are important enough that their individual names are given, which is not the case in John. Although the Twelve in the Synoptics are routinely baffled by Jesus' words and actions, they remain his constant companions. Jesus sends them out as apostles and gives them authority to cast out demons and cure diseases (Mark 3:14–15; Matt 10:1–4; Luke 9:1–2). In Matthew and Luke it is a watershed moment in their collective career when they are promised thrones from which to judge the twelve tribes of Israel (Matt 19:28; Luke 22:30).

Such a scene would be entirely out of place in John's Gospel, in which true disciples are individuals who believe in and follow Jesus. Discipleship is thus a broader category in John's Gospel than in the Synoptics. G. M. Burge rightly observes that "John is particularly interested throughout his gospel to reduce the significance of the Twelve, not to demote them, but to emphasize the general importance of the individual believers."[84] F. J. Moloney goes further than this in

---

[83] The familiar characters of Peter, Nathanael, Thomas Didymus, and BD are joined by the previously unmentioned sons of Zebedee and one unnamed disciple.

[84] G. M. Burge, *The Anointed Community: The Holy Spirit in the Johannine Tradition* (Grand Rapids: Eerdmans, 1987), 120 n. 26. See also Cullmann, *Johannine Circle*, 67.

saying that "[t]he group plays no significant role in the Gospel's theology of discipleship, but the grouping of 'twelve' is by now traditional. The author uses it here to differentiate between 'many of the disciples' (vv. 60, 66) and a smaller group who have come to authentic belief in the word and person of Jesus."[85]

If I am right in believing that the Fourth Evangelist is familiar with the story of Peter's confession as it appears in Matthew 16:16–19 (see chapter 2), it may be that Peter is presented as spokesman for the Twelve in the confession scene because he appears this way in the inherited tradition (cf. also Mark 8:27–30 and Luke 9:18–21). John certainly presupposes in his audience some familiarity with the Twelve, for they are introduced without explanation or comment at the end of the Bread of Life Discourse (6:67), an event that takes place more than a year into Jesus' ministry.[86] I agree with C.S. Keener that the Twelve are on hand for Peter's confession in John's Gospel essentially because John's original readership *expects them to be*: "Undoubtedly reflecting knowledge of historical tradition, Peter plays a role similar to that preserved in the Synoptic tradition, as spokesman for the disciples."[87]

As we saw in our survey of the Johannine literature, the idea that Peter and the Twelve represent a strand of Christianity distinct from Johannine Christianity is pervasive in modern scholarship. To a considerable extent, theories that seek to reconstruct Johannine community history depend on the idea that Johannine theology and Christology are distinguishable from the theology and Christology embraced by Peter and Apostolic Christians.[88] Yet Peter appears as spokesman for the Twelve on one occasion only, and, as mentioned, he never appears this way in John 21. Would not the Redactor, in compiling a chapter concerned with ecclesial issues (including Peter's post-Easter pastoral responsibilities), mention the Twelve if he were interested in reminding us of Peter's connection to this group? If, as many argue, Peter receives praise in John 21 as a roundabout way of extending an olive branch (or

---

[85] F. J. Moloney, *Gospel of John* (SP 4; Collegeville: Liturgical Press, 1998), 231.

[86] Barrett, *St. John*, 306, suggests that John's audience is familiar with the Twelve through their acquaintance with Markan tradition.

[87] C. S. Keener, *The Gospel of John: A Commentary* (2 vols.; Peabody, Mass.: Hendrickson, 2003), 1.697.

[88] For R. E. Brown, as we have seen, the doctrine of Jesus' pre-existence is the major concept they fail to grasp. Perkins, "John," 945–46, modifies Brown's theory of community development only slightly when she describes the community drawing its boundaries against three groups: the *followers of John the Baptist*, the *Jews*, and *other Christians*. Peter and the Twelve represent a fourth group: "Christians of Apostolic communities outside the Johannine church." This group is indirectly impugned on the many occasions when Peter's "faith and closeness to Jesus" is shown to be inferior to that of BD. In the mind of O'Grady, *According to John*, 132, the Johannine community frowns upon the Apostolic churches for being "preoccupied with corollaries to Christianity instead of emphasizing the essentials of faith and love."

the hand of fellowship) to the Apostolic church, why not restore "the Twelve" to prominence as well? There is little reason for readers to connect Peter closely to the Twelve or Apostolic Christians when the Evangelist and the Redactor do not do so.

Rather than focusing on the Twelve, the Evangelist and the Redactor show Peter congregating with disciples in groups of various sizes. In 1:35–51 he appears in a group of five disciples, in 21:1–25 he is the leader of a group of seven disciples, and, in the many instances in which he is teamed with BD, he is one of two disciples who follow Jesus. Like BD, he is not portrayed as one who is "sent out" (i.e. serves as an *apostle*), but as a disciple who struggles to follow Jesus and express faith in an appropriate manner. One of the messages of the Gospel is that Peter is a representative of Johannine Christianity and not the leader of a rival or competing movement.

JOHN AND THE SYNOPTICS

In a recent monograph on Petrine traditions in the primitive church, F. Lapham makes the following observation about the characterization of Peter in the canonical Gospels: "[v]arious important traditions in all four Gospels link together Peter's bravado (Luke 22:33), his slowness to understand (Mark 8:32), and his ultimate disloyalty (John 18:25–27). All of these traditions are associated in some way with the disciples' failure to come to terms, during Jesus' lifetime, with the necessity of persecution and suffering, whether for Jesus or for themselves."[89]

While this is to some extent true, and there is some degree of continuity in the characterization of Peter across all four Gospels, it is also true that the Fourth Gospel presents us with a very different picture of Peter than the Synoptics.[90] We have already noted that the Fourth Gospel includes many

---

[89] F. Lapham, *Peter: The Myth, the Man and the Writings: A Study of Early Petrine Text and Tradition* (JSNTSup 239. Sheffield: Sheffield Academic Press, 2003), 8.

[90] Perkins, *Peter*, 97, argues that Matthew and Luke reshaped "the Markan image of Peter so that Christians could see Peter as a model for discipleship," but that John, in making BD into the paradigmatic disciple, "departs from this trend." The statement is in line with Perkins' belief that Peter is demoted by the Fourth Evangelist; it seems also to presuppose John's familiarity with Matthean and Lukan redaction of Mark. The most exhaustive study to date on John and the Synoptics remains D. M. Smith's *John Among the Gospels* (2nd ed.; Columbia: University of South Carolina Press, 2001). A slightly updated bibliography on the subject appears in K. Scholtissek, "The Johannine Gospel in Recent Research," in *The Face of New Testament Studies: A Survey of Recent Research* (ed. S. McKnight and G. R. Osborne; Grand Rapids: Baker Academic, 2004), 444–72. Also helpful in this volume is C. L. Blomberg's "John and Jesus," 209–26. While most scholars continue to argue for Johannine independence, a few hold out for John's knowledge of the Synoptics. For a particularly forceful defense of the idea that John

scenes involving Peter that are not in the Synoptics. It is also true that many well-known scenes from the Synoptics in which Peter is a key player are missing from John. These include the appointing of the Twelve (Mark 3:1–19; Matt 10:2–5; Luke 6:14–16), the transfiguration (Mark 9:2–6; Matt 17:1–5; Luke 9:28–33), Peter's declaration that the Twelve have left 'everything' (πάντα) to follow Jesus (Mark 10:28; Matt 19:27; Luke 18:28), the healing of Jairus' daughter (Mark 5:37; Luke 8:51), Peter's brief walk on the Sea of Galilee (Matt 14:2–31), the conversation about the Temple tax (Matt 17:24–27), the question about forgiveness within the church (Matt 18:21), Peter's admission to being a sinful man (Luke 5:8), and the disciples' sleepiness in Gethsemane during Jesus' agony (Mark 14:32–42; Matt 26:36–46; cf. Luke 22:39–46).

Because the Fourth Gospel shares so little Petrine material with the Synoptics—the major exception being John's and Matthew's handling of the call/naming/confession pericope—it will usually be possible to analyze Peter's function in John's Gospel without referring to the Synoptic Gospels. In fact, there is such a high degree of variance between John's portrait of Peter and the Synoptic portraits that a relatively simple question comes to mind: "Is there such a person / literary character as the *canonical* Peter?" Even taking into account Lapham's point about Petrine continuity across the four Gospels, John presents us with a character that bucks so many Synoptic trends that one wonders whether questing for the "canonical Peter" is a worthwhile pursuit or a wild goose chase!

IDENTITY OF THE BELOVED DISCIPLE

Although speculating on the identity of BD is something of a rite of passage in Johannine scholarship, and a brief review of the literature turns up all manner of colorful theories identifying BD with the various named characters in John's Gospel or other parts of the NT (e.g. John son of Zebedee, Lazarus,

---

knows *and* uses the Synoptics, see F. Neirynck, "John and the Synoptics 1975-1990," in *John and the Synoptics* (ed. A. Denaux; BETL 101; Leuven: Leuven University Press, 1992), 3–62. In "John and the Synoptics in Recent Commentaries," *ETL* 74 (1998): 386–97, Neirynck updates his 1990 thesis—essentially to say it is catching on—although the evidence suggests that it is primarily German scholars who are subscribing to this idea with regularity. U. Schnelle, for example, in his recent NT introduction, *The History and Theology of the New Testament Writings* (trans. M. E. Boring; Minneapolis: Fortress, 1998), argues that "John's adoption of the gospel genre and the compositional analogies speak in favour of John's knowledge of the Synoptics" (p. 499). Similar positions are adopted in the recent commentaries of L. Schenke, *Johannes* (Düsseldorf: Patmos, 1998) and U. Wilckens, *Das Evangelium nach Johannes* (NTD 4; Göttingen: Vanderhoeck & Ruprecht, 2000). Scholars who have, at one time or another, argued for John's dependence on Mark (but probably not Matthew and Luke) include C. K. Barrett, M. E. Glasswell, W.G. Kümmel, and R. H. Lightfoot.

Nathanael, Mary Magdalene, Martha, Thomas, Joseph of Arimathea, the rich young ruler, Matthias, Paul),[91] I am content to respect the wishes of the author(s) and let him remain anonymous. As we will see, much of his power and paraenetic function is due to his anonymity.[92] Although it will take the full length of this study to learn all of BD's habits and qualities and determine the dynamics of his relationship with Peter, three basic observations can be made about him at this point:

First, due to the fact that only male personal and demonstrative pronouns are used to describe him (13:23–25; 18:15–16; 20:3–10; 19:26–27 [here BD is referred to as the spiritual "son" (υἱός) of Jesus' mother]; 20:3-10; and 21:21–25), it seems fair to conclude that BD is male.[93] If *he* is actually a *she*, it is odd that Peter refers to *her* only as "him" / "this (male) one" (οὗτος; 21:21) and that Jesus also refers to *her* only as "he" or "him" (e.g. αὐτόν in 21:22). The narrator, too, relies exclusively on male pronouns to describe BD (numerous). To argue against BD being male requires that a great deal be read into the text.[94]

Second, BD appears to be a real person and not a representational figure or symbol of pious discipleship for the Johannine church (contra Loisy, Lindars and many others).[95] The Evangelist and the Redactor each understand him to be

---

[91] Charlesworth, *Beloved Disciple*, 127–224, provides a far more extensive list of possibilities, though opts himself for Thomas.

[92] The benefits of anonymity in the case of BD are listed by, among others, Bauckham, "Beloved Disciple," 46–68; and Watty, "Significance of Anonymity," 209–12.

[93] Here I agree with Reinhartz, *Befriending the Beloved Disciple*, 23. In a spirited defense of the idea that υἱός need not be seen as proof of BD being male, Ringe, *Wisdom's Friends*, 17, points out that Hellenistic philosophers, "whose discussions might well have been part of the cultural context of John's community," sometimes considered a person who takes on the "filial or familial responsibilities" of a sick or dying friend to be a "substitute 'son' of the family."

[94] In my opinion, an inclusive reading of John's Gospel does not necessitate leaving open the question of BD's gender. As is well known, many of Jesus' most important conversations in the Gospel take place with women, and women are among his closest disciples (see 4:9–26; 11:21–45; 12:2–3; 19:25). At no time does the Evangelist seek to confuse us about the gender of these characters by throwing in the odd male personal pronoun.

[95] See A. Loisy, *Le quatrième Évangile* (Paris: Alphonse Picard et Fils, 1903), 123–39; and B. Lindars, *John* (Sheffield: JSOT Press, 1990), 22. See also M. E. Boring and F. B. Craddock, *The People's New Testament Commentary* (Louisville: Westminster John Knox, 2004), 334–35; and S. M. Schneiders, *Written that You May Believe: Encountering Jesus in the Fourth Gospel* (New York: Crossroad, 1999), 227–29. Schneiders maintains that BD is "an epithet that fits all believers that manifest certain qualifications during the lifetime of Jesus, in the time of the Johannine community, and down through the ages" (p. 228). A. Meyer, *Kommt und seht: Mystagogie im Johannesevangelium ausgehend von Joh 1,35–51* (Würzburg: Echter Verlag, 2005), 77, maintains that "[d]er Geliebte Jünger verkörpert die *corporate identity* der joh Gemeinde, hinter seiner Gestalt liegt etwas vom

the authenticator of many (all?) of the traditions behind the Gospel (19:35; 21:24) *as well as* a paradigmatic practitioner of the Christ faith. In other words, he is remembered as well as revered. In my opinion, John 21 was written primarily to address the issue of BD's death. An authority of no less stature than Jesus is required to make a final resurrection appearance and, in a conversation with Peter, another iconic figure, convince the community that BD's inability to survive until the Parousia is not a reason for undue concern. A central message of the chapter is that BD's witness endures even when the disciple does not. If members of the community will only *follow* Jesus (21:19, 22), then participation in his ongoing life—and by extension the eternal life of God (10:38; 14:10; 17:21)—will take care of itself.

Third, BD is most likely a Jerusalemite who enters the story at the Last Supper (13:23ff) and whose intimacy with Jesus is so pronounced that the Evangelist chooses to introduce him as one whose natural position is to recline upon Jesus' breast (κόλπος), evoking the image of Jesus dwelling in the bosom / breast (κόλπος) of the Father (1:18). To imagine that BD is the anonymous disciple of 1:35–40 and therefore a participant in Jesus' ministry from the call narrative onward is to imagine that he has nothing to say about Peter's extended confession in 6:68–69. Is such a scenario credible? Elsewhere in the Gospel it is not BD's habit to stay beneath the radar, as it were, when Peter is expressing solidarity with Jesus by following or professing faith in him (18:15–16; 20:2–20; 21:7, 20–23). In fact, BD's actions often prompt actions in Peter or are prompted *by* them. Would BD, if he were present for the confession, pass up an opportunity to modify, affirm, improve, or otherwise supplement it? It seems to me unlikely. If, however, he is a Jerusalemite who becomes active in the ministry only on the eve of Jesus' execution, it is understandable he has nothing to say about an event that transpired one year earlier in or near Capernaum.

As we examine Peter's relationship with BD in the chapters that follow, I will attempt to show that the two practice together the three activities fundamental to Johannine discipleship: *following*, *believing*, and *testifying*. While their faith is demonstrated in different ways, they each have a fundamental role to play as inspirational founding members of the Johannine church.

---

ursprünglich-originären Traditions-hintergrund der joh Theologie und Sprache im JohEv."

CHAPTER 2

PETER'S CALL, NAMING, AND CONFESSION

INTRODUCTION: PETER IN JOHN 1–6

For a disciple who figures in more scenes than any other disciple in John's Gospel, Peter is introduced with little fanfare. Unlike in the Synoptic Gospels, it is Andrew and not Peter who first confesses Jesus as "Messiah" (John 1:41; cf. Mark 8:29; Matt 16:16; Luke 9:20). Andrew also engages in the Gospel's first explicit missionary endeavor when he finds and brings Peter to Jesus (1:41–42).[1] Unlike Andrew, Philip (1:45), and Nathanael (1:46), all of whom have something to say to or about Jesus in the opening call narrative, Peter says nothing. In contrast to Andrew, Philip, and, by way of proclamation, John the Baptist (1:29–36), Peter does not engage in any sort of missionary activity.[2] Pressed into service by Jesus, he silently takes up the call to follow.[3] It is, to put it mildly, not a rousing start.

---

[1] One can, of course, equate proclamation with witness and argue that John the Baptist acts as the first missionary when he exclaims, "Behold the lamb of God!" (ἴδε ὁ ἀμνὸς τοῦ θεοῦ), but he does not physically bring people to Jesus, as do Andrew and Philip.

[2] According to J. L. Staley, "What Can a Postmodern Approach to the Fourth Gospel Add?" in *Jesus in Johannine Tradition* (ed. R. T. Fortna and T. Thatcher; Louisville: Westminster John Knox, 2001), 53, "[t]his peculiarly Johannine motif of meeting Jesus through an agent is not found in the Synoptic Gospels, where association with Jesus normally comes instead through direct personal contact with him." Staley goes on to argue that the "motif of agency" as described in 1:35–51 belonged to the "original opening of the narrative" and not a later editorial phase. Bultmann, *Gospel of John*, 97–108, argues similarly, as does E. Ruckstuhl, *Die literarische Einheit des Johannesevangeliums: Der gegenwärtige Stand der einschlägigen Forschungen* (Göttingen: Vandenhoeck & Ruprecht, 1987), 113–16. S. G. Sinclair, on the other hand, in *The Road and the Truth: The Editing of John's Gospel* (Vallejo, CA: BIBAL Press, 1994), 19–23, attributes the conversion stories of John 1:35–51 to a Johannine 'editor' who opens the canonical Gospel with a "recapitulation of the Christian life."

[3] His active discipleship is not explicitly recorded until 6:68. See Moloney, *Gospel of John*, 59, for the spiritual and physical meanings of ἀκολουθέω.

Yet there are at least three signs in the opening call narrative that Peter will figure prominently in the Gospel. First, despite the fact that Andrew enters the narrative ahead of Peter, he is introduced as "Simon Peter's brother" (Ἀνδρέας ὁ ἀδελφὸς Σίμωνος Πέτρου, 1:40; cf. 6:8), which suggests that John's implied reader already knows something about Peter.[4] Second, after Andrew has stayed with Jesus for a day and become convinced of his Messianic status, he makes evangelization of Peter his "first" (πρῶτον) priority. Third, Jesus needs only to look at Peter to know that he "will be called" Cephas (translated into Greek as Πέτρος in 1:42). Although the naming scene is designed primarily to emphasize Jesus' foreknowledge (cf. 2:24; 4:18; 5:6; 6:64; etc.), it drops a hint that Peter's role will expand as the story continues.

When, in 6:68–69, Peter finally does speak—and this is perhaps an entire year later in the Gospel timeline—he shows that he has not been idle in his discipleship.[5] In fact, he has gone from being one who must be "brought" (ἤγαγεν, 1:42) to Jesus to one who speaks for Jesus' closest group of followers. Peter confesses that the Twelve "have come to believe" (πεπιστεύκαμεν) and "have come to know" (ἐγνώκαμεν) that Jesus has the "words of eternal life" and is the "Holy One of God" (6:68–69). What is perhaps most impressive about Peter's confession is its complexity and timing. On behalf of the Twelve, he swears allegiance to Jesus at a time when "many" disciples are finding his teachings difficult and fleeing his ministry. The tripartite confession, made up of catechetical-sounding statements about the loyalty of true followers (6:68a), the unique content of Jesus' revelation (6:68b), and Jesus' status as an agent of God (6:69), has the dual effect of stemming the exodus of disciples from the ministry and shifting the topic of conversation from the health of the ministry to the movements of a single traitorous individual (Judas). It is an impressive turnaround for a disciple who, a year before, had nothing to say when brought face to face with Jesus, and shows the manner in which faith accrues in one who centers his or her life in Christ.

THE CALL OF THE FIRST DISCIPLES: 1:35–40

Of the two disciples in the opening call narrative who peel off from the ministry of John the Baptist to follow Jesus (1:35–39), we are given the identity of only one: Andrew (1:40; cf. 6:8; 12:22). Andrew and his unnamed companion are so captivated by the Baptist's statement, "Behold the lamb of God" (ἴδε ὁ ἀμνὸς τοῦ θεοῦ, 1:36; cf. 1:29),[6] that they set out to follow Jesus.[7] They are not

---

[4] Meyer, *KomMatt und seht*, 118.

[5] One year as measured as the time between the first two Passovers of Jesus' ministry.

[6] According to H. Conzelmann, *An Outline of the Theology of the New Testament* (trans. J. Bowden; London: SCM, 1969), 337, "lamb of God" and "Son of God" are

long in this endeavor when Jesus turns and puts to them a seemingly simple question: "What are you searching for?" The question works on two levels: it conveys Jesus' curiosity about the motivations of would-be followers and invites would-be followers to divulge to him their innermost desires. R. A. Culpepper is probably correct to characterize *"What are you searching for?"* as "one of the great existential questions of life."[8] Rather than being disappointed with the disciples when they express a pragmatic desire to know where Jesus is currently staying, Jesus tells them to "come and see" (ἔρχεσθε καὶ ὄψεσθε, v. 39). They stay with him for the remainder of the day, at which point Andrew makes an informed decision to go and find Peter and tell him that they have found the Messiah (vv. 41–42).[9]

The identity of Andrew's anonymous companion has long been mulled over by scholars. The tradition of the early Church was to regard him as BD, typically thought to be John son of Zebedee and the authority behind the Gospel.[10] While this argument continues to draw its notable proponents (e.g., J. H. Bernard, J. A. T. Robinson, R. A. Culpepper, and A. J. Köstenberger), it is no longer adopted as a matter of course.[11] A popular offshoot of the argument continues to see the anonymous disciple and BD as one and the same person, but holds that this person is not John son of Zebedee. J. H. Charlesworth, for example, believes the anonymous disciple is Thomas (cf. 19:35; 21:24).[12] R. T. Fortna maintains that Andrew's companion is "anonymous and evidently to be ignored at the pre-Johannine level," but is, at the Johannine level, BD.[13] R. E. Brown says something similar in arguing that the anonymous disciple of 1:35–40 *becomes*

---

synonymous terms in the mind of the Baptist (cf. 1:34). It is not clear whether Andrew and his unnamed companion are in the Baptist's company in 1:34, however, and the fact that they address Jesus as "Rabbi" in 1:38 probably suggests they do not yet recognize him as the Son of God.

[7] Quast, *Peter and the Beloved Disciple*, 28, sees the phrase ἐκ τῶν μαθητῶν αὐτοῦ δύο (1:35) as a partitive ablative, describing two of John's disciples peeling off from a larger contingent. But the correct image to keep in mind, I believe, is not Andrew and his companion breaking away from a larger group of disciples but parting company with the Baptist, who "must decrease," and taking up with Jesus, who "must increase" (3:30).

[8] R. A. Culpepper, *The Gospel and Letters of John* (IBT; Nashville: Abingdon, 1998), 122.

[9] J. Becker, *Das Evangelium nach Johannes, Kapitel 1-10* (ÖTK 4/1; Gütersloh: Verlagshaus Mohn, 1991), 122.

[10] See the discussion in S. K. Ray, *St. John's Gospel: A Bible Study Guide and Commentary for Individuals and Groups* (San Francisco: Ignatius, 2002), 62–65.

[11] Bernard, *John*, 1.53; J. A. T. Robinson, *Priority of John* (London: SCM, 1985), 180–81; Culpepper, *John Son of Zebedee*, 59; Köstenberger, *John*, 76.

[12] Charlesworth, *Beloved Disciple*, 329–30.

[13] R. T. Fortna, *The Fourth Gospel and its Predecessor: From Narrative Source to Present Gospel* (Edinburgh: T & T Clark), 37 n. 68.

BD at Jesus' "hour" (13:1ff.), which is to say at that moment when his final identity can be achieved "in a Christological context."[14]

As I mentioned in the introduction to this study, I am of the opinion that the anonymous disciple of 1:35–40 and BD are *not* one and the same person (so F. Neirynck, B. Lindars, F. Filson, M. E. Boismard, J. R. Michaels, and R. Schnackenburg, among others),[15] but that BD is a Jerusalemite who enters the story at the Last Supper (13:23ff.) and whose intimacy with Jesus is so pronounced that the Evangelist seems almost to delight in introducing him as one whose natural inclination is to lean against Jesus' breast (κόλπος) at supper (13:23). The anonymous disciple of 1:35–40, on the other hand, is introduced to us as a disciple of John the Baptist, and one whose habit is to follow Andrew, not Peter. Andrew's anonymous companion is clearly meant to remain anonymous, and functions in the call narrative as the second witness to the proclamation of John the Baptist that Jesus is the "Lamb of God," thereby making the testimony valid according to Jewish law (cf. 8:17).[16]

---

[14] Brown, *Community of the Beloved Disciple*, 33.

[15] In a rather terse response to scholars who claim the linguistic similarities between 1:35–42 and 13:23–25 point to BD being the central character in each scene, Neirynck, "The Anonymous Disciple in John 1," *EThL* 66 (1990): 5–37, argues convincingly that the asyndetic use of ἦν (1:40 and 13:23) is the *only* striking parallel between the passages. B. Lindars, "John," in *The Johannine Literature* (ed. B Lindars, R. B. Edwards, and J. M. Court; Sheffield: Sheffield Academic Press, 2000), 42–46, also believes the linguistic similarities between John 1 and John 13 are too weak to support the contention that BD is the anonymous disciple in 1:35–40. F. V. Filson, "Who was the Beloved Disciple?" *JBL* 68 (1949): 84, argues against the anonymous disciple being BD primarily to support his (ultimately unconvincing) argument that BD is Lazarus, but his observation that "it would hardly have occurred to the first readers" of the Gospel to make an explicit connection between the anonymous disciple of chapter one and BD is astute. Boismard, *Du Baptême à Cana [Jean 1.19–2.11]* (Paris: Cerf, 1956), 72–73, and J. R. Michaels, *John* (NIBC; Peabody, Mass.: Paternoster, 1989), 37, each contend that the anonymous disciple is Philip, whose movements are often linked to Andrew's (6:5–9; 12:21–22) and who, along with Andrew and Peter, comes from Bethsaida (1:44). Schnackenburg, "Der Jünger den Jesus liebte," 97–100, thinks the whole idea of forging a link between the activities of the anonymous disciple and BD is "fragwürdig" (dubious). He depends for his characterization of BD on material in chapters 13, 20 and 21 only.

[16] Meyer, *Kommt und seht*, 105, sees a dramatic literary function in the arrival of two disciples at this point in the story: "Symmetrisch zu den zwei prophetischen Lehrern Johannes und Jesus ist es das einzige Mal innerhalb von Joh 1,35–51, dass zwei Jünger als Paar auftreten."

Peter Meets Jesus: 1:40–1:42

⁴⁰One of the two who heard John speak and followed him was Andrew, Simon Peter's brother. ⁴¹He first found his brother Simon and said to him, "We have found the Messiah" (which is translated 'the Christ'). ⁴²He brought Simon to Jesus, who looked at him and said, "You are Simon son of John. You are to be called Cephas" (which is translated Peter). (⁴⁰ἮΗν Ἀνδρέας ὁ ἀδελφὸς Σίμωνος Πέτρου εἷς ἐκ τῶν δύο τῶν ἀκουσάντων παρὰ Ἰωάννου καὶ ἀκολουθησάντων αὐτῷ· ⁴¹εὑρίσκει οὗτος πρῶτον τὸν ἀδελφὸν τὸν ἴδιον Σίμωνα καὶ λέγει αὐτῷ· εὑρήκαμεν τὸν Μεσσίαν, ὅ ἐστιν μεθερμηνευόμενον χριστός. ⁴²ἤγαγεν αὐτὸν πρὸς τὸν Ἰησοῦν. ἐμβλέψας αὐτῷ ὁ Ἰησοῦς εἶπεν· σὺ εἶ Σίμων ὁ υἱὸς Ἰωάννου, σὺ κληθήσῃ Κηφᾶς, ὃ ἑρμηνεύεται Πέτρος.)

We have seen that Andrew and his anonymous companion remain with Jesus for only a day before bringing to Peter their message, "We have found the Messiah." Their decision to follow Jesus all the way to his dwelling place should not be construed as a response to the Baptist's proclamation, "Behold the Lamb of God," but to Jesus' invitation to "come and see" where he "abides" (μένω, 1:39).[17] Elsewhere in the Gospel Jesus is said to *abide* in the Father (μενεῖτε, 15:10), the Father is said to *abide* in Jesus (μένων, 14:10), and Jesus promises to build heavenly *abodes* (μοναί) for his disciples (14:2–3), and therefore readers cannot be faulted for suspecting that Jesus is inviting the pair into a lasting relationship and not on a short-term excursion.[18]

In 1:40–42, as in 4:7–29, 39–43; 6:68–69; and 9:1–38, faith in Jesus expands in proportion to time spent in his company and gives rise to a confession that speaks to some aspect of his person or work.[19] Because the title

---

[17] P. Barnett, *Jesus and the Rise of Early Christianity: A History of New Testament Times* (Downer's Grove, Illinois: InterVarsity, 1999), 233, takes it for granted that Peter, like Andrew, is a member of the Baptist's inner circle, but nothing in the text suggests this.

[18] In 8:31 Jesus defines a "disciple" (μαθητής) as one who "abides" (μένω) in his word. Waetjen, *Beloved Disciple*, 105, makes the following incisive observation: "Even as the Spirit descended and *remained* upon Jesus, these disciples will remain with Jesus, and as the author continues to use the verb μένειν (to stay, remain), it will gradually develop into a spirituality of relationship between Jesus and his disciples that will culminate in a union of interdependence."

[19] S. O. Abogunrin, "The Three Variant Accounts of Peter's Call: A Critical and Theological Examination of the Texts," *NTS* 31 (1985): 596, contends that an overnight stay in Jesus' company is required to convince the disciples that the cost of discipleship is "nothing less than total obedience and abiding in him forever." Moloney, *Gospel of John*, 60, is not receptive to this idea that Andrew comes to a decision about Jesus' person and

bequeathed to Jesus by Andrew and his companion gives expression to *Jewish messianic* hopes (Μεσσίας is a transliteration unique to John's Gospel in the NT; cf. also 4:25), the Evangelist may be suggesting that Andrew and his companion speak for Israel as much as for themselves when they say "*We* have found (εὑρήκαμεν) the Messiah," and that Jesus is at this particular point in the story is more of a national figure than a universal one (cf. 1:31).[20]

It is fair to infer from the accusative adverb πρῶτον (v. 41) that Andrew, upon spending a day in Jesus' company and becoming convinced of his messianic status, makes evangelization of Peter his "first" order of business.[21] After he brings the good news about Jesus to Peter, he physically brings (ἄγω) Peter to Jesus, letting Jesus determine the course of the relationship. Because Jesus' invitation to Andrew and his companion to "come and see" the truth about him had the effect of instilling faith in Andrew, the reader may well imagine that Andrew hopes the same will happen in Peter's case.[22] A. Meyer argues persuasively that Andrew is as much a mediator in the scene as a missionary: "Andreas bringt seinen Bruder mit Jesus Christus in Kontakt, er vermittelt die Begegnung mit dem Mysterium."[23] As Schnackenburg points out, the fact that Peter is called after his brother Andrew should not be construed as an attempt by the Evangelist to minimize his importance:

> There is no question of Peter's being disparaged in the present text, either by the fact that he is not one of the first two disciples to follow Jesus, or that he only comes to follow Jesus through the mediation of another, his brother Andrew. On the contrary, since the evangelist has passed over in silence Jesus' conversation with the first disciples, Peter

---

role before deciding to proselytize Peter, but prefers to see Jesus as the focus of the scene, or the one whose initiative (1:38–39, 42) leads to Peter's discipleship.

[20] See the discussion in C. K. Barrett, *The Gospel of John and Judaism* (London: SPCK, 1975), 8–9. In the opinion of J. Ferreira, *Johannine Ecclesiology* (JSNTSup 160; Sheffield: Sheffield Academic Press, 1998), 136 n. 108, the nationalistic nomenclature of 1:41 (cf. 4:25) is ultimately overwhelmed by the idea that the "Johannine Jesus is certainly rather the Christian Christ who comes to save the world."

[21] This could mean that he recruits Peter (1) immediately after leaving Jesus' company or (2) before recruiting anyone else (i.e., Philip or Nathanael). Compared to πρῶτον, which appears in the great majority of ancient manuscripts, πρῶτος (which would describe Andrew evangelizing Peter before anyone else has a chance to) is weakly attested (ℵ* R K L U W^{sup} Δ and Λ). Due to the fact that three of the Old Latin manuscripts (*b, e, r*) read *mane* (early in the morning), the assumption is made by Bernard, *John*, 1.58, that the original Greek of the passage was πρωΐ but that the text was corrupted at an early date.

[22] See Simon, *Petrus und der Lieblingsjünger*, 129.

[23] Meyer, *KomMatt und seht*, 117.

PETER'S CALL, NAMING, AND CONFESSION

is distinguished by the words addressed to him and the prediction of his future rank.[24]

Considering that Andrew is introduced to us as Simon Peter's brother and makes evangelization of Peter his first priority, Schnackenburg's assessment is persuasive. There is also much to recommend the statement of T. L. Brodie that in the adverb πρῶτον there is an "intimation or suggestion that Simon is in some sense first" among the disciples.[25]

When Jesus meets Peter, he initially hails him as "Simon son of John" (Σίμων ὁ υἱὸς Ἰωάννου, v. 42b), but then informs him that he "will be called" (κληθήσῃ) Cephas (Gk = Πέτρος, v. 42c). The closest Synoptic parallel is Matt 16:16–19, in which Jesus refers to Peter by the patronymic Σίμων Βαριωνᾶ before telling him that he is the "rock" (πέτρα) upon which he "will build" (οἰκοδομήσω) his church. The name change is effective immediately in Matthew's Gospel even though the investiture of ecclesial authority is reserved for a later (i.e., post-Easter) date. But while Matthew suggests that Peter earns the nickname and office by receiving the Father's revelation about Jesus, John presents no such action / reward dynamic. Other than following Andrew, Peter accomplishes no great task prior to meeting Jesus. He does not come to Jesus of his own initiative but, as mentioned, is *brought* (ἤγαγεν) to him. The Fourth Evangelist uses the aorist indicative of ἄγω on three other occasions in the Gospel, always to describe someone being moved against their will.[26] Nothing in our passage indicates that Andrew *forces* Peter to come along with him to meet Jesus, but the use of ἤγαγεν makes it clear that following Jesus is not Peter's idea.

What, then, does Peter do—or *will* he do—to warrant the name change? The bestowal of a nickname in a scene of this context would not have been understood by John's original audience to be a casual event; that is, they would not have suspected that Jesus makes the switch from "Simon" to "Cephas" simply because the latter name rolls more easily off the tongue. Set in a call narrative in which Israel's long-awaited Μεσσίας is the central player, the naming episode would have evoked OT stories in which a character's name change marks "the beginning of a new relation to God," e.g., Jacob becoming Israel in Gen 32:28, Abram becoming Abraham in Gen 17:5, or Sarai becoming Sarah in Gen 17:15.[27] (One also thinks of Isa 62:2–12, in which a repentant

---

[24] Schnackenburg, *St. John*, 1.312.

[25] Brodie, *Gospel according to John*, 161. So Brown, *John*, 1.75; and Schnackenburg, *St. John*, 1.311.

[26] In 19:13 Jesus is forcibly *brought* outside by Pilate for inspection by οἱ Ἰουδαῖοι, in 18:13 he is *brought* to Annas, and in 7:45 certain of the Temple police are scolded for *not bringing* Jesus to the Pharisees.

[27] Bernard, *St. John*, 1.60.

Jerusalem is promised a new name from the Lord, such as "My Delight is in Her" [v. 4] or "Sought Out, a City not Forsaken" [v. 12].)[28] Although J. Fitzmyer has discovered in the Elephantine papyri evidence that Κηφᾶς was used as a proper name in the Mediterranean world as early as the fifth century B.C.E., most scholars believe that it was not used in Jesus' day and that Peter receives the nickname in recognition of some aspect of his "character or career."[29]

If R. E. Brown and others are correct that "Cephas" translates best into English as the American nickname "Rocky," then the Petrine trait in question may be *stability* or *permanence*.[30] We saw in our exegesis of 1:40 that John presupposes in his reader one basic fact about Peter: he is better known than Andrew. We are not constrained to imagine that the reader's familiarity with Peter ends there. In the Fourth Gospel supplement (John 21), for example, the Redactor presupposes the reader's familiarity with crucifixion as the manner of Peter's death (vv. 18–19). And if "following" (ἀκολουθέω) in 13:37 is a veiled reference to martyrdom, which I argue in the next chapter is the case, then the Evangelist does as well. If Peter's kinship to Andrew and his martyrdom are known biographical facts about him, it is not unreasonable to imagine that the reader also knows something about the history behind the name change, including the trait in Peter it signifies.[31]

---

[28] See also Mark 3:17, in which the sons of Zebedee are named *Boanerges* (Sons of Thunder).

[29] See Brown, *John*, 1.76.

[30] Ibid., 1.75–76. See also R. E. Brown, K. P. Donfried, and J. Reumann, eds., *Peter in the New Testament* (Minneapolis: Augsburg; New York: Paulist, 1973), 31 n. 279. Wiarda, *Peter in the Gospels*, 114–15, believes the positive traits that earn Simon his new nickname are "outspokenness," "confidence," and "loyalty." A similar conclusion is reached by Cullmann, *Peter*, 20–28. For a radically different take on the naming, see Droge, "The Status of Peter," 308, who thinks Peter is awarded the name change not because he is the rock of the church but because of his "obtuseness and persistent inability to understand Jesus."

[31] Brown, *John*, 1.76; Haenchen, *John 1*, 164–65. E. Drewermann, *Das Johannes-Evangelium: Bilder einer neuen Welt, Erster Teil: Joh 1–10* (Düsseldorf: Patmos, 2003), 94, sees Peter's identity beginning to change upon meeting Jesus: "Doch einem Mann wie Jesus zu begegnen, das bedeutet, angesprochen zu werden auf seine Wirkliche Berufung. Da wird aus dem, was einmal 'Simon' war, eine Stütze und ein Halt für andere Menschen...." The suggestion of D. W. Riddle, "The Cephas-Peter Problem, and a Possible Solution" *JBL* 59 (1940): 169–180, that Simon and Cephas were two early Christian leaders whose names became conflated when the language of the church moved from Aramaic to Greek, has not caught on. (But see the list of disciples in the Ethiopic text of the *Epistula Apostolorum*, which names "Peter" *and* "Cephas" as early disciples.) K. Lake, "Simon, Cephas, Peter," *HTR* 14 (1921): 95–97, also investigates the idea that Peter and Cephas are two people, but reaches no firm conclusions.

As mentioned, I believe that John is well acquainted with *Matthew's* version of Peter's call, naming, and confession—however that knowledge may have been translated around the Mediterranean crescent. His version of events is much closer to Matthew than Mark, and in fact shows knowledge of Matthew's expansions of Mark. There is not enough linguistic overlap between John and Matthew to *prove* that one knows the other, but the thematic overlap is so pronounced that it strongly suggests a literary interdependence.[32] Assuming the events recalled in John and Matthew are rooted to some degree in history, I believe Matthew preserves an earlier form of call-naming-confession tradition than does John, keeping the events tied closely together and providing much in the way of geographical and chronological context, which, one imagines, would have accompanied the narrative tradition in its earliest incarnation. John strips away much of the context, however, seeming almost to want to camouflage the parallels. In contrast to Matthew, for example—who goes to great lengths to link Simon bar-Jonah's new name (Peter) to the disciple's recent revelation and future ecclesial office—John sets the naming in the beginning of the Gospel without a wisp of context.[33] Why? The fact that his readers are already familiar with Peter is not in itself a reason to separate the name change from the confession. In fact, an audience expecting the events to dovetail might well be mystified to find the name change isolated in the call narrative, five chapters removed from the confession!

While I recognize the wisdom in the statement of K. Quast that "indubitably nearly every interpretation of this naming involves a certain amount of 'grasping at straws' because the evangelist does not provide any leads,"[34] I would like to propose three reasons why John shifts the naming to the front of his Gospel but saves the confession for a later scene. First, it supports his Christology, emphasizing Jesus' foreknowledge; second, it allows Peter's confession—when it does occur (6:68–69)—to stand as a timely pledge of loyalty and not simply an(other) exercise in Christological nomenclature; and third, it highlights the calls of Andrew, Philip, and Nathanael, characters whose missionary activity is crucial to the initial community-building phase of the ministry but whose stars are destined to fade relative to Peter's.

---

[32] Seven distinct *thematic* parallels between Matt 16:16–19 and John 1:40–42; 6:68–69 are listed and briefly discussed in the excursus to this chapter.

[33] According to M. D. Goulder, "John 1:1–2:12," in *John and the Synoptics* (ed. A. Denaux; BETL 101; Leuven: Leuven University Press, 1992), 216, "all the *eclat* of the Matthean 'Blessed art thou, Simon bar-Jonah' [and] all splendour of the Petrine promise has dissolved, and like the baseless fabric of a vision, left not a wrack behind." While I strongly disagree with Goulder's anti-Petrine reading of the Gospel and his claim that John 1:42 "is the beginning of a long series of humiliations which John plans to inflict on the leader of the Jerusalem church" (p. 216), I cannot fault him for pointing out that John's version of the story is less colorful than Matthew's.

[34] Quast, *Peter and the Beloved Disciple*, 39.

In analyzing the Fourth Evangelist's treatment of these scenes, let us first address his Christological motive for transplanting the naming episode to the front of the Gospel. By having Jesus award a new name to a character who is *brought* to him—i.e., one he has never before met and with whom he enjoys no relationship—John highlights both Jesus' general foreknowledge (cf. 4:25; 6:6; 14:26; 16:30, etc.) and his specific foreknowledge concerning the fates of the disciples (14:16; 15:20 and 16:32). All that is known to the Father is known to Jesus (10:15), and therefore Jesus has only to "look at" (ἐμβλέψας) Peter to know that his future actions warrant an epithet.[35] "Cephas" does not appear to be a nickname that Jesus chooses to describe Peter's *current* attributes, for Peter has not shown any! To put it another way, Peter does not receive his new name because he is *presently* stout, trustworthy, or in some other way "rock-like," but in anticipation of being a rock-like fixture of the ministry (see 6:68–69; 13:23–25, 37; 18:15–16; 20:1–10; cf. also 21:7, 11, 15–19, 22–23). It is the case that "Jesus' promise to Simon is different from those he makes in verses 39, 50, and 51. While the promise to Simon refers to his future mission, the other promises refer to the ongoing revelation of God in Jesus, which the disciples will gradually see as they journey with Jesus."[36]

A second benefit of moving the name change to the front of the Gospel is that it allows Peter's confession in John 6 to serve as a *pro*fession of loyalty in a time of crisis. In Matthew's Gospel, as is well known, Peter receives a dominical blessing and an ecclesial office in recognition of his confession that Jesus is *Messiah* and *Son of the Living God*. (Matthew is clear about crediting the Father for the inspiration of the confession; it is the Father and not "flesh and blood" that makes Jesus' identity known.) In John's Gospel, Peter's confession ends with but does not begin with Christology. The first part of the confession, "Lord, to whom shall we go?" is a rhetorical masterstroke, tacitly acknowledging the presence of other spiritual leaders in the area (cf. 1:35–40; 3:25) while affirming Jesus as the one leader worth following. The message to the Johannine community seems to be obvious: true disciples align themselves with Jesus (cf. 3:18; 11:25; 17:20). More is said on the timing of Peter's confession below.

Finally, by bringing the name change to the front of the Gospel but leaving the confession in its "original" context (i.e., at that point in the story when questions are being raised about Jesus' identity and the viability of his ministry

---

[35] Ray, *St. John's Gospel*, 66, imagines (in highly colloquial style!) the thoughts of Jesus as he meets Peter: "Ah, it's you; my Father chose you before time began to follow me and to be the foundation of my Church. I am going to rename you now, to fit the office I have chosen you to fill."

[36] R. M. Chennattu, *Johannine Discipleship as a Covenant Relationship* (Peabody: Hendrickson, 2006), 33.

[see esp. Matt 16:13-20; cf. Mark 8:27-30; Luke 9:18-21]), John introduces the familiar character of Peter without letting him overshadow Andrew, Philip, and Nathanael. These three characters give initial momentum to the ministry by following Jesus and proselytizing. After John the Baptist, they are the earliest links in the chain of witness, hailing Jesus as, respectively, "Messiah" (1:41), "the one about whom Moses and the prophets wrote" (1:45), and the "Son of God" (1:49). While John places Peter's naming in the context of the first confession of Jesus as "Messiah," and so provides us with a distinct echo of Matt 16:16-19, he gives the "Messiah" part of Peter's confession as it occurs in the Matthean tradition to Andrew and the "Son of God" part to Nathanael. The result is that a powerful chain of witness takes shape early in Jesus' ministry, with the call-response mechanism of discipleship functioning in a variety of individuals.

The many scholars who believe that John (1) has some knowledge of Synoptic tradition and (2) holds Peter in low regard—even seeking to denigrate him—are quick to point out one other result of the editing: all that is left for Peter in the Johannine narrative is a nickname! His "Matthean" achievements have been democratized away, they say, with the aim of expediting the community-building phase of Jesus' ministry and minimizing Peter's role.[37] If this interpretation is correct, however, and the Fourth Evangelist is whittling away at Matthean tradition here in order to downgrade Peter's call, naming, and confession, why does he drop the subsequent Matthean scene in which Jesus calls Peter "Satan" (Matt 16:23; cf. Mark 8:33)? Why does he make Judas rather than Peter the disciple who devils the ministry in the wake of Peter's confession? And why does he omit the scene in which Peter is called by Jesus a "stumbling block" (σκάνδαλον), as happens in Matt 16:23? As will be shown throughout this study, the case against Peter is greatly overdone.

PETER'S CONFESSION: 6:66-71

⁶⁶Because of this many of his disciples turned back and no longer went about with him. ⁶⁷So Jesus asked the twelve, "Do you also wish to go away?" ⁶⁸Simon Peter answered him, "Lord, to whom can we go? You have the words of eternal life. ⁶⁹We have come to believe and know that you are the Holy One of God." ⁷⁰Jesus answered them, "Did I not choose you, the twelve? Yet one of you is a devil." ⁷¹He was speaking of Judas son of Simon Iscariot, for he, though one of the twelve, was going to betray him. (⁶⁶Ἐκ τούτου πολλοὶ [ἐκ] τῶν μαθητῶν αὐτοῦ ἀπῆλθον εἰς τὰ ὀπίσω καὶ οὐκέτι μετ' αὐτοῦ περιεπάτουν. ⁶⁷εἶπεν οὖν ὁ Ἰησοῦς τοῖς δώδεκα· μὴ καὶ ὑμεῖς θέλετε ὑπάγειν; ⁶⁸ἀπεκρίθη αὐτῷ Σίμων Πέτρος· κύριε, πρὸς τίνα ἀπελευσόμεθα; ῥήματα ζωῆς αἰωνίου

---

[37] See § 4.

ἔχεις, ⁶⁹καὶ ἡμεῖς πεπιστεύκαμεν καὶ ἐγνώκαμεν ὅτι σὺ εἶ ὁ ἅγιος τοῦ θεοῦ. ⁷⁰ἀπεκρίθη αὐτοῖς ὁ Ἰησοῦς· οὐκ ἐγὼ ὑμᾶς τοὺς δώδεκα ἐξελεξάμην; καὶ ἐξ ὑμῶν εἷς διάβολός ἐστιν. ⁷¹ἔλεγεν δὲ τὸν Ἰούδαν Σίμωνος Ἰσκαριώτου· οὗτος γὰρ ἔμελλεν παραδιδόναι αὐτόν, εἷς ἐκ τῶν δώδεκα.)

The exodus of disciples from Jesus' ministry in 6:66 is sometimes thought to reflect a moment of crisis in his historical ministry, or a moment when desertion was contemplated.[38] The way John tells it, desertion is a response to the "hard" (σκληρός) sayings Jesus delivers in the Bread of Life Discourse (esp. 6:53–58). In his book *The Hard Sayings of Jesus*, F. F. Bruce considers the invitation to drink the blood of Jesus to be the original *hard saying*: "For Jews the drinking of any blood, even the eating of flesh from which the blood had not been completely drained, was taboo."[39] D. M. Smith speculates that the "characterization of Jesus' word, presumably about eating and drinking his flesh and blood, as a hard one may reflect the fact that participation in the distinctively Christian rite would constitute a public confession that would take one out of the synagogue (cf. 9:22; 12:48)."[40]

Both arguments are persuasive. The Jewish aversion to drinking blood is understandable enough in light of the prohibitions of Gen 9:4; Lev 3:17; 17:14 and 17:26, and we know from many extra-biblical sources that cannibalism was widely reviled in the Mediterranean world (e.g., Herodotus, *Hist.* 1.123; Plutarch *Cic.* 10:3; 49:2; Philostratus *Hrk.* 25:15). It may be the case that the exodus of disciples in this scene speaks to a situation in the Johannine church in which public confession of Jesus invited persecution.[41] What seems beyond doubt in the latter verses of John 6 is that dissatisfaction with Jesus grows among his

---

[38] See especially C. H. Dodd, *The Interpretation of the Fourth Gospel* (Cambridge: Cambridge University Press, 1953), 344–45, and by the same author, *Historical Tradition in the Fourth Gospel* (Cambridge: Cambridge University Press, 1963), 221–22. See also Bernard, *St. John*, 1.221.

[39] Bruce, *The Hard Sayings of Jesus* (London: Hodder and Stoughton, 1983), 21. In many well-known commentaries on John (e.g. Bultmann, Brown, Schnackenberg, and Culpepper), "drinking blood" is seen to represent the consumption of Eucharistic wine. A number of scholars do not see John 6 as sacramental, however. See especially J. D. G. Dunn, "John VI—A Eucharistic Discourse?" *NTS* 17 (1971), 328–38; and P. D. Borgen, *Bread from Heaven: An Exegetical Study of the Concept of Man in the Gospel of John and Writings of Philo* (Leiden: Brill, 1965), 150–58.

[40] Smith, *John*, 161.

[41] Keener, *Gospel of John*, 1.696. D. Rensberger, *Johannine Faith and Liberating Community*. (Philadelphia: Westminster Press, 1988), 75, argues persuasively that John 6:51c–58 is a "critique of Jewish Christians who were unable to accept either the Christology [of the Bread of Life discourse] or its eucharistic implications."

opponents *and* his disciples (but not the Twelve) to the point that his ministry suffers greatly from attrition. Schnackenburg sums up the situation in stark terms: "The falling away of the many Galilean disciples is envisaged as a permanent abandonment of Jesus."[42]

Οἱ Ἰουδαῖοι are the first to take issue with Jesus during the Bread of Life Discourse, complaining (γογγύζουσιν) at his statement, "I am the bread that came down from heaven" (6:41; cf. 6:31–35). At this point of the discourse the sapiential theme is still dominant and Jesus sounds much like personified Wisdom in Pr 9:5 or Sir 24:19-21, occasions when she "speaks in terms of 'feeding' and 'drinking' of her teaching."[43] When Jesus announces plans to give his flesh for the life of the world (6:52), however, the grumbling of οἱ Ἰουδαῖοι turns into quarrelling / fighting (ἐμάχοντο).[44] When the offensive terminology becomes exclusivist and Jesus says that "those who eat my flesh and drink my blood have eternal life, and I will raise them up on the last day" (6:54), many of his own disciples grow uncomfortable with his teaching. At first they limit their protest to a remark—"this is a hard teaching; who can accept it?" (6:60)—but soon abandon him physically (6:66).

In v. 66, ἐκ τούτου can be translated as "because of this" or "from this time." The former is preferred by a slight majority of scholars but the latter is attractive in that it matches precisely the temporal use of the phrase in 19:12. Barrett and Moloney are probably right to suggest that the Evangelist means to convey both ideas.[45] The phrase "to walk about with someone" (μετ' αὐτοῦ περιεπάτουν) is a Semitic expression meaning to share in another's company,[46] and therefore when the disciples choose "no longer" (οὐκέτι) to "walk about" with Jesus they are in effect giving notice that they have severed ties with him. It is not an exaggeration to say that many of the same followers who earlier forced Jesus up the mountain in their zeal to make him king (6:15) now head for the hills themselves.[47] Jesus does not rail against their faithlessness (cf. 5:38; 6:36) or ponder aloud the effect the mass exodus will have on his ministry, but turns to the Twelve, the ministry's surviving remnant, to see if they, too, will abandon him.

---

[42] Schnackenburg, *St. John*, 2.74.

[43] W. R. Domeris, "The Confession of Peter According to John 6:69," *TynBul* 44 (1993): 163. See also T. L. Inbody, *The Many Faces of Christology* (Nashville: Abingdon, 2002), 131.

[44] See, for example, G. R. Beasley-Murray, *John* (2nd ed.; WBC; Nashville: Thomas Nelson, 1999), 97.

[45] Barrett, *St. John*, 306; Moloney, *Gospel of John*, 231.

[46] Lightfoot, *St. John's Gospel*, 170.

[47] If ἀπῆλθον εἰς τὰ ὀπίσω comes from the Hebrew נסוג אחור, it could mean either that the crowd "turned back" (cf. Isa 50:5) or "were repulsed" (cf. Isa 42:17). See Barrett, *St. John*, 306. It may be that both ideas apply.

One could argue that by including the negative particle μή in his question, μὴ καὶ ὑμεῖς θέλετε ὑπάγειν; ("Do you also wish to go away?" [6:67]), Jesus expects a negative answer. Put into the vernacular, his question sounds something like this: *You, of course, will not leave me also, will you?* The only other time in the Gospel he prefaces a question with μή is in the post-resurrectional scene of 21:5, in which he knows that the disciples have fished all night without success but asks them about their catch anyway, forcing them to confront the absurdity of self-reliance. But we should perhaps be wary of attaching too much significance to the negative particle in 6:67, letting it lull us into thinking that a confident Jesus is asking rhetorically about the faith of the Twelve, knowing all the while that it is strong. To the contrary, there is a perceptible tension in the scene; as Jesus waits to hear what the Twelve will say, so the reader waits with him.

To suspend that tension for one moment longer, we should, before analyzing the component parts of Peter's confession, say a little bit more about the role of the Twelve in John's Gospel. What do they—and what do they not—represent?[48] Other than in this scene, the Fourth Evangelist does not show a particularly strong interest in the Twelve.[49] Discipleship is a broader category in John's Gospel than in the Synoptics. One of the central messages of the Fourth Gospel is that if one believes in and follows Jesus, one is a disciple in the truest sense (1:12; 10:38; 14:11, etc.). The Twelve are not mentioned in John 1, when the first disciples are called and named, nor are they mentioned in John 21, in which seven disciples (who I will argue are the true seeds of the Johannine church) are privy to the final resurrection appearance. John mentions the Twelve only here (6:66, 71) and on one occasion in chapter 20 (v. 24). They do not accomplish anything in an *active* sense, as in, say, Mark 3:14; 6:7; 11:11; Matt 10:1–4; or Luke 9:1–2, but are a relatively passive collective. Peter *speaks* for them in 6:68–69 and Judas and Thomas are said to *belong* to them in 6:70–71 and 20:24.[50] John certainly assumes among his readership a basic familiarity with the Twelve, for they are introduced in 6:67 without comment.[51]

To borrow from the vernacular of baseball, when Peter finally *does* confess Jesus, he touches all the bases. In a few words he professes the loyalty of the Twelve, notes the unique quality of Jesus' revelation, and acknowledges Jesus

---

[48] The topic is treated briefly in the introduction to this study.

[49] See especially the discussion in Cullmann, *Johannine Circle*, 67.

[50] "Undoubtedly reflecting knowledge of historical tradition, Peter plays a role similar to that preserved in the Synoptic tradition, as spokesman for the disciples." Keener, *Gospel of John*, 1.697. Becker, *Evangelium nach Johannes*, 262, puts it this way: "Simon Petrus (vgl. 1,42) ist wie selbstverständlich der Sprecher der Zwölf."

[51] Barrett, *St. John*, 306, suggests that John's audience is familiar with the Twelve through their acquaintance with Markan tradition.

as God's holy agent. Each part of the confession builds on the previous part: the Twelve follow Jesus because he is the only practical choice; he is the only practical choice because he has the words of eternal life; he has the words of eternal life because he is the Holy One of God, consecrated and empowered to speak for God.[52]

Buried in the first part of Peter's confession ("Lord, to whom else can we go?") is the implication that the Twelve have choices about whom they follow but that they are not terribly attractive choices. As Peter will soon make clear, Jesus alone has the words of eternal life. In one respect, Peter's words do not come as a surprise to John's reader because many charismatic leaders claimed followings in those days. We recall that Andrew and his anonymous companion were introduced as disciples originally belonging to John the Baptist (1:35–40), and we know from Acts 5:36–37 and 21:28 that charismatic leaders arose in first century Palestine from time to time claiming—as Luke puts it in the case of Theudas—"to be somebody" (εἶναί τινα ἑαυτόν), and so gained followers (cf. also Jos. *Ant.* 20.97–102; 167–72; *War* 2.261–63; 6.285, 437–53). But in another respect Peter's words *are* startling, for they remind the reader that the burden of discipleship rests on the would-be follower, not on Jesus. Jesus extends the invitation to follow; it is up to the disciple to accept (e.g., 9:38; 11:25; 20:29; 21:18–22) or refuse (e.g., 5:4–47; 8:45; 10:25).[53]

The phrase "words of eternal life" (ῥήματα ζωῆς αἰωνίου, 6:68) is *anarthrous*, which leads Barrett to suggest, and I think correctly, that Peter's confession is not a Johannine iteration of some early Christian formula (cf. 6:63).[54] Although the tenor and structure of the confession appear creedal—and may have developed in that direction—the confession itself builds on the unique experience of the Twelve. It is Peter and his associates who "have come to believe" (πεπιστεύκαμεν) and "have come to know" (ἐγνώκαμεν) important truths about Jesus.[55] It is not clear that they have "left everything" (ἀφήκαμεν πάντα) to

---

[52] According to F. Lapham, *Peter*, 8, Peter's three statements when taken together are "the Johannine equivalent of the Synoptic story of Peter's celebrated acclamation of the Christ," and yet included in the Johannine confession is an implied promise of group loyalty and a comment about the nature of Jesus' revelation, not found in the Synoptic Gospels.

[53] I agree with S. Ringe, *Wisdom's Friends*, 55, that the "entire Gospel narrative is the story of the interplay of the acceptance and rejection of Jesus."

[54] Barrett, *St. John*, 306.

[55] Jesus' disciples in 16:30 (not said to be the Twelve) take this confession a step further when they declare that they have come to know (οἴδαμεν) and believe (πιστεύομεν) that Jesus knows *all things* and is from God. They have an advantage over Peter (as he appears in John 6) in that they have heard Jesus speak "plainly" (παρρησία) about his origins. In 17:7–8, part of the so-called "priestly prayer," Jesus testifies to the mature state of the disciples' faith, saying: "Now they know that everything you have given me is from you for the words that you gave to me I have given to them, and they

follow Jesus, as Peter himself says to be the case in Mark 10:28 and Matt 19:27, but they have thrown in with him during a dangerous time, when grumbling turns easily to fighting and disciples turn away. E. Haenchen describes the manner in which the perfect active indicative verbs πεπιστεύκαμεν and ἐγνώκαμεν function in Peter's confession:

> The words "we have believed and have come to know" stand amicably beside each other as though they could not designate two different and mutually hostile certainties. But for John they really express one and the same certainty and subject matter. For him, the one who believes really knows God, who remains closed, inaccessible, unrecognized to the one who lacks faith. But this knowing is not concurrence in some mathematical, logical proposition. It is rather faith: the surrender of the whole man to the one who is known and to his will....[56]

Interestingly, two different types of "surrendering" appear to be taking place here, one concerned with apostasy and the other with passionate discipleship. In the first case, the many Galilean disciples who have traveled with Jesus this far now *surrender* their positions in his ministry, unable to accept the "hard" sayings of the Bread of Life Discourse. In the second case, Peter and the Twelve *surrender* themselves to God's will, revealing themselves to be Jesus' most intimate supporters.

As for the title Peter assigns to Jesus, "Holy One of God" (6:69; cf. Mark 1:24; Luke 4:34), many scholars, including renowned commentators such as Bultmann and Brown, maintain that it throws into bold relief Peter's "low" Christology.[57] Compared with the confessions of Martha (11:27), and Thomas (20:28), it is argued, Peter's confession does not do a particularly good job of unpacking Johannine theology.[58] The criticism levied against Peter is that his words speak more to Jesus' divinely-sanctioned authority than to his filial relationship with the Father, that they say nothing about his preexistence, and that they are used of mere mortals in the Old Testament (Jdgs 13:7; Ps 106:16; cf. also Gk *Apoc Ezra* 5:10). In Cullmann's opinion, when Peter speaks he

---

have received them and know in truth that I came from you; and they have believed that you sent me." See the discussion in G. Strecker, *Theology of the New Testament* (Louisville: Westminster John Knox, 2000), 503.

[56] E. Haenchen, *John 1: A Commentary on the Gospel of John Chapters 1–6* (trans. R. W. Funk; Philadelphia: Fortress, 1984), 307.

[57] See the introduction to this study, 1.3.

[58] σὺ εἶ ὁ ἅγιος τοῦ θεοῦ is the reading in B P^{75} ℵ C* L W D, which I take to be original. Peter's confession includes a messianic component (ὁ χριστὸς ὁ ἅγιος τοῦ θεου) in P^{66} and in a few later manuscripts, including f^1 33 and 565, but this probably reflects a desire to expand the confession's Christological significance.

reveals himself to be on the outside of the "Johannine Circle" looking in.[59] He represents a group of Christians (Apostolic Christians) who have courage enough to confess Jesus publicly but who do not understand the deepest truths about him.

But in the context of the aftermath of the Bread of Life discourse, the Christological appellation *Holy One of God* is an entirely appropriate description of Jesus. Peter has already announced that Jesus has the words of eternal life (6:68b). Now we hear him extrapolate on that thought: Jesus has been set apart—i.e. made a holy one of God (ἅγιος τοῦ θεοῦ)—in order to bear these revelatory words.[60] Far from betraying a weak or "low" Christology, "Holy One of God" describes Jesus as Jesus has been describing himself in the Bread of Life Discourse, as one sent into the world by the Father (6:57) to do the Father's will (6:38), which in this case means bringing to the disciples the words of "spirit and life" (6:63).

In looking closely at this word "holy," Schnackenburg makes the astute observation that it "expresses the closest possible intimacy with God, a participation in God's deepest and most essential being. Peter's confession is therefore the appropriate responsory (σὺ εἶ) to the revelatory formula ἐγώ-εἰμι which John transfers from God to Christ, who reveals himself and the Father."[61] When Peter acknowledges Jesus' holiness, he is conveying a contention of the Fourth Evangelist that Jesus has been *set apart* for God's redemptive work.[62] (See also 17:19, in which Jesus sanctifies (ἁγιάζω) himself for the sake of the disciples, and 10:36, in which he is sanctified (ἡγίασεν) by the Father.) I agree with B. Witherington that "in light of this wisdom tradition, which closely associates wisdom with the holy, the title 'the Holy One of God' is perhaps the most appropriate title for one portrayed as Wisdom come in the flesh to earth...."[63] It may also be the case that Peter's choice of Christological appellation, "Holy One of God," serves the dualistic themes of the Gospel, for it sets Jesus apart from Judas—soon to be described as possessed by Satan (6:70)—and over and against the evil associated with the world (7:7).

---

[59] See Cullmann, *Johannine Circle*, 91–94.

[60] See Hoskyns and Davey, *Riddle of the New Testament*, 302–3.

[61] Schnackenburg, *St. John*, 2.76.

[62] It may be the case that the "of God" part of Peter's confession is a delayed response to Jesus' I AM declaration in 6:20. If O. Cullmann, *The Christology of the New Testament* (trans. S. C. Guthrie & C. A. M. Hall; London: SCM, 1959), 285, and Conzelmann, *Outline*, 337, are correct that "Holy One of God" is an exact synonym for "Son of God," there is even less reason to castigate Peter's Christology.

[63] B. Witherington, *John's Wisdom: A Commentary on the Fourth Gospel* (Louisville: Westminster John Knox, 1995), 161. According to M. M. Thompson, *The God of the Gospel of John* (Grand Rapids: Eerdmans, 2001), 124, what proves "most illuminating in interpreting the Gospel's Christology, particularly with respect to how God is made known, are those figures that unite agent (Jesus) and sender (God) most closely."

Some scholars particularly dedicated to the task of denigrating Peter's Christology do not merely compare his confession to the confessions of other Johannine characters to expose its deficiencies but argue that it pales in comparison to his own confession in the Synoptic Gospels. A. G. Brock speaks for many when she says that Peter's confession in John's Gospel "does not carry the same christological significance" as his confession in the Synoptics, for it fails to identify Jesus as *Christ* (Mark 8:29; Matt 16:16; Luke 9:20) or *Son of God* (Matt 16:16).[64] According to M. Goulder, "[i]n place of Peter's high insight (in the Synoptic Gospels), 'You are the Christ,' all he can rise to in John is 'we have believed, and have come to know, that you are the Holy One of God' (6:69)."[65] D. H. Gee argues that "whereas in the accounts given in the Synoptic Gospels Peter hails Jesus specifically as the Christ, in the Johannine account the title accorded is vaguer and less decisive."[66] A. H. Maynard is quite caustic in suggesting that Peter's confession in John is "tainted with the demonic" because it echoes the confession of Mark 1:24 (=Luke 4:34)![67]

In my opinion, comparing the Christological language Peter employs when confessing Jesus in John's Gospel to the language he employs in the parallel scene in the Synoptics is precisely like comparing apples to oranges. Peter's confession in the Synoptics (esp. Mark 8:29 and Matt 16:16) is a crucial turning point because it testifies to Jesus' messianic status and paves the way for Jesus to begin teaching openly about his upcoming suffering, death, and resurrection. In John's Gospel, his confession is also a turning point, but because it keeps the ministry from losing critical mass.[68] In the aftermath of the Bread of Life Discourse, what Jesus needs most is *not* a(nother) Christological title but a pledge of loyalty. The question he puts to the Twelve is *not* "Who do you say that I am?," as in the Synoptic Gospels, but "Do you also wish to go away?" He

---

[64] Brock, *Mary Magdalene*, 42.

[65] Goulder, *St. Paul vs. St. Peter*, 21. Goulder goes on to say that Peter "makes a goat of himself" and "gets the wrong end of the stick" during the foot-washing in chapter 13, laying bare the Evangelist's anti-Petrine bias. Similar disaffection for the Johannine Peter is voiced by Snyder in "Anti-Petrinism," 5–15.

[66] Gee, "Why Did Peter Spring into the Sea?" 484. Waetjen, *Beloved Disciple*, 222, offers a similar analysis in saying that Peter's "titular designation of Jesus as 'the Holy One of God' is certainly feeble, but on this occasion, at this moment, it may be adequate."

[67] Maynard, "Role of Peter," 543. Maynard also makes the startling assertion that because John's negative portrayal of Peter is the perfect opposite of the positive Synoptic image, "we must assume John knew the Synoptics" (p. 537).

[68] F. Porsch, *Johannes-Evangelium* (Stuttgart Kleiner Kommentar—Neues Testament 4; Stuttgart: Verlag Katholisches Bibelwerk, 2001), 65, aptly describes the large emigration of disciples from the ministry as a "Massenabfall," and notes that it results from a "Glaubenkrise."

is concerned with group loyalty rather than group Christology.[69] Peter does not reveal himself as one possessing a watered down Christology but answers the question put to him in the clearest possible terms. "As a lesson in true faith, this answer of Peter's is of undying importance."[70]

If one compares the positive sequence of events of 1:35–51 (the initial expansion of Jesus' ministry) with the generally negative sequence in 6:35–66 (the ministry's contraction), one discovers that the latter sequence is in many respects a negative image of the former, and that it is only Peter's confession that prevents the outflow of disciples in chapter six from reversing completely the positive missionary trend established by his brother Andrew in chapter one. Looking closely at this trend we see that in the expansion sequence interest in Jesus is sparked initially by the exultant proclamation of John the Baptist: "Behold the Lamb of God!" This, in turn, leads to two disciples following Jesus, staying with him, confessing him as "Messiah," and finally bringing others to meet him. At the heart of the cycle is a naming episode: Jesus looks into the future (or otherwise employs his omniscience) and sees that Simon *will be called* Peter.

In the contraction sequence of John 6, disenchantment with Jesus is expressed at a number of points, but most clearly by the disciples (not the Twelve) in 6:60, when they say: "This is a hard teaching; who is able to accept it?" After this many disciples "turn back" from Jesus and then "no longer go about" with him. Ending the cycle is another naming episode. This time it is Peter who speaks, looking not to the future but to the past, to the experiences of the Twelve, concluding that Jesus has demonstrated that he is the consecrated

---

[69] In regard to the timing and importance of Peter's confession as *Matthew* understands it, W. D. Davies and D. C. Allison, *A Critical and Exegetical Commentary on the Gospel According to Saint Matthew* (3 Vols.; ICC; Edinburgh: T & T Clark, 1988), 2.603, have this to say: "The primary function is to record the establishment of a new community, one which will acknowledge Jesus' true identity and thereby become the focus of God's activity in salvation-history. The event has been occasioned by the rejection of Jesus by corporate Israel...." One wonders if the same could not be said about Peter's confession in John's Gospel, for in John 6 this same sort of community-building takes place, and in the same three stages: first, corporate Israel abandons Jesus; second, Peter acknowledges Jesus' true identity; and third, the Twelve—the remnant of the "old" ministry—are installed as the seed of the "new" ministry. In John's Gospel, of course, the Twelve do not last long as a paradigmatic faith community but are superseded by individuals who make personal decisions about believing in Jesus. The fact remains, however, that in all the Gospels Peter's confession settles an issue about Jesus' identity and establishes Jesus' closest group of supporters as the core of the faith community.

[70] Schnackenburg, *St. John*, 2.75.

bearer of revelation, which is to say the "Holy One of God."[71] The similarities / contrasts are perhaps easier to see in table format:

TABLE 2.1

THE MINISTRY BEGINS		THE MINISTRY STALLS	
1:35	"Behold the Lamb of God!"	6:60	"This is a hard teaching"
1:37	they followed Jesus	6:66a	many disciples turned back
1:39	they came and saw / remained	6:66b	they no longer went with him
1:41	"We have found the Messiah!"	6:67	"Do you wish to go away?"
1:42	Jesus: *You are to be called Cephas*	6:69	Peter: *You are the Holy One of God*

Interestingly, no words of commendation from Jesus follow Peter's confession in John's Gospel. He receives from Jesus neither a blessing nor an ecclesial office, as in Matthew's Gospel. If, as I believe, John is working from Matthew or a tradition extremely similar to Matthew's, and if he also wishes to portray Peter in a favorable light, why does he drop Jesus' laudatory response?

The short answer is, he doesn't. He rearranges it and, in so doing, camouflages it. We see this happening in three ways. First, as has already been discussed, John shifts the "naming" part of the response forward in his Gospel to suit his Christological agenda. One result of this is that Peter is named in anticipation of becoming a rock-like figure in Jesus' ministry and (perhaps) a cornerstone of the post-Easter Johannine church (cf. 21:15–17).[72] Second, while John does not say as clearly as Matthew that it is the Father and not "flesh and blood" (human agency) that reveals to Peter the truth about the identity of Jesus,

---

[71] In his commentary on John's Gospel, Calvin notes that "although the twelve did not at once understand all that Christ was teaching, it was enough for them, according to the measure of their faith, to confess Him as the author of their salvation and submit to Him in everything." *Calvin's New Testament Commentaries: John 1–10* (trans. T. H. L. Parker; Grand Rapids: Eerdmans, 1995), 178.

[72] S. van Tilborg, *Das Johannes-Evangelium: Ein Kommentar für die Praxis* (Stuttgart: Verlag Katholisches Bibelwerk, 2005), 26, describes 1:40 as the scene in which "[d]as Lamm begegnet dem Fels...."

he does preface Peter's confession with the statement of 6:44a that "no one can come to me unless drawn by the Father who sent me" (cf. 6:65), which may suggest that Peter's strong desire to remain with Jesus is, at least in part, divinely inspired. Third, while John (6:70) and Matthew (16:23; cf. Mark 8:33) follow Peter's confession with a statement from Jesus that one of the disciples is a devil/adversary (Mark/Matt = σατανᾶ), John identifies this devil (διάβολος) as *Judas*, and so alters the inherited tradition, keeping Peter in a positive light.[73]

Of course this does not explain why the Fourth Evangelist is so subtle about awarding praise to Peter in the aftermath of his confession. Why should readers have to read between the lines of these pericopae to know that Jesus thinks well of Peter's confession? Why doesn't the Johannine Jesus incorporate the praise into an extended dominical blessing, as the Matthean Jesus does?

I suspect that the Fourth Evangelist scatters Jesus' praise of Peter throughout the Gospel to avoid giving the impression that confessors of Jesus should be allowed to bask for long in the glow of their achievements. Without exception, confessions in John are met by Jesus not with praise but with requests for deeper professions of faith (1:49–50; 4:20–23; 9:17–38; 20:28–29). The *act* of confessing is what is important to John. As is well known, the noun "faith" (πίστις) never appears in the Gospel. As a static commodity it is not terribly important. *Believing* in Jesus is certainly important, but believing is an active process that gains relevance through reflection, witness, proclamation, and proselytizing. The tripartite confessions of Peter and Martha are as valuable as they are because they teach the new believer—and, one may infer, the young church—how to express and propagate belief. As soon as confessional words leave a person's lips in the Fourth Gospel, it is time to test that person's faith all over again. Witness the confessions of Nathanael (1:49–50), the Samaritan woman (4:19–26), the man born blind (9:17–41), Martha (11:27–40), and Thomas (20:28–29): in all cases the characters confess Jesus but with language that encourages him to probe the boundaries of their faith or issue the promise that their faith will deepen with more time spent in his company.

Thus while Peter delivers a confession that restores equanimity to Jesus' ministry, establishing the Twelve as the temporary seed of the new faith community, and that would seem to merit at least a pat on the back (if not a dominical blessing), John has Jesus respond not with praise but with a warning that the Twelve are still plagued by a "devil." Jesus' ability to see clearly the

---

[73] "This synoptic episode will certainly have been known to the fourth evangelist, and we must therefore assume that he has made a deliberate change. Instead of a humiliation of Simon Peter, he echoes the synoptic report by including a derogatory remark about the traitor." Schnackenburg, *St. John*, 2.78.

future and know that Judas will betray him is an attribute of his divinity.[74] As Moloney notes, "Jesus has chosen the Twelve but there is a larger design in God's leading some to Jesus (cf. v. 64), and each believer is free to accept or refuse the gift. The fragility of human response remains, even among believers. More than a confession of faith is called for. If there is a betrayer, there will be a betrayal."[75] Hoskyns puts it this way: "The misunderstanding of Peter, which causes the Lord to identify him with Satan immediately after his confession (Mark 8:33; Matt 16:23), is omitted, as in Luke. Subsequent history proved that Judas, not Peter, was the veritable demon."[76]

Conclusion

When one looks closely at the call narrative (John 1:35–51) and focuses not only on Peter's actions but also on the actions he elicits from others—particularly Jesus but also Andrew—one gets the impression he is being groomed for some sort of consequential role. As soon as Andrew realizes that Jesus is the Messiah (1:41), he makes evangelizing Peter his first priority. When Jesus meets Peter in 1:42 and tells him, "You are Simon son of John. You are to be called Cephas," readers familiar with OT "naming stories" sense that Peter will accomplish something in his career worthy of the epithet, perhaps developing a new relationship with God. Readers already familiar with certain aspects of his story (cf. 1:40–42, 13:36–38; 21:18–19) may also assume he is being named in anticipation of becoming the "rock-like" fixture of the ministry (6:68–69; 13:23–25) and perhaps a cornerstone of the post-Easter Johannine church (21:7, 11, 18–19, 22; cf. also 13:36–38). As C. S. Keener notes, "Epithets were usually positive, and 'rock' makes sense in connection with a saying about 'building' one's church, language which would have been familiar in Jewish thought and coheres well with other known teachings of Jesus, especially his almost certainly authentic use of the cornerstone image from the Hallel (Ps 118:22)."[77]

Six chapters into the Gospel, Peter finally does confess Jesus (6:68–69), revealing that he has not been idle during the Galilean phase of the ministry but has been contemplating his own call and Jesus' identity. We spent a good deal

---

[74] See R. Bauckham, "Monotheism and Christology in the Gospel of John," in *Contours of Christology in the New Testament* (ed. R. N. Longenecker; Cambridge, England: Eerdmans, 2005), 160.

[75] Moloney, *Gospel of John*, 229. It is worth noting that Jesus does not blame Peter for presenting a flawed confession, i.e., one that advocates perfect loyalty among the Twelve even as Judas' treachery is taking shape, but takes responsibility for choosing the Twelve.

[76] Hoskyns, *Fourth Gospel*, 303.

[77] Keener, *Gospel of John*, 479.

of time expounding the exquisite timing of Peter's confession, finding that his words draw much of their power from their context: Peter speaks as the ministry is suffering from attrition, when many disciples have turned their backs on Jesus because they cannot accept the "hard" teaching that his flesh is true food and his blood true drink. In focusing so tightly on the title Peter awards to Jesus, "Holy One of God," and demoting it for its supposed inability to unpack Johannine Christology, too many scholars pay too little attention to the sublime timing of the pledge of loyalty he makes on behalf of the Twelve. Peter's pledge establishes the Twelve—the faithful remnant of the "old" ministry—as the temporary core of the "new" and revitalized ministry.[78] The very words the crowds find offensive are recognized by Peter to be words of eternal life, which is an early indication that he and the Twelve are to be numbered among Jesus' "sheep" (τὰ πρόβατα), hearing and responding to his voice (cf. 10:4, 27). Peter's confession makes clear that he understands the Bread of Life discourse to be an invitation to participate in the ongoing life of Jesus, whatever form that may take. He and the Twelve are prepared to draw sustenance from Jesus.[79] They have learned that "[g]oing away from Jesus would mean parting from the one person who can show them the path, point them the way."[80]

To the extent that "believe" and "know" are recognized by the Fourth Evangelist as synonyms (cf. 4:42; 10:38), the phrase "we have come to believe and know" is a *hendiadys* that expresses "the firmness of conviction arrived at by the Twelve as a result of a thoroughgoing process."[81] In responding individually to a question put to the Twelve, however, Peter shows himself not only to be the group's spokesman but Jesus' paradigmatic *listener*. G. A. Phillips sums up the situation this way: "Simon Peter is presented as *the* disciple who accepts and properly fills the listening post vis-à-vis Jesus. If the strategy of the narrator is to identify an acceptable discoursive partner for Jesus, it is now revealed to be one-like-Simon Peter."[82]

---

[78] The Evangelist does not return to the theme of the Twelve being the seed of the new ministry, but concentrates on the witness, faith, and testimony of individuals. In John 21, the Redactor describes a group of *seven* individuals serving as the collective progenitor of the Johannine church.

[79] "Nur ein kleiner Kreis kann sich von diesen Worten nähren. Die anderen gehen weg. Das Brot, das sie bekommen, die Wunder, die sie gesehen haben, nähren sie nicht. Jene, die bleiben (symbolisiert durch den Zwölferkreis), finden zu einer neuen Klarheit. Sie wissen nun, warum sie da sind und warum sie bleiben: Sie haben gefunden, was nährt." R. Grünenfelder and B. L. Grünenfelder, *Erde und Licht: Mit dem Johannesevangelium auf den Spuren unserer Lebenswünsche* (Stuttgart: Verlag Katholisches Bibelwerk, 2004), 69.

[80] Schnackenburg, *St. John*, 2.75

[81] Köstenberger, *John*, 221.

[82] G. A. Phillips, "'This is a Hard Saying: Who Can Be Listener to It?': Creating a Reader in John 6," in *Narrative Discourse in Structural Exegesis: John 6 and 1*

Excursus

Johannine-Matthean Parallels in Peter's Call, Naming, and Confession

Writing over a half-century ago, P. Gardner-Smith offered the following warning to exegetes looking to adduce Matthean-Johannine parallels as evidence of a literary relationship between the Gospels:

> No two gospels could differ more widely than Matthew and John; their history is different, their teaching is different, their vocabulary is different. To conclude from the common use of a single saying that St. John was acquainted with Matthew is hazardous in the extreme, for the two passages in John in which the saying is contained must be set against innumerable passages in which Matthew is ignored or contradicted by the fourth evangelist.[83]

Although I take that warning to heart, and in fact do not believe that John writes with an entire copy of canonical Matthew (or any of the Synoptic Gospels) laid out before him—there is simply not enough linguistic overlap to make a case for broad, intimate familiarity—it is clear that several *Petrine* traditions involving Peter in Matthew's and John's Gospels share vital details, and can probably be traced to a common source. Seven of the most dramatic thematic parallels are listed in the table below. What is most fascinating about them is that neither Luke nor (the hypothetical) Q shows knowledge of *any* of them, and that Mark shows knowledge of only one (item 6). Much of what John duplicates from Matthew is Matthean expansion of Mark, which suggests that *John knows portions of Matthew's Gospel dealing with Peter*, as opposed to pre-Matthean tradition.

Thessalonians (ed. Daniel Patte; *Semeia* 26; Chico, Calif.: Scholar's Press, 1983), 51. Reinhartz, *Befriending the Beloved Disciple*, 59, argues similarly that Peter's response "emphasizes that hearing Jesus' words is a more important conduit to and component of faith than viewing his miraculous acts."

[83] P. Gardner-Smith, "St. John's Knowledge of Matthew," *JTS* 4 (1953): 35.

TABLE 2.2
PETER'S CALL, NAMING, AND CONFESSION IN JOHN AND MATHEW

1.	Peter's father is named. The name given is Jonah / John.	(Matt 16:17 // John 1:42)
2.	A name change from Simon to Peter / Cephas takes place in close proximity to the scene of the first confession of Jesus as "the Messiah."	(Matt 16:16–17 // John 1:41–42)
3.	Peter is introduced into the confession scene as "Simon Peter," a common term for John but a *hapax legomenon* in Matthew's Gospel.	(Matt 16:16 // John 6:68)
4.	Jesus makes a *verbal* response to Peter's confession.	(Matt 16:17–19 // John 6:70)
5.	"Flesh and "blood" are discussed by Jesus as being inferior to revelation as a source of knowledge about the divine.	(Matt 16:17 // John 6:63, 65)
6.	The confession scenes are preceded by a discussion about bread. In Matthew, the disciples lack physical bread to eat and learn they must subsist on the teachings of Jesus. In John, Jesus is the "true bread," of which only the Twelve agree to partake immediately. In both Gospels Peter's confession is delivered after the disciples become aware of their absolute dependence on Jesus.[84]	(Matt 16:5–12 // John 6:5–58)
7.	Jesus makes Peter the *rock* of the church in Matthew, the *shepherd* of the flock in John.	(Matt 16:18 // John 21:15–19).[85]

While there is not time here to unpack the parallels, I would like to suggest that the reason they tend to escape the notice of many lay readers and academics

---

[84] Mark 8:14, which says that the disciples have "one loaf of bread" (ἕνα ἄρτον), is altered by Matthew to read that they have no bread. Matthew's message, in striking similarity to John's, is that Jesus in and of himself supplies the sustenance necessary for survival.

[85] Items 1–2, 5, and 7 appear in Brown, *John*, 302. See also the discussion in Davies and Allison, *Matthew*, 2.608.

is that they are obscured by the evangelists' very different theological and organizational agendas. We have already explored how John's theology causes him to separate Peter's naming and call from his confession. Now let us look briefly at ways in which the evangelists' organizational preferences (including decisions about geographical staging) blur commonalities between the Gospels.

Matthew, the great arranger of teaching material and a devotee of tightly-constructed scenes, encapsulates Peter's confession material into a single pericope. In the span of a few verses, he teaches that Peter's career included a three-fold denial of Jesus and a confession of him as "Messiah" and "Son of God," and that Peter is alternately a stumbling block in Jesus' earthly ministry and the foundation of his post-Easter church. John, on the other hand—given to dispersing thematically-related material throughout his Gospel with a free hand (the speeches of 5:10–18 and 7:14–20 are nearly identical but take place a year apart!)—breaks up the naming and confession scenes to exalt Jesus and underscore Peter's loyalty. The reader who is familiar with Matthew's tightly-constructed story and then comes to John's Gospel expecting the naming and confession scenes to dovetail is sure to be confounded.

Geographical context also obscures the parallels. Matthew sets the confession in Caesarea Philippi, a collection of villages nestled in the foothills of Mt. Hermon in Iturea. It is an elevated setting, the sort of place where Matthew's audience would expect to find Jesus teaching (5:1–7:29; 28:16–20). (Mark says only that Jesus is on the *way* [ὁδὸς] to Caesarea Philippi when Peter confesses Jesus, not that he is actually in the village complex.) I suspect that Matthew sets the confession in Caesarea Philippi for reasons having to do with Palestinian political jurisdiction. Located in Iturea, Caesarea Philippi fell during Jesus' lifetime under the purview of Philip the tetrarch of Iturea, not Herod Antipas, ruler of Galilee. It may have occurred to Matthew that Caesarea Philippi was a safer place than Galilee to have Jesus field theories about his identity. After all, it is not long before the confession episode that Matthew describes in graphic detail the execution of John the Baptist by Herod Antipas (14:3–12). Matthew is the only one of the four evangelists to mention John's status as a prophet in the course of narrating his death (14:5), which is in line with his habit of underscoring the dangerous nature of the prophetic profession (Matt 5:12; 23:29–34, 37). By taking Jesus out of the hostile region of Galilee and even off the road that connects it to Caesarea Philippi, Matthew gives him a safe place to hear Peter's extensive confession.

John, on the other hand, seems largely unconcerned with geographical context when framing Peter's confession. The few details he does give materialize only in retrospect, gleaned by the reader from the preceding narrative. If we assume that 6:66 picks up from 6:65, the climax of the Bread of Life Discourse, it is possible to situate Peter's confession in the vicinity of Capernaum, the destination toward which the boats set out in 6:24 and where

Jesus teaches in 6:59. But it is by no means clear that 6:66 describes a single event, which is to say a fast-moving, chaotic, Capernaum-based exodus. In fact, ἐκ τούτου (6:66) is a temporal connective that seems to describe the ministry unraveling slowly. Only when the ministry loses critical mass does Jesus turn to the Twelve to confirm their status as supporters.

Is the Johannine Peter in Capernaum when this happens or somewhere else? Has he traveled as far north as Caesarea Philippi? John does not tell us. The reader familiar with the Matthean version of Peter's confession does not find any geographical marker in John to indicate that the evangelists are discussing the same event. Unlike Matthew, who gives us the highs and lows of Peter's discipleship in a single passage, John asks us to build our portrait of Peter slowly, from scattered episodes. The parallels are present but hidden.

Are there other parallels involving Peter buried even more deeply in the two Gospels? I believe so. One question I hope to pursue in a future study is whether Peter's departure from the boat and walk across the Sea of Galilee to the earthly Jesus in Matt 14:28-31 is related literarily to Peter's departure from the boat and swim across the same lake to the risen Jesus in John 21:7. Drawing out the finer points of the many parallels between the pericopae would be a substantial task—certainly beyond the scope of this study—but would, I think, be one way of exploring the literary relationship between John and Matthew.

CHAPTER 3

THE FOOT WASHING, THE PREDICTION OF THE DENIALS, AND PETER'S PROMISE TO FOLLOW JESUS

INTRODUCTION: PETER IN JOHN 13

After he confesses Jesus to be the Holy One of God in John 6:69, we do not hear from Peter again until the night before Jesus' crucifixion, which means that six chapters of the Gospel pass—or one year in the storyworld timeline—before he next engages Jesus in conversation (13:6–9).[1] As was discussed in the introduction to this study, one result of Peter being given a relatively minor role in the early phases of Jesus' ministry is that many colorful "Synoptic" scenes involving Peter and Jesus do not appear in John's Gospel, including the appointing of the Twelve (Mark 3:16–19; Matt 10:2–5; Luke 6:14–16), the transfiguration (Mark 9:2–6; Matt 17:1–5; Luke 9:28–33), Peter's declaration that the Twelve have left "everything" (πάντα) to follow Jesus (Mark 10:28; Matt 19:27; Luke 18:28), the healing of Jairus' daughter (Mark 5:37; Luke 8:51), Peter's brief walk on the Sea of Galilee (Matt 14:28–31),[2] the conversation about the Temple tax (Matt 17:24–27), the question about forgiveness within the church (Matt 18:21), and Peter's admission to being a sinful man (Luke 5:8). Although a few scholars maintain that John purposely omits these scenes as a way of blurring the Synoptic focus on Peter and minimizing his achievements,[3] R. E. Brown speaks for the scholarly majority when he says that "[t]his difference of material involving Peter is part of the radical variance of Gospel outline which divides John from the Synoptics and which has caused scholars to suggest that the Fourth Evangelist drew on a tradition independent of the Synoptics and / or their sources."[4]

---

[1] One year as measured from the time of the second Passover of Jesus' ministry (6:4) to the third (12:1).

[2] But see 2 § 6.

[3] Cullmann, *Peter*, 27; Käsemann, *Testament of Jesus*, 29; Watty, "Significance of Anonymity," 211.

[4] Brown et al, *Peter in the New Testament*, 129–30. If it is in fact the case that John does know these scenes and omits them, I would imagine it is not because he wants to denigrate Peter but because his focus in these chapters is on Jesus' *opponents*, specifically identified as "the Jews" (οἱ Ἰουδαῖοι; 7:1–35; 8:22–59; 9:18–10:33; and 11:8–36). In underscoring the versatility of the term οἱ Ἰουδαῖοι, J. Ashton and S.

Although the reader is free to imagine that Peter and Jesus build a relationship in between the time of Peter's confession and the final trip to Jerusalem, the text does not suggest this. In fact, the Evangelist waits to flesh out Peter's character until the arrival of Jesus' "hour," when Jesus knows he is about to depart the world to return to the Father (13:1). Given that Peter is portrayed in John's Gospel as one who struggles to protect Jesus from degradation, physical maltreatment, and death, it is perhaps appropriate that he emerges as a central character in the story only when Jesus' death is approaching and the disciples are being instructed about how to conduct themselves in his absence. Rather than stepping squarely between Jesus and the cross by entreating him not to go to Jerusalem, as happens in Matthew (16:21–23) and Mark (8:31–33), Peter seeks to prevent Jesus from engaging in a ritual that *prefigures* that atoning work: the footwashing (13:6–8). Although many see in Peter's desire to keep Jesus free from degradation symptoms of his deficient (i.e., Apostolic) Christology, what is more likely is that this scene tells us something about Peter's misunderstanding of his own role as a disciple.

John 13 is an especially important chapter in our study of Peter not only because he appears in three distinct scenes—alternately challenging, protecting, and aligning himself with Jesus—but because he appears for the first time in the company of BD. From the moment BD is introduced to us in 13:23, we do not doubt that he enjoys a special relationship with Jesus, for he sits in the place of honor at the supper table, reclining on Jesus' breast (ἐν τῷ κόλπῳ). In this same introductory scene, however, he is portrayed as one who works closely with Peter to elicit the identity of the traitor (13:23–25), which is the first of five episodes in which he and Peter appear together. The message to the reader is that BD is an intimate associate of Jesus *and* a colleague of Peter.[5]

Motyer each point out that it can describe an ethnic group (4:22; 11:55; 18:20), or Jews living in Judea (11:7–8), or Jewish religious leaders hostile to Jesus' revelation (11:47–53; 18:4; 19:12–15). See J. Ashton, *Understanding the Fourth Gospel*, 152; and S. Motyer, "The Fourth Gospel and the Salvation of Israel," in *Anti-Judaism and the Fourth Gospel* (ed. R. Bieringer, D. Pollefeyt, and F. Vandercasteele-Vanneuville; Lousiville: Westminster John Knox, 2001), 83–100. Motyer argues convincingly that οἱ Ἰουδαῖοι should be understood primarily as referring to "scrupulous adherents of the religion of Judaea, those especially associated with the life of the Temple before 70 C.E., who were most particular about Temple purity and all that went with it, and who, after the loss of the Temple, by which they were especially affected, became leading lights of the movement that reemphasized a scrupulous Torah-centered lifestyle as the essential response to that disaster" (p. 96).

[5] See the previous chapter for my rejection of the idea that BD is the anonymous disciple who trails Andrew in 1:35–40.

Jesus Prepares to Wash the Disciples' Feet: 13:1–5

Famously in John's Gospel, the Last Supper incorporates a footwashing ritual and not a Eucharistic scene, as in the Synoptic Gospels (Mark 14:22–25; Matt 26:26–29; Luke 22:15–20).[6] Scholars are divided as to whether the footwashing has sacramental overtones or John purposely eschews sacramental theology in order to deliver a lesson about selflessness and corporate humility.[7] Although one can imagine that early Christians would have found in the footwashing scene echoes of the baptismal liturgy as presented in Acts 22:16,

---

[6] For a discussion of footwashing in antiquity as well as a historical reconstruction of what the ritual might have looked like in the Johannine community, see J. C. Thomas, *Footwashing in the Johannine Community* (JSNTSup 61; Sheffield: Sheffield Academic Press, 1991). On Footwashing in John 13 see also A. J. Hultgren, "The Foot-washing (John 13:1–11) as Symbol of Eschatological Hospitality," *NTS* 28 (1982): 539–46; P. Jeffrey, "Do You Mind if I Wash Your Feet? John 13 as Pattern for Ecumenism," *Pacific Journal of Theology* 3 (1990): 17–22; R. A. Culpepper, "The Johannine *Hypodeigma*: A Reading of John 13," *Semeia* 53 (1991): 133–52; and M. L. Coloe, "Welcome into the Household of God: The Foot Washing in John 13," *CBQ* 66 (2004): 400–15. L. W. Countryman, *The Mystical Way in the Fourth Gospel: Crossing Over into God* (rev. ed.; Harrisburg, Penn: Trinity Press International, 1994), 96–97, speculates that foot-washing was practiced to forgive post-baptismal sin, which echoes the argument of Ambrose in *On the Mysteries* (16.32).

[7] If the Eucharistic scene is omitted by design, it may be because John already has a Eucharistic scene in the Gospel: 6:53–58 (see also 6:11). For an eloquent (but not altogether persuasive) argument that John's Last Supper is a true Eucharistic meal, see J. Jeremias, *The Eucharistic Words of Jesus* (trans. N. Perrin; London: SCM, 1966), 43–53. For the contrasting (and prevailing) view that the meal is not a Eucharist, see especially Bultmann, *Gospel of John*, 471–72; J. D. G. Dunn, "The Washing of the Disciples' Feet," *ZNW* 61 (1970): 11–16; and G. H. C. MacGregor, *Gospel of John* (MNTC; London: Hodder and Stoughton, 1928), 272–73. Brown, *John*, 559, argues that *baptism* is a faint background theme in the passage, a view held by many others, including C. K. Barrett, *Church, Ministry and Sacraments in the New Testament* (Carlisle, England: Paternoster, 1983), 72–73, and Moloney, *Gospel of John*, 375. The issue is almost skirted by Lindars, "John," 50, when he suggests that 13:10 refers to baptism "briefly and allusively." What can only be termed rampant eisegesis informs the century-old opinion of C. Fouard, *Saint John and the Close of the Apostolic Age* (London: Longmans, Green and Co., 1906), 192–93, that the institution of the Eucharist is the *central element* in John 13. As happens with full theological agendas, Fouard explains, John focuses on the central rite even as he leaves out the "details"!

Titus 3:5, and 1 Cor 6:11 (cf. also Eph 5:26; Heb 10:22),[8] it is not clear that John intends for baptism to register as a background theme.[9]

What can be said about the footwashing is that it illuminates Johannine Christology in three ways. First, it symbolizes the true cleansing the disciples are to receive through the sacrificial death of Christ on the cross.[10] "The public act of Jesus on the cross and the private act in the Upper Room are, in essence, deeds which are motivated by the love of Jesus for mankind."[11] The fact that the ritual does not occur until the hour when Jesus is "to depart from this world and go to the Father" (13:1)—at which time the devil infects Judas' heart and convinces him to betray Jesus to the enemy (13:2)—strongly suggests that the sacrifice prefigured in the ceremony is Jesus' death and not some lesser offering. Although *self-emptying* is not a recurrent theme in John's Gospel (cf. Phil 2:7), Jesus' activity here presages the crucifixion and illustrates that what he "pours out is himself."[12]

The second way in which the footwashing illuminates Johannine Christology is by revealing Jesus to be one who is willing to assume a humble position before the disciples in order to model lowly service. John's first-century audience would have understood that what Jesus washes from the disciples' feet is not only the dust of the road—which was often shaken off in ritualistic fashion by Jewish travelers as a way of symbolizing decontamination from the pagan world (see Mark 6:11; Matt 10:14; Luke 9:5; 10:11; Acts 13:51; cf. also

---

[8] J. McPolin, *John* (Dublin: Veritas, 1979), 147.

[9] For a recent and creative treatment of this topic, see J. S. Webster, *Ingesting Jesus: Eating and Drinking in the Gospel of John* (Academia Biblica 6; Atlanta: Society of Biblical Literature, 2003), 101–16. I agree with B. J. Malina and R. L. Rohrbaugh, *Social-Science Commentary on the Gospel of John* (Minneapolis: Fortress, 1998), 220, that the footwashing is a "prophetic action that symbolizes forgiveness."

[10] Barrett, *St. John*, 436. Witherington, *John's Wisdom*, 237, generally concurs but emphasizes (*contra* Barrett) that the footwashing is not a reference to "later sacraments such as baptism which look back retrospectively on Christ's cleansing death." So Dunn, "Washing," 11-16.

[11] W. M. Eshbach, "Another Look at John 13:1–20," *Brethren Life and Thought* 14 (1969): 121.

[12] Brodie, *Gospel According to John,* 447. When water is next poured from Jesus (19:34), it comes not from a pitcher but from his body, which leads Beasley-Murray, *John*, 436, to observe that John's reader is ultimately able to look back on the footwashing as pointing "directly to the redemptive death of Jesus, rather than the rite which is a reflection of it." Barrett, *St. John,* 436, says the foot-washing is "based on the synoptic tradition that Jesus was in the midst of the disciples as ὁ διακονῶν [Luke 22:27]," but he spends little time pursuing the idea. In his article "The Footwashing in John 13 and its Relation to the Synoptic Gospels," *ETL* 58 (1982): 279-308, M. Sabbe argues boldly that John knows all three Synoptic Gospels and that the inspiration for the foot-washing comes from the anointing scene in Mark 14:3–9; Matt 26:6–13, and Luke 7:36–50.

Isa 49:23; Nah 1:3)—but animal and human *waste*. While the former was a constant contaminant on roads, there is evidence that the latter was poured from windows onto village streets at least once each day.[13] In humbling himself to perform such a seemingly degrading chore, Jesus models the "loving condescension" he expects the disciples to practice in his absence.[14] The scene is especially poignant because Jesus, the one who is about to ascend to the Father and to whom all authority will be given, temporarily "descends to the lowest place of service."[15]

The third thing the reader learns about Johannine Christology is that faith in Jesus must be appropriated with actions as well as words. L. P. Jones uses an ingestion metaphor to make this point when he notes that "one must drink of him, commit to him with faith."[16] B. Witherington opts for an inheritance metaphor, suggesting that participation in the eternal life of Christ is a useful inheritance only for those heirs who stake a claim.[17] Both images are helpful. What can safely be said about 13:1–11 is that faith-building is described as a two-stage process. In the first stage, carried out in the presence of the earthly Jesus, the disciples participate in Jesus' life by acquiescing to his will, which means permitting his self-oblation. In the second stage, which is to take place only after Jesus departs to the Father, they are to participate by ministering to one another and recapitulating his loving kindness. (On the love commandment, see 13:34 and 15:12–17; cf. also 1 Jo 3:11, 16; 4:7–12; 2 Jo 1:5.)[18]

The footwashing can perhaps be considered a Johannine σημεῖον in its own right insofar as the outward ritual—the cleansing of dirt from the disciples' feet—has a deeper prophetic significance: it points both to his sacrificial death and the propriety of charitable service in the Christian profession.[19] Even the

---

[13] See the discussion in Malina and Rohrbaugh, *Social-Science Commentary*, 219–20.

[14] Barrett, *St. John*, 440. Witherington, *John's Wisdom*, 236, identifies the footwashing, the last discourse, and Jesus' "testamentary dispensations for his mother and the Beloved Disciple" as communicating clearly Jesus' love for his disciples.

[15] Dodd, *Interpretation of the Fourth Gospel*, 401. R. Bultmann, *Theology of the New Testament* (2 vols; trans. K. Grobel; London: Bloomsbury, 1955), 49, is quick to point out that "Jesus' life on earth does not become an item of the historical past, but constantly remains present reality. The historical figure of Jesus, i.e., his human history, retains its significance of being the revelation of his 'glory' and thereby God's."

[16] L. P. Jones, *The Symbol of Water in the Gospel of John* (JSNTSup 145; Sheffield: Sheffield Academic Press, 1997), 228.

[17] Witherington, *John's Wisdom*, 236.

[18] See D. M. Smith, *Johannine Christian*ity (Edinburgh: T & T Clark, 1984), 216.

[19] The defense of this idea as presented in Dunn, "Washing," 247–52, is entertaining as well as persuasive. In addition to Dunn, see Maloney, *Gospel of John*, 378, and Brown, *John*, 2.551. C. H. Talbert, *Reading John: A Literary and Theological Commentary on the Fourth Gospel and the Johannine Epistles* (New York: Crossroad, 1988), 191, finds a

constitutive actions of the footwashing—Jesus' disrobing, his girding again, the filling of the basin with water—point to or are later reflected in other episodes in the Gospel, and therefore have a sign-like quality. In Jesus' act of laying aside (τίθημι, v. 4) his robe and taking it up again (λαμβάνω, v. 12), for example, we are reminded of the Good Shepherd laying aside (τίθημι) his life so that he may once more take it up (λαμβάνω).[20] The verb διαζώννυμι (v. 4)—used to describe Jesus girding himself prior to the humble act—is employed by the Redactor in 21:7 to describe Peter dressing himself to swim to (and subsequently serve) the risen Jesus. The Redactor also uses the cognate verb ζώννυμι to describe Peter being harnessed / dressed for martyrdom (21:18), which is evocative of Jesus girding himself to perform the footwashing. When the Evangelist describes Jesus "getting up" from the table to minister to the disciples in 13:4, he employs the passive form of ἐγείρω (ἐγείρεται), which is generally reserved in the Gospel for descriptions of the resurrection (2:22; 21:14; cf. 5:21).[21] J. S. Webster is right to observe that when "Jesus 'arises' to wash the disciples' feet and lays down his garments in order to take them up again, the Gospel points to his imminent death and resurrection."[22]

PETER'S REACTION TO THE FOOTWASHING: 13:6–11

[6]He then came to Simon Peter, who said to him, "Lord, are you going to wash my feet?" [7]Jesus answered, "You do not know now what I am doing, but later you will understand." [8]Peter said to him, "You will never wash my feet." Jesus answered, "Unless I wash you, you have no share with me." [9]Simon Peter said to him, "Lord, not my feet only but also my hands and my head!" [10]Jesus said to him, "One who has bathed does not need to wash, except for the feet, but is entirely clean. And you are clean, but not all of you." [11]For he knew who was to betray him; for this reason he said, "Not all of you are clean." (⁶ἔρχεται οὖν πρὸς Σίμωνα Πέτρον· λέγει αὐτῷ· κύριε, σύ μου νίπτεις τοὺς πόδας; ⁷ἀπεκρίθη Ἰησοῦς καὶ εἶπεν αὐτῷ· ὃ ἐγὼ ποιῶ σὺ οὐκ οἶδας ἄρτι, γνώσῃ δὲ μετὰ ταῦτα. ⁸λέγει αὐτῷ Πέτρος· οὐ μὴ νίψῃς μου τοὺς πόδας εἰς τὸν αἰῶνα. ἀπεκρίθη Ἰησοῦς αὐτῷ· ἐὰν μὴ νίψω σε, οὐκ ἔχεις μέρος μετ' ἐμοῦ. ⁹λέγει αὐτῷ Σίμων Πέτρος· κύριε, μὴ τοὺς πόδας μου μόνον ἀλλὰ καὶ τὰς χεῖρας καὶ τὴν κεφαλήν. ¹⁰λέγει αὐτῷ

---

prophetic symbolism in John 13:4–5 that leads him to compare the passage with Isa 8:1–4 Jer 13:1–11 ; and Ezek 12:1–7.

[20] In John 10, vv. 11, 15, 17 and 19 employ both words.

[21] Webster, *Ingesting Jesus*, 107. In 7:52, when the crowds express astonishment about the possibility of a prophet "rising" from Galilee, John may be conveying a double meaning.

[22] Ibid., 108.

ὁ Ἰησοῦς· ὁ λελουμένος οὐκ ἔχει χρείαν εἰ μὴ τοὺς πόδας νίψασθαι, ἀλλ' ἔστιν καθαρὸς ὅλος· καὶ ὑμεῖς καθαροί ἐστε, ἀλλ' οὐχὶ πάντες. ¹¹ᾔδει γὰρ τὸν παραδιδόντα αὐτόν· διὰ τοῦτο εἶπεν ὅτι οὐχὶ πάντες καθαροί ἐστε.)

If one understands οὖν in 13:6 to be a simple conjunctive, one could make a case that Peter is the first of the disciples to have his feet washed. Taking the last part of v. 5 with the first part of v. 6, the Greek might be translated as, *"he began to wash...and so came to Simon Peter."*[23] But because the previous verse describes Jesus beginning to wash *and* dry the disciples' feet, meaning that individual acts of service take place with a distinct beginning and end, it is clear that οὖν is transitional and that the ritual is well underway by the time Jesus comes to Peter.[24] "In fact, it is possible that Peter is the last one to receive the washing, for immediately after his encounter with Jesus over the matter the disciples are pronounced to be clean."[25]

When Peter realizes in 13:6–8 that it is his turn to participate in the solemn act, he reacts with disbelief and, it occurs to the reader, panic. A fair inference to be drawn is that Peter finds cognitive dissonance in the image of Jesus, the one he has proclaimed as the "Holy One of God" (6:69), engaging in a menial chore. At one level the disconnect he experiences is understandable. The *Midrash Mekhilta* on Ex 21:2, for example, notes that even slaves were not expected to wash their masters' feet.[26] In *Joseph and Asenath* (20:2–4), Joseph protests dramatically when Asenath prepares to wash his feet. In one of Aesop's tales, a noblewoman attempts to hide her identity by girding herself with a towel, filling a basin with water, and in other ways pretending to prepare to wash the feet of a peasant.[27] As we will see, what Peter finds to be beneath Jesus' station is not Jesus washing feet *per se* but washing *his* (Peter's) feet.

The absence of the negative particle μή in Peter's exclamation of 13:6, οὐ μου νίπτεις τοὺς πόδας, tells us that Peter knows his turn for washing is at hand and that Jesus intends to go through with it. (Unlike the woman in Aesop's tale, Jesus is not bluffing.) Yet Peter does not yet object to the ritual, perhaps because he is lost in astonishment. One is reminded of the astonishment the Samaritan shows in 4:9 when Jesus, a Jew—whom she previously understood not to have dealings with Samaritans—asks her for a drink. There is a palpable disconnect. Peter seems to experience a similar sort of cognitive dissonance. In 4:9 and in our scene, the experiences of Jesus' conversation partners do not align with their

---

[23] So B. F. Westcott, *The Gospel According to St. John* (Grand Rapids: Eerdmans, 1975), 90–91. This idea is considered but not endorsed by Bernard in *St. John*, 460.

[24] See Wiarda, *Peter in the Gospels*, 107.

[25] Thomas, *Footwashing in John 13*, 90.

[26] Smith, *John*, 252.

[27] See Koester, *Symbolism in the Fourth Gospel*, 131.

convictions about him. As is the case with the Samaritan woman, Peter's actions are governed by pre-conceived ideas about how Jesus should behave. He is not comfortable with the Holy One of God stooping to lowly service, and so mistakes Jesus' selfless act for a reckless act of self-disregard.

Many scholars assume that Peter is speaking for all the disciples when he expresses astonishment at the prospect of Jesus engaging in a footwashing ritual. Some believe he represents Apostolic Christians who are unable to comprehend the meaning of the ritual and the requirements of Johannine discipleship.[28] C. S. Keener goes so far as to speculate that *all* the disciples balk at the ritual, recognizing it to be beneath Jesus' station, but that, for some reason, this detail is left out of the story.[29] What is clear about the text is that only Peter is described as putting up any kind of resistance. As mentioned above, a certain number of footwashings take place before Peter's discussion with Jesus, and yet Peter makes no attempt to stop Jesus from washing the feet of the other disciples. If a deficient Christology were to blame for his resistance to the ritual, would he not attempt to block Jesus from carrying out the procedure with the other disciples, thereby safeguarding Jesus from dishonor or adversity (as in 13:23–25 and 18:10–11)? As it is, he lets the early phase of the ritual pass without complaint. This indicates that what he finds particularly objectionable is the prospect of Jesus washing *his* feet, which in turn means that he misunderstands his own place / value in the ministry.

Recognizing this, J. H. Bernard imagines Peter experiencing such revulsion at the thought of the Holy One of God washing his feet that, as Jesus approaches, Peter draws up his feet in "impulsive humility."[30] This is certainly a case of reading between the lines, but the image Bernard provides is not absurd. Although both personal pronouns employed by Peter in 13:6 (σύ and μου) are emphatic, the stress is on μου since it follows immediately after σύ. What Peter says to Jesus, then, is just this: "You intend to wash *my* feet?" He does not pause to consider the possibility that Jesus is prefiguring his atoning death and that by

---

[28] On the former idea, see M. de Jonge, *Jesus: Stranger from Heaven and Son of God* (trans. J. E. Steely; Missoula, Mont.: Scholar's Press, 1977), 16; Wilckens, *Evangelium nach Johannes*, 208; and Keener, *Gospel of John*, 2.908. On the latter idea see Crosby, "*Do You Love Me?*," 156. For the idea that foot-washing is more a symbol of hospitality than of humility—and that Peter understands neither aspect—see Coloe, "Welcome into the Household of God," 414.

[29] "Interactions in ancient Mediterranean culture proceeded according to status differences, so that one might expect the disciples to staunchly protest Jesus' taking the role of their servant." Keener, *Gospel of John*, 2.908. Although Gen 18:4 in the MATT reads, "Let a little water be brought, and wash your feet, and rest yourselves under the tree," in the *Targum Neofiti* Abraham himself performs the chore as a demonstration of hospitality.

[30] Bernard, *St. John*, 2.460. Bernard's subsequent statement that Peter's "pseudo-reverence" in this scene is "near akin to irreverence" would seem to go too far.

failing to submit to the footwashing Peter risks losing a share in that death. Peter reacts emotionally, as in many other passages in the Gospel (e.g. 13:36–38; 18:10–11; and 21:7). He has accepted the invitation to follow Jesus (6:68–69) and has heard Jesus describe himself as the shepherd who "goes ahead (ἔμπροσθεν + πορεύεται) of the sheep" (10:4). He understands "following" to be a profession in which disciples must adopt a subservient role to Jesus.[31]

Knowing Peter's mind better than the disciple does—and perhaps having a better opinion of his intrinsic value—Jesus handles this initial exclamation with equanimity, saying: "You do not know now what I am doing but afterward (μετὰ ταῦτα) you will understand" (13:7).

There is no shortage of theories among scholars as to what, precisely, is meant by μετὰ ταῦτα.[32] After *what* things? After the *footwashing*? This does not seem likely, for some of the disciples have already had their feet washed and dried, and thus Peter has seen phases of the ritual completed, yet he lacks understanding. After *Pentecost*? This is a slightly better interpretation because the combination of cross, resurrection, and Holy Spirit has been promised to illuminate Jesus' teachings after he departs to the Father (7:39; cf. 14:25–26),[33] but it is not entirely convincing, for the event prefigured by the footwashing is Jesus' death on the cross and not the visitation of the Spirit. After *Peter's own denials and reinstatement*? This is the interpretation of A. Schlatter, but, again, it is unconvincing, for nothing about Peter's denials and subsequent professions of love for Jesus brings to mind this episode.[34] The best scholarship interprets μετὰ ταῦτα to mean *after the Passion and resurrection* (cf. 2:22; 12:16; 16:13; 20:9).[35] For Peter and the other disciples, it will be impossible to understand Jesus' humble act of service until his glorification is made manifest in the crucifixion and resurrection.[36]

Unfortunately, Peter is not satisfied by the promise of future understanding. He is upset at the unsavory prospect of Jesus adopting a subservient position toward him. When he now launches his protest, it is with vigor: "You shall never wash my feet!" (οὐ μὴ νίψῃς μου τοὺς πόδας εἰς τὸν αἰῶνα). The οὐ μή emphatic negative is a powerful phrase in Greek. It is used to similar effect by Peter in Matt 16:22, when he seeks to prevent Jesus from going to Jerusalem, and in Matt 26:35 (= Mark 14:31), when he dismisses Jesus' prediction that he

---

[31] On teacher/disciple dynamics, cf. Just. *Dialogue* 8.3; Diogenes Laertius 2.48; Jos. *Ant.* 8.354.

[32] See the discussion in Brown, *John*, 2.563–65.

[33] See Beasley-Murray, *John*, 233; Wilckens, *Evangelium nach Johannes*, 208.

[34] A. Schlatter, *Der Evangelist Johannes* (2nd ed.; Stuttgart: Calwer, 1948), 282.

[35] See the discussions in Jones, *Symbol of Water*, 187–89; Michaels, *John*, 240; and Brown, *John*, 2.553.

[36] See M. de Jonge, "The Radical Eschatology of the Fourth Gospel and the Eschatology of the Synoptics," in *John and the Synoptics* (ed. A. Denaux; BETL 101; Leuven: Leuven University Press, 1992), 484.

will betray him.³⁷ As in John 13:6, μου in 13:8 appears as an emphatic pronoun, preceding τοὺς πόδας in the sentence.³⁸ This is a further indication that what concerns Peter is not Jesus washing feet *per se* but washing *his* feet. As J. C. Thomas notes, "Despite Jesus' words, Peter will have none of it and uses the strongest form of negation possible in Greek grammar."³⁹ Peter seems to attach more value to Jesus' dignity than to his own, which is also the case in 18:10–11 and 21:7, and yet the irony of the scene is that his gracious action pales in comparison to the selflessness of Jesus' act, which is to model lowly service and adumbrate his own death. According to S. M. Schneiders, Peter is not so much dismayed at the prospect of allowing Jesus to adopt a subservient role as he is at the prospect of changing his own role:

> First, Peter was not merely objecting to having his feet washed by another but specifically to the reversal of service roles between himself and Jesus: 'Lord, do *you* wash *my* feet?' Secondly, his protest was not simply an embarrassed objection to Jesus' action but a categorical refusal to accept what this reversal of roles implied. 'By *no means* will you wash my feet *ever*' (lit. 'unto the ages,' meaning 'unto eternity'). In some way, Peter grasped that complicity involved acceptance of a radical reinterpretation of his own life-world, a genuine conversion of some kind which he was not prepared to undergo.⁴⁰

But Schneiders' second point assumes that Peter sees far enough into the future to realize that his role in the ministry must change, and that he is jittery at this prospect. Yet foresight is not a virtue of the Johannine Peter! I suspect that what

---

³⁷ Except for the angel (a non-human figure) in Luke 1:13 and the "Jews" (a group) in John 8:56, the only characters other than Jesus to use the phrase οὐ μή in the Gospels are Peter, who uses it four times, and Thomas, who uses it once (John 20:25). Because the angel in Luke 1:15 quotes the words of the angel in Jgs 13:4 and the Jews in John 8 quote Jesus' own words back to him, Peter and Thomas can be said to be the only characters other than Jesus to use οὐ μή as a product of individual expression. Of these two, only Peter uses the expression multiple times; it is always used in conversation with Jesus and it is always used as a corrective (see John 13:8; Mark 14:31; Matt 16:22, 35). Considering that the four evangelists reserve almost exclusively this powerful expression for Jesus (57 of 63 occurrences), one wonders if some historical memory of Peter challenging Jesus with such a phrase (or its Aramaic equivalent) is preserved here.

³⁸ This is the reading according to P⁶⁶ B Cᶜ W and L. Other manuscripts, including ℵ A M U and Λ, put μου at the end of the sentence, modifying the scene so that Peter's concern is that his *feet* (as opposed to other, cleaner parts) are going to come into contact with Jesus.

³⁹ J. C. Thomas, "Jesus Washes the Disciples' Feet," *Living Pulpit* 9 (2000), 28.

⁴⁰ S. M. Schneiders, "The Foot Washing (John 13:1–20): An Experiment in Hermeneutics," *CBQ* 43 (1981): 83.

he is focused on is the inappropriateness of his Lord performing a seemingly degrading chore, and that he does not see beyond this.

Jesus responds to Peter's brash declaration with words that are at once compassionate and threatening: "If I do not wash you, you have no part (μέρος) in me" (13:8). Brown translates μέρος as "heritage" on the grounds that it is often used in the LXX to translate the Heb. *heleq*, or "God-given heritage of Israel."[41] Bultmann opts for the translation "fellowship."[42] J. S. Webster, in a bold but, I think, astute move, suggests that both scholars err in conflating μέρος with μερίς, the latter being the more frequent septuagintal synonym for "inheritance." She chooses to translate μέρος as "portion."[43] However one translates the Greek noun, it appears in the NT most frequently in the book of Revelation, where it describes both the heavenly resting place of the elect (20:6 and 22:19) and the place of eternal torment of the condemned (21:8 and 22:19; cf. also Matt 24:51 and Luke 12:46). It may be the case that it carries eschatological connotations in our scene. What is at stake is Peter's participation in the ongoing life of God, made available through the salvific work of Jesus.

In keeping with the Fourth Gospel's emphasis on *realized* eschatology, however, Jesus does not warn Peter that he risks losing a share in him at some future date but risks losing a share in him *now*: "Unless I wash you, you have (ἔχεις) no share in me." G. F. Snyder does well to point out that "the focus of the narrative in vss. 1–9 falls on Peter who refuses to accept the self-giving of Jesus and therefore has blocked any possibility of receiving the glory."[44] Although Peter in John 6 offered an impressive Christological confession of Jesus, Snyder asserts that he has not yet discovered the proper way of serving him. C. S. Keener takes the criticism of Peter a step further—and, I would say, a step too far—when he notes that Peter's objections to having his own feet washed by Jesus are evocative of the objections raised by Judas to Mary's washing of Jesus' feet (12:4; cf. 11:2): "Mary and Jesus embody sacrifice and servanthood; Judas and Peter, impending betrayal and denial!" (emphasis in original).[45] The problem with this analysis is that Peter embodies sacrifice to a greater extent than any disciple in the Gospel (esp. 18:10 and 21:18–19). Far from drawing a parallel between the actions of Judas and Peter, as Keener suggests, the Fourth Evangelist returns here to the practice of drawing a contrast between these characters, a process he initiated in 6:70 and will return to in 18:3–11. I agree with M. Sabbe that in both scenes, "Peter's readiness to give his life for Jesus is opposed to the attitude of the betrayer."[46]

---

[41] Brown, *John*, 2.565.
[42] Bultmann, *Gospel of John*, 468.
[43] Webster, *Ingesting Jesus*, 111–12.
[44] Snyder, "Anti-Petrinism," 6.
[45] Keener, *Gospel of John*, 2.909.
[46] M. Sabbe, "Footwashing in John 13," 303.

Jesus' warning to Peter that he risks losing a share in him if he blocks the oblation rouses Peter from his stupor. He suddenly realizes "the paradox that, in the spiritual kingdom, the way to climb high is to come down, and that to attain the first place you must choose the last."[47] As a consequence he blurts out, "Lord not my feet only, but also my hands and my head!"[48]

It has been observed that this remark provides a moment of "comic relief" in the increasingly tense scene.[49] Particularly for modern readers familiar with all four canonical Gospels and their consistent reporting of Peter's penchant for exuberance (Mark 9:5 [=Matt 17:4; Luke 9:33]; Matt 14:28–29; Luke 24:12; John 13:37; 18:10; 20:3–4, 6; 21:17), this assessment may ring true. For Peter, however, the words reflect only a sudden change of heart. What he initially dismissed as a repugnant image, his Lord engaging in a humiliating act, he now sees as the key to intimate fellowship. When he scrambles to rectify the situation, he displays his characteristic impulsiveness.[50] If water brings life with Jesus, it appears to us he reasons, more water will bring more life, and so he requests a soaking.[51] This is not a true *Johannine misunderstanding* in which Jesus and a dialogue partner engage in one conversation but speak to different topics (cf. 3:4–9; 4:9–15, etc), for *life in Jesus* is understood by both parties to be the topic. Peter's confusion stems from the fact that he is focused on water and not the prophetic action it supports. Yet, as M. W. G. Stibbe observes, the reader is not without sympathy for him, and wonders if he is not "the victim of Jesus' elusive actions...."[52] L. Simon is correct to point out that Peter suffers no devaluation (*Abwertung*) here, and that it is not a goal of the author "ein

---

[47] C. Spicq, "Priestly Virtues in the New Testament," in *Sacraments in Scripture* (ed. T. Worden; London: Geoffrey Chapman, 1966), 194.

[48] There is much textual variation when it comes to recording where and how Peter's name is introduced in this verse. The four most common readings are: Πέτρος Σίμων B; Πέτρος D; Πέτρος Σείμων W; Σίμων Πέτρος P^{66} ℵ* A C K L M f^1 f^{13}. Although Peter's name appears in some way, shape, or form in all these manuscripts, the textual discrepancies may suggest that the verse originally began with λέγει αὐτῷ only, and that industrious scribes reached different conclusions about how and where to insert his name.

[49] W. Howard-Brook, *Becoming Children of God: John's Gospel and Radical Discipleship* (Maryknoll: Orbis, 1999), 297. N. P. Madsen, *John* (BBC; Nashville: Abingdon, 1988), 107, also notes the comic irony in Peter's request for "a good scrubbing." Van Tilborg, *Johannes-Evangelium*, 193, suggests Peter remains likeable to the reader even in the midst of his misunderstanding: "Wie sympathisch dies auch bei den Leser/-innen ankommt, es offenbart doch zuglech sein totales Missverstehen."

[50] See Smith, *John*, 252.

[51] Haenchen, *John 2*, 107, sees Peter at his most obtuse here, embracing the idea that salvation lies "in the quantity of the water."

[52] Stibbe, *John*, 147.

negatives Bild des Menschen Petrus zu entwerfen, der aus eigenem Verschulden die Aufgabe der Mission Jesu nicht versteht."[53]

Rather than rebuking Peter for missing the point, Jesus delivers a lecture to all the disciples about the benefits of true discipleship (13:10–20) and alerts them for the second time to the presence of an unclean one in their ranks: "One who has bathed does not need to wash, except for the feet, but is entirely clean. And you are clean, though not all of you."[54] The word "bathing" almost certainly refers to the Jewish ritual practice of bathing the entire body before participating in a festive meal and not to the more mundane practice of washing hands before a meal, because the active verb changes from νίπτω to λούω, which describes a comprehensive washing (cf. Acts 9:37). It is a confusing verse, to be sure, but the message to the disciples seems plain enough: the true washing they have received is *spiritual*; they have bathed in the "ministry, teachings, and presence" of Jesus.[55] The one disciple who receives a footwashing but remains spiritually unclean is Judas, who is now in league with the devil (διάβολος; 13:2, 27) and whose plans for treachery will shortly be revealed (13:23–25).[56]

Curiosity About the Traitor: 13:21–26

²¹After saying this Jesus was troubled in spirit, and declared, "Very truly, I tell you, one of you will betray me." ²²The disciples looked at one another, uncertain of whom he was speaking. ²³One of his disciples—the one whom Jesus loved—was reclining next to him;

---

[53] Simon, *Petrus und der Lieblingsjünger*, 192.

[54] The specification "except for the feet" (εἰ μὴ τοὺς πόδας) is omitted in ℵ 579 vgst.

[55] Jones, *The Symbol of Water*, 189. For the opposite view (i.e., that the ritual bathing leaves the disciples without a need for additional washing), see Moloney, *Gospel of John*, 375. Culpepper, *Gospel and Letters of John*, 208, paraphrases Jesus' instruction to Peter and his associates this way: "Do (foot-washing/serve/love/die) for one another as I am doing for you."

[56] Jesus is said in 13:11 to know the identity of the betrayer, which makes understandable his statement in 13:10: "not all of you are clean." It is interesting that reference is made to both the "devil" (13:2) and the "betrayer" (13:2, 11) in the same pericope in which Peter confronts Jesus and seeks to prevent him from prefiguring his sacrificial work. In Mark 8:33 and Matt 16:23, Peter plays the role of Satan / adversary (σατανᾶ) when he steps between Jesus and the cross. In John 6:69, as we discussed in the second chapter of this study, John reserves for Judas the negative appellation shared by Judas *and* Peter in the Synoptic tradition. Philo, in commenting on Jewish sacrificial laws, makes note of the symbolic nature of foot-washing: "And by the command that the feet of the victim shall be washed, it is figuratively shown that we must no longer walk upon the earth, but soar aloft and traverse the air" (*Spec. Leg.* 1.207). Traversing the air is particularly appropriate for the future of Jesus, who is to soon rejoin the Father (19:30; cf. 7:33; 8:14; 8:21), but the reader familiar with the Fourth Gospel supplement (esp. 21:18–19) may wonder if Peter is not also being cleansed for death.

²⁴Simon Peter therefore motioned to him to ask Jesus of whom he was speaking. ²⁵So while reclining next to Jesus, he asked him, "Lord, who is it?" ²⁶Jesus answered, "It is the one to whom I give this piece of bread when I have dipped it in the dish." So when he had dipped the piece of bread, he gave it to Judas son of Simon Iscariot. (²¹Ταῦτα εἰπὼν [ὁ] Ἰησοῦς ἐταράχθη τῷ πνεύματι καὶ ἐμαρτύρησεν καὶ εἶπεν· ἀμὴν ἀμὴν λέγω ὑμῖν ὅτι εἷς ἐξ ὑμῶν παραδώσει με. ²²ἔβλεπον εἰς ἀλλήλους οἱ μαθηταὶ ἀπορούμενοι περὶ τίνος λέγει. ²³ἦν ἀνακείμενος εἷς ἐκ τῶν μαθητῶν αὐτοῦ ἐν τῷ κόλπῳ τοῦ Ἰησοῦ, ὃν ἠγάπα ὁ Ἰησοῦς. ²⁴νεύει οὖν τούτῳ Σίμων Πέτρος πυθέσθαι τίς ἂν εἴη περὶ οὗ λέγει. ²⁵ἀναπεσὼν οὖν ἐκεῖνος οὕτως ἐπὶ τὸ στῆθος τοῦ Ἰησοῦ λέγει αὐτῷ· κύριε, τίς ἐστιν; ²⁶ἀποκρίνεται [ὁ] Ἰησοῦς· ἐκεῖνός ἐστιν ᾧ ἐγὼ βάψω τὸ ψωμίον καὶ δώσω αὐτῷ. βάψας οὖν τὸ ψωμίον [λαμβάνει καὶ] δίδωσιν Ἰούδᾳ Σίμωνος Ἰσκαριώτου.)

We have seen Jesus "troubled in spirit" twice before in the Fourth Gospel: once before raising Lazarus (finding Lazarus' family and friends distraught [11:33]), and once afterwards (contemplating his own fast-approaching "hour" [12:27]).⁵⁷ Now, with the betrayal imminent, we are given another glimpse of his inner turmoil. Except for Peter, none of the disciples takes his words about the upcoming betrayal as an invitation for discussion. Informed that one of them will betray him, they react by looking quizzically at one another across the table, like children feigning innocence when charged by a parent with some domestic offense. This is very different from the scene in Mark 14:19 and Matt 26:22, in which the disciples go around the table seeking to remove suspicion from themselves by putting to Jesus the rhetorical question, "Not I?" (μήτι ἐγώ). In John's Gospel, only Peter takes a proactive stance, arranging an inquiry into the traitor's identity.

We can imagine that Peter is portrayed as apparently troubled by the news that one of Jesus' closest disciples is about to betray him because he earlier vouchsafed for the loyalty of Jesus' innermost circle of followers (6:68-69), the remnant that kept Jesus' ministry afloat after the Bread of Life Discourse.⁵⁸ As we saw in the footwashing episode, his inclination is to protect Jesus from adversity whether or not Jesus agrees that he has properly assessed the threat. Despite the fact that Jesus has made it clear he is under the Father's care (3:35;

---

⁵⁷ Daniel is said to be troubled in spirit (בְּרוּחִי) when he sees the vision of the son of man coming with the clouds of heaven in Dan 7:13–15, and Pharaoh is similarly "troubled" (niphal of פעם) in Gen 41:8, but it is not a common expression in the biblical corpus.

⁵⁸ The Twelve are not mentioned specifically in John 13. We know only that Jesus has gathered "his own" (τοὺς ἰδίους). While it is possible that τοὺς ἰδίους refers to the Twelve—said by Jesus in 6:70 to have been "chosen" (ἐκλέγομαι) by him—it is also possible this phrase describes his closest disciples, those who believe in his name.

5:20; 10:17), and that he is therefore in safer custody than Peter could ever provide, Peter takes it upon himself to identify the faithless element in the group.

His method is to signal "the disciple whom Jesus loved" (ὃν ἠγάπα ὁ Ἰησοῦς), who reclines on Jesus' breast, to ask Jesus to which disciple he is referring.[59] It is only here, halfway into the Gospel, that we meet BD. In one respect he is introduced with little fanfare, appearing out of thin air as he does on the fishing boat in 21:7. Yet in another respect his seating assignment is impressive and commands our respect: as he reclines on Jesus' bosom / breast (κολπός), we are reminded of Jesus dwelling in the bosom (κολπός) of the Father (1:18).[60]

Depending on whether one translates πυθέσθαι as an aorist middle infinitive or an infinitival imperative, Peter either enlists BD's cooperation in rooting out the traitor or issues him a command to help. Because πυθέσθαι is coupled with an indirect question (τίς ἂν) and a relative clause (περὶ οὗ), it initially appears to be an infinitive. When we consider that it is attached to the active verb νεύω (to motion or signal), however, it becomes clear it is an infinitival imperative. Peter wants his question passed along to Jesus and, with a gesture, *instructs* BD to do it. The presence of the adverb οὕτως ("therefore," "without much ado")[61] in v. 25 lends support to this idea that πυθέσθαι functions as an imperative here, for it describes BD passing along Peter's question without hesitation or deliberation.

The fact that Peter does not put the question to Jesus directly has led many scholars to raise questions about the nature of his relationship with Jesus and BD. Most conclude that he is a less intimate associate of Jesus than BD is and that—in relying on BD to get a question to Jesus—he reveals himself to be a somewhat impotent figure in the ministry.[62] More than a few scholars go further than this and insist that Peter appears in this scene as BD's subordinate: he prompts BD to put a question to Jesus about the traitor because his own

---

[59] There is a good deal of textual variation in this verse. P[66*] B C L 1071 and W describe Peter signaling to BD *and* speaking to him: νεύει οὖν τούτῳ Σίμων Πέτρος καὶ λέγει αὐτῷ εἰπὲ τίς ἐστιν περὶ οὗ. P[66c] A K M U Δ Λ Π f[1] and f[13] report Peter signaling but not speaking, which I believe preserves the original text since it seems to be Peter's poor seat at the table that makes signaling necessary in the first place.

[60] See L. Schenke, *Das Johannesevangelium* (Stuttgart: Kohlhammer, 1992), 110.

[61] "Without much ado" is the free rendering of Brown, *John*, 2.575.

[62] According to Perkins, *Peter*, 96: "The Beloved Disciple, the source of the Johannine tradition, clearly has both loyalty to Jesus and insight into his person that surpasses Peter's....Peter must ask him to ask Jesus for an explanation of his words about the disciple who is going to betray him (13:21–25)." Quast, *Peter and the Beloved Disciple*, 63, focuses on the mechanics of the situation when he says that "Peter is constrained to query the Lord through the Beloved Disciple."

relationship with Jesus (represented by his assigned seat at the table) is poor.[63] As we will see, this is reading too much into the text.

A question worth asking at this point is whether Peter relies on BD to put his question to Jesus because he himself is unable to ask the question or because he is unwilling. Given his proclivity for speaking his mind to Jesus (13:4–11, 37; 21:15–19), the latter is a possibility only if we imagine him so chagrined by the memory of the foot-washing debacle that he is temporarily speechless and therefore willing to cede the limelight to his colleague.[64] Considering that he will shortly challenge Jesus on the issue of his readiness to follow him (13:36–38), however, penitence or shame does not seem to be the force / mood that stifles him. If he is *unable* to put the question to him, though, what is it that restricts him? One possibility is that he has spoken to Jesus once already and is waiting for his next opportunity. In commenting on Essene tradition, Josephus (*J. War* 2.8.5.132) describes members of the community speaking in rotation at meals (cf. 1QS 6.10). Because Peter motions rather than whispers to BD, however, we get the impression his inability to question Jesus is logistical: he is not within speaking distance of either one of them. Simply put, he does not have a particularly good seat at the table.[65]

---

[63] See, for example, Kragerud, *Lieblingsjünger*, 21–25; O'Grady, *According to John*, 35; and Maynard, "Role of Peter," 543–45. Crosby, *"Do You Love Me?"* 161, insists that the "hard-of-understanding" Peter motions to BD because he is clueless as to the nature of the betrayal Jesus is talking about and requires an interpreter. According to Perkins, *Peter*, 97, "Beginning at the Last Supper, Peter's deficiencies are highlighted as he is consistently contrasted with the Beloved Disciple." Chennattu, *Johannine Discipleship*, 101, sees BD's intimacy with Jesus in this scene as the first indicator that he "represents the covenant relationship and community that is expected from the disciples and the subsequent readers of the gospel..." In each case, the mediating disciple is assigned a greater symbolic importance than the disciple who initiates the inquiry into the traitor's identity.

[64] So Aquinas, *Catena Aurea: A Commentary on the Four Gospels, Volume 4: St John* (trans. J. H. Newman; London: St. Austin Press, 1997), 435: "Peter had been just reproved, and therefore, checking the customary vehemence of his love, he did not speak himself now, but made John speak for him."

[65] We know that in formal gatherings in first-century Palestine guests were often seated at meals with regard to social status. If we are interested in trying to envision where Peter sits vis-à-vis BD, we should perhaps begin by imagining a table (*mensa*) surrounded by three mats (*triclinium*), a traditional seating arrangement at formal suppers. (Malina and Rohrbaugh, *Social-Science Commentary*, 220; see also Webster, *Ingesting Jesus*, 102–05.) As host, Jesus occupies the middle mat (*medius*). It is fair to assume that BD sits on this same mat, immediately to Jesus' right or his left, for this allows him to be in position to lean upon Jesus' breast (13:23). Insofar as it was customary for guests to recline on the left elbow and pick food from the table with the right hand, we might at first assume that he sits on Jesus' right. But because the seat to the host's immediate *left* was deemed to be the seat of highest honor, it is also possible he sits in that position. What is most

If seating were the whole story here, we could perhaps postulate some sort of hierarchical relationship between BD and Peter and establish a crude "pecking order" in Jesus' ministry, an exercise undertaken by many scholars (see below). But more important than Peter's position at the table is his activity. He does not fret about his seat at his Lord's table but takes advantage of BD's intimate positioning vis-à-vis Jesus to help identify the traitor. Receiving Peter's signal, BD puts forward a simple question to Jesus: "Lord, who is it?" Köstenberger rightly notes that "one is struck by the noncompetitive relationship between Peter and John (BD)...."[66] Schnackenburg argues persuasively that Peter's act of motioning to BD underscores the latter disciple's importance but also reinforces "Peter's acknowledged authority and his intimacy and closeness to Jesus."[67]

Interestingly, nothing in the text suggests that BD considers putting this question to Jesus before being prompted by Peter, or, to put it another way, it does not occur to him to make use of his intimate friendship with Jesus (cf. also 19:26; 21:2, 7, 20) to expose the enemy. This point is generally ignored by scholars who identify BD as Peter's superior and hail his abilities as mediator.[68] While it is possible that Jesus' love for BD so distracts BD that he is blind to external threats against Jesus, and that his inaction is therefore a paradoxical byproduct of his pious discipleship, it is equally likely that he shies away from

---

important to recognize about BD is that he sits next to Jesus, leaning against him, with the inference that BD's intimacy with Jesus is akin to Jesus' intimacy with the Father (1:18), and that Jesus keeps the one he loves close to him just as the Father keeps the Son close (10:30, 36; 14:6; 16:32; 17:11). As for Peter, he probably sits on the left mat (*summus*) or the right mat (*imus*). To imagine that he sits next to Jesus on the *medius* requires that we concoct a scenario in which he leans around Jesus to pass a question to BD that is ultimately meant to return to Jesus, which is absurd. Wherever Peter sits, it is far enough from BD that signaling to him is the only practical way of getting his attention without attracting the attention of the others. So Cullmann, *Peter*, 27. Dschulnigg, *Petrus im Neuen Testament*, 125, observes that "[d]ies zeigen auch sein bevorzugter Platz an der Seite Jesu und die Bitte des Petrus an ihn, durch die Frage an Jesus die gespannte Situation zu lösen."

[66] Köstenberger, *John*, 415. With many others, Köstenberger holds that BD is John son of Zebedee (see introduction).

[67] Schnackenburg, *St. John*, 3.30.

[68] See, for example, Perkins, *Peter*, 96. Charlesworth, *Beloved Disciple*, 54, contends that the Beloved Disciple "obliges Peter" by passing along his question, and that he is "superior to Peter, who must ask him to obtain insight from Jesus concerning the meaning of some of his words" (118), but this interpretation does not give credit to Peter for instigating the investigation into the traitor's identity. Also ignoring Peter's role as catalyst is J. GniLukea, *Johannesevangelium* (ed. J. GniLukea and R. Schnackenburg; NEchtB; Würzburg: Echter Verlag, 1983), 109, who lauds BD for being the one to put the question to Jesus, noting that only he can obtain from Jesus the "gewünschte Antowrt."

the topic of the betrayal because it is—in a word—dangerous. In 18:10, as we will see shortly, BD mysteriously disappears when the Roman cohort confronts Jesus (and Peter), although earlier in the evening he was quite comfortable sitting between them. In 18:17–27, BD again goes missing, this time at the precise moment when Peter is accosted by members of the chief priest's household and accused of complicity with Jesus.[69] In 20:5–8 he wins the race to the empty tomb but waits to go inside until Peter can enter and reconnoiter the site. Does piety overwhelm his sense of adventure or does it conceal a chronic timidity? We have only just been introduced to him and cannot yet make wholesale judgments, but one theory to be considered in subsequent chapters is that his sublime piety has a weakness, and only when he is teamed with Peter does he represent the ideal Johannine disciple.

Looking briefly at the last part of the pericope (13:26–28), we find that the act of cooperation between Peter and BD achieves a positive result: with the issue of the traitor's identity raised, Jesus exposes Judas by giving him a piece of bread to eat, at which time Satan enters into his heart. W. Wrede describes the transfer of the morsel as "a satanic sacrament, which Judas takes to himself."[70] In urging Judas to do what he must do quickly, Jesus reveals that his own surrender to the will of the Father is absolute (see also 5:19, 36; 8:28; 10:15, 18, 38; 12:27; 14:31; 15:1; 18:11). When Judas flees the room and the fellowship is purged of its unclean element, Jesus issues to the disciples the love commandment (13:34) and engages in a lengthy monologue about his approaching glorification, as well as the consequences it will have for the disciples (chapters 14–17).[71]

---

[69] One can argue that the situation is reversed in 19:26ff., when BD stands beneath the cross and all other male disciples, including Peter, have deserted Jesus. Yet at that point in the story the danger of being an associate of Jesus has lessened somewhat. Associates and relatives of crucified Jews were often encouraged by Roman authorities to attend the executions in order to establish them as "a deterrent against Jewish nationalism." See J. B. Green, "Death of Jesus," in *Dictionary of Jesus and the Gospels* (ed. J. B. Green, S. McKnight and I. H. Marshall; Downer's Grove, Illinois: InterVarsity, 1992), 148.

[70] W. Wrede, *Vorträge und Studien* (Tübingen: Mohr [Siebeck], 1907), 136.

[71] Bultmann, *Gospel of John*, 459–61, believes the Gospel in its earliest incarnation placed the discussion about Peter's denials after the Last Discourse. He reconstructs the Gospel by putting chapters 13–17 in the following order: 13:1–30; 17:1–26; 13:31–35; 15:1–16:33; 13:36–14:31. For the idea that the example of lowly service that Jesus "gives" to the disciples has a parallel in 13:34, in which he "gives" the love commandment (in both cases δίδομι), see Y. Simoens, *La gloire d'aimer: Structures, stylistiques et interprétatives dans le discourse de la Céne: John 13–17* (AnBib 90; Rome: Biblical Institute Press, 1981), 92.

Peter's Promise to Follow Jesus: 13:33–38

³³"Little children, I am with you only a little longer. You will look for me; and as I said to the Jews so now I say to you, 'Where I am going, you cannot come.' ³⁴I give you a new commandment, that you love one another. Just as I have loved you, you also should love one another. ³⁵By this everyone will know that you are my disciples, if you have love for one another." ³⁶Simon Peter said to him, "Lord, where are you going?" Jesus answered, "Where I am going, you cannot follow me now; but you will follow afterward." ³⁷Peter said to him, "Lord, why can I not follow you now? I will lay down my life for you." ³⁸Jesus answered, "Will you lay down your life for me? Very truly, I tell you, before the cock crows, you will have denied me three times." (³³τεκνία, ἔτι μικρὸν μεθ' ὑμῶν εἰμι· ζητήσετέ με, καὶ καθὼς εἶπον τοῖς Ἰουδαίοις ὅτι ὅπου ἐγὼ ὑπάγω ὑμεῖς οὐ δύνασθε ἐλθεῖν, καὶ ὑμῖν λέγω ἄρτι. ³⁴Ἐντολὴν καινὴν δίδωμι ὑμῖν, ἵνα ἀγαπᾶτε ἀλλήλους, καθὼς ἠγάπησα ὑμᾶς ἵνα καὶ ὑμεῖς ἀγαπᾶτε ἀλλήλους. ³⁵ἐν τούτῳ γνώσονται πάντες ὅτι ἐμοὶ μαθηταί ἐστε, ἐὰν ἀγάπην ἔχητε ἐν ἀλλήλοις. ³⁶Λέγει αὐτῷ Σίμων Πέτρος· κύριε, ποῦ ὑπάγεις; ἀπεκρίθη [αὐτῷ] Ἰησοῦς· ὅπου ὑπάγω οὐ δύνασαί μοι νῦν ἀκολουθῆσαι, ἀκολουθήσεις δὲ ὕστερον. ³⁷λέγει αὐτῷ ὁ Πέτρος· κύριε, διὰ τί οὐ δύναμαί σοι ἀκολουθῆσαι ἄρτι; τὴν ψυχήν μου ὑπὲρ σοῦ θήσω. ³⁸ἀποκρίνεται Ἰησοῦς· τὴν ψυχήν σου ὑπὲρ ἐμοῦ θήσεις; ἀμὴν ἀμὴν λέγω σοι, οὐ μὴ ἀλέκτωρ φωνήσῃ ἕως οὗ ἀρνήσῃ με τρίς.)

Jesus' affection for the disciples is revealed in his use of the diminutive τεκνία, a *hapax legomenon* in the Gospels (but frequent in 1 John [2:1, 12, 28; 3:7, 18; 4:4; 5:21]) that "recalls both the promise that those who receive the incarnate word will become children of God (1:12) and the characterization of Jesus' task as gathering God's 'scattered children' (11:52)."[72] Whereas οἱ Ἰουδαῖοι were in an earlier scene unable to follow Jesus because they lacked faith in him (8:21), the disciples are now unable to follow him because he is going to the Father.[73] The world will know that they are his disciples only when they reciprocate among themselves the service and loving kindness that he demonstrated in the footwashing and will demonstrate on the cross. The message is thoroughly in keeping with the overarching Gospel message that love is a binding force without parallel, drawing together not only Father and Son, but Father, Son, and believers (see 14:15, 21–24, 31; 15:9; 17:26; 21:15–17).

---

[72] Coloe, "Welcome into the Household of God," 410.
[73] Porsch, *Johannes–Evangelium*, 149, describes Jesus as being "auf seinem (Kreuz-) Weg zum Vater."

What the reader quickly comes to realize, however, is that Peter has not read the Gospel! Rather than spending time reflecting on possible layers of meaning in Jesus' words about "departing," he boldly asks him where he is going, echoing the question of the Pharisees in 7:35 and οἱ Ἰουδαῖοι in 8:22.[74] Whereas moments earlier Jesus spoke of the disciples' collective inability to follow him (ὅπου ἐγὼ ὑπάγω ὑμεῖς οὐ δύνασθε ἐλθεῖν; 13:33), he now employs the second person singular to inform Peter about the future of his own discipleship: ὅπου ὑπάγω οὐ δύνασαί μοι νῦν ἀκολουθῆσαι, ἀκολουθήσεις δὲ ὕστερον. Peter will indeed follow Jesus, even to death, but not yet. "Das ist ganz wörtlich gemeint: Petrus wird ihm folgen zum Kreuzestod. Dann wird auch er es verstanden haben, daß der Weg zur Herrlichkeit ist."[75] Schnackenburg emphasizes the positive nature of Jesus' promise: "It is seen to be a concealed announcement of death as a witness or martyrdom and acceptance into Jesus' community with the Father."[76] One might imagine that Peter would react to news of his future loyalty—even when taking into consideration the terrible personal cost—with jubilation, for this has been his goal. But he does not. Having confused "following" Jesus with maintaining a close proximity to him, he focuses only on that part of the message that foretells their near-term separation.

When he again speaks, it is to ask why he cannot follow Jesus *now*, and to express a willingness to lay down his life for him. Although S. K. Ray observes that "[i]n the comfortable setting of the upper room, such boisterous courage is easy," this is giving Peter too little credit.[77] Through the specific language he assigns to the disciple, the Fourth Evangelist wants it to be known that Peter is sincere in his pledge to die for Jesus. When Peter says that he will follow Jesus "now," he uses the word ἄρτι (at once; immediately) rather than νῦν, the latter term being much more common in the Fourth Gospel, but that would, in this case, fail to convey adequately Peter's sense of urgency.[78] Also, when Peter employs the preposition ὑπέρ in vowing to die on behalf of Jesus, he intimates that he envisions giving himself over to a sacrificial death,[79] perhaps one in which he and Jesus die together or in which he follows Jesus into the hands of

---

[74] The question he puts to Jesus in the Vulgate, "Domine, quo vadis?," is identical to that which he poses in their meeting outside the gates of Rome in the apocryphal *Acts of Peter and Paul*. Schnackenburg, *St. John*, 3.55, astutely resists comparing Peter to the Pharisees because Peter's question is delivered sincerely and not ironically.

[75] De Boor, *Evangelium des Johannes*, 94.

[76] Schnackenburg, *St. John*, 3.56.

[77] Ray, *St. John's Gospel*, 263.

[78] D and W have both νῦν *and* ἄρτι, emphasizing the extent of Peter's desire to stay close to Jesus.

[79] On this use of ὑπέρ, see BDAG, s.v., 1030.

the enemy. As F. Lapham observes, "there appears to be some recognition by Peter that martyrdom might first be required."[80]

But that martyrdom will not come now. Peter's pledge to give his life for Jesus is sincere, but the courage needed to carry out the act is not yet mature. As Haenchen puts it, Peter "exhibits a self-confidence that is unjustified."[81] Jesus informs him that his discipleship will take a decidedly negative turn in the near future: "Will you lay down your life for me? Very truly, I tell you, before the cock crows, you will have denied me three times."[82] As the reader knows by now, the first question is rhetorical; Peter will indeed lay down his life for Jesus. (Chapter 21 reveals the particulars of the event: he dies by crucifixion and so glorifies God [21:18–19]).[83] The second part of the message is what is new: Peter will deny Jesus three times, an event that takes place in all the Gospels (John 18:17–25; cf. Mark 14:66–72; Matt 26:69–75; Luke 22:56–62) and is examined in the next chapter. But while Jesus' words are harsh, there is little reason to accept the opinion of Ridderbos that they are delivered "almost contemptuously" as a way of mocking Peter's overly optimistic pledge to follow.[84] If anything, the prediction of the denials is less damaging to the reader's overall opinion of Peter than it is in the Synoptic Gospels because John, unlike the Synoptists, precedes the bad news with the positive message that Peter will ultimately prove faithful.[85]

---

[80] Lapham, *Peter*, 8 n. 13. See also Cullmann, *Peter*, 87; and Brown et al., *Peter in the New Testament*, 133.

[81] Haenchen, *John 2*, 118.

[82] Curiously, Jesus' statement in 16:5, "But now I am going to him who sent me; yet none of you asks me, 'Where are you going?,'" appears to assume no knowledge of Peter's question in John 13:36. Brown, *John*, 2.614, may be correct in asserting that they are "variant forms of the same incident." The prophetic warning, ἀμὴν ἀμὴν λέγω σοί is a favorite phrase of the Fourth Evangelist's (cf. 3:3, 5, 11; cf. also 21:18 [the work of the Redactor]) and gives a sombre feel to the occasion. A shorter version of the warning, ἀμὴν λέγω σοί, appears in Jesus' prediction of Peter's denials in Mark 14:30.

[83] Writers as early as Tertullian (*Adv. Ser.* 15.3) interpreted 21:18–19 to be a reference to Peter's crucifixion: "In Rome Nero was the first to stain with blood the rising faith. Peter was girded about by another when he was made fast to the cross." (For other ancient writers who describe crucifixion as the manner of Peter's death, see the discussion in chapter 6.)

[84] H. N. Ridderbos, *The Gospel According to John* (trans. J. Vriend; Grand Rapids: Eerdmans, 1997), 478.

[85] Concurring with this assessment is Dschulnigg, *Petrus*, 127. Luke 22:31–34, like John 13:36–38, predicts Peter's redemption and/or eventual faithfulness before foretelling his denials. In contrast to John, Luke describes Jesus praying for rather than predicting Peter's ultimate faithfulness. If we accept that Jesus' prayers are not vain petitions in Luke, the distinction is perhaps trivial. See Sabbe, "Footwashing," 279–308, for the idea that much of John 13 is dependent on Luke 7:36–50. As is discussed in the following

Conclusion

We have seen that Peter plays a major role in the three scenes that constitute John 13: the footwashing, the discussion about the identity of the traitor, and Peter's own promise to follow Jesus regardless of the consequences.

The first action he takes in the chapter, rejecting the footwashing, is, to put it simply, disastrous. By refusing to participate in a ritual that prefigures Jesus' sacrifice on the cross, he risks losing a share in Jesus' glory. While it is clear he misunderstands or under-appreciates the Christological significance of the footwashing, what is even more apparent is how uncomfortable he is with the idea of Jesus washing his (Peter's) feet. He does not attempt to curtail the ritual in its earliest stages, when the other disciples are having their feet washed and dried, but expresses misgivings only when Jesus comes to him with the basin. His devotion to Jesus involves a desire to protect him from what he considers to be degradation or danger. To the extent that the Evangelist affords us a look inside his mind, Peter seems to find great degradation in the "Holy One of God" washing the feet of his confessor.

In this pericope, as in several others in the Gospel, Peter acts on impulse. When he learns that his own submission to the footwashing ritual will not denigrate Jesus but will in fact increase Peter's own share in him, he reverses course completely and requests that his head and hands be washed as well.[86] There is no reason to accept the suggestion of M. H. Crosby that "given the Johannine community's concern about the Petrine community's predilection for hierarchical patterns rejected by Jesus, there may be reason to believe his acquiescence was more reluctant than fervent."[87] The community Peter represents in the Fourth Gospel is the *Johannine Community*. Anti-Petrine polemic is not on the Evangelist's mind. And "fervent" is precisely the right word to describe the manner in which Peter ultimately submits to the footwashing. A "reluctant" disciple might dip a toe in the basin to keep his master happy, but would not request a comprehensive soaking. Certainly the scene has humorous overtones, but it casts Peter in a generally favorable light. He is slow to understand his role in the ministry and the significance of the prophetic action, yet he is willing to be redirected into a proper relationship with Jesus.

---

chapter, the Evangelist in this pericope is preparing the reader to adopt a forgiving attitude toward Peter in advance of the denials.

[86] Thomas, in *John 13*, 96, finds Peter's request for his head to be washed especially significant: "In ancient Greek κεφαλή came to represent the whole person, life itself...Peter's request that his head be washed expresses the view that the head represents the person."

[87] Crosby, *"Do you Love me?,"* 156.

Peter's attempt to identify the traitor (13:23–26), which has the unforeseen effect of culling Judas from the fellowship, is better received by Jesus. Not much time passes between Peter's decision to begin an inquiry into the identity of the traitor and Judas' graceless departure. But what is more interesting than the revelation of impending treachery—a topic broached in 6:70—is the fact that Peter and a new character, BD, work together to learn who it is Jesus is talking about. There is no such scene in the Synoptic Gospels, for there the disciples seek only to remove suspicion from themselves. In John's Gospel, Peter does not say out of desperation to BD, "Asks him if he means me!," but enlists BD to help identity the faithless disciple. Thus John introduces BD to us as one who is loved by Jesus, who is trusted by Peter, and who trusts Peter.

In the final scene in John 13 (vv. 36–38), Peter's future discipleship is the topic of discussion. His near-term destiny is to deny Jesus three times, a cowardly act that is recorded in all the Gospels. His long-term destiny is far brighter, however: he will follow Jesus, ultimately to martyrdom, although the Evangelist, unlike the Redactor (cf. 21:18–19), does not give us the graphic details. Peter's vow to follow Jesus "at once" (ἄρτι) has a sense of desperation about it, and it marks the second time in the chapter that he seeks to cultivate an intimacy with Jesus that is conditional. He tries to shield Jesus from adversity and therefore keep him available for fellowship (cf. also 13:36–38; 18:10–11, 15–27). It is Bultmann, of all people—not one normally given to underscoring Peter's accomplishments in the Gospel—who reminds us that John 13 ends on a positive note as far as Peter is concerned. Behind all Peter's fretting, Bultmann emphasizes, "lies the disciple's readiness to follow Jesus, and thus he receives the promise, ἀκολουθήσεις δὲ ὕστερον, admittedly a promise that in the first place only tells him to wait."[88]

---

[88] Bultmann, *Gospel of John*, 596.

CHAPTER 4

SWORDPLAY AND DENIALS

INTRODUCTION: PETER IN JOHN 18

Not long after Jesus prays to the Father to bring the disciples "to complete unity to let the world know that you sent me and have loved them even as you have loved me" (John 17:23), Peter breaks ranks with the other disciples and strikes out at the opposition, cutting off the ear of the servant of the high priest. As in chapter thirteen, the only unity Peter seeks is unity with Jesus, and this is a special brand of unity that requires that Jesus be kept safe and available for earthly fellowship. Of the four evangelists, only John names Peter as the disciple who attacks the servant of the high priest, a fact that is often adduced by scholars as evidence of the Evangelist's low regard for him. Although I will endeavor to prove that this is a mistaken reading of the text, there is no disputing the fact that Peter's hostile action in the garden is poorly conceived and antithetical to Jesus' mission, which is drinking the cup (ποτήριον) the Father has given him (John 18:11b; cf. Matt 26:39; Mark 14:36; Luke 22:42).

Things do not improve for Peter in John 18 once he sheathes his sword. As in the Synoptic Gospels, he denies Jesus three times in the courtyard of the high priest (18:17–27; cf. Matt 26:69–75; Mark 14:67–72; Luke 22:54–62). John, like the Synoptists, builds tension in the scene by interspersing images of Jesus speaking openly about himself and receiving punishment for his confession with images of Peter denying Jesus and keeping warm by a fire.[1] It is beside this fire that Peter's swordplay comes back to haunt him, for a relative (συγγενής) of the servant maimed in the garden steps out of the shadows and identifies him as the attacker and thus an associate of Jesus (18:26), prompting the final denial. Unlike in the Synoptic Gospels (Matt 26:75; Mark 14:72; Luke 22:62), the Fourth Evangelist does not include a scene of Peter weeping in response to his shameful act, which is for some further evidence of the Evangelist's low opinion of him.

For a study that seeks to portray Peter as a heroic character in the Gospel whose faith matches up well against BD's and who teaches positively about *Johannine* discipleship (as opposed to being a representative of the less-

---

[1] Matthew (26:69–75) has Peter huddled with the servants of the high priest in the courtyard but says nothing about him warming himself.

Christologically-attuned Apostolic Christians), John 18 presents some obvious exegetical challenges! It is not my intention to throw a coat of whitewash over the chapter and explain away Peter's blunders as random blemishes on an otherwise spotless career, however. The Fourth Evangelist allows for us to see Peter at his most fragile here.

As was discussed in the introduction, all the mistakes Peter makes in the Gospel take place in the span of a few hours on the night of Jesus' arrest, and most of these are recounted in chapter eighteen. However, he is not portrayed as timid, hapless or buffoonish, as some believe; there are positive intentions behind his actions. Throughout the chapter the Fourth Evangelist contrasts Peter's strengths (zeal, curiosity, fidelity, and courage) with his weaknesses (overzealousness, misunderstanding, and cowardice), underscoring his humanity and showing him to be in a state of confusion about his own discipleship. Peter is as willing to defend Jesus as he is to deny him. He lashes out at enemies with a sword and then huddles with them around a warming fire. Through Peter's example and through the example of BD—who pursues Jesus and assists Peter as long as it is convenient—the reader learns that discipleship is easier in theory than practice.[2]

Jesus and the Disciples in the Garden: 18:1–9

Of the four evangelists, John is the only one who describes a "garden" (κῆπος) as the place of Jesus' arrest. The garden lies to the East of Jerusalem, "beyond the winter-flowing Kidron Valley." Although John does not name the place of arrest as Gethsemane, as Mark (14:32) and Matthew (26:36) do, commentators are probably correct to combine the geographical marker in John 18:1 with the remark in 18:2 ("Jesus often met there with his disciples" [cf. 8:1; cf. also Luke 22:39]) to locate the garden on the Mount of Olives.[3] Among NT authors, κῆπος is only used by John (18:1, 26; 19:41; cf. κηπουρός in 20:15) and Luke (13:19), and describes a private garden as opposed to a farm or field used for commercial growing (cf. ἀγρόν in Mark 13:16; Matt 6:28–30; 22:5; Luke 15:25; 17:7). Such private gardens were typically enclosed, which may explain why Jesus is described as *entering into* (εἰσέρχομαι) it. The Evangelist skips over scenes in the Synoptics in which Jesus is troubled and prays in the moments before the arrest (Mark 14:33–36; Matt 26:37–39; Luke 22:41–42) and

---

[2] Wiarda, *Peter in the Gospels*, 174–75, summarizes Peter's situation in John 18 this way: "Peter's misunderstanding of Jesus' mission and his readiness to defend Jesus through violence are both essential to preparing the way for Jesus' affirmation that his suffering is a matter of obedience. Quick initiative and courage befit the scene."

[3] The NIV and NLV are perhaps too free in their translations of κῆπος as "olive grove" or "grove of olives," respectively.

catches his disciples sleeping (Mark 14:37–40; Matt 26:40–43; Luke 22:45),[4] focusing instead on the fact that Jesus and his loyal disciples enter the garden immediately ahead of Judas and the opposition (18:2–3).

After the slow pace of action in chapters 14–17, in which Jesus speaks in long and often repetitive speeches about himself and the future of the disciples,[5] the action comes swiftly in John 18. Familiar with the location of the garden from previous visits (18:2), Judas brings a "cohort" (σπεῖρα) of soldiers—or about one-tenth of a Roman legion (approximately 600 men)[6]—and some officials of the chief priests and the Pharisees to arrest Jesus. Only John places both Pharisees and Romans at the arrest, which may convey his belief that collaboration between Jewish and Gentile authorities began well before the transfer of Jesus from Caiaphas to Pilate (cf. 18:28).[7] The arresting party carries lanterns and torches, another detail peculiar to the Fourth Gospel. W. Howard-Brook believes the "open flames suggest a more wild anger at Jesus, while the lanterns a more 'sophisticated' approach."[8] Another possibility is that artificial light is needed to penetrate the "Johannine darkness" that routinely engulfs the ignorant and the opponents of Jesus (3:2; 6:17; 13:30; 21:3). The simplest explanation, of course, is that lights are necessary to negotiate the darkness of night!

One major consequence of Judas' betrayal is that Jesus is "confronted in the garden by representatives of the entire non-believing world, Gentile and Jew (1:10–11; cf. Acts 4:25–28)."[9] Unlike in Mark and Matthew, in which Judas

---

[4] See § 5 of the introduction to this study for a discussion of the relationship of John to the Synoptics. As far as the events of chapter 18 are concerned, many scholars note that John follows Mark's sequence of events fairly closely but employs very different vocabulary. The images he provides of Peter toiling in the garden and courtyard also differ from those in Mark's Gospel. For the idea that the overlap between John and canonical Mark owes to John's dependence on fixed oral tradition or a pre-Markan written source, see C. E. Evans, "'Peter Warming Himself': The Problem of an Editorial 'Seam,'" *JBL* 101 (1982): 245–49, and R. T. Fortna, "Jesus and Peter at the High Priest's House: A Test Case for the Question of the Relation between Mark's and John's Gospels," *NTS* 24 (1978): 371–83.

[5] 16:4–33 duplicates nearly all of 14:1–31.

[6] See U. Busse, *Das Johannesevangelium: Bildlichkeit, Diskurs und Ritual* (BETL 162; Leuven: Leuven University Press, 2002), 236.

[7] A. Grün, *Jesus: Tür zum Leben* (Stuttgart: Kreuz Verlag, 2002), 129, thinks it highly unlikely that Jews and Romans would cooperate in carrying out an arrest order. He imagines them assembled together for another reason: "Johannes denkt hier weiter: Der Tod Jesus geschieht für die ganze Welt, für Juden und Römer." M. Goguel, "Juifs et Romains dans l'histoire de la Passion," *RHR* 62 (1910): 181, is of a similar opinion, believing that the Evangelist added Jews to the arresting party to implicate Jewish religious leaders as well as Romans.

[8] Howard-Brook, *Becoming Children of God*, 374.

[9] Talbert, *Reading John*, 232–33.

identifies Jesus with a kiss (Mark 14:45; Matt 26:49),[10] in John he stands idly by while the officials question Jesus. As in other scenes in John's Gospel in which Jesus' prescience is highlighted (7:8; 12:27; 13:1, 11, 21, 38; 16:1–4), the arrest in 18:4 does not take Jesus by surprise. The Evangelist tells us that "Jesus, knowing all that was to happen to him, came forward and asked them, 'Who are you looking for?'" The message is plain enough: Judas is the leader of the arresting party but Jesus is in control. When the opposition answers that they seek "Jesus of Nazareth," Jesus responds with the divine self-designation formula ἐγώ εἰμι (cf. John 4:26; 6:20; cf. Mark 14:62; Matt 14:27; cf. also Ex 3:14), knocking the enemy to the ground with the force of the words.[11] The question and answer process is repeated in 18:7–8, at which time Jesus also commands the enemy to let the disciples go (cf. 11:44). This marks a significant turn of events from 6:67, in which the disciples' "going away" (ὑπάγειν) was a cause of concern for Jesus. Now, with his hour close at hand, he acts to safeguard the charges given him by the Father (18:9).

Swordplay: 18:10–11

[10]Then Simon Peter, who had a sword, drew it, struck the high priest's slave, and cut off his right ear. The slave's name was Malchus. [11]Jesus said to Peter, "Put your sword back into its sheath. Am I not to drink the cup that the Father has given me?" (Σίμων οὖν Πέτρος ἔχων μάχαιραν εἵλκυσεν αὐτὴν καὶ ἔπαισεν τὸν τοῦ ἀρχιερέως δοῦλον καὶ ἀπέκοψεν αὐτοῦ τὸ ὠτάριον τὸ δεξιόν· ἦν δὲ ὄνομα τῷ δούλῳ Μάλχος. εἶπεν οὖν ὁ Ἰησοῦς τῷ Πέτρῳ· βάλε τὴν μάχαιραν εἰς τὴν θήκην· τὸ ποτήριον ὃ δέδωκέν μοι ὁ πατὴρ οὐ μὴ πίω αὐτό;).

The coordinating conjunction οὖν is all that links Peter's aggressive action in 18:10 with the arrival and activity of the arresting party. If οὖν were to be understood inferentially (i.e., *therefore, so*), then Peter's action could be interpreted primarily as a response to the mob's specific treatment of Jesus. Because the inferential οὖν is rare in John, however (see 6:13, 30), a better translation is "then" or "at that time," with οὖν serving as a temporal connective (cf. 1:22; 2:18; 5:10; 6:60, 67; 8:13, 21).[12] Is this a matter of splitting exegetical

---

[10] In Luke 22:47–48, Judas' attempt to kiss Jesus is rebuffed.

[11] Dan 2:46; 8:18; Luke 5:8 and Rev 1:17 all describe individuals falling to the ground in response to divine revelation. In LXX Exod 3:14; Isa 45:5–7 and 48:12, ἐγώ εἰμι is the phrase that triggers the response. For a brief but lively discussion of theophany and its effects, see S. K. Ray, *St. John's Gospel*, 316. Bauckham, "Monotheism," 161, notes that "[t]he formula of divine identity reminds us that this was Jesus' own sovereign accomplishment of what he had purposed—that is, that his disciples, seeing what he had predicted had occurred, should now believe that he is 'I am he' (13:19)."

[12] BDAG, s.v., 736-37. D substitutes τότε for οὖν, supporting this reading.

hairs? Perhaps. All that the reader really needs to know is that Peter has time to think about how to respond. It is *after* Jesus' discussion with the enemy and *after* Jesus shows he can paralyze them with a few spoken words that Peter lashes out.

The attack on the high priest's servant is one of the few events in the NT attested by all four evangelists, and yet each describes it very differently. We have already seen that John is the only NT writer to put the sword in Peter's hand. He is also the only one to provide the name of the wounded servant: Malchus.[13] Mark's account is the simplest of the four, saying that "one of those who stood by drew his sword, and struck the slave of the high priest, cutting off his ear" (14:47).[14] The Markan Jesus has no words for his defender, which is not the case in the other Gospels. Matthew (26:52–53) contains the famous response of Jesus to his would-be defender, "Put your sword back into its place; for all who take the sword will perish (ἀπόλλυμι) by the sword," as well as the solemn declaration from Jesus that the Father could send "more than twelve legions of angels" should Jesus request heavenly assistance. In Luke 22:50–51, Jesus speaks *and* acts in response to the attack on the servant: he calls out to the attacker "no more of this!" before healing the slave's wounded ear.

One way of interpreting the language of John 18:10 is to imagine that Peter draws a sword because he happens to be carrying one (ἔχων μάχαιραν εἵλκυσεν αὐτήν), which is to say his attack is a knee-jerk response to the appearance of the armed and hostile mob. But the situation is not so simple. As mentioned, there is no indication that Peter is rushed for time in trying to decide how to respond to the arrival of the mob. Despite the presence of six hundred-plus men in a small and enclosed garden, the action unfolds slowly. Before Peter lashes out, Jesus and the authorities twice go over the question of his identity. Jesus then knocks the enemy to the ground with his words. After that he demands the release of the disciples. Next the Evangelist interjects himself into the story—or at least calls attention to himself as narrator—when he explains Jesus' plea for the release of the disciples to be an act that fulfils prophecy. Only after all this do we get the description of Peter drawing his sword.

It is quite common for scholars to describe Peter's attack on Malchus in extremely negative language, saying that it is emblematic of his naiveté or oafish disposition. T. L. Brodie, for example, notes that "[w]ithin the context of the arrest scene as a whole, his 'sword' stands in literary continuity not with

---

[13] Attempts are occasionally made to see John 18:10 as a fulfillment of the prophecy in Zech 11:6, "I will cause them, every one, to fall each into the hand of a neighbor, and each into the hand of the king (מַלְכּוֹ)." However, Brown, *John*, 2.812, points out that Malchus was a common name in the first century, appearing several times in the writings of Josephus and in the Palmyrene and Nabatean inscriptions.

[14] Like Mark 14:47, the best Johannine manuscripts (B ℵ C* L W) use the diminutive ὠτάριον.

Jesus but with the final focal detail in the description of the assembled forces of darkness—their weapons (v. 3)."[15] R. G. Maccini attributes Peter's swordplay to a "lack of understanding of Jesus' words and deeds."[16] A similar analysis is offered by U. Busse: "Zudem gibt Jesus Petrus erneut (12,27) zu verstehen, dass er sein gewaltsames Geschick freiwillig (10,17) und ohne Zögern (diff. Mark 14,36 parr.) auf sich nimmt und dessen kontraproductive Befreiungsbemühungen mißbilligt."[17] Peter's swordplay is seen by A. J. Droge to be a by-product of his "obtuseness and inability to comprehend" Jesus.[18] A. H. Maynard observes boldly that Peter's militant gesture is a sign of the Evangelist's low opinion of him: "[t]he total impact of the incident is again to cast Peter in a bad light."[19]

While I disagree that the Evangelist has portrayed Peter as an impetuous bumbler, I agree that his response seems ill-conceived. It also appears to be premeditated. To suggest as J. H. Bernard does that "there was something of a scuffle, and then Peter hit out," is to characterize the encounter between Jesus and the opposition as a pitched battle, which it is not.[20] Peter's action is wholly unnecessary; Jesus has demonstrated that he has the situation well in hand and can paralyze the enemy at will. As I read the text, Peter lashes out to demonstrate his own willingness to die for Jesus (cf. 13:36–37) as much as he does to defend him. The fact that he cuts off the *right* ear of Malchus (cf. Luke 22:50) is probably not a random detail but serves to underscore the deliberate, aggressive nature of the action, for John's readers would have known that indemnity laws of the period compensated the loss of a right limb / organ more handsomely than a left one.[21]

---

[15] Brodie, *Gospel According to John*, 527. Brodie also says that Peter's "darkness of mind" in chapter 13 is "cast in the context of the Satanic darkness of Judas," but this is a very difficult proposition to accept in light of the fact that Peter is the one who spearheads the movement to identify the traitor (13:23–25).

[16] Maccini, *Her Testimony is True*, 156.

[17] Busse, *Johannesevangelium*, 236–37. Van Tilborg, *Johannes-Evangelium*, 264, says something similar of Peter's action, calling it "eine große Demonstration des Missverständnisses zwischen Jesus und Petrus."

[18] Droge, "Status of Peter in the Fourth Gospel," 310.

[19] Maynard, "Role of Peter," 538. As R. F. Collins, "Beloved Disciple," 208, monitors Peter's activities in John 18, beginning with the attack on Malchus and ending with the denials, he makes the following observation: "Throughout these events, the bumbling and impetuous Peter shows himself to be a disciple who really does not comprehend what Jesus is about." He goes on to say that BD "is a figure intended to contrast with Peter. In his anonymity and stylization, the Beloved is the epitome of discipleship; he is the disciple par excellence."

[20] Bernard, *St. John*, 2.588–89.

[21] See Brown, *John*, 2.812. D. E. Garland, "John 18–19: Life through Jesus' Death," *RevExp* 85 (1988): 487, suggests that Peter's choice to attack the right ear of Malchus was less an act of defense than of defiance: "Malchus may have been singled out by Peter

According to P. Perkins, "the damning evidence of Peter's failure" does not materialize until 18:36, when Jesus tells Pilate, "My kingdom is not from this world. If my kingdom were from this world, my followers would be fighting to keep me from being handed over to the Jews. But as it is, my kingdom is not from here."[22] Although it is not self-evident that Jesus' words in 18:36 are a subtle castigation of Peter, it is certainly the case that 18:11 and 18:36, when viewed together, reveal the extent of Peter misunderstanding of Jesus' selfless nature (cf. 5:30; 10:11) and sacrificial mission (cf. 8:28–29; 13:6–7, 36). At this point in the story, the kingdom of Jesus is, in Peter's mind, an earthly kingdom, capable of being defended by conventional weapons.[23] His delusion that conventional weapons can protect Jesus mirrors the delusion of the arresting party that conventional weapons (ὅπλα, 18:3) can subdue Jesus. His attack on the servant of the high priest reinforces the "portrait of Peter as one who, while acting out of loyalty and devotion, fails to see his own dependence and the necessity of Jesus' sacrifice."[24]

But while Peter's action is wrongheaded in many respects, it does not completely take the reader by surprise. I agree with J. H. Bernard that John expects the reader to believe that Peter carries the sword into the garden as a prophylactic measure, having listened to the Last Discourse and heard Jesus enumerate the myriad threats facing himself and the disciples.[25] Among Jesus'

---

for a particularly suggestive form of violence directed at the high priest through his servant. Jewish history records incidents when the high priest was deliberately disqualified from office by having his ear mutilated. In this case, the high priest would not have been deliberately disqualified, but Daube (see reference below) pointed out that in a shame/honor society, 'he would be seriously and suggestively disgraced by having his servant mutilated in this particular manner.'" See D. Daube, "Three Notes Having to Do with Johanan ben Zaccai," *JTS* 11 (1960): 61. Haenchen, *John 2*, 166, says that this "is cutting things a bit too fine, especially since Peter could not have known during the tumult in the dark with whom he was struggling."

[22] Perkins, *Peter*, 99.

[23] Droge, "Status of Peter," 311, suggests that in light of 18:36, "Peter's action reveals that he is not a 'subject' of Jesus' heavenly kingdom, and thereby confirms the truth of his 'denial' of being Jesus' disciple." One cannot assume the converse of Jesus' statement about subject and kingdom is true, however. Jesus does not imply that "because Peter fights, he is not my follower." The negative final clause with ἵνα μή and the aor. pass. subj. of παραδίδωμι combine to reveal the hypothetical nature of the entire statement. Jesus concocts a scenario in which armed resistance would be appropriate. Peter is not absolved of blame but neither is he denied status as Jesus' ὑπηρέτης.

[24] Wiarda, *Peter in the Gospels*, 139. De Boor, *Evangelium des Johannes*, 181, notes that Peter, as in Matt 16:23, "denkt 'menschlich' und nich 'göttlich' und achtet nicht auf das Tun seines Herrn...."

[25] Bernard, *St. John*, 2.588. In Luke the disciples bring *two* swords with them (22:38a). The Lukan Jesus is aware of the weapons and, although he does not endorse armed resistance, he does not order their removal (22:38b). Considering that it was illegal for

predictions during the Last Discourse were that many disciples would be expelled from the synagogue (16:2), scattered (16:32), and killed (16:2). Concerns about Jesus' future and the direction of the ministry were expressed by a number of disciples during the Last Discourse, including Philip (14:8–9), Thomas (14:5), and Judas (not Isacariot; 14:22). It is not unreasonable to imagine that Peter, alternately depicted as the spokesman (6:68-69; 13:23–25) and leader (20:2; 21:2–4, 11) of the disciples, shared some of those concerns and armed himself as a consequence.[26]

Let us assume for just a moment that the Fourth Evangelist *does* expect us to believe that Peter was paying attention during the Last Discourse, that some of the prophecies *did* alarm him, and that he *did* arm himself before entering the garden, eager to place himself between Jesus and danger (and disregarding the legal stipulation against carrying a weapon at Passover).[27] Which of the prophecies made during the Last Discourse might the Evangelist expect us to believe Peter finds most troubling?

One of the first things that stands out about the "sword episode" is that Peter does not attack the enemy until immediately *after* he hears Jesus issue a command (ἄφετε) to the opposition to let the disciples go (18:8). The command is said by the Evangelist in 18:9 to fulfill an earlier prophecy of Jesus: "I did not lose a single one of those whom you gave me." While it is possible that this prophecy is contained in 6:39, 10:11 or 10:28, most scholars believe it comes from 17:12, a verse of the Last Discourse in which Jesus declares that he has protected all those given to him by the Father, except "the one doomed for destruction."[28] If this is the case, Peter is hearing for the second time in one

---

Jews to carry weapons on feast days in biblical times, it is difficult to believe the Johannine Jesus is not, like the Lukan Jesus, aware of the fact that one of the disciples carries a weapon. Some Johannine scholars will be quick to point out that in John the Last Supper is not a Passover meal, which would mean that Peter is not in violation of any law. Does the presence of an armed disciple in the garden support the theory that John's chronology of the Last Supper and crucifixion is more accurate than the Synoptic chronology? Bernard, *St. John*, 2.588–89, thinks so. It is also possible that John borrows the sword from his Passion "source" but moves up the Last Supper by a day, allowing Jesus' death to coincide with the slaughter of the paschal lambs.

[26] Simon, *Petrus und Lieblingsjünger*, 262, wonders if Peter strikes out on behalf of all the disciples in 13:10 and again acts for them in following Jesus into the high priest's courtyard: "Aus dem Schwertstreich des P ergibt sich der Verteidigungswille des Sprechers der Jünger. Auch nach seiner Verhaftung ist Jesus ist nicht etwa von seinem Jüngern verlassen, sondern P folgt dem Verhaftungstrupp in den Hof des Hohenpriesters."

[27] See *m. Šabb.* 6.4. If the Last Supper in John takes place a day before Passover, it is not clear whether carrying a weapon on this day would have been allowed. Brown, *John*, 2.812, suggests Peter's sword was really a concealable dagger, allowing for his attack on Malchus to be "unforeseen."

[28] See the discussion in Barrett, *St. John*, 521.

evening about Jesus' plans to safeguard the disciples, and he may be trying—however misguidedly—to assist him by removing the proximate threat. After all, we have seen him step forward before to shore up Jesus' ministry during times of crisis (6:68–69; 13:23–25), and John may expect us to infer that the combination of the arrival of the Roman cohort, Peter's memories of the Last Discourse, and his penchant for safeguarding Jesus are what trigger the attack on Malchus.[29]

Another verse in the Last Discourse that John *might* expect the reader to imagine is reverberating in Peter's mind as the cohort confronts Jesus is 15:13, in which Jesus says that "no one has greater love than this, to lay down one's life for one's friend" (cf. 10:11, 15, 17; 1 John 3:16). One can imagine that an overeager disciple such as Peter (see, for example, 13:9; 21:7; cf. also Mark 14:29–30; Matt 14:28–30) would take a proleptic statement about Jesus' own sacrificial death and misconstrue it as an invitation to lay down his own life in defense of him. For example, we saw in 13:1–11 the manner in which he takes a lesson about humility and self-sacrifice and mistakes it for an opportunity to safeguard Jesus from debasement. An attack by one man against six hundred soldiers is surely a recipe for suicide, and yet a suicidal plunge into enemy lines satisfies (albeit in an odd way!) the description of brotherly love set forth by Jesus in 15:13. A suicidal act of resistance would also allow Peter to make good on his pledge of 13:37: "I will lay down my life for you." The fact that Jesus has demonstrated an ability to vanquish enemies with a few spoken words (18:6) does not deter Peter from lashing out. He seems to subscribe to the belief that selfless service to Jesus is the *sine qua non* of discipleship, and that self-sacrifice qualifies as the *sine qua non* of selfless service (cf. 21:18–19).[30]

Admittedly, the Evangelist does not afford us a look inside Peter's mind, so the above analysis is speculative. But I submit that he subtly encourages us to make inferences about Peter's motives such as those suggested here. He arranges his material so that Peter's pledge to give his life for Jesus immediately precedes the Last Discourse (with its link between brotherly love and martyrdom) and so that the Last Discourse immediately precedes Peter's decision to arm himself and attack the opposition. The result is that the words and actions of Peter bracket the Last Discourse. When we consider that, during the discourse, disciples other than Peter (Philip, Thomas and Judas [not Iscariot]) voiced concerns about certain of Jesus' prophecies, and that Peter's

---

[29] With many others, Brown, *John*, 2.812, notes that Peter's action "fits his impetuous character."

[30] Keener, *Gospel of John*, 2.1083, questions Peter's courage when he says that "[l]oyalty with a weapon in one's hand and hope of messianic help is not the same as loyalty when self-defense is impossible." Yet nothing in the text suggests that Peter expects to be saved before the opposition retaliates. The inference of 13:36–38 is just the opposite: he envisions that self-sacrifice in the act of defending Jesus will be a foolproof way of "following" him.

habit is to put himself between Jesus and danger and degradation (6:68–69; 13:4–10), it is not difficult to foresee a scenario in which Peter will be upset about "an arrangement in which he is dismissed to safety while Jesus suffers arrest."[31] I am not suggesting that we are being prompted to absolve Peter of all responsibility for the violent action, but the Evangelist does imply that Peter was put on edge by the warnings of the Last Discourse and that he is, at least in one sense, an early casualty of the plot against Jesus.[32]

Jesus is not at all impressed by Peter's action and speaks to him solemnly: "Put your sword back into its sheath. Am I not to drink the cup that the Father has given me?" The rebuke of Peter is plain enough, although it is not as intense as the one delivered by the Matthean Jesus in Matt 26:52, in which the anonymous swordsman is told that those who pick up the sword will perish by the sword. In fact, in combining the aorist subjunctive of $\pi\acute{\iota}\nu\omega$ with the double negative οὐ μή, Jesus seems to expect that Peter's response will be affirmative, although it is also the case that "Jesus ist der einzige, der weiß, daß er den Kelch seines Vaters bis zum Boden leertrinken muss."[33] In vowing to drink the cup given him by the Father, Jesus not only corrects Peter's mistaken ideas about his sacrificial mission but returns to the "motif of self-giving."[34] Peter does not attempt again in the Gospel to come between Jesus and his salvific work, but in the very next episode denies Jesus and momentarily tarnishes his image as Jesus' staunchest ally.

THE THREE DENIALS: 18:15–27

Much of the power of the denial pericope in John's Gospel comes from the interspersing of scenes of Jesus' interrogation before Annas and Caiaphas with scenes of Peter's denials before the servants in the Courtyard (cf. Mark 14:53–65; Matt 26:57–68; Luke 22:54–71).[35] John interrupts the denials to report on Jesus' situation at one point (18:18–24), something that does not happen in the Synoptic Gospels. Much has been written about the "cutaway" narrative technique in which the tension in both scenes is heightened by affording Jesus and Peter equal time on the proscenium. The contrasts between Jesus and Peter are plentiful and stark. At the moment when Jesus is being taken into the high priest's house (18:13), Peter is kept waiting outside by the gate (v.15). When Jesus is being beaten (v. 22), Peter is keeping warm by the fire (v. 25). When

---

[31] Wiarda, *Peter*, 110.
[32] Wiarda, *Peter*, 175, finds one positive function Peter plays as swordsman: He "provides the occasion for Jesus' rejection of armed resistance and his affirmation that the cross is the way of obedience."
[33] Van Tilborg, *Johannes-Evangelium*, 264.
[34] Brodie, *Gospel According to John*, 527.
[35] See Moloney, *Gospel of John*, 486–87; and Brown, *John*, 2.842.

Jesus is emphasizing to the authorities that he has not taught in secret and that "those who heard what I said to them" are able to testify to this (v. 21), Peter is refusing to answer questions about Jesus, keeping their relationship secret (vv. 17, 25-27).

A fourth contrast takes shape when Jesus' three ἐγώ εἰμι confessional statements (vv. 5, 6, and 8) are contrasted with Peter's two οὐκ εἰμί denials (vv. 17 and 25). Although a third οὐκ εἰμί denial from Peter would make the contrast perfectly symmetrical, John's point is not lost on the reader: Jesus is the only proper refuge of the believer (cf. 10:1-14). Peter understood this in 6:68-69 and will again in 20:2-20 and 21:15ff, but for the moment he wilts before the opposition, putting distance between himself and Jesus. BD stays at Peter's side long enough to see him safely into the courtyard, but then disappears when interrogators begin to query Peter about his relationship with Jesus.

ARRIVAL AT THE COURTYARD AND THE FIRST DENIAL: 18:15-17

> [15]Simon Peter and another disciple followed Jesus. Since that disciple was known to the high priest, he went with Jesus into the courtyard of the high priest, [16]but Peter was standing outside at the gate. So the other disciple, who was known to the high priest, went out, spoke to the woman who guarded the gate, and brought Peter in. [17]The woman said to Peter, "You are not also one of this man's disciples, are you?" He said, "I am not." [18]Now the slaves and the police had made a charcoal fire because it was cold, and they were standing around it and warming themselves. Peter also was standing with them and warming himself.
> ([15]Ἠκολούθει δὲ τῷ Ἰησοῦ Σίμων Πέτρος καὶ ἄλλος μαθητής. ὁ δὲ μαθητὴς ἐκεῖνος ἦν γνωστὸς τῷ ἀρχιερεῖ καὶ συνεισῆλθεν τῷ Ἰησοῦ εἰς τὴν αὐλὴν τοῦ ἀρχιερέως, [16]ὁ δὲ Πέτρος εἱστήκει πρὸς τῇ θύρᾳ ἔξω. ἐξῆλθεν οὖν ὁ μαθητὴς ὁ ἄλλος ὁ γνωστὸς τοῦ ἀρχιερέως καὶ εἶπεν τῇ θυρωρῷ καὶ εἰσήγαγεν τὸν Πέτρον. [17]λέγει οὖν τῷ Πέτρῳ ἡ παιδίσκη ἡ θυρωρός· μὴ καὶ σὺ ἐκ τῶν μαθητῶν εἶ τοῦ ἀνθρώπου τούτου; λέγει ἐκεῖνος· οὐκ εἰμί. [18]εἱστήκεισαν δὲ οἱ δοῦλοι καὶ οἱ ὑπηρέται ἀνθρακιὰν πεποιηκότες, ὅτι ψῦχος ἦν, καὶ ἐθερμαίνοντο· ἦν δὲ καὶ ὁ Πέτρος μετ' αὐτῶν ἑστὼς καὶ θερμαινόμενος.)

As in 13:24-25, 20:2-9, and 21:7-8, Peter and BD engage in activities that are, for the most part, complementary.[36] As they will do during the race to the

---

[36] This is assuming that by "another disciple" John means BD. The best manuscripts (B ℵ* A W Ψ P66*) say only that ἄλλος μαθητής accompanies Peter to the courtyard. Later important manuscripts (C* θ ℵc K L M U) add a definite article (ὁ ἄλλος μαθητής) to make it clear that the "other disciple" is BD (so John Chrysostom, Cyril, and the Textus Receptus). The identity of this other disciple remains a topic of debate, however.

empty tomb (20:2–10), they break off from the larger contingent of disciples to follow Jesus. Only in John's Gospel is Peter accompanied into the courtyard of the high priest by another disciple. In the Synoptic Gospels (Mark 14:54; Matt 26:58; Luke 22:54), Peter follows Jesus "from afar" (μακρόθεν).[37] In contrast to John, who devotes a fair amount of time to narrating Peter's detention at the gate, Mark says that Peter "went right into the courtyard of the high priest" (ἠκολούθησεν αὐτῷ ἕως ἔσω εἰς τὴν αὐλὴν τοῦ ἀρχιερέως). Matthew edits the Markan text to read ἕως τῆς αὐλῆς τοῦ ἀρχιερέως καὶ εἰσελθὼν ἔσω, creating an image of Peter pausing briefly at the gate before going in. John is thus closer to Matthew in this detail, for both describe Peter's entry as a non-fluid process. For John, as we will see, the fact that Peter pauses several times on his journey into the courtyard is significant.

Before the Fourth Evangelist informs readers about the delay Peter encounters in entering the courtyard (18:16), he explains that BD enters without incident. Because BD is "known to the high priest" (γνωστὸς τῷ ἀρχιερεῖ, 18:15; cf. 18:16), he gains currency with the gatekeeper and is ushered in. Γνωστός is rarely used in the NT to describe friendship. Luke uses the term to describe *known things* or *known circumstances* (Acts 1:19; 2:14; 4:10, 16; 9:42; 13:38; 19:17; 28:22, 28:28), and Paul uses it to describe *known truths* about God (Rom 1:19). The fact that the high priest's knowledge of BD serves as a practical visa for Peter (see below) suggests that BD and the high priest are more than mere acquaintances.[38] The double compound verb συνεισέρχομαι draws our

---

Howard-Brook, *Becoming Children of God*, 384, contends that it is Nicodemus, the only person in the Gospel who clearly bridges the "worlds of discipleship and priesthood." Bernard, *St. John*, 2.594, argues for Nicodemus or Joseph of Arimathea. Brodie, *Gospel According to John*, 529, and Charlesworth, *Beloved Disciple*, 341-47, maintain that the other disciple is Judas, who is frequently grouped with Peter (6:68–71; 13:1–11, 21–30) and whose relationship with the high priest has been established (18:3). However, most Johannine commentators do not see the "other disciple" as a perfidious character or shadow disciple but as BD. In my opinion, the Evangelist confirms the fact that the "other disciple" in 18:15–16 is in fact BD, but only after the fact, in 20:2, when he describes Peter's competitor in the race to the tomb as both "other" *and* "beloved" (τὸν ἄλλον μαθητὴν ὃν ἐφίλει ὁ Ἰησοῦς). F. Neirynck, "The 'Other' Disciple in John 18,15–16," *ETL* 51 (1975): 113–41, builds a compelling case for BD being the "other disciple" by showing that the excursions of Peter and BD to the courtyard of the high priest and to the empty tomb are "consciously put in parallel by the evangelist." So Schnackenburg, *St. John*, 1.186.

[37] GNV, KJV, NLV are right to translate μακρόθεν as "afar off" or "from afar" (cf. μακρόθεν in Mark 15:40; Luke 23:49; Rev 18:10, 15, 17). "At a distance," one of the more popular NT translations (NRSV, NIV), obscures the degree to which Peter's fear or resistance to the idea of denying Jesus impedes his movements.

[38] Cf. Luke 2:44, in which Joseph and Mary search for Jesus among their γνωστοῖς (close friends) in the caravan. When one considers both that BD does not appear in John's Gospel until Jesus arrives in Jerusalem for the final time (13:23) and that he is

attention not because it describes BD entering into the courtyard with Peter, who remains mired at the gate, but because it describes BD entering *with Jesus*.[39] Jesus' prediction in 16:32 that all the disciples will scatter and abandon him is (briefly) defied by BD.

As Jesus predicted in 13:36, Peter's short-term plan to follow him without regard to his own personal safety proves overly optimistic.[40] We do not know when it is that BD first notices that Peter is not beside him. Due to the fact that he must go back outside (ἐξέρχομαι) the gate to retrieve Peter, we can infer that he travels some distance into the courtyard before discovering he is alone. The coordinating conjunction οὖν is used inferentially here (rare in John; see § 3 above), indicating that Peter's tardiness is what forces BD to retrace his steps, but it does not tell us whether BD is unwilling or afraid to enter by himself, or if he returns to assist Peter out of charity.[41] R. T. Fortna is convinced that a considerable amount of time elapses before BD (called by Fortna "the unnamed disciple") returns to chaperone Peter, and that he only goes back to get him because the interrogation of Jesus has turned into "mistreatment at the hands of the high priest's officer."[42] Although the idea that Peter is summoned to come to Jesus' aid is exciting, evoking images of a daring rescue attempt in which BD knows Peter must prominently figure, it is not supported by the text. The only thing we know is that BD refuses to proceed without Peter.

Εἰσάγω in v. 15 should be translated as "lead" or "bring" (cf. Luke 22:54; cf. also Acts 7:45 and 9:8). BD does not merely speak a word of introduction to the gatekeeper to earn Peter passage inside, he *collects* him and *leads* him into the courtyard. (We remember how Andrew collected and brought Peter to Jesus

---

friends with the high priest, one is led to the conclusion that he is a Jerusalemite. See Cullmann, *Johannine Circle*, 62–85; Brown, *Community of the Beloved Disciple*, 31–34; and Smith, *John*, 334–35. Scholars who hold that BD is John the son of Zebedee typically find it a challenge to explain the circumstances by which a Galilean fisherman would come to be friends with Annas or Caiaphas. Although Smith supports the idea that BD is a Jerusalemite, he offers a practical scenario by which the high priest *might* cultivate a relationship with a fishmonger: he has a taste for fish! (*John*, 335.)

[39] In John's Gospel, συνεισέρχομαι denotes not only simultaneous movement but intimate association. In 6:22 the crowd is surprised that Jesus does not enter into the boat with (συνεισέρχομαι) his disciples, probably because they had earlier assisted him in the feeding of the 5,000 (6:12–13).

[40] *Contra* Brodie, *Gospel According to John*, 529, Peter's decision to follow Jesus in the wake of the prophecy of 13:37–38 does not constitute "impetuosity" or "sinfulness." His penchant for following Jesus is an established positive characteristic, first demonstrated in the earliest phase of the ministry (6:68-69; cf. 1:42).

[41] In John 20 he is first to arrive at the empty tomb but waits to explore its confines until Peter goes inside and surveys the scene. In 21:7 he sights Jesus on the shore and proclaims his presence but does not join Peter in swimming across the lake to reach him.

[42] Fortna, "Jesus and Peter," 380.

in 1:40–41.) An interesting piece of information we are given is that the doorkeeper (θυρωρός) to whom BD appeals on Peter's behalf is female. Although it is difficult to find in the biblical corpus another clear example of a woman serving in a similar position of authority (see perhaps 2 Sam 4:6 [LXX]; Acts 12:13; cf. also *TestJob* 6:4–5; Jos., *Ant* 7:48), it is the case in all the Gospels that the first person to interrogate Peter is a woman (e.g., Mark 14:66 [μία τῶν παιδισκῶν τοῦ ἀρχιερέως]; Matt 26:69 [μία παιδίσκη]; Luke 22:56 [παιδίσκη]). It may be that John is simply economizing by having the female accuser double as the gatekeeper.

Were it not for the fact that Peter and BD function in the Gospel as allies, BD's act of whispering to the gatekeeper immediately before she decides to confront Peter would have to be viewed with suspicion. What does he say to her that convinces her to allow Peter access to the courtyard but also prompts her to investigate his ties to Jesus? Does he precipitate her accusation? Does he vouch for Peter, as is routinely assumed, or does he incriminate him? T. L. Brodie argues for the latter idea, finding in the first denial scene "overtones of the original fall," with BD playing the role of serpent, the female gatekeeper playing Eve, and Peter playing Adam.[43] But that scenario is, I fear, unduly imaginative. If BD were interested in betraying Peter, one suspects he would have tipped off the gatekeeper about Peter's relationship to Jesus on his first pass through the gate, but he does not. Another improbable theory is that the female porter allows BD inside—all the while knowing him to be a disciple of Jesus—but then stops Peter because she is "surprised that another disciple would want to be admitted to the hearing before Annas."[44] Nothing in the text suggests that BD is recognized as a follower of Jesus or that he *wants* to be recognized as such. For that matter, nothing suggests that the gatekeeper has the authority to allow one of Jesus' supporters inside but not multiple supporters. What is most likely is that BD returns to the gate to vouch for Peter because he is eager to regain his fellowship before pursuing Jesus (cf. 20:6–10; see discussion below).

After BD assists Peter in entering the courtyard, however, he vanishes. Most scholars insist that he escapes with his probity intact, and that the first denial scene manages to showcase him as a disciple with connections to the priestly caste and an ability to negotiate important doors.[45] Peter, on the other hand, is routinely seen to be an impotent figure blocked by important doors.[46] K.

---

[43] Brodie, *Gospel According to John*, 529.

[44] Waetjen, *Beloved Disciple*, 21.

[45] See, for example, Haenchen, *John 2*, 167.

[46] See, for example, Droge, "Status of Peter," 307–10; Culpepper, *Anatomy*, 120; and Maynard, "Role of Peter," 538. Howard-Brook, *Becoming Children of God*, 384, offers a very bleak assessment of Peter in this pericope: "People from the social peak (the high priest) and the pit (a woman servant) must conspire through the mediation of this mysterious other disciple for Peter's discipleship journey to continue. How far this 'head' apostle has fallen in the course of the fourth gospel!"

Wengst maintains that BD's sole purpose in the pericope is to gain Peter admission to the courtyard, and that after that he is free from responsibilities: "Das gab ihm die Funktion, Petrus im den Hof zu bringen. Diese Funktion hat er erfüllt. Nun wird er nicht mehr gebraucht und tritt also auch nicht mehr auf."[47] G. Stanton breaks the scene down into two very simple components: "Peter enters the courtyard only to deny Jesus, the 'beloved disciple' enters with Jesus and does not deny him."[48] An even more benevolent interpretation finds BD vanishing from the courtyard in order to make his way to Golgotha, readying himself to take up a position beneath the cross and receive custody of Jesus' mother (19:26–27).[49] E. Haenchen believes that the Evangelist underscores BD's "superiority" to Peter throughout the pericope: "Since the 'other disciple' goes into the courtyard with Jesus unhindered, while Peter has to remain outside, he evidences a superiority already with respect to Peter. This superiority is sustained when the 'other disciple' returns, speaks with the gatekeeper, and then conducts Peter into the courtyard."[50]

But surely it is a mistake to regard BD's exit strategy without at least a modicum of suspicion! Although he is perfectly willing to intercede with the gatekeeper to help gain Peter entry—even going so far as to retrace his steps through the courtyard and collect him—he does not speak a word in Peter's defense when this same gatekeeper accosts Peter and accuses him of complicity

---

[47] K. Wengst, *Das Johannesevanglium* (2 vols; Stuttgart: Kohlhammer, 2001), 208. But this describes BD not primarily as one wishing to follow Jesus but as one wishing to assist Peter, which surely misrepresents the truth of the situation. Because 18:15 describes BD entering the courtyard *with* Jesus (συνεισέρχομαι)—and therefore ahead of Peter—assisting Peter cannot be BD's primary goal.

[48] G. Stanton, *The Gospels and Jesus* (2nd ed.; Oxford: OUP, 2002), 114. Stanton speaks for many scholars when he says that this narrative together with the empty tomb narrative shows BD "being given precedence over Peter." According to M. Stibbe, *John*, 184, "[t]hrough the subtle use of settings, the narrator equates the roles of Jesus, Judas, Peter and the beloved disciple with certain roles in the shepherd discourse of John 10. Obviously, Jesus plays the part of the good shepherd, and Judas of the thief in 18.1–11. In 18.15–27, however, the beloved disciple plays the part of the shepherd who walks in and out of the fold, and the girl at the gate plays the gatekeeper. This leaves Peter, who runs away in the hour of danger in 18.15–27. Here the flight is not a literal desertion but a metaphorical flight from confession. This means that Peter can only be equated with one role in the shepherd discourse: the role of the hired hand, who runs away in the hours of danger (10.12–13)." But it is the case that in John's Gospel, unlike in the Synoptics, Peter is not described as leaving the courtyard.

[49] See particularly Minear, "Beloved Disciple," 199–200. Minear is among a handful of scholars who find more similarities between Peter and Judas than between Peter and BD: "His (BD's) courage and openness stand in sharpest contrast to the double-dealing of Judas and the double-take of Peter" (199).

[50] Haenchen, *John 2*, 173. Haenchen presents his rationale for equating this 'other disciple' with BD on pp. 167–68.

with Jesus. Is there not the faintest implication that he assists Peter when it is convenient?[51] Is "assistance" even the right word to describe his activity as facilitator? As Haenchen points out, "His recommendation did not help Peter."[52] As in the Synoptic Gospels, Peter is the only disciple who lingers long enough in the courtyard to attract the sustained interest of the high priest's staff and police. Not only is he the only disciple who denies Jesus on the night of the arrest, he is the only disciple *in a position* to deny him. The others, including BD, vanish.[53]

This is not to suggest that John portrays BD as a coward, of course, for a coward would not be entrusted with the care of Jesus' mother following the crucifixion. In one respect, BD's overall status is slightly improved in the pericope, for as in 13:23–25, 19:26–27; 20:2–10 and 21:7, he shows himself to be one whose first instinct is to maintain a close proximity to Jesus and whose faith can quite literally open doors.[54] But he is wholly lacking in dimension, appearing and disappearing like a vapor—albeit a saintly vapor. He is no better at "following" Jesus in the Johannine sense of the word than Peter is, for, although he does not deny Jesus in the courtyard, neither does he confess him, and confession is the essence of Johannine discipleship.

I must therefore disagree with Wengst that BD is free from responsibility once he helps Peter into the courtyard.[55] Frankly, BD's treatment of Peter is bizarre. He plucks him from the proverbial frying pan only to set him down in the fire. The reader may well come to the conclusion that Peter would have been better off if he had been left cooling his heels on the doorstep than being "assisted" by BD! We cannot fault BD for escorting Peter inside, for, as we have begun to learn, he is predisposed to pursue Jesus in the company of Peter, but neither should we disregard the fact that he abandons Peter just as the enemy closes in, which is what Peter does to Jesus. Both disciples are shown to have a fierce desire to follow Jesus, but both fail to confess him in the presence of the enemy.

---

[51] According to Wilckens, *Evangelium des Johannes*, 275: "Er handelt nicht mit Petrus zusammen, sondern vermittelt lediglich den Enlaß des Petrus in den Innenhof, danach verschwindet er....[d]er Lichtkegel der Erzählung fällt allein auf Petrus, der die Frage der Magd, ob er nich einer der 'Jünger dieses Menschen' sei...."

[52] Haenchen, *John 2*, 167.

[53] Inexplicably, Waetjen, *Beloved Disciple*, 383, has Peter in this scene disowning "any connection with Jesus or the disciple who interceded for his admission..." It is a remarkable reading of the text to conclude that Peter abandons or disowns BD here! All signs point to the opposite being the case.

[54] On the Johannine understanding of faith and BD's role, see F. Hahn, "Das Glaubenverständnis im Johannesevangelium," in *Glaube und Eschatologie* (ed. E. Grässer and O. Merk; Tübingen: Mohr [Siebeck], 1985), 51–69.

[55] See note 47.

The idea is occasionally proposed that BD and the gatekeeper are introduced into the pericope as auxiliary characters to explain the process by which a Galilean fisherman[56] might enter the guarded Jerusalem compound of a high-ranking religious official.[57] The Synoptists do not describe the method by which Peter negotiates the gate. Might it be that John is attending to a detail overlooked by Matthew, Mark, and Luke? It is doubtful. Θυρωρός is a loaded term in John's Gospel, not at all suited to resolving logistical matters. Jesus is the true θυρωρός (John 10:3), the gatekeeper who seeks to control the movements of his sheep in an effort to protect them (10:3, 7, 9). It is hard to believe that John would use a significant Christological term to remind his readers of the historical fact that the courtyard of the high priest in first-century Jerusalem maintained a guard. More plausible is the idea that the gatekeeper is essential to the story, a flesh-and-blood obstacle that stands in Peter's way when persecution is no longer just theoretical, once again reminding the reader that following Jesus is simpler in theory than in practice.[58]

John suggests that Peter tarries on the doorstep because he has been denied access by the gatekeeper, but he does not make this explicit. If we imagine that this *is* the reason for his delay, are we to conclude that Peter is being portrayed as a hapless figure or a stalwart one? Does John emphasize that Peter has no friends among the hostile religious hierarchy or that he is no friend *of* the hostile religious hierarchy? If it is fear and not the gatekeeper that blocks Peter's path, is it fear of being interrogated and punished, which would signal cowardice, *or* is it fear of denying Jesus and thus fulfilling the prophecy of 13:38, which might signal a residual desire on Peter's part to remain faithful to Jesus? The implications for our overall opinion of Peter are very different. What cannot be inferred from the scene, I feel, is that Peter is the representative of cowardice or impotence or some other "non-Johannine" trait while BD is the representative of courage and devotion. John makes two things quite clear: Peter *cannot* enter the courtyard without assistance from BD, and BD *will not* venture deeply into the courtyard without Peter. As in 13:23–25, 20:2–10, and 21:7, they are most comfortable serving Jesus as a team.

Although John earlier told us that Peter would ultimately prove successful in following Jesus (13:36–38), he does not minimize the awful significance of his denials. As we have already discussed, the language Peter uses (οὐκ εἰμί) in attempting to remove suspicion from himself as an associate of Jesus during this first denial is the antithesis in both letter and spirit of the confessional formula used by Jesus in 18:5–8 (ἐγώ εἰμι). Circumstances have changed greatly since 6:68–69, when Peter pledged loyalty to Jesus and stanched the flow of

---

[56] That Peter's profession is a fisherman is implied in John 21:2ff.

[57] See the discussion in Neirynck, "Other Disciple," 126.

[58] On Johannine "following" in general see esp. 1:43; 6:2; 10:4–5, 27; 6:67–69; 12:26; 13:36; and 21:19–22.

disaffected disciples from his ministry. Now he follows the lead of the other disciples in abandoning him.

THE SECOND AND THIRD DENIALS: 18:25–27

> [25]Now Simon Peter was standing and warming himself. They asked him, "You are not also one of his disciples, are you?" He denied it and said, "I am not." [26]One of the slaves of the high priest, a relative of the man whose ear Peter had cut off, asked, "Did I not see you in the garden with him?" [27]Again Peter denied it, and at that moment the cock crowed. ([25]Ἦν δὲ Σίμων Πέτρος ἑστὼς καὶ θερμαινόμενος. εἶπον οὖν αὐτῷ· μὴ καὶ σὺ ἐκ τῶν μαθητῶν αὐτοῦ εἶ; ἠρνήσατο ἐκεῖνος καὶ εἶπεν· οὐκ εἰμί. [26]λέγει εἷς ἐκ τῶν δούλων τοῦ ἀρχιερέως, συγγενὴς ὢν οὗ ἀπέκοψεν Πέτρος τὸ ὠτίον· οὐκ ἐγώ σε εἶδον ἐν τῷ κήπῳ μετ' αὐτοῦ; [27]πάλιν οὖν ἠρνήσατο Πέτρος, καὶ εὐθέως ἀλέκτωρ ἐφώνησεν.)

Despite the fact that 18:17 and 18:18 are consecutive verses, 18:18 should probably be seen as belonging to the second "half" of the denial scene, the fireside interrogation of Peter (vv. 25–27), for it describes him assembling with the assorted slaves and police of the high priest in order to keep warm. Unlike in Mark and Luke, in which all three denials are issued beside the fire, in John's Gospel Peter does not stop to warm himself until after issuing the first denial.[59] Although he has time to consider what he has done and realize that his allegiance to Jesus is now suspected, he moves deeper into the courtyard. John tells us that it is cold (ψῦχος). We know from vv. 2–4 that it is dark and from elsewhere in the Gospel that darkness is a Johannine symbol for ignorance and despair (cf. 3:1–9; 8:12; 9:4; 11:10; 21:4). After setting the stage for the second and third denials, John cuts away to Jesus' hearing before Annas (18:19–24).

When he returns to Peter's story, six verses later, he presents 18:25 as an abridged version of 18:18, even reduplicating the periphrastic imperfects ἑστὼς and θερμαινόμενος, as if concerned his "cutaway" technique has left the reader confused and Peter's situation needs updating. But Peter has not moved. He is still warming himself, even as Jesus suffers mistreatment before Annas.[60] By

---

[59] Bernard, *St. John*, 2.598, attributes the detail of it being "cold" to the memory of an eye-witness, but then weakens his argument by observing casually that "it is chilly at midnight in springtime" in Jerusalem.

[60] Viewed together, 18:18 and 18:25 evoke the scene in Mark 14:53 in which Peter mixes with servants of the high priest while warming himself (ἦν συγκαθήμενος μετὰ τῶν ὑπηρετῶν καὶ θερμαινόμενος πρὸς τὸ φῶς). As we have seen, the parallel scene in Luke (22:55) has a fire but says nothing about Peter warming himself. The Matthean scene (26:57–58) makes no mention of a fire. The repetition of the detail that "Peter was warming himself" (John 18:18, 25) is thought by some scholars to expose a "seam" that binds together two separate stories: Jesus' trial and Peter's denials. Particularly for

cutting away to Jesus' hearing before Annas and then returning to Peter's story, John neatly contrasts Jesus' honesty and physical discomfort with Peter's dishonesty and physical comfort. The contrast becomes starker when Peter is approached by a group of servants and officers and again distances himself from Jesus with the phrase οὐκ εἰμί.⁶¹

The fact that Peter stands (ἑστώς) with the servants of the high priest in the courtyard as opposed to sitting (συγκαθήμενος) with them—as happens in Matt 26:69 and Luke 22:56—may be significant. Regardless of how closely John knows the tradition behind Matthew and Luke, he conveys the idea that Peter never settles in with the opposition and waits passively for the drama to unfold. John's use of ἵστημι emphasizes Peter's transient status.⁶² Peter pauses / stands (ἑστώς) with the guards beside the fire in the same way he paused / stood (εἰστήκει) outside the gate before entering. Whether we are to infer that his restlessness is due to nervous energy or to a disinclination to abandon Jesus is not clear, but what can safely be said is that he is not paralyzed by the spectacle. I must therefore disagree with M. Stibbe that everywhere in John 18 one finds "indications of Peter being controlled by his circumstances."⁶³ What is tragic

---

scholars who believe John borrows directly from Mark, questions relating to the origin of the seam are intriguing. See Evans, "'Peter Warming Himself,'" 245–49; and J. Donahue, "Are You Christ?" *The Trial Narrative in the Gospel of Mark* (SBLDS 10; Missoula, Mont: Scholar's Press, 1973), 9. N. J. McEleney, "Peter's Denials—How Many? To Whom?" *CBQ* 52 (1990): 472, maintains that the "Markan scene" is the basis for much of John 18:15-27, but he acknowledges that an "unexplained discrepancy of detail" exists between the two accounts. Despite the fact that Mark's story (Mark 14:53 and 14:67) has at its center the same θερμαινόμενος doublet that appears in John, orality may account for the overlap, for there is more that is *different* about John's and Mark's narration of Peter's travails than is similar. Consider the following: Mark's συγκαθήμενος (cf. Luke 22:55) is absent from John; John opts for ἀνθρακία in place of Mark's φῶς; Peter's Galilean "accent" is not mentioned in John; Mark does not put a relative of the wounded servant in the role of accuser and says nothing about a gatekeeper; the denials in John do not come as responses to accusations (as in Mark) but as answers to questions; and the cock crows twice in Mark (14:72) but once in John (18:27). The fact that Peter sits with (συγκαθήμενος) the servants of the high priest in the courtyard scene in Mark (cf. Luke 22:55; Matt 26:58) but stands (ἑστώς) with them in John is at once a subtle and significant discrepancy. One does not get the sense in John's Gospel that Peter ever settles in with the opposition.

⁶¹ In Mark 14:70 and Matt 26:73, multiple "bystanders" (παρεστῶτες) also elicit the second denial.

⁶² Matthew and Luke use κάθημαι.

⁶³ M. W. G. Stibbe, *John's Gospel* (London: Routledge, 1994), 181. It is in the Synoptic denial scenes that Peter actively lets Jesus' trail run cold. We have already seen that Mark and Luke allow him to settle in around the campfire with the high priest's guards. There are other signs of capitulation. In Mark, for example, he flees *backward* to the gate (καὶ ἐξῆλθεν ἔξω εἰς τὸ προαύλιον) when the interrogations begin to pile up

about Peter's situation in John 18 is that he controls many of his own circumstances, wearing and then using a sword, moving about between the denials, warming himself when it becomes cold, and of course making a series of poor decisions about how—or whether—to display allegiance to Jesus.

Unlike in Mark (14:70) and Matthew (26:73), it is not Peter's Galilean accent that gives him away but another individual's memories of his aggressive behavior in the garden. A relative of Malchus appears out of the shadows to accuse Peter of being Malchus' attacker and therefore of being an associate of Jesus (18:26). The result of the appearance is that Peter stands accused of attempted murder as well as sedition. He responds by denying his association with Jesus a third time, at which time the cock crows, fulfilling the prophecy of 13:38. Although Peter does not deny that Jesus is *Lord*—which, at least according to 1 John 2:22, is the most egregious form of denial possible for a disciple—he denies *knowing* him, which is every bit as shocking because his confession in 6:68–69 was based on having come to "know" (γινώσκω) Jesus as God's Holy One. Now, we are led to believe, it occurs to him that the dangers of associating with God's consecrated agent outweigh the benefits. P. Dschulnigg neatly summarizes Peter's plight in the aftermath of the third denial: "Er hat zwar sein Leben gerettet, dabei aber auch tragisch versagt und sein Gesicht verloren."[64]

Unlike in the Synoptic Gospels, Peter does not shed any tears in the wake of this final denial (cf. Mark 14:72; Matt 26:75; Luke 22:62). For scholars who believe John portrays Peter unfavorably, this is grist for the mill, for the lack of tears is interpreted as a lack of remorse.[65] Assuming that John does know the tradition in which Peter weeps after the denials, it is still not clear that by omitting the scene he means to put Peter in a bad light. It is possible, for example, that John denies Peter a (cathartic?) weeping scene because such a scene would send a mixed message to the reader, who has thus far been instructed that there is no substitute for confession (cf. 4:42; 6:68–69; 9:38; 11:27).[66] It is also possible that the Evangelist leaves the tearful episode out

---

(14:68). In Luke 22:59, an interval of one hour passes between the second and third denials, with Peter not taking advantage of the time to close the gap between himself and Jesus. In Matt 26:58 Peter is the epitome of the bystander: he sits with the guards "to see the end."

[64] Dschulnigg, *Petrus*, 130.

[65] The apotheosis of Petrine vilification appears in Maynard, "The Role of Peter," 531–48, in which the disciple is portrayed as coward and fool. A similar portrait appears in Snyder, "Anti-Petrinism," 5–15.

[66] Both Brown, *Community of the Beloved Disciple, passim,* and Martyn, *History and Theology in the Fourth Gospel, passim,* describe the historical situation of the Johannine community as one in which self-preservation depended upon an internal component of confession and an external component of steadfast resistance to persecution by Jewish religious leaders. Without examining the Johannine epistles or the Book of Revelation,

because—unlike in the Synoptic Gospels—Peter's ultimate faithfulness has already been predicted, and there is therefore no urgent need to build sympathy for him. What seems fair to say is that "John neither emphasizes the vehemence of the third denial (Mark 14:71) nor the agony of repentance that followed; for him it is enough that Jesus' prediction has been fulfilled."[67]

Interestingly, scholars who believe John is familiar with Synoptic tradition and omits the weeping scene in order to demonize or denigrate Peter consistently fail to report that John also omits the subsequent Synoptic scene in which Peter invokes a curse against Jesus[68] after the third denial (cf. Mark 14:71; Matt 26:74).[69] Is this not employing a double standard? If one is willing to adduce the omission of a scene sympathetic to Peter as proof of the Fourth Evangelist's low regard for him, one should, it seems to me, be willing to explain why he omits a follow-up scene that emphasizes his cowardice.

Conclusion

Not long after Peter's near-term apostasy is predicted by Jesus in John 13:38, Peter begins to encounter obstacles. Most of these are described in chapter 18. As he attempts to follow Jesus, he is confronted by an armed mob (vv.1–11), a gatekeeper (vv. 15–17), a group of the high priest's servants (v. 25), and a hostile relative of the man he injured in the garden (v. 27). He is assisted but then abandoned by BD. As in all the Synoptic Gospels, he denies Jesus three times, the last time immediately before cockcrow, fulfilling Jesus' prediction.

His decision to bring a sword into the garden may be construed as brave and premeditated, but it is also foolish and impractical, and begins the process of his unraveling. From a tactical standpoint, Peter's assault on Malchus makes no

---

works consulted heavily by Brown and Martyn, one can find in the Gospel of John alone examples of confession serving as a cohesive force (4:42; 6:68–69; 9:38; 11:27) and of persecution as a divisive force (11:48; 12:42; 16:2, 32–33). Keener, *Gospel of John*, 2.1092, notes that "[t]he text strikes a note of severe warning to John's audience: regardless of the opposition, they must maintain their faith...."

[67] MacGregor, *Gospel of John*, 332–33.

[68] Despite the fact that most NT translations report Peter cursing *himself* in the aftermath of the denials, the implicit object of καταθεματίζειν in the Gospels of Mark and Matthew is *Jesus*. Peter's cursing of himself would not serve to reinforce the denial, which is the point of the scene. According to Pliny the Younger (*Ep.* 10.96) and Justin Martyr (*1 Apol.* 31:6), people suspected by the Romans of being Christians were asked to deny their affiliation to Jesus two or three times and then reinforce those denials by invoking a curse against Jesus.

[69] See for example R. Kysar, *John's Story of Jesus* (Philadelphia: Fortress, 1984), 80; and Maynard, "Peter in the Fourth Gospel," 543. Maynard includes Peter's failure to weep as one of fifteen "incidents which depreciate Peter or reduce his Synoptic Role," yet he fails to explain the omission of the cursing scene.

sense because Jesus has demonstrated an ability to defend himself, even to the point of being able to paralyze the opposition with a single utterance. From a theological standpoint, Peter's action fails because it shows that he does not fully comprehend Jesus' selfless nature (5:30; 10:11) and sacrificial work (8:28–29; 13:6–7, 36). Peter's belief that Jesus can be defended with conventional weapons mirrors in a perverse way the belief of Judas and the arresting party that he can be subdued with conventional weapons. As in 13:4–9, Peter ignores recently-revealed Christological truths about Jesus' destiny to focus on the business of protecting him.[70]

The foolishness of the attack on Malchus does not compare with the sin of the threefold denial, however.[71] Peter's desire to protect Jesus melts away as the members of the household of the high priest close in on him and as the previously-obliging BD vanishes into the night. Three times Peter is asked if he knows Jesus or has associated with him; three times he answers "no." The drama plays out as Jesus provides truthful answers about himself to the Jewish religious leadership. The final denial is elicited by a question from a relative of Malchus, the man Peter injured in the garden, re-establishing the swordplay as a foolish endeavor.

But, as bad as things get for Peter in John 18, the Evangelist does not encourage us to write him off as a faithless or weak disciple. I have suggested that the Evangelist expects readers to believe that Peter acts in the garden with memories of the Last Discourse fresh in his mind, particularly the verse in which Jesus says that "no one has greater love than this, to lay down one's life for one's friends" (15:13). His attack on Malchus—carried out in the presence of six hundred armed Roman soldiers—seems to be an attempt to lay down his life for Jesus. Ironically, he ends up momentarily placing himself between Jesus and the cross, as in Mark 8:32 and Matt 16:22.

John credits him with zeal even as he reveals the inadequacies of his faith, and so the reader learns the challenges of discipleship by making careful note of Peter's accomplishments and mistakes. Peter is presented as an authentic disciple, which is to say one who is called to follow Jesus but must make up his gameplan as he goes, and who is genuine and three-dimensional in the extreme, defined as much by his rough edges as by his faith. As T. Wiarda notes, Peter's "emphatically expressed positive intentions engender a degree of reader identification and make him an example of certain attitudes which even sincere

---

[70] In 13:4–9 he protects Jesus from what he believes to be debasement.

[71] Going well beyond the text, J. Vanier, *Drawn into the Mystery of Jesus through the Gospel of John* (London: Darton, Longman and Todd, 2004), 309, interprets Peter's two οὐκ εἰμί statements as meaning much more than "I am not." Vanier says they mean "I have no existence." He explains: "As a disciple Peter was filled with Jesus. Now he is empty and lost...he is not just denying Jesus but denying also all that he had seen, heard and lived during those years with him. He is denying his own self and his own experience! That is why he has lost his identity" (310–11).

followers of Jesus might fall into....all these traits contribute further by adding colour to the portrayal of Peter; this encourages reader identification and increases the impact made by his example of mistaken thinking."[72]

Although John is clear about the fact that Peter fails Jesus in denying him, in several respects he paints a more sympathetic picture of Peter in the denial scene than do the Synoptists.[73] First, Peter's inability to successfully follow Jesus in the near-term is predicted ahead of the denial scene (13:38), which means that his failure to penetrate the depth of the courtyard and stand in solidarity with Jesus does not come as a surprise to the reader. (The reader already knows that Peter will ultimately prove faithful [13:37].) Second, Peter pauses at the gate and again at the bonfire as he makes his way into the center of the courtyard, conveying a reluctance to deny Jesus. Third, the first two accusations made against him incorporate the negative particle μή, which portrays the enemy as trying to coax or "tempt" denials out of him.[74] Fourth, he needs help from another person (BD) just to get into position to deny Jesus. Peter does not rush headlong into the denial process, disavowing Jesus in a vigorous attempt to protect himself; the denials are extracted in a slow process.

As for BD, it is difficult to justify his behavior toward Peter. Nothing suggests he parts company with Jesus in between the Last Supper and Jesus' interrogation in the household of the high priest, yet he is not mentioned during the arrest pericope (18:1–11). He does not interact with Peter in the garden, either to assist him or prevent him from striking out with the sword. He appears again suddenly in 18:15–16, following Jesus and interceding with the gatekeeper to facilitate Peter's entry into the courtyard, but then disappears when the opposition confronts Peter. He is portrayed as one whose first instinct is to follow Jesus, but enough questions are raised by his behavior to prevent us from hailing him as the hero of the pericope to Peter's villain, as is done by Droge, Goulder, Maynard, Minear, and many others.[75]

A major message of the chapter is that Peter and BD are colleagues and not competitors (cf. 13:23-25, 20:2-9, and 21:7-8), and that, although both expose

---

[72] Wiarda, *Peter in the Gospels*, 173.

[73] So Schnackenburg, *St. John*, 3.236: "Peter comes off best in John; he does not speak a word directly against Jesus (synoptics: 'I do not know him')."

[74] See Haenchen, *John 2*, 167.

[75] Can one argue from silence in chastising BD for his timidity, noting that in danger-filled moments he conveniently manages to absent himself from the narrative? There is some high-calibre scholarly precedent for arguing from silence when analyzing the motives of characters in John's Gospel. For example, Raymond Brown, *Community of the Beloved Disciple*, 83, equates Peter's absence in 19:25 (the crucifixion scene in which BD alone of the male disciples stands with Jesus beneath the cross) with *cowardice*, noting that he scatters with all the other males disciples until the crucifixion can completely play out, and so is guilty of the twin crimes of "cowardice" and "abandoning Jesus" to the enemy.

themselves to danger in following Jesus—Peter more so than BD—they are of little service to Jesus or themselves when they are outside Jesus' company. Neither man confesses Jesus before the enemy. Peter *will not*. BD, having vanished, *cannot*. In the race to the tomb pericope, to which we next turn, both disciples bring a sense of urgency to the task of investigating Mary Magdalene's report that Jesus' body has been removed, as if they realize their performance on the night of the arrest does not meet the high standards of Johannine discipleship.

CHAPTER 5

THE RACE TO THE EMPTY TOMB

INTRODUCTION: PETER IN JOHN 20

As if suddenly concerned that his previous attempts to follow Jesus have failed and his standing as a loyal disciple is in jeopardy, Peter literally races off after Jesus—or Jesus' body—in John 20. Precipitating his action is a report from Mary Magdalene that "the Lord" has been removed from the tomb and moved to an undisclosed location (John 20:1).[1] As in John 18:15–16, BD accompanies

---

[1] Much of the information in John 20:2–10 also appears in Luke 24:12, including Peter's journey to the tomb, his observation of the discarded linen garments, and his decision to return home afterward. BD's presence in the Johannine pericope is the major item that distinguishes John's story from Luke's, but there are a few other differences, such as the fact that male rather than female disciples enter the tomb (John 20:6, 8; cf. Luke 24:3; Mark 16:5), belief in the resurrection occurs prior to an encounter with the risen Jesus (20:8), and the resurrection is said to fulfil scripture (20:9). Luke 24:12 is one of the nine "Western non-interpolations" designated by B. F. Westcott and J. F. A. Hort in their classic work *The New Testament in the Original Greek* (2nd ed.; London: MacMillan, 1896), 175–77. The inclusion of this verse in P^{75}, discovered after the publication of Westcott-Hort, has convinced many that Luke 24:12 is authentic, but the debate about the origin of the verse and its literary connection to John 20:2–10 is far from settled. In my opinion, John and Luke work off common "Petrine traditions" both in reporting this story and in reporting the "miraculous catch of fish" story (John 21:1–11 // Luke 5:1–11). Of the many scholars who have endeavored to explain the relationship between John 20:1–10 and Luke 24:12, the works of only a few can be cited here. Among the most colorful are: K. Aland, "Neuetestamentliche Papyri II," *NTS* 12 (1966): 206ff.; H. Thyen, "Johannes und die Synoptiker: Auf der Suche nach einem neuen Paradigma zur Beschreibung ihrer Beziehungen anhand von Beobachtungen an Passions- und Ostererzählungen," in *John and the Synoptics* (ed. A Denaux; BETL 101; Leuven: Leuven University Press, 1992), 81–107; J. A. Fitzmyer, *The Gospel According to Luke* (2 vols; AB; New York: Doubleday, 1981, 1985), 2.1542; B. D. Ehrman, *The Orthodox Corruption of Scripture: The Effect of Early Christological Controversies on the Text of the New Testament* (Oxford: Oxford University Press, 1993), 212–17; A. Dauer, "Zur Authentizität von Luke 24,12," *ETL* 70 (1994): 294–318; B. M. Metzger, *A Textual Commentary on the New Testament* (2nd ed.; Stuttgart: Deutsche Bibelgesellschaft, 1994), 157–58; F. Neirynck, "Once More Luke 24:12," in *Evangelica III* (ed. F. Neirynck; BETL 150; Leuven: Leuven University Press, 2001), 549–71; W. L. Craig, "The Inspection of the Empty Tomb: Luke 24:12–24," 614–19; J. D. Crossan, *The Cross that Spoke: The Origins of the Passion Narrative* (San Francisco: Harper and Row,

Peter in the search for Jesus and outdistances him for a while but, upon arriving at the tomb, waits for Peter to arrive before investigating the situation. As we will soon see, most scholars believe BD wins the race to the tomb because he is propelled by superior love for Jesus, greater zeal, or younger legs. And because only BD is said to "believe" when the two disciples see the discarded facecloth, the additional case is often made that only he represents Johannine Christians, whose faith is strong enough to discern the presence or power of Christ in the bleakest of situations. Peter, often thought to be the representative of Apostolic Christianity, is usually described as plodding along as best he can, eager to reconnect with Jesus but slow of foot and slower on the uptake. D. M. Smith speaks for many when he says of Peter during the tomb experience that he "fares none too well, coming in a clear second."[2]

But while the race to the tomb *is* a "race" in the sense that both disciples are running quickly, it is *not* a race in the sense that one disciple emerges as the winner and the other as the loser. I argue in this chapter that it is no more helpful to think of BD as the winner of the race *to* the tomb than it is to think of Peter as the winner of the race *into* the tomb. Both descriptions may be technically accurate, but both fail to describe the event as a joint endeavor. In running to the tomb to ascertain the veracity of Mary's report, both disciples reestablish themselves as loyal disciples who seem eager to make up for their less-than-stellar performance in the courtyard of the high priest on the night of Jesus' arrest.

Although it is true that BD is gripped by an incipient faith upon seeing the facecloth, it is also true that his faith is just that: incipient. Like Peter he does not yet understand the scripture that Jesus "must rise from the dead" (δεῖ αὐτὸν ἐκ νεκρῶν ἀναστῆναι; 20:9), and so does not spread word of his revelation. This means he does not share the good news with Peter or with the mother of Jesus, with whom he now lives.[3] The adventure ends with both disciples returning "to their own homes" (πρὸς αὐτούς). Mary Magdalene, after her Christophany (20:14–17), is the only one of the three tomb witnesses to spread the word that Jesus has risen. Not until the final chapter of the Gospel will BD proclaim Jesus as Lord (21:7) and Peter profess his love for Jesus (21:15–17).

1988), 289; Goulder, *Luke: A New Paradigm*, 776–79; and Quast, *Peter and the Beloved Disciple*, 105–06.

[2] Smith, *John*, 374. Gnilka, *Johannesevangelium*, 149, argues similarly, saying that while the pericope establishes Peter as a witness to the empty tomb, "[d]ie Priorität des Lieblingsjüngers gegenüber Petrus ist deutlich."

[3] Willingness to communicate one's faith is an important Johannine trait. See, for example, 4:29, in which the Samaritan woman tells the men of her city what she has seen in Jesus; 5:15, in which the paralytic tells the Jews that he has been made well by Jesus; and 1:41, in which Andrew tells Peter that he and his companion "have found the Messiah."

Mary Magdalene Reports to Peter and the Beloved Disciple: 20:1–2

¹Early on the first day of the week, while it was still dark, Mary Magdalene came to the tomb and saw that the stone had been removed from the tomb. ²So she ran and went to Simon Peter and the other disciple, the one whom Jesus loved, and said to them, "They have taken the Lord out of the tomb, and we do not know where they have laid him." (¹Τῇ δὲ μιᾷ τῶν σαββάτων Μαρία ἡ Μαγδαληνὴ ἔρχεται πρωῒ σκοτίας ἔτι οὔσης εἰς τὸ μνημεῖον καὶ βλέπει τὸν λίθον ἠρμένον ἐκ τοῦ μνημείου. ²τρέχει οὖν καὶ ἔρχεται πρὸς Σίμωνα Πέτρον καὶ πρὸς τὸν ἄλλον μαθητὴν ὃν ἐφίλει ὁ Ἰησοῦς καὶ λέγει αὐτοῖς· ἦραν τὸν κύριον ἐκ τοῦ μνημείου καὶ οὐκ οἴδαμεν ποῦ ἔθηκαν αὐτόν.)

A helpful way of beginning our study of the race to the tomb will be to construct a loose chronology of the morning's events, paying particular attention to Mary's movements. They can be broken down in the following manner: (1) On the first day of the Sabbath, while it is still dark (πρωῒ σκοτίας), Mary arrives at the tomb before anyone else and sees that the stone has been rolled away [v. 1]; (2) without the advent of an angelophany to enlighten her to the nature or significance of the morning's events, she rushes off to find Peter and BD and inform them of the body's theft / removal [v. 2];[4] (3) she returns to the tomb with them, maintaining a low enough profile that her presence must be read back into the story from details in v. 11; (4) Peter and BD investigate the tomb [vv. 3–10]; (5) Mary remains at the tomb after their departure, weeping [v. 11];[5] (6) Mary experiences an angelophany [vv. 12–14] and then a Christophany [vv. 14–17], taking news of the Lord back to the disciples.[6]

---

[4] Because Mary is able to discern that the body has been removed without looking inside in 20:1 but then *does* look inside in 20:11, one suspects the details of her story have been juggled to make room for the insertion of the Petrine account. Canonical criticism suggests that John has moved Mary's angelophany from its original position during her "first visit" to the tomb (John 20:1–2; cf. Mark 16:5–7; Matt 28:2–7; Luke 24:4–7) to her "second visit" (John 20:11ff.), inserting Peter's tomb visit into the resulting gap.

[5] Cf. *The Gospel of Peter* in which women also weep outside the tomb.

[6] According to W. L. Craig, "The Empty Tomb of Jesus," *NTS* 31 (1985): 53, the angelophany in this series of events is "oddly superfluous." It may be that John preserves it out of respect for his source or because it introduces the scene of Mary's conversation with the risen Jesus (20:15–18). Some scholars postulate a literary relationship between John 20:17, in which Jesus commands Mary to report the resurrection to his "brethren" in

In John's Gospel, then, pride of place for being the first disciple to see the risen Jesus goes to Mary Magdalene (20:14–18), which is at variance with Paul's report in 1 Cor 15:5 that Peter was the first to see the Lord (cf. also Mark 16:7; Luke 24:34).[7] The meeting between Mary and Jesus transpires only after earlier visits to the empty tomb by her (20:1; cf. Mark 16:1–2; Matt 28:1; Luke 24:1–3; 10) and by Peter and BD (20:3–10).[8] The fact that Mary reports the disappearance of Jesus' body in the first person plural (οὐκ οἴδαμεν ποῦ ἔθηκαν αὐτόν) in 20:2 and then her meeting with the risen Jesus in the first person singular (ἑώρακα τὸν κύριον) in 20:18 leads many scholars to conclude that two separate narratives have been combined, one involving a visit to the tomb by Mary and other women (cf. Mark 16:1; Matt 28:1; Luke 24:1, 10) and the other a post-Easter conversation between Jesus and Mary (John 20:15–18; cf. Matt 28:9).[9] While it is true that in first-century Palestine the "value of women as witnesses (*M. Shebu.* 4.1; *Sif. Deut.* 19.17; *b. Bab. Kam* 88a; *Ant.* 4.219) was negligible,"[10] we can still imagine that both traditions would have had important apologetic value for early Christians who were seeking to assemble witnesses to the events of Easter morning. A further visit to the tomb by Peter, culminating in the discovery of Jesus' neatly discarded clothing (cf. Luke 24:12), would have had great apologetic value as well, especially in anti-docetic polemic.[11]

Galilee, and Matt 28:9–10, in which he issues a similar command to Mary Magdalene and "the other Mary" (ἡ ἄλλη Μαρία [Matt 18:1]). A particularly insightful study of this subject is offered by F. Neirynck, "Note on Matt 28:9–10," *ETL* 71 (1995): 161–65.

[7] Barrett, *St. John*, 466, considers John 20:2–10 to be dependent on the tradition preserved in 1 Cor 15:5 *and* Mark 16:1–8. R. Bultmann, *Synoptic Tradition* (Oxford: Blackwell, 1972), 259, argues that "Peter's experience of Easter was the time when the early Church's messianic faith was born." This position is also maintained by E. Stauffer, *New Testament Theology* (trans. J. Marsh; New York: Macmillan, 1955), 31–34.

[8] See BDAG., s.v., 482–83. Would a woman venture outside the walls of first-century Jerusalem in darkness? Most scholars think not, and maintain that the darkness of John 20:1–2 is Johannine "spiritual darkness," which results from the deprivation of Jesus (cf. 21:2–4). See the remarks of Charlesworth, *Beloved Disciple*, 69 (esp. n. 145).

[9] No doubt in an effort to smooth over the discrepancy, manuscripts S and 579 replace οἴδαμεν with οἶδα.

[10] C. Rowland, *Christian Origins: An Account of the Setting and Character of the most Important Messianic Sect of Judaism* (London: SPCK, 1985), 191.

[11] According to B. Lindars, *Gospel of John* (NCB; London: Oliphants, 1972), 597, the "motive for the tradition of Peter's visit to the tomb is to establish the fact that, though it was empty, the body of Jesus could not have been stolen, because the grave clothes were still there." Simon, *Petrus und der Lieblingsjünger*, 272, speaks to the anti-docetic flavor of the scene: "Das Zeugnis des P (Petrus) und des LJ (Lieblingsjünger) ist vor allem aus antidoketistischen und apologetischen Gründen wichtige. Die Leinenbinden und das Schweißtuch weisen auf den Tod und damit auf die menschliche Natur Jesu hin."

What is not easy to discern about this pericope is whether the authority of one witness is being elevated above that of the others. W. Marxsen believes that John 20:2–10 "has been edited to stress the priority of Peter," and that the "Beloved Disciple's prestige in this matter is enhanced by noting his proximity to Peter."[12] D. A. Lee, on the other hand, argues that Mary's decision to remain at the tomb after the male disciples leave reveals her more powerful "determination to meet the Lord."[13] As will be discussed shortly, many scholars point to the speed and intuitive powers of BD as signifying his leadership role.

In my opinion, the Evangelist does not assign a priority to any one of the witnesses but celebrates the manner in which three of Jesus' closest disciples—male and female—go to and inspect the empty tomb. Insofar as all three are later blessed by encounters with the risen Christ, the Evangelist is, I think, conveying a belief that these three disciples comprised for a time the nucleus of the nascent post-Easter faith community.[14]

The fact that Mary takes the news about the empty tomb to Peter first indicates that he is, despite his denials, still considered by those closest to Jesus to be the leader of the disciples.[15] (This will become clearer in 21:2–11, when

---

[12] W. Marxsen, *The Resurrection of Jesus of Nazareth* (Philadelphia: Fortress, 1970), 59. Quotation taken from W. T. Kessler, *Peter as the First Witness of the Risen Lord: An Historical and Theological Investigation* (Rome: Gregorianum, 1998), 57.

[13] D. A. Lee, "Partnership in Easter Faith: The Role of Mary Magdalene and Thomas in John 20," *JSNT* 58 (1995): 40. Maccini, *Her Testimony is True*, 208, takes a more neutral position toward Mary, noting that her "inability to perceive the significance of the empty tomb leaves her metaphorically in the dark, but such a metaphor can make sense only against her accurate visual perception of the empty tomb." E. Schüssler Fiorenza, *In Memory of Her: A Feminist Theological Reconstruction of Christian Origins* (New York: Crossroad, 1983), 306, finds in the actions of Peter and Mary clues about the attitudes of the early church toward women: "Patristic Christianity downplayed the significance of women, especially Mary Magdalene, as the primary witness of the resurrection, and highlighted figures like Peter, Paul and the twelve, whereas the non-canonical gospels claimed women disciples as apostolic authorities for the reception of revelation and secret teaching. Apocryphal writings of the second and third centuries which speak of the competition between Peter and Mary Magdalene reflect the tension that existed on the question of primacy of apostolic authority." For a survey of the literature dealing with the relative importance of the visits to the tomb by Mary Magdalene and Peter, see G. O'Collins and D. Kendall, "Mary Magdalene as Major Witness to Jesus' Resurrection," *TS* 48 (1987): 631–46; and Brock, *Mary Magdalene*, 41–60.

[14] The number swells to seven in the Redactor's supplemental chapter.

[15] Van Tilborg, *Johannes-Evangelium*, 298, points out that the Greek of 20:2 (τὸν ἄλλον μαθητὴν ὃν ἐφίλει ὁ Ἰησοῦς) can be taken to mean "the other disciple whom Jesus loved," instead of the traditional reading "the other disciple, whom Jesus loved," which would mean that Peter is the first disciple whom Jesus loved (*erster Jünger ist, den Jesus*

Peter leads a post-Easter fishing expedition to which six other disciples sign on.) By tracking Mary's movements we discover that Peter has not disappeared or been driven into hiding by shame. As de Boor points out, "Maria weiß, wo Petrus in Jerusalem zu finden ist."[16]

After bringing the news to Peter, Mary next goes to BD, who—despite the fact that he was not present for the first two years of Jesus' ministry—has quickly emerged as a major character in the Gospel.[17] Unlike in 18:15–16, in which the Evangelist leaves a small degree of doubt about the identity of Peter's companion, here he tells us plainly that it is the "one whom Jesus loved" (ὃν ἐφίλει ὁ Ἰησοῦς). Brown speculates that the Fourth Evangelist makes BD's identity clear in this pericope to convey to readers the fact that profound love for Jesus is a sacred possession that "gives one the insight to detect his presence."[18] One wonders if the reverse is not also true: John does *not* name BD explicitly in 18:15–16 because in that scene his profound love does *not* generate insight. In fact, BD abandons Peter in that scene and fails to confess Christ!

THE FOOTRACE: 20:3–5

³Then Peter and the other disciple set out and went toward the tomb. ⁴The two were running together, but the other disciple outran Peter and reached the tomb first. ⁵He bent down to look in and saw the linen wrappings lying there, but he did not go in. (³Ἐξῆλθεν οὖν ὁ Πέτρος καὶ ὁ ἄλλος μαθητὴς καὶ ἤρχοντο εἰς τὸ μνημεῖον. ⁴ἔτρεχον δὲ οἱ δύο ὁμοῦ· καὶ ὁ ἄλλος μαθητὴς προέδραμεν τάχιον τοῦ Πέτρου καὶ ἦλθεν πρῶτος εἰς τὸ μνημεῖον, ⁵καὶ παρακύψας βλέπει κείμενα τὰ ὀθόνια, οὐ μέντοι εἰσῆλθεν.)

Although they set out for the tomb together (ὁμοῦ, 20:4a), BD outruns (προτρέχω) Peter and reaches the tomb first (hence the genitive Πέτρου in 20:4b).[19] Προτρέχω is used elsewhere in the NT only in Luke 19:4, where it

---

liebte) and BD is the second one (*zweiten*). But only BD is described by the Evangelist as being loved by Jesus. No statement is made in the Gospel about Jesus' love for Peter.

[16] De Boor, *Evangelium des Johannes*, 228.

[17] The probability that she makes separate trips to visit the disciples is indicated by the double use of πρός in 20:2.

[18] Brown, *John*, 1005.

[19] In 20:3, εἰς seems to describe them *entering* the tomb, although it is the case that they are only just setting out on the journey. Brown, *John*, 2.984–85, surmises that the confusion owes to hasty editing or the misuse of koine Greek (i.e., εἰς for πρός). While both suggestions are plausible, the latter may be more so, since John also misuses εἰς in 20:1 to describe Mary arriving *at* the tomb.

also means to "run on before" or "outrun."[20] When it is combined with the adverb ταχύς, a pleonastic expression results. In John's tautology there is purpose, however, for it allows him to emphasize the eagerness BD brings to this earliest phase of the endeavor.

Throughout the centuries all manner of theories have been introduced to explain how it is that BD finishes ahead of Peter even though the two set out for the tomb at the same time. The most popular theory has been and remains that he is propelled by superior love for Jesus, emblematic of the love that all Johannine Christians hold for their Lord.[21] This theory will be discussed (but not endorsed!) as the chapter proceeds. As for other theories, there is time enough here to summarize only the most influential.

Identifying Peter with the Gentiles and BD with the synagogue, it was the habit of Gregory the Great to equate Peter's slowness with the slowness of Gentiles to come to faith in Jesus.[22] Ishodad of Merv (bishop of Hedhatta, c. 850) credits BD's faster speed to the fact that he was unmarried![23] Writing in our own time period, J. H. Bernard argues that BD (a.k.a. John son of Zebedee) runs faster than Peter because he has younger legs, a view shared by A. J. Köstenberger and J. Redford.[24] Although T. L. Brodie does not believe BD is necessarily younger than Peter, he deduces from the text—with considerable sleight of hand, it seems to me—that he is in "better running condition."[25] U.

---

[20] Cf. also 1 Macc 16:21.

[21] See, for example, B. Byrne, "The Faith of the Beloved Disciple," 86; Beasley-Murray, *John*, 372; Perkins, "John," 983; Smith, *John*, 374; Underhill, *Saint Peter*, 120–21. Brown, *John*, 2.2007, says that the "two disciples' running to the tomb is expressive of their concern upon hearing Magdalene's report; such concern touches upon love. So naturally the Beloved Disciple outdistances Peter—he loves Jesus more." As has been pointed out several times in this study, however, the reader is never told that BD loves Jesus. It is not exactly an appalling exegetical misstep to assume that he does, since love is most valuable when reciprocated, but it bears emphasizing that his special identifying characteristic in the Gospel is that he is loved *by* Jesus. It is *Peter* who is said to love Jesus (21:15-17). These facts support a major tenet of this study: Peter and BD *together* represent the paradigmatic Johannine Christian, one who loves Jesus and is loved by him.

[22] *Homily on John xxii*, as quoted in Aquinas, *Catena Aurea: A Commentary on the Gospels, Vol. 4: John* (trans. J. H. Newman; Southampton: Saint Austin Press, 1997), 597. Gregory does not use "slowness" in a pejorative sense but to describe Gentiles coming to worship God through Christ *after* the earliest Jewish Christians did.

[23] See the discussion in Brown, *John*, 2.985.

[24] Bernard, *St. John*, 2.658. A. J. Köstenberger, *Encountering John: The Gospel in Historical, Literary, and Theological Perspective* (Grand Rapids: Baker Academic, 1999), 182. J. Redford, *Bad, Mad or God?: Proving the Divinity of Christ from St. John's Gospel* (London: St. Paul's, 2004), 311.

[25] Brodie, *Gospel According to John*, 561, says that "in a gospel where discipleship is connected with images of 'following,' (1:37–38), of physical movement, being in better

Busse offers a similarly eisegetical analysis when he says that the "physisch schwächere" Peter arrives at the tomb after BD.[26] In the opinion of J. F. O'Grady, "the Beloved Disciple is a representative figure embodying the best of what it means to be a follower of the Lord," and so it is no surprise that he is quickest in the pursuit of Jesus.[27] B. Lindars maintains that BD is a literary creation (so Loisy, Jülicher, and Goguel) and explains his first-place finish as a literary device designed to build dramatic tension.[28] That is, by having BD arrive first but enter second, the Evangelist is giving the reader time to speculate about what will be BD's response to the missing body. When BD sees and believes, this is, for Lindars, the climax of the story.

Many scholars find traces of early Christian polemic in the competitive dynamic. Typically, Peter and BD are said to represent competing strains of Christianity, whether these are described as Jewish and Gentile,[29] Petrine and Johannine,[30] official and spiritual,[31] fleshly and spiritual,[32] and so on. In all the scenarios, BD is seen to win the race because he has the more refined faith.[33] A related idea is that the race symbolizes competition for *internal* control of the

---

running condition is of considerable significance; it indicates that what is ultimately in better condition is the essence of his discipleship."

[26] Busse, *Johannesevangelium*, 251.

[27] J. F. O'Grady, "The Role of the Beloved Disciple," *BTB* 9 (1979): 61.

[28] Lindars, *John*, 22–24. Lindars also argues this in his commentary, *Gospel of John*, 600-01.

[29] Bultmann, *Gospel of John*, 685.

[30] Perkins, "John," 945; Charlesworth, *Beloved Disciple*, 388; Quast, *Peter and the Beloved Disciple*, 24. In his 1970 commentary, *John*, 2.1007, R. E. Brown argues against a polemical interpretation of the passage. However, in a later work, *The Community of the Beloved Disciple* (1979), he changes tack, locating a mild polemic underlying the passage: "In counterposing their hero over against the most famous member of the Twelve, the Johannine community is symbolically counterposing itself over against the kinds of churches that venerate Peter and the Twelve...." (p. 83).

[31] Kragerud, *Lieblingsjünger*, 82.

[32] Summarized but not endorsed by Brown, *John*, 2.1007.

[33] W. Trilling, "Zum Petrusamt im Neuen Testament: Traditionsgeschichtliche Überlegungen anhand von Mätthaus, 1 Petrus und Johannes," in *Studien zur Jesusüberlieferung* (Stuttgart: Katholisches Bibelwerk, 1988), 131. According to Maynard, "Role of Peter," 540, "Peter is said to have arrived after—literally 'following'—the Beloved Disciple. Since the term 'to follow' is a technical term for becoming a disciple in the Fourth Gospel, it is probably that it is here used to subordinate Peter to the Beloved Disciple...Peter does not fare well in this story!" Brock, *Mary Magdalene*, 48, argues similarly. Porsch, *Johannes-Evangelium*, 210–11, notes that the rivalry between Peter and BD is unmistakeable (*unverkennbar*). As he sees it, the respective heads of the Petrine and Johannine churches have different speeds, which match their "verschiedenes 'theologisches Tempo.'"

THE RACE TO THE EMPTY TOMB 113

community. In *Befriending the Beloved Disciple*, for example, A. Reinhartz argues that BD wins the race and thus demonstrates his "superiority in the hierarchy of community leadership."[34]

By putting Peter and BD into a situation that appears to so many scholars to be competitive, the Evangelist must take responsibility for inviting polemical interpretations. Yet I do not believe he actively encourages us to see the race as a win / lose event, or that he depicts Peter and BD as rivals. I agree with C. K. Barrett that it is unwise to read too much into the pericope and equate "fleetness of foot with apostolic pre-eminence."[35] Peter and BD, as we will see, move past each other at various stages in the race; Peter is first to get the news about Jesus, he begins running, he is passed by BD, but he manages to enter the tomb first. The enthusiasm of both disciples is thus accentuated. Indeed, they replicate this sort of two-pronged pursuit of Jesus throughout the Gospel, with BD typically being propelled by faith in Jesus and the love *of* Jesus and Peter by the desire to follow Jesus and prove his love through physicality (13:23–25; 18:15–16; 21:7, 11, 15–17, 18-22). The following observation of Ridderbos is particularly helpful in that it describes the overarching dynamic of the pericope as cooperation rather than competition:

> It is, indeed, remarkable how graphically the Evangelist describes the two disciples going together and then being together at the tomb. Recent exegetes have made much of this, especially focusing on the difference between the two disciples' approach to the tomb. "The other disciple ran ahead of Peter and reached the tomb first" (vs. 4); this is said to indicate his "priority" in the narrative and, especially in connection with the conclusion in vs. 8 ("he saw and believed"), to mark him here as the ideal disciple. This does not take into account that Peter is the first to enter the tomb and takes careful note of the situation there (vv. 5–7), which is of no less importance for the intent of the narrative.[36]

Ridderbos attaches little significance to the fact that BD runs faster than Peter, pointing out instead the manner in which the urgency and care the two disciples

---

[34] Reinhartz, *Befriending the Beloved Disciple*, 126–27. Culpepper, *John the Son of Zebedee*, 69, makes a similar argument before offering his theory about how Peter and BD came to be interjected into the tomb story: "In short, the tradition of Peter's running to the empty tomb is a secondary development in the empty tomb/appearance traditions, but it can be traced to tradition known to both Luke and the Fourth Evangelist. The Fourth Evangelist then added the role of the Beloved Disciple with the effect that his authority was elevated over that of Peter."

[35] Barrett, *St. John*, 563.

[36] Ridderbos, *Gospel of John*, 632.

bring to the task of investigating Mary's report about the empty tomb is "designed to put all the stress on the reliability of their testimony."[37]

In v. 5 we see that BD arrives first but does not immediately enter, reserving by design or default that privilege for Peter. We cannot know why he waits, but a pattern has by now begun to develop in which he pauses to investigate Jesus' whereabouts or interact with him until he can first gain the company of Peter. Reading quite a bit into the text, W. Howard-Brook argues that BD arrives first but enters second because he is stopped in his tracks at the mouth of the tomb by "a wall of fear or sacred awe or some other unnamed emotion."[38] P. Billerbeck suggests BD is a good Jew who is mindful of Levitical purity laws and therefore halts outside the tomb to prevent coming into contact with a corpse.[39] R. H. Lightfoot offers an analysis of the scene that is equally speculative and even provides psychologies for the characters: "We are perhaps to understand that a natural reverence and reserve at first prevent the Beloved Disciple from entering the tomb; only when his companion, who is of a different temperament, has entered, does he follow."[40]

One thing that does seem safe to say is that BD does not loiter at the mouth of the tomb, absently killing time while he waits for Peter to arrive and conduct the initial survey of the tomb's interior. He stoops down and looks inside (παρακύψας βλέπει) and glimpses the linen garments (τὰ ὀθόνια κείμενα) that had been used to wrap Jesus' body.[41] Nothing is said about his faith at this point. He sees (βλέπει), but not with sufficient clarity to believe. As with Peter and Mary, BD is still on the outside of the post-Easter faith looking in; he does not yet recognize the tomb or the wrappings as signs pointing to the resurrection.[42]

---

[37] Ibid., 633.

[38] Howard-Brook, *Becoming Children of God*, 443.

[39] P. Billerbeck, *Kommentar zum Neuen Testament aus Talmud und Midrash* (8th ed.; Munich: C. H. Beck, 1983), 2.584.

[40] Lightfoot, *St. John's Gospel*, 332. See also Busse, *Johannesevangelium*, 250–51.

[41] In the LXX, παρακύπτειν usually has the meaning of "peering," as through a crevice or window (cf. Gen 26:8; Judg 5:28; 1 Kgs 6:4; 1 Chron 15:29; and Prov 7:6).

[42] According to M. Grant, *Saint Peter: A Biography* (New York: Scribner, 1995), 97, "early Christians would have regarded the Resurrection as unconvincing without the Empty Tomb, and the conviction that it was found empty helped to encourage the belief in the subsequent Appearances." Rowland, *Christian Origins*, 192, says something similar: "It should not be the appearance of the risen Christ which should be the starting place for examination of the resurrection faith but the stories of the empty tomb."

THE RACE TO THE EMPTY TOMB

ENTRY INTO THE TOMB: 20:6–10

⁶Then Simon Peter came, following him, and went into the tomb. He saw the linen wrappings lying there, ⁷and the cloth that had been on Jesus' head, not lying with the linen wrappings but rolled up in a place by itself. ⁸Then the other disciple, who reached the tomb first, also went in, and he saw and believed; ⁹for as yet they did not understand the scripture, that he must rise from the dead. ¹⁰Then the disciples returned to their homes. (⁶ἔρχεται οὖν καὶ Σίμων Πέτρος ἀκολουθῶν αὐτῷ καὶ εἰσῆλθεν εἰς τὸ μνημεῖον, καὶ θεωρεῖ τὰ ὀθόνια κείμενα, ⁷καὶ τὸ σουδάριον, ὃ ἦν ἐπὶ τῆς κεφαλῆς αὐτοῦ, οὐ μετὰ τῶν ὀθονίων κείμενον ἀλλὰ χωρὶς ἐντετυλιγμένον εἰς ἕνα τόπον. ⁸τότε οὖν εἰσῆλθεν καὶ ὁ ἄλλος μαθητὴς ὁ ἐλθὼν πρῶτος εἰς τὸ μνημεῖον καὶ εἶδεν καὶ ἐπίστευσεν· ⁹οὐδέπω γὰρ ᾔδεισαν τὴν γραφὴν ὅτι δεῖ αὐτὸν ἐκ νεκρῶν ἀναστῆναι. ¹⁰ἀπῆλθον οὖν πάλιν πρὸς αὐτοὺς οἱ μαθηταί.)

In keeping with other Johannine scenes in which enthusiasm or impetuousness propels Peter (13:9; 18:10; 21:7), he enters the tomb without pausing to look in.[43] He immediately sees the linen wrappings previously observed by BD (v. 5; cf. Luke 24:12), but he sees another garment as well: the facecloth (σουδάριον), which had been "rolled up in a place by itself." Not only are burial clothes present, they are in pristine condition. The Evangelist is often thought to provide this detail to quash rumors that thieves absconded with the body (cf. Matt 27:64; cf. also *GosPet* 5:30; Justin, *Trypho* 108.2; Tertullian, *Apology* 23).[44] In describing the contents of the tomb in such a way, the Fourth

---

[43] "Peter, on the other hand, immediately—in character!—went in and saw not only the linen cloths lying there but also 'the cloth that had been on Jesus' head'...." Ridderbos, *Gospel of John*, 633.

[44] John Chrysostom notes matter-of-factly that thieves would not take the time to strip a body before removing it (*Homily* 85.4). During Claudius' reign, Rome allowed punishments as severe as death for tomb desecration carried out in Palestine. Was this also the case during the reign of Tiberius? One thing that can be assumed is that thieves would have found particularly laborious the task of removing the linens from (the Johannine) Jesus, for John tells us that they had been soaked in "one hundred pounds [λίτρας ἑκατόν] of myrrh and aloes" (19:39)! If Chrysostom and others are right and the Evangelist is presenting evidence against a "stolen body" argument here—countering anti-Christian propaganda in which Jesus' disciples removed the body to instil belief in a "false" resurrection (cf. Matt 27:64; 28:13-15)—it is interesting that he builds his case on forensic evidence alone. Is he aware of the "Jewish conspiracy theory" outlined in Matthew (27:64; 28:13-15)? It does not seem likely. If he were—given his hostile attitude to those Jews who do not confess Jesus—one suspects he would mention it.

Evangelist gives us our first clue that Jesus has escaped "the trappings of death."[45]

By this time readers begin to suspect that here Jesus' resurrection is a different sort of phenomenon than Lazarus' resuscitation (11:44-45). Lazarus came out of the tomb still wearing his linen burial clothes (κειρία) and facecloth (σουδάριον), powerless to pick up the pieces of his life until Jesus could issue the command to bystanders to "unbind him and let him go" (11:44). Lazarus was no more capable of removing his own burial garments than of rolling away the stone that sealed his tomb. The story of his reanimation emphasizes his total dependence on the power of Jesus.[46] The story of the empty tomb is different: the reader suspects that something more profound than reanimation has taken place. Unlike in the Lazarus story, burial garments are not even temporarily appropriate to clothe Jesus in his new life.[47]

It is not to Peter's credit that he fails to grasp this fact. One cannot excuse his failure to believe on a rushed inspection of the garments. John uses the verb θεωρέω rather than the more common βλέπω (cf. v. 5) to emphasize the careful manner in which Peter studies the facecloth.[48] Examining it for clues to the whereabouts or condition of Jesus, Peter fails to realize that it is itself a sign pointing to Jesus' resurrection (see below). Peter's presence inside the tomb testifies to his desire to follow Jesus, but, as in 18:15–27, he is unable to convert that desire into physical or spiritual reattachment to Jesus.[49]

---

[45] Moloney, *Gospel of John*, 520.

[46] Schneiders, *Written that You May Believe*, 186, asserts that it is more appropriate to draw comparisons with Ex 34:33–35 than with the Lazarus episode: "Like Moses, who put aside the veil when he ascended to meet God in glory, Jesus, the new Moses, has put aside the veil of his flesh as he ascends to God to receive from God that glory which he had with the Father before the world was made."

[47] Gnilka, *Johannesevangelium*, 150, suggests that Jesus leaves behind the facecloth as a *"Zeichen des neuen Lebens."*

[48] According to the BDAG, s.v., 454, θεωρέω means to "observe something with sustained attention." The verb is used by John in 20:14 to describe Mary Magdalene's observation of the risen Jesus. It is also used in Acts 10:11 to describe Peter carefully observing the "great sheet" (ὀθόνην μεγάλην) that descends from the heavens in his vision.

[49] Quast, *Peter and the Beloved Disciple*, 117, argues persuasively that Peter's failure to come to belief in 20:6–7 actually underscores his value as a witness to the empty tomb: "Peter did not immediately understand the significance of what he saw, therefore his witness can be regarded as an objective report of the actual physical situation. There was no anticipation or incipient faith to cloud his vision." Of course, this does not mean that the Fourth Evangelist strips Peter of belief in order to make him a more credible witness. Like Luke (24:12), the Fourth Evangelist seems to believe that Peter comes away from the empty tomb without a belief in the resurrection. Bultmann, *Gospel of John*, 684, is one of the few scholars who believes that the Johannine Peter *does* come to belief during

BD, on the other hand, *does* seem to find something about the facecloth compelling. Emboldened by Peter's entry into the tomb, he steps inside and, as the Evangelist describes the action in the aorist tense, "saw and believed" (εἶδεν καὶ ἐπίστευσεν).[50] Although 20:8c is rich in verbs, it is devoid of objects. *What* BD sees and *what* he believes are not spelled out for us. I concur with most scholars that the object of his sight is most likely the σουδάριον (Latin = *sudarium*: "sweat cloth"), which is not mentioned specifically in 19:40 (the verse in which Joseph of Arimathea and Nicodemus prepare Jesus' body for burial) but which we assume is part of the burial ensemble.[51] Because it has been "rolled up in a place by itself," we are perhaps to assume that BD was unable to see it from his original vantage point outside the tomb (20:5). The appearance of the cloth is the only piece of forensic information he gathers in between the time he first looks into the tomb and sees the ὀθόνια (20:5) and the time he comes to believe (20:8), and it is therefore fair to assume that it is this object that catalyzes his belief. Paradoxically, the presence of discarded garments in the tomb makes it seem all the more empty.

As to *what* it is BD believes when he sees the cloth, commentators are divided. Many contend it is the physical event of the resurrection, which was foretold in 2:19-22 and 12:32 and will be stated as an accomplished act in 21:14.[52] Although this seems to me the best interpretation (see below), it must be said that it is challenged frequently enough to resist being casually classified as

---

the tomb experience: "[i]f the writer had meant otherwise, and if the two disciples were set over against each other with respect to their πιστεῦσαι, it would have had to be expressly stated that Peter did not believe." While it would be nice for once to concur with Bultmann concerning Peter's performance in the Gospel, I fear the text does not support his conclusion.

[50] Rather than ἐπίστευσεν, which is reported in the most reliable ancient manuscripts, three manuscripts from the f^{13} group (69, 124 and 788) read ἐπίστευσαν, describing Peter coming to belief at the same time as BD. Is this a case of fudging the data to support the desired result?

[51] In discussing the preparation of corpses for burial, the *Mishnah* (*Shab.* 23.5) ordains that caretakers "tie the chin, not so that it will go up, but so it will not droop further." See Jacob Neusner, *The Mishnah: A New Translation* (New Haven: Yale University Press, 1988), 207. F. Filson, "Who was the Beloved Disciple?" 83–88, maintains that BD is riveted by the σουδάριον because he is none other than Lazarus, and therefore intimately familiar with such burial accoutrements. For more on the impact of the facecloth on BD's faith, see W. E. Reiser, "The Case of the Tidy Tomb: The Place of the Napkins of John 11:44 and 20:7," *HeyJ* 14 (1973): 47–57; and F. J. Moloney, *Glory not Dishonor: Reading John 13-21* (Minneapolis: Fortress, 1998), 161–62.

[52] See, for example, Brown, *John*, 2.1004–08; Bultmann, *Gospel of John*, 684; Cullmann, *Peter*, 28; Lindars, *Gospel of John*, 602; Culpepper, *Gospel and Letters of John*, 240; Wengst, *Johannes-Evangelium*, 279.

the majority opinion. D. A. Lee believes there is a danger in removing ambiguity from the passage by assigning an object to BD's belief, for it forces the Evangelist's hand. She sees John 20:8–10 as a "prolepsis, pointing forward to the meeting with the risen Christ in John 21...."[53] Still popular among scholars is the theory of Augustine and certain other early church leaders that the object of BD's belief is Mary Magdalene's testimony about the tomb being empty.[54] The "Augustinian interpretation" goes a long way toward explaining why BD returns home (20:10) after coming to believe rather than taking the good news to his fellow disciples. Simply put, the news he has to impart is not good: Jesus is gone but not necessarily raised. There are two problems with this interpretation, however. First, if the only thing being confirmed in 20:8 is Mary's report about the tomb being empty, it is really a *re*-confirmation of the discovery made by BD himself in 20:5, and yet in that verse nothing is said about his belief. Second, if Mary's testimony about the tomb being empty is the object of belief, why does Peter not also become a believer? One does not doubt that his careful examination (θεωρέω) of the garments and facecloth reveals to him that the tomb is empty, but he is not said to believe. The safest conclusion to draw is that the neatly-discarded σουδάριον triggers belief in BD but not in Peter, and that it is not belief about the condition of the tomb.

S. M. Schneiders maintains that believing in 20:8 "suggests primarily an active spiritual state of personal adherence to Jesus the revealer and readiness for whatever he will do" (cf. Martha's belief in 11:21–40).[55] She does not say that BD believes in the *resurrection*—the event through which Jesus returns to his own—but that the σουδάριον is a sign of his *glorification*, the event that "takes place on the cross when Jesus goes to his Father...."[56] Among those who share this belief are G. W. MacRae and A. J. Dewey.[57] But could mundane objects such as discarded burial wrappings serve as outward signs of Jesus' glorification and reunion with the Father without also signifying his

---

[53] Lee, "Partnership in Easter Faith," 40. If I am correct that a Redactor is responsible for John 21 and that his additions are not anticipated by the Evangelist, Lee's theory faces challenges.

[54] See the discussions in Moloney, *Gospel of John*, 523, and M. Edwards, *John* (Blackwell Bible Commentaries; Oxford: Blackwell, 2004), 192.

[55] Schneiders, *Written that You May Believe*, 186.

[56] Ibid.

[57] A. J. Dewey, "The Eyewitness of History: Visionary Consciousness in the Fourth Gospel," in *Jesus in Johannine Tradition* (ed. R. T. Fortna and T. Thatcher; Louisville: Westminster John Knox, 2001), 65. G. W. MacRae, *Invitation to John: A Commentary on the Gospel of John with Complete Text from the Jerusalem Bible* (Garden City, N.Y.: Image Books, 1978), 219. Witherington, *John's Wisdom*, 325, argues rather audaciously that BD's familiarity with the stories of Moses and Elijah would have led him to believe that Jesus had been "taken up into heaven bodily."

resurrection? If BD detects that Jesus has been glorified, surely he detects that he has been raised from the dead. And if his immediate focus is on the "trappings of death" that Jesus has escaped (Moloney), then the resurrection is in all probability the event that *first* occupies him.[58] De Boor imagines BD speaking softly to himself as he looks at the discarded garments and sees evidence of Jesus' resurrection: "sie sind nicht mehr nötig, Jesus bedarf ihrer nicht mehr, Jesus ist auferstanden."[59]

Due to the inherent ambiguity of Johannine signs, Peter studies the σουδάριον but fails to see its significance. BD's sensitivity to the presence of Christ is greater than Peter's (cf. 21:7). John does not say how BD comes to believe, but the condition of the facecloth seems to be significant. In telling us that it had been "folded up in a place by itself" (ἐντετυλιγμένον = perf. pass. ptc. of ἐντυλίσσω), the Evangelist implies that God has intervened in the story.[60] "The Beloved Disciple does not see the risen Lord and yet he comes to faith on the basis of what he sees in the tomb, which for him is a genuine sign leading to faith."[61] Byrne says that for BD "the neatly folded, separately placed facial cloth would appear to be the culminating indication of this totally self-possessed, majestic act of Jesus."[62] Peter, whose confession of Jesus in 6:68–69 was cobbled together from observations made during their earthly experiences together in Galilee and Judea, is powerless to perceive the power of God where Jesus is absent from sight.

This is perhaps a good time to point out that John does not disparage sight-based belief in his Gospel, as exegetes sometimes conclude from the "doubting Thomas" episode in 20:25–29. Rather, he gives it a mixed review. On a few occasions, sight-based belief is actually endorsed in the Gospel. In 1:34, for example, John the Baptist testifies that he knows Jesus to be the son of God because he has seen (ἑώρακα) the evidence for it: the spirit descending on Jesus (1:33). The man born blind (9:1–38) receives his sight (ἀναβλέπω) *before* he confesses faith in Jesus, and so reveals sight to be a useful attribute in the pilgrimage of faith. Nathanael is promised he will see "greater things" the more time he spends in Jesus' company, and that these will continually lead to deeper belief (1:50).

---

[58] So Haenchen, *John 2*, 208.

[59] W. de Boor, *Evangelium des Johannes* (Wuppertaler Studienbibel; Wuppertal: R. Brockhaus Verlag, 1970), 230.

[60] Moloney, *John*, 520.

[61] Byrne, "Faith of the Beloved Disciple," 89. I am in agreement with Gnilka, *Johannesevangelium*, 150, that "[d]as leere Grab ist nur Zeichnen, Siegestrophäe, die auf den auferweckten Christus verweist." On the tomb as "sign," see also F. J. Matera, "John 20:1-18," *Int* 43 (1989): 402–06.

[62] Byrne, "Faith of the Beloved Disciple," 88.

In my opinion, rather than disparaging sight-based belief in 20:25–29, Jesus suggests that it is not the ultimate type of faith to which true disciples should aspire. The faith for which Jesus holds the most respect is faith generated by the testimony of believers (cf. 1:41, 45; 4:29; 9:1–38; cf. 19:35; 20:31), which, not coincidentally, is the faith that must sustain the Johannine community when his appearances cease (21:24–25). Interestingly, it is also the case that *sign-based* faith, like sight-based faith, gets mixed reviews in the Gospel. Jesus urges his followers not to build their faith on signs alone (3:2–3; 4:43–54; 6:26), and yet signs consistently evoke faith (6:2; 10:19–21, 41-42; 20:30).[63]

How, then, should we categorize BD's belief in 20:8, since it appears to be predicated on both seeing *and* signs? Perhaps the safest thing to say is that his belief in the resurrection is real—related in some manner to his sensitivity to Jesus—but that it is uninformed by scripture and therefore incapable of being promulgated.[64] When he sees the σουδάριον, BD does "not yet know the scriptures that Jesus must rise from the dead" (20:9; on this use of δεῖ see also 3:14; 12:34; cf. Mark 8:31; Matt 27:62; Luke 22:37; 24:7 and Acts 1:16),[65] which is one explanation for why he does not spread news of his belief. Both BD and Peter lack knowledge of the "scripture" (γραφή) pertaining to the resurrection. Moloney offers a credible analysis of the scene in saying that both disciples "are in a 'not yet' situation of ignorance that will be overcome by a later generation of believers who will read the scripture and recognize the revelation of the action of God in the resurrection of Jesus."[66]

---

[63] It has been said by Brodie, *Gospel* of John, 63, that "failure to believe is associated precisely with a refusal to pay heed to signs (11:47; 12:18–19, 37)."

[64] This is my reading of the text. The opening Greek words of the verse, οὐδέπω γὰρ ᾔδεισαν, lend themselves to other interpretations. For instance, it is possible that BD is being *praised* by the Evangelist for believing without being able to confirm his beliefs with reference to scripture or for believing *prior* to confirming them. The latter idea is supported by M. J. J. Menken, "Interpretation of the Old Testament and the Resurrection of Jesus in John's Gospel," in *Resurrection in the New Testament* (ed. R. Bieringer, V. Koperski and B. Lataire; BETL 165; Leuven: Leuven University Press, 2002), 203. But if BD is being praised for developing a mature belief in the resurrection without the advent of scripture, why is he not subsequently described as spreading news of his discovery? I submit that what he experiences is a flash of revelation and that sustainable faith comes only with the appearance of the risen Jesus (21:7).

[65] Perhaps anticipating 20:9, the reading of 20:8 in D^{supp} is "he saw and did *not* believe" (εἶδεν καὶ οὐκ ἐπίστευσεν). Boring and Craddock, *People's New Testament Commentary*, 356, point out that "[f]or the Fourth Gospel's theology, resurrection faith is supported by rereading the Old Testament as illumined by the insight provided by the post-Easter gift of the Holy Spirit (see 2:17, 22; 7:39; 12:16; 14:15–17, 25–26; 15:26–27; 16:7–15)."

[66] Moloney, *John*, 520. See also Chennattu, *Johannine Discipleship*, 145–46. Attempts are occasionally made to locate a specific passage in the OT to which 20:9 might be

The sudden shift from the third person singular (ἐπίστευσεν, v. 8) to the third person plural (ᾔδεισαν, v. 9) reinforces this interpretation of events. Simply put, the faiths of BD and Peter are, at the end of the story, once more on the same plane.[67] BD has had his moment of insight, but it has not proven robust enough to foster transmission.[68] This is made most clear in v. 10, the concluding verse of the pericope, in which BD and Peter are said to return "to their own homes" (πρὸς αὐτούς).[69] Nothing in the text suggests that BD treads more lightly than Peter on the way home, buoyed by his newfound belief. To put it simply, he does not "run" as he did on the way over. This is, I think, an observation that warrants highlighting: BD runs to the tomb to ascertain the veracity of Mary's report about it being empty but does not run back to report that the empty tomb is a faith-generating "sign." If the discovery rates as "good news," to put it modestly, why not report it? Does the Evangelist wish the reader to infer from BD's silence that the experience has left him confused or too amazed to speak?[70] Or, as I have speculated, is BD's faith too fragile to be shared quite yet, unsubstantiated by scripture or by physical observation of the risen Jesus? What is the reader to conclude?

One thing that is certain is that there is not even an implication that BD shares news of his faith with Peter or with Jesus' mother, who is now a guest in BD's home (19:27).[71] His great confessional statement of 21:7, "It is the Lord!"—which he does share with Peter—comes only *after* Jesus materializes in dramatic fashion on the shore of the Sea of Tiberias. In the race to the tomb pericope, BD's burst of belief is indicative of his facility to detect the power or presence of the Lord, but it is only a single step in his pilgrimage of faith, for it is as yet incapable of being promulgated.

The majority of Johannine commentators are not convinced of this, however, but continue to see the empty tomb pericope as the clearest indicator of the Evangelist's low regard for Peter vis-à-vis BD. In addition to the many

---

referring (e.g., Ps 16:10). However, by "scripture" (γραφή) John may be referring to the whole "Jesus story" that he himself is reporting (not his particular version of events but the sacred story itself). We know from 10:16 that he is aware of other communities familiar with the Jesus story.

[67] Hence the interpretation of Ridderbos, *Gospel of John*, 634, that the Evangelist keeps silent on the issue of Peter's faith "in order to describe a situation that is unclear to both disciples."

[68] The fact that εἶδεν and ἐπίστευσεν are aorist verbs does not mean that BD's faith in 20:8 is "mature," as is argued by Byrne, "Faith of the Beloved Disciple," 34.

[69] On this reflexive use of the pronoun, see Josephus *Ant.* 7.4, 6.

[70] Cf. Luke 24:12.

[71] *Contra* Bernard, *St. John*, 2.662, who emphatically (and inexplicably!) states that BD *does* share and celebrate the news of the resurrection with Jesus' mother. One can only ask: *Where?*

scholars we have already heard from, L. Schenke declares succinctly that, as the pericope draws to a close, "[w]ieder ist der 'geliebte Jünger' dem Petrus überlegen."[72] Schnackenburg goes further, saying that "the point of the narrative" is to depict BD as the ideal disciple, as opposed to Peter, who sees and does not believe.[73] Haenchen takes the criticism of Peter a step above this, noting that, during the empty tomb pericope, BD "once again shows that he is superior to Peter."[74]

I do not believe the text supports these interpretations. The Evangelist does not tip the balance in favor of BD, but honors the disciples equally. The urgency they bring to the task of investigating Mary Magdalene's report about possible desecration of the tomb—which involves running to the tomb and carefully inspecting the discarded linens—testifies to the special affection they hold for Jesus. I agree with Ridderbos that *both* BD and Peter appear in this pericope as "beloved disciples," with Peter's "*belovedness*" not deriving from Jesus' affection for him but from the intimate stature assigned him by the Johannine Community.[75] Manifest in the joint endeavor of Peter and BD is an expression of faith and loyalty that members of the Johannine community are meant to emulate.

Conclusion

Let us conclude the study of Peter's role in the empty tomb pericope by once again recapitulating the events of Easter morning, this time focusing on the activities of all three disciples rather than just Mary:

1. Mary arrives first at the tomb. It is still dark, but there is enough light to show her that the stone has been rolled away. She takes this to be a sign (not yet a *Johannine sign*, for such typically lead to faith rather than despair [cf. v. 8]) that Jesus' body has been removed or stolen.

2. Mary seeks out Peter first and then BD (repeated πρός) to report her finding, which reveals to the reader these men hold positions of great importance in Jesus' ministry, for they warrant notification.

3. Peter and BD set out for the tomb together (ὁμοῦ).

---

[72] Schenke, *Johannesevangelium*, 111.

[73] Schnackenburg, *St. John*, 3.310. Schnackenburg goes on to describe BD's faith as "clear and strong" (3.312), which is remarkable given the fact that (1) he is not said to share it with Peter or the mother of Jesus, and (2) the narrator makes it clear that he does not yet understand the scripture that Jesus must rise from the dead!

[74] Haenchen, *John 2*, 208.

[75] Ridderbos, *Gospel of John*, 633.

4. Their expedition quickly turns into a footrace, or, perhaps, a joyful "free-for-all," with BD outrunning (προτρέχω) Peter and arriving at the tomb first.

5. Rather than exploiting his first-place finish and entering the tomb first, BD defers to and/or waits for Peter, who arrives second but proceeds immediately into the tomb. As he waits for Peter to arrive, BD peers into the tomb and sees the linen garments (ὀθόνια), but does not yet come to faith.

6. Peter sees the linen garments and also the facecloth (σουδάριον), yet these fail to provoke an explicit emotional or spiritual response.

7. Following Peter's lead, BD enters the tomb and, upon seeing the σουδάριον, believes.

8. BD keeps the discovery to himself, perhaps because he is unable to make full sense of it without knowledge of the pertinent scripture that speaks of Jesus rising from the dead.

9. Peter and BD return to their individual homes, making no report of their discoveries.

10. Mary Magdalene receives her private angelophany and Christophany, afterward becoming the first disciple to spread news of the resurrection.

Setting aside for a moment the momentous contribution of Mary Magdalene, it is clear that the race to the tomb and its subsequent exploration by Peter and BD is logistically too complex to serve as a metaphor for inter-community competition in early Christianity. How is one to quantify the contributions each man makes, set them in opposition, and transform the race into a metaphor for an early Christian rivalry? The "race" is not an orderly event.[76] There is no consistent frontrunner. Starting out for the tomb, Peter and BD appear to be in lock-step; neither is described as initiating the journey and neither deserves sole credit for beginning the pilgrimage of faith. BD is the first to arrive at the tomb but Peter is the first to enter. The σουδάριον inspires belief in BD, yet this belief is not propagated and lacks evangelical value.

While T. L. Brodie builds an elegant case that Peter and BD do not represent two branches of Christianity but relate "to the whole church,"[77] and in

---

[76] If one had to characterize the empty tomb story with a single sports metaphor, "endurance contest" might be a better fit than "race," and Mary Magdalene would surely be declared the winner. Of the three disciples, only Mary's determination to solve the mystery of Jesus' disappearance is so stubborn that it results in a tomb-side encounter with him. Her weeping, far from being a symptom of helplessness, is fortuitous: it delays her departure from the tomb until she can experience the angelophany (vv. 12–13) and the Christophany (vv. 14–17).

[77] Brodie, *Gospel According to John*, 563. According to Brodie, BD and Peter "represent two faces of the church, the contemplative and the official" (p. 564). A similar argument is put forward by Dschulnigg, *Petrus im Neuen Testament*, 132: "Petrus wird gleichsam in amtlicher Funktion vorgestellt, und der Vorzugsjünger erkennt

so doing speaks for a large number of commentators, I believe the two disciples' primary function in the story is to demonstrate *Johannine* ideals. We have been exploring for some time the idea that the Johannine Community claims both of these disciples as their inspirational co-founders *and* as disciples whose traits should—particularly when combined—be emulated. The race to the tomb is a case in point. As in 13:24–26, 18:15–16 and 21:7, Peter and BD act in a spirit of cooperation. They have different attributes, but these are not inimical to one another or to the overarching goal of coming to faith in Jesus.

In 20:2–10, as in earlier parts of the Gospel, BD's story is about *believing* more than anything else. *Following* is an activity basic to his discipleship, but it is not his true forte. (We saw this most recently in 18:16, when he disappeared from the courtyard of the high priest at the moment of Peter's inquisition.)[78] Although his effort to investigate Mary's report (i.e. follow Jesus' trail) is initially impressive, it falters when he reaches the mouth of the tomb, and it ends up being *Peter* he follows, as is also the case in 13:23–25 and 21:19–22. His perceptual powers, on the other hand, are formidable. W. T. Kessler may well be correct when he says that they stem from the love Jesus holds for him: "Beyond his historical reality, he has an important symbolic value in John as a disciple of exemplary faith who enjoyed a special place in the affections of Jesus."[79] It is clearly to BD's credit that he recognizes the σουδάριον as a sign of the resurrection, but, because he does not spread news of his discovery, the example he sets of a believing disciple falls just short of the Johannine ideal, which mandates that believers promulgate faith (see especially 1:7; 4:39; 6:69; 9:38; 12:42; 17:20; 19:35).[80]

In contrast to BD, Peter's story is less about *believing* than *following*. He does not have the same sensitivity to Jesus that BD has. BD perceives the presence or power of the Lord in the darkest of situations (cf. 21:7); Peter does not. Despite the energy Peter expends seeking Jesus' body, he does not perceive the discarded σουδάριον as a sign pointing to the resurrection. His determination to follow Jesus—or in this case Mary Magdalene's report about him—is what is impressive. Rather than wrapping himself in shame after the denials and hiding in the shadows of Jerusalem, he goes to a place where Mary Magdalene easily

---

diesbezüglich seinen Vorrang an. Er überagt ihn aber bei weitem in der Klarsicht des Glaubens und kommt als erster zur Erkenntnis der Auferstehung Jesu."

[78] *Contra* Brown et al, *Peter in the New Testament*, 136, who believe BD alone is depicted throughout the Gospel as the "true follower" of Jesus, particularly when he appears beneath the cross (19:26–27).

[79] Kessler, *Peter as the First Witness*, 56.

[80] "But for the disciple whose heart was uplifted by faith there was no more to see or to do at the tomb than for the disciple whose heart was full of bewilderment. So the disciples went away again to their own homes." Temple, *Readings in St. John's Gospel*, 379.

finds him (20:2). Mary's decision to reveal to him first the news about the empty tomb before revealing it to anyone else—including BD—suggests that she still considers him to be the leader of the disciples (cf. 6:68–69; 13:23–25; 21:2–4). Peter follows her line of investigation all the way into the tomb. His plunge inside is bold and spontaneous, paving the way for the entrance of BD.

As T. Wiarda observes, "Peter is shown to be the one who *acts boldly, who influences others, and who is stimulated to action by anything affecting Jesus*" (emphasis in original).[81] His bold foray into the tomb is not only in keeping with the Evangelist's portrait of him, it foreshadows his behavior in the Redactor's "supplemental" chapter, when, breaking ranks with the other disciples, he plunges over the side of the fishing boat in order to expedite the reunion with the risen Jesus (21:7).

---

[81] Wiarda, *Peter in the Gospels*, 115.

CHAPTER 6

JOHN 21 AS GOSPEL SUPPLEMENT

INTRODUCTION: THE PLACE OF JOHN 21 IN THE FOURTH GOSPEL

Nearly all scholars agree that Peter fares better in John 21, the final chapter of the Gospel, than in any other chapter or in the Gospel as a whole. He single-handedly hauls to shore a large catch of fish, which, as will be shown, attests metaphorically to his missionary skills, and he is charged by the risen Jesus with pastoral responsibilities, specifically the care and feeding of Jesus' "lambs" (ἀρνία) and "sheep" (πρόβατά).[1] He issues a threefold profession of love for Jesus that mitigates some of the sting of his threefold denial and, more importantly, qualifies him for his pastoral duties. He also manages to follow Jesus without wavering, finally making good on his pledge to give his life for Jesus (13:36–38), dying a martyr's death (alluded to after the fact in 21:18–19).

The improvement in Peter's fortunes is thought by many scholars to be so dramatic that they describe John 21 as his "rehabilitation."[2] No longer the "bumbler" of earlier chapters who refuses foot-washings, relies on BD to get questions to Jesus, lashes out at opponents with a sword, fails to enter important courtyards, loses footraces, and denies Jesus, this "new" Peter is recognized as a skilled missionary and pastor. Indeed, it is partly by seeing John 21's treatment of Peter as markedly different from his treatment in the rest of the Gospel that scholars are able to construct complex theories about the development of the Johannine community. For example, it is argued by many that the Johannine community, beset by persecution (expulsion from the synagogue) and despair (a reaction to the death of one of their two iconic leaders, BD), attempted at or near the end of the first century to stabilize itself by improving its relations with the Apostolic churches. Peter's "rehabilitation" is alternately seen to reflect this

---

[1] This may be Johannine shorthand for proselytes and second generation believers. See the following chapter.

[2] See, for example, Haenchen, *John 2*, 234; Perkins, *Peter*, 97; Brown, *Community of the Beloved Disciple*, 84; Talbert, *Reading John*, 261; Brodie, *Gospel according to John*, 589. Waetjen, *Beloved Disciple*, 14, states that in "the addendum of chapter 21 Simon is restored to a more complete ministry than that which he was originally called to fulfil in the narrative world of the Fourth Gospel."

change in attitude or be a literary device designed to garner the friendship of Apostolic Christians.[3]

While I agree that the chapter portrays Peter in a positive light and that someone other than the Evangelist is responsible for it (see below), I strongly disagree that it should be considered his "rehabilitation." As we have seen, Peter fares quite well in the first twenty chapters of the Gospel, and is shown by the Evangelist to possess many positive traits. I have argued that Peter and BD should be seen as composite halves of the ideal Johannine Christian, with BD representing insightful faith and Peter representing praxis. John 21 continues to portray the two disciples in this positive manner. While it is true that John 21 affirms Peter's growing ecclesial significance in the Johannine (and perhaps wider) post-Easter church, this affirmation is not evidence of a reconciliatory overture by Johannine Christians to the Apostolic church or any other "rival" church or faction.[4] In fact, there is no evidence in the text that the positive attitude toward Peter represents a more open attitude toward the outside world. Even as the author acknowledges Peter's ecumenical credentials—as fisherman missionary he safely brings to Jesus a large number of fish / novitiates—he adopts a proprietary attitude toward him. Peter is portrayed as the leader of a fishing expedition in which the Twelve are nowhere to be found but in which two uniquely Johannine characters (BD and Nathanael) figure. He is the *new shepherd* who assists the Good Shepherd in caring for the Johannine flock. He is paired even more closely with BD than in other parts of the Gospel. In fact, the portrait of these two following Jesus at the end of the chapter is an intimate one and celebrates the final acts of loyalty of the community's two favorite sons. The message to the reader is that the true Johannine Christian—again, understood to be an amalgam of these two characters—succeeds in following Jesus only through perseverance.

Having said that, I would like to use the balance of this chapter to examine the place and function of John 21 in the overall Gospel, leaving our study of Peter's specific actions for chapters seven and eight. This will allow me to substantiate my claim that John 21 is the work of someone other than the Evangelist, namely a community scribe (called here the "Redactor") charged

---

[3] See especially Brown, *Community of the Beloved Disciple*, 82–88; Martyn, *Gospel of John in Christian History*, 120; Perkins, *Peter*, 98–99; Charlesworth, *Beloved Disciple*, 391; O'Grady, *According to John*, 36; and Pesch, "Position and Significance of Peter," 31.

[4] Here I agree with Bultmann, *Gospel of John*, 713. Witherington, *John's Wisdom*, 355, is another who does not detect a "rivalry between the Petrine and Johannine communities. Indeed, it is doubtful that any rivalry is depicted in these narratives at all. What we do find in vv. 15–19 is the story of the restoration of Peter's relationship with Jesus and renewed commission to teach the Christian community."

with appending the Gospel.[5] If Peter's role in the chapter were a little smaller and if all scholars agreed that John 21 was the product of someone other than the Evangelist, this could perhaps be accomplished in an excursus. As it is, Peter is a central figure in the chapter, and a vocal minority of scholars insists that John 21 is the work of the Evangelist.

Included in the changes that point to John 21 being a Gospel "supplement" written by someone other than the Evangelist are the addition of a "second ending" (21:25; cf. 20:28–29), the change in setting from Jerusalem to Galilee, the introduction of new characters (the sons of Zebedee), new vocabulary (28 *hapax legomena*), new themes ("fishing" as a missionary metaphor, BD's death, and new details about Peter's death and ecclesial responsibilities), and a new type of "sign," which points not to the unity of Father and Son but to the relationship between Jesus and the church.[6]

By understanding the provenance and purpose of John 21 and by becoming familiar with its unique characteristics, we will, I hope, be in a good position to analyze Peter's complex role in the chapter.

REASONS FOR ASCRIBING JOHN 21 TO A REDACTOR

THE DOUBLE ENDING: 21:1–25 // 20: 28–31

In various and significant ways, John 21 reads like a conclusion on top of a conclusion. Although John 20 ends in Jerusalem with Thomas receiving a thinly-veiled rebuke from Jesus for basing his faith on a visual inspection of the wounds of the cross, and with Jesus declaring as *blessed ones* (μακάριοι) "those who have not seen and yet have come to believe" (20:29),[7] John 21 opens in

---

[5] As I stated in the methodology section of the introduction to this study, I consider a "redactor" to be the person ultimately responsible for putting a written work in its final form, readying it for publication. In the case of the Johannine Redactor, I believe this process involved little more than affixing a supplementary chapter.

[6] So Bultmann, *The Gospel of John*, 700–06; Dodd, *The Interpretation of the Fourth Gospel*, 431; Brown, *John*, 2.1063ff; Gnilka, *Johannesevangelium*, 156–57; van Tilborg, *Johannes-Evangelium*, 307–08; and Jones, *The Symbol of Water in the Gospel of John*, 36. P. N. Anderson, "The Having-Sent-Me Father: Aspects of Agency, Encounter, and Irony in the Johannine Father-Son Relationship," in *God the Father in the Gospel of John* (ed. A. Reinhartz; *Semeia* 85; Atlanta: SBL, 1999), 47, credits nearly one-third of the Gospel (the prologue as well as chapters 6, 15–17, and 21) to writers other than the Evangelist.

[7] By making 20:29b (ὅτι ἑώρακάς με πεπίστευκας;) into an affirmation—"you have believed because you have seen me"—M. J. J. Menken, *Old Testament Quotations in the Fourth Gospel: Studies in Textual Form* (CBET 15; Kampen: Kok Pharos, 1996), 182, removes the element of reproach from Jesus' words to Thomas. Most scholars translate

Galilee with the disciples once again encountering the risen (and very visible) Jesus.[8] Despite the fact that the disciples are conveniently adrift on the Sea of Tiberias, no demand is put on them to navigate their way to Jesus by faith. Rather—in a scenario that Thomas might have dreamt up—Jesus provides them with a wealth of sensory data about himself: he stands by a signal fire on the shore (v. 4), directs them to a school of fish and empowers them to net them (v. 6), and bids them to join him for breakfast (v. 10).

Not only does the return to the motif of sight-based belief (cf. 4:48; 6:30, 36; 20:25) represent a departure from the implicit exhortation of 20:29 to believe without seeing, it backtracks on the statement of 20:30 that "Jesus did many other signs (σημεῖα) in the presence of his disciples, which are not written in this book." If the author of John 21 and the Evangelist are one and the same person, why does this person not regard the appearance of the risen Christ to the disciples and the miraculous catch of fish as falling under the rubric of "signs"?[9] If the same person wrote John 21 as John 20, why not excise 20:30–31 to create a seamless transition between the Jerusalem resurrection appearances (20:19–23, 26–29)[10] and this one in Galilee? And, finally, if one individual is responsible for both chapters, why does this individual twice say that not everything Jesus did is written in the Gospel? The disclaimer is appropriate in 20:30–31, for it justifies the editorial decision to omit a certain number of σημεῖα from the Gospel, but it is redundant in 21:25.

20:29b as a question, however, and consider that Thomas is under some mild form of indictment.

[8] Bernard, *St. John*, 2.687, describes John 21 in its entirety to be an "anticlimax." The statement of Waetjen, *Beloved Disciple*, 8, that "[i]n all likelihood, chapter 21 is an appendix to the Fourth Gospel, and, very probably attached by a later editor," is supported by the majority of scholars. So many commentators adhere to this belief, in fact, that it would be a pointless exercise to list them. That said, Haenchen, *John 2*, 229, would appear to go too far in saying that "[t]he view that chapter 21 stems from the author of chapters 1–20 has been all but give up by modern scholarship." In the twenty or so years since he published his monumental commentary, the minority of scholars who argue for John 21 belonging to the original blueprint of the Gospel has grown somewhat larger and certainly more vocal. See below.

[9] On the nature of Johannine σημεῖα, see note 45.

[10] John 21:14 states that the resurrection appearance in Galilee was the third made "to the disciples" (τοῖς μαθηταῖς), which means that the Redactor does not consider Mary Magdalene a disciple or that he assigns her resurrection experience (20:14–17) to a separate category. Only the first option can be ruled out with confidence. Disciples in John's Gospel are those who "follow" and "believe," which are certainly habits of Mary (19:25; 20:1, 16–18). Within a century or so of the writing of John's Gospel, certain Gnostic texts began treating Mary as a disciple of very special status, describing her receiving from Jesus kisses on the mouth (*Gospel of Peter* 55b) and lips (*Second Apocalypse of James* (Nag Hammadi, Codex V, 270) as expressions of love. See Charlesworth, *Beloved Disciple*, 89.

Despite these "redundancies" a vocal minority of commentators shrug off the "double ending" as an exegetical illusion, something that is visible to the (poorly focused) scholarly eye but would have been *in*visible to John's original audience.[11] Although their argument is supported by the fact that no extant copy of the Fourth Gospel omits chapter 21, it is not ultimately convincing. In addition to the changes in vocabulary, theme, and characterization that occur in the chapter (discussed below), 21:1 is itself a sort of *aporia*. Simply put, the author does not seem sure about where to begin.[12] Eager to address the death of BD and the new ways in which his perpetual significance to the community should be understood, he employs transitional language that is vague and confusing.[13] And, as has been said, the second ending is extraordinarily anticlimactic. After the community has been prepared to live in the absence of Jesus, infused with the power of the Holy Spirit to go out into the world and forgive sins, Jesus appears again—visible, voluble, and eating fish. It is a strange turn of events, and seems not to be a continuance of the events of John 20. When this "second ending" is viewed in combination with the linguistic and thematic changes of John 21, to which we now turn, it appears that a new author is appending the Gospel.

---

[11] See, for example, E. Ruckstuhl, *literarische Einheit*, 146ff.; J. H. Bernard, *St. John*, 2.687–90; F. F. Segovia, "The Final Farewell of Jesus: A Reading of John 20:30–21:25," *Sem* 53 (1991): 167–90; S. S. Smalley, "The Sign in John 21," *NTS* 20 (1974): 275–88; U. Busse, "Die 'Hellenen' Joh 12,20ff. und der sogennante 'Anhang' Joh 21," in *The Four Gospels* (ed. F. van Segbroeck et al; Leuven: Leuven University Press, 1992), 2083–2100; J. Breck, "John 21: Appendix, Epilogue or Conclusion?" *SVTQ* 36 (1992): 27–49; Grün, *Jesus: Tür zum Leben*, 146–47; Keener, *Gospel of John*, 1219–22; and Ridderbos, *Gospel of John*, 655–58. S. Bezobrazov, "John 21," *NTS* 3 (1956-57): 136, finds the shared pastoral imagery of John 10 and John 21 to be the "organic connexion" that binds the last chapter to the Gospel. P. Minear, "The Original Functions of John 21," *JBL* 102 (1983): 85–98, builds his case for unity on the fact that all known ancient Gospel manuscripts include chapter 21, and that Tertullian (*Scorp.* 15) and Origen (*Commentary on John*) also demonstrate knowledge of it. Brown, *John*, 2.1077, reports that a Syriac manuscript (British Museum cat. add. no. 14453) dating to the 5th–6th century ends at 20:25, but he is probably right to conclude that this is because it has "lost the final folios."

[12] An ἀπορία in the strictest sense is a philosophical puzzle or perplexing situation. The Greek verb ἀπορέω is used in John 13:22 to describe the disciples looking helplessly at one another during the Last Supper, "uncertain" (NRSV) or "doubting" (KJV) of whom Jesus speaks. (As we saw in our exegesis of the larger passage, Peter attempts to resolve the tension in the scene by having BD ascertain the identity of the traitor from Jesus.) Still, it seems acceptable to use the noun ἀπορία here because the Redactor seems uncertain about how to stitch together the two resurrection traditions.

[13] According to Haenchen, *John 2*, 222, "[t]he redactor who added chapter 21 to the Fourth Gospel took care not to obliterate the text that lay before him; he preferred to settle for internal tension."

CHANGES IN THE STRUCTURE AND LANGUAGE

As it stands, John 21 is attached to the ending of John 20 with transitional language that is chronologically vague. The Greek of 21:1, Μετὰ ταῦτα ἐφανέρωσεν ἑαυτὸν πάλιν ὁ Ἰησοῦς τοῖς μαθηταῖς ("After these things Jesus again showed himself to the disciples"), begs a simple question: After *what* things? After the Jerusalem resurrection appearances, which together make up the bulk of chap. 20? After Pentecost? After all the events of the Gospel? The language itself does not suggest an obvious answer. While this phrase μετὰ ταῦτα is used on five other occasions in the Gospel (5:1, 14; 6:1; 7:1; 13:7) and is therefore a relatively common Johannine connective, it does not fit the Evangelist's pattern of affixing precise timeframes to the events of the crucifixion and resurrection. In narrating these events, for example, the Evangelist uses precise markers to establish a chronology, including "it was about the sixth hour" (19:14), "it was the Jewish day of preparation" (19:42), "early on the first day of the week" (20:1), "evening on that day, the first day of the week" (20:19), and "a week later" (20:26).[14] The author of John 21 does not share this same attention to detail.

The adverb πάλιν (also 21:1) is similarly ill-equipped to describe with any precision the sequence of events leading up to the Galilean resurrection appearance. A survey of the earliest manuscripts reveals that copyists had trouble deciding where (or whether!) to place πάλιν in v. 1, which introduces the possibility that πάλιν did not belong to the original text of the chapter but was inserted at a later date to emphasize the chronological priority of the Jerusalem appearances.[15] Taken together, πάλιν and μετὰ ταῦτα form an awkward transitional phrase that does not help the reader know where, exactly, to place the Galilean resurrection appearance on the post-Easter timeline. Are we to imagine that Peter and the others have been fishing for months when Jesus appears to them in Galilee, and have thus ignored the mandate to go out into the world and forgive sins, empowered by the Holy Spirit (20:21–24)? Or are we to conclude that this is their first endeavor following the other resurrection appearances, a business cruise of sorts, with captain and crew trying to work out a good evangelical program? Whatever the case, the ambiguity is not characteristic of the Evangelist.

---

[14] Michaels, *John*, 351. Brown, *John*, 2.1067, is dismissive of the idea that μετὰ ταῦτα was ever part of the original Gospel or of the Evangelist's unfinished blueprint, calling it a "stereotyped connective conveniently used to attach extraneous matter."

[15] ἐφανέρωσεν ἑαυτὸν πάλιν B C* H U M 700 1071 Δ *f*13 | ἐφανέρωσεν πάλιν ἑαυτόν ℵ | ἐφανέρωσεν ἑαυτὸν ὁ Ἰησοῦς πάλιν W Ψ 69. Πάλιν omitted in G and 1424.

If the language is chronologically unspecific, it is geographically precise: the Sea of Tiberias (Sea of Galilee) is given as the location for the newest resurrection scene. Seven disciples (down from twelve in 6:67–71 and 20:24) appear in the pericope and behave as though they have been unaffected by the miraculous events in Jerusalem. Peter's announcement that he is going fishing brings aboard ship six other disciples, all of whom are either fishermen or have enough free time on their hands to commit to an overnight voyage (21:3–4). This is the first time in John's Gospel that Peter or anyone else has been described as "going fishing," and yet the Galilean voyage is mentioned casually (λέγει αὐτοῖς Σίμων Πέτρος· ὑπάγω ἁλιεύειν), as if the author presupposes his audience's familiarity with Peter's (Synoptic) profession.[16] The collocation of Peter, the sons of Zebedee, a boat, and fishing nets is reminiscent of fishing expeditions and Galilean seaside scenes in the Synoptics (e.g., Matt 4:18–22; Mark 1:16–20; Luke 5:1–11) but comes as a surprise in John's Gospel. In fact, the sons of Zebedee have not been mentioned at all in this Gospel, yet they are deposited without comment into the boat alongside the familiar characters of Peter, BD, Nathanael, and Thomas Didymus.[17]

I agree with the majority of scholars that the sons of Zebedee are able to embark on the expedition with these familiar Johannine characters because the Redactor is combining two distinct traditions.[18] The sons of Zebedee are brought on board, as it were, from a Galilean fishing story, while BD, Nathanael of Cana, and Thomas Didymus have been placed in the boat as favorite Johannine characters. Peter is the only disciple who belongs to both traditions, equally at home on the water and in the pages of John's Gospel.[19] While it is not surprising

---

[16] Witherington, *John's Wisdom*, 354.

[17] One other, unnamed disciple participates in the voyage (see next chapter). P. F. Ellis, "The Authenticity of John 21," *SVTQ* 36 (1992): 17–25 contends that the overlap in names and terms between 1:19–51 and 21:1–25 (including "Simon Son of John," "Jesus," "Son of God," "Nathanael," "Cana," "follow me," "bear witness," and "turned and saw following") is evidence that one person wrote the Gospel and that John 21 was included as a "fitting conclusion." In my opinion, it is easier to believe that certain names and themes in John 21 were inserted to evoke earlier images and establish continuity with the Evangelist's portion of the Gospel than it is to believe John 1:19–51 was written in anticipation of 21:1–25.

[18] See R. F. Brown, *Gospel and Epistles of John: A Concise Commentary* (Collegeville: Liturgical Press, 1988), 100. Whether the Galilean strain of the tradition incorporates a fishing story from the earthly ministry of Jesus (cf. Luke 5:1–11) or a Synoptic call narrative set by the sea (cf. Mark 1:16–20; Matt 4:18–22; cf. Luke 5:1–11)—or whether it existed originally as a resurrection narrative—is a topic of much debate. See the discussion in the following chapter.

[19] One of the Twelve in the Synoptic Gospels is called Thomas (Greek = "twin"; Mark 3:18; Matt 10:3; Luke 6:15), but it is not clear if this is the same individual identified by John as Thomas Didymus (lit. "twin-twin"; 11:16; 20:24; 21:2).

to find BD in an important scene in John's Gospel, it is quite surprising to find him in Galilee, for thus far his appearances have been confined to Jerusalem, the city in which he has connections to the religious authorities (18:15–16) and where he knows the local terrain (18:15; implicit in 19:26).

As might be expected of an author who wishes to create a sense continuity with the "original" edition of the Gospel, the Redactor borrows certain words and phrases from the vocabulary of the Evangelist. These include φανερόω, (1:31; 2:11; 3:21; 9:3; 17:6); θαλάσσης τῆς Τιβεριάδος (6:1); Θωμᾶς ὁ λεγόμενος Δίδυμος (11:16; 20:24); Ναθαναήλ (1:45, 48-49); Κανὰ τῆς Γαλιλαίας (2:1, 11; 4:46); ἀνθρακιά (18:18); and διαζώννυμί (13:4-5).[20] What is altogether *unexpected*, however, is the large number of new words that appear. There are 28 *hapax legomena* in all: αἰγιαλός, ἁλιεύειν, ἀποβαίνειν, ἀριστᾶν, ἀρνίον, βόσκειν, γηράσκειν, γυμνός, δίκτυον, ἐκτείνειν, ἐξετάζειν, ἐπενδύτης, ἐπιστρέφειν, Ζεβεδαῖος, ζωννύναι, ἰσχύειν, ἰχθυς, μακράν, νεώτερος, οἴεσθαι, πῆχυς, ποιμαίνειν, προβάτιον, προσφάγιον, πρωΐα, σύρειν, τολμᾶν, and τρίτον.[21] In addition to these *hapax legomena*, several important words or cognates are used differently by the author of John 21 than by the Evangelist, including ἐπιστραφείς instead if στραφείς in v. 20 (cf. 1:38; 20:14, 16), ἐξετάζειν in place of ἐρωτᾶν in v. 12; partitive ἀπό instead of ἐκ in v. 10, causative ἀπό in v. 6; πλέον in place of μᾶλλον in v. 15 (cf. 3:19; 12:43), ἰσχύω for δύναμαι in v. 6; ἕως in v. 22 instead of compound terms such as ἕως ὅτου (9:18) or ἕως οὗ (13:38), and ἀδελφοί for μαθηταί in v. 23.[22]

J. H. Bernard, a subscriber to the theory that the same person wrote John 1–21 as John 21, explains the new vocabulary as the result of the Evangelist's striking out on his own without the reminiscences of the recently-deceased John son of Zebedee to guide him. But this explanation relies on the dubious assumption that John's eyewitness testimony was delivered with such rigorous syntax that the Evangelist was left with no option but to alter his vocabulary, style, and thematic concerns when affixing the supplement.[23] I am inclined to agree with W. G. Kümmel that it is easier to explain certain recurring words in John 21 as "conscious or unconscious literary adaptations" of preceding material than it is to account for the vast number of new words and idiomatic expressions that appear in John 21.[24]

---

[20] Howard-Brook, *Becoming Children of God*, 466.

[21] Barrett, *St. John*, 576.

[22] See the discussions in W. G. Kümmel, *Introduction to the New Testament* (London: SCM, 1965), 149; Barrett, *St. John*, 576-77; and Haenchen, *John 2*, 228.

[23] Bernard, *St. John*, 2.688.

[24] Kümmel, *Introduction*, 148. This is contra M. Davies, *Rhetoric and Reference in the Fourth Gospel* (JSNTSup 69; Sheffield, Sheffield Academic Press, 1992), 263, who maintains that the style, vocabulary, and themes of John 21 are consistent with those presented in chapters 1–20.

NEW IMAGES AND THEMES

R. Schnackenburg argues that while John 21 "did not belong to the original plan of the Gospel, it certainly belongs to the Evangelist's tradition."[25] His statement is supported by the fact that many themes and images from the main body of the Gospel are carried forward to John 21. Examples include the disciples actively working in Galilee (numerous in chapters 1–12) and seeing Jesus from a boat during an unsuccessful voyage (6:16–18), the onset of a food shortage (6:5–7), Jesus distributing food to end the shortage (6:11), Peter and BD working closely together (13:24; 18:15–16; 20:4–10), Peter being referred to as "Son of John" (1:42), and Jesus speaking tenderly of his "sheep" (10:2–27). The expectation that true disciples will "follow" (ἀκολουθέω) Jesus (21:7, 11, 19–22) is perhaps the most important theme carried forward from the main body of the Gospel (cf. 1:43; 10:4–5; 10:27; 12:26; 13:36–37).

In addition to these familiar images, however, several important new images and themes appear in John 21. These include a change from optimism to pessimism in the Johannine community (reflected in the early misfortune of the fishing party), the replacement of the Twelve by seven disciples, the death of BD, the precise ecclesial significance of Peter and the identification of crucifixion as the manner of his death, the omission of Father-Son language, and the introduction of a new kind of σημεῖον, which points to the relationship between the risen Christ and the church as opposed to the relationship between the Father and the Son. There is time enough here to explore these phenomena only briefly.

Assuming the members of the Johannine community are represented to some extent by the disciples in John 21, as in other parts of the Gospel, one gets a sense from vv. 2-4 that the community suffered through a period of despair in between the time the Gospel was written and the supplement added.[26] When the Evangelist wrote John 20, completing what might be termed loosely as the "first edition" of the Gospel, the Johannine community had at least four reasons to be optimistic about the future: first, Jesus had assured them the Paraclete was coming to guide and teach them (14:16–17, 26; 15:26; 16:7); second, the Father had sanctified the Church (17:17–19); third, Jesus had promised to return and

---

[25] R. Schnackenburg, *The Church in the New Testament* (London: Burns and Oates, 1974), 108. See also de Boor, *Evangelium des Johannes*, 2.251, who gives credit for the chapter to a "circle of friends and students" (*Kreis der Freunde und Schüler*) of the Evangelist steeped in his teachings and eager to continue reporting Jesus' word after his death.

[26] I accept the statement of Ferreira, *Johannine Ecclesiology*, 198, that "the present history of the community is represented by Jesus and the disciples in the Gospel." Ferreira closely links the "sending" of the disciples in John 20:21 with the mission of the Johannine community, but he also sees missionary themes in 4:38, 13:20 and 17:18.

not leave them "orphans" (14:18); and fourth, BD was expected to survive until the Parousia, providing perpetual witness (inferred from 21:22–23).[27] As if all this were not enough to build feelings of optimism, the members of the community—again, represented by Jesus' disciples—had been given a warrant allowing them to minister to the world (20:21) and forgive sins while empowered by the Holy Spirit (20:22–23). At the end of John 20, the Evangelist informs the reader that there is no need to include more traditions about Jesus because the community has enough material to aid its belief and foster belief in others (20:28–29), which is one way of saying that the stage has been set for a period of evangelism in which faith will be propagated not by sightings of the risen Christ but by testimony and anamnesis.

Then comes John 21. The disciples are back in Galilee, their bountiful spiritual gifts replaced by empty fishing nets and darkness. Although they have supposedly been infused with the Holy Spirit, they cannot perform so simple a task as catching a single fish.[28] They are not busy forgiving sins or evangelizing, fulfilling the mandate issued by the risen Jesus in 20:20–23, but are looking for their next meal![29] What has happened, the reader wonders? Has some calamity befallen them? Did the combination of reassurances and empowerment in 20:21–31 precipitate an overly optimistic mood in which the community felt it could, through sufficient confessing and believing, generate a centripetal ecclesial force that would keep it together? What are readers to think?

In my opinion, the implication of 21:21–23 is that a calamity *did* befall the community in between the writing of John 1–20 and John 21: the death of BD.[30] When Peter asks Jesus about BD's fate in 21:21, Jesus gives the following response: "If it is my will that he remains until I return, what is that to you? Follow me!" Before Peter has time to respond, the author, calling attention to himself as narrator, quickly explains that Jesus did not mean by that statement that BD would *necessarily* survive as a perpetual witness but that he would

---

[27] Charlesworth, *Beloved Disciple*, 298, maintains that Thomas is the Beloved Disciple and also the Paraclete! Finding the Thomas/Paraclete character to be largely indistinguishable from the Holy Spirit of 20:21, Charlesworth argues that Thomas is the individual/spirit who was originally meant to sustain the community εἰς τὸν αἰῶνα.

[28] This is not to suggest that fish would throw themselves into the nets of individuals infused with the Holy Spirit. Rather, the reader is meant to take notice of the changing fortunes of the disciples, who are transformed from empowered to powerless.

[29] I disagree with Barrett, *St. John*, 579, that the disciples are fishing for people (evangelizing) here. It is they who are in need of "good news," which does not come until the appearance of Jesus (21:5ff.) Aquinas, *Commentary on John*, 616, makes a practical observation about the disciples: "They were not forbidden by their Apostleship from earning their livelihood by a lawful craft, provided they had no other means of living.'"

[30] Haenchen, *John 2*, 228, says that it "is all but impossible to conclude from this verse that that disciple was still living and that his (eventual) death is spoken of only by way of prevention, so to speak, so that verse 23 could even still be ascribed to him."

survive if it were Jesus' will (v. 23). Obviously it was not Jesus' will. Were BD still alive at the time of the writing of John 21 it would not have made sense to refer to his *in*ability to withstand the passage of time as a "rumor that spread in the community" (ἐξῆλθεν οὖν οὗτος ὁ λόγος εἰς τοὺς ἀδελφοὺς). Indeed, the situation caused by his passing seems to be have been so dire that two iconic characters, Jesus and Peter, are recalled by the Redactor and placed into a conversation to put the event in perspective.[31] In view of the fact that expectations for Christ's imminent return were often high in the first century (cf. 1 Thes 4:15; 1 Cor 15:51), it is easy to imagine that the death of one rumored to survive until the Parousia would have had a distressing effect.[32] Haenchen explains why the death of this particular individual would have troubled the Johannine community:

> It is quite clear that the author is not thinking merely of a symbolic person, but of a particular disciple, who died at an extremely old age—to the general consternation. For, while in Paul's day it appeared certain that the overwhelming number of Christians would experience the parousia, and while it could still be said in Mark 9:1: "There are some standing here who will not taste death before they see the kingdom of God come with power," this disciple was evidently the last supporting pillar of the imminent expectation that the parousia would yet come in his lifetime.[33]

Peter speaks for the Johannine community when he voices concern about BD's death; Jesus speaks for himself when he reminds Peter (i.e., the community) that following and not fretting should be the primary responsibility of disciples. The message is that BD's death is not grounds for despair. Yes, he has died, but he will continue to lead people to Jesus through his role as authenticator of the traditions in the Gospel (21:24; cf. 19:35).[34]

The specific manner in which Peter is said to die (crucifixion) is the next new theme / image we encounter in the Gospel supplement.[35] While 13:36–37 makes it clear that Peter will eventually make good on his promise to lay down

---

[31] "The evangelist explains the saying because of the misunderstanding within the Johannine community about the Beloved Disciple's life span, which on any showing had already been considerable. The explanation suggests perhaps some considerable dismay in the community that the Beloved Disciple had died before Jesus returned." Witherington, *John's Wisdom*, 357.

[32] See the discussion in Lightfoot, *St. John's Gospel*, 340.

[33] Haenchen, *John 2*, 233.

[34] So Ridderbos, *Gospel of John*, 672: "Nowhere more clearly than in 21:24 is the beloved disciple referred to as a historical person and not a symbolic figure."

[35] A very small minority of scholars doubts that 21:18–19 describes Peter's martyrdom, whether by crucifixion or some other means. See chapter eight of this study.

his life for Jesus and successfully "follow" him, it is not until 21:18–19 that readers are given the details of his arrest and execution.[36] In his old age, after he "stretches out his hands," someone will fasten a belt around him and take him to a place he does not wish to go. The Redactor notes that Peter will "glorify God" through this specific manner of death, which seems a clear enough reference to martyrdom.[37] In discussing Peter's martyrdom, the Redactor combines the themes of "taking up the cross" (v. 18) and "following" (vv. 19, 22). In the main body of the Gospel, the Evangelist reserves the cross for Jesus; it is the instrument of his glorification (3:14; 8:28; 12:32), and no one, not even Simon of Cyrene (cf. Mark 15:21; Matt 27:32; Luke 23:26) helps him carry it. In fact, the "Synoptic" theme of *taking up the cross and following* (Mark 8:34; Matt 16:24; Luke 9:23) does not appear anywhere in chaps 1–20 of John's Gospel, perhaps because the Evangelist does not wish to mix images of the cross of glory with the cross of obedient discipleship.[38] The insistence on reserving the cross—or at least *a* cross—for Jesus does relent in John 21, however, where Peter's crucifixion and successful act of "following" Jesus is a major topic.[39]

Not only does Peter die a martyr's death, he is invested with pastoral responsibilities (tending Jesus' lambs and sheep, vv. 15–17) and is shown to be a successful missionary (v. 11). In the same way that Jesus does not lose a single one of the charges given him by the Father (17:12), Peter does not lose any of the fishes (novitiates) put into his care by Jesus. This is made clear by his handling of the un-torn net.[40] Not only does he evangelize, he is given the further responsibility of nourishing those who come into the fold (vv. 15–17). He is the *new shepherd* who assists the Good Shepherd (cf. 10:1–15). As I will

---

[36] The event is discussed after the fact. Most scholars contend that the historical Peter died a generation or more before work on the Gospel began. See especially O. Cullmann, *Peter*, 86–87; Culpepper, *Gospel and Letters of John*, 249; Köstenberger, *John*, 599. See also the discussion in chapter eight.

[37] Cullmann, *Peter*, 87. See also Haenchen, *John 2*, 226–27. O. Glombitza, "Petrus – Der Freund Jesu: Überlegungen zu Joh 21:15 ff.," *NovT* 6 (1963): 284, agrees: "Petrus ist schließlich der, der in ergebener Gelassenheit die verordneten Wege geht bis ins Martyrium zur Verherrlichung des Gottes...." Koester, *Symbolism in the Fourth Gospel*, 251, takes the reference to crucifixion to be historical evidence that Peter was killed by Roman and not Jewish authorities.

[38] Of course, it is also possible that he does not know the tradition! But this is not the easiest explanation since 13:36 almost certainly alludes to Peter's death. See chapter 3.

[39] "In light of Jesus' words in 21:18–19, his call to Peter to follow him now takes on a new and deeper meaning. The rest of Peter's life must be lived in the shadow of the cross, just as Jesus' was." Köstenberger, *John*, 599.

[40] As for Peter transferring the net to shore unassisted, Bultmann, *Gospel of John*, 709, has this to say: "It will hardly be doubted that the intention is to portray Peter as the leader of the churchly fellowship, since it is he (and this representation presumably is due to the redactor) who draws the net to the land." For my theory that Peter is entrusted with the care of both novitiates and second generation believers, see the following chapter.

argue in the following two chapters, this new focus on Peter's ecclesial significance does not represent a period of ecumenical outreach but is part of a general explication and celebration of the post-Easter roles of both Peter and BD.

Interestingly, although the author of John 21 tells us a good deal about the post-Easter roles of Peter and BD and their relationship with Jesus, nothing is said about the relationship between Jesus and the "Father." To be more specific, "Father-Son" language is not explicitly employed in John 21. If the author of John 21 is actually the Evangelist, this is a truly remarkable fact, for in all but one of the Gospel's other chapters (John 7 being the exception) extensive and explicit use is made of the "Father-Son" paradigm, usually to convey the idea that the Son is "sent" by the Father or that the Father and Son are one.[41] And even in John 7 the Father-Son relationship is implicit in the speech Jesus makes during the festival of Booths: "Then Jesus cried out as he was teaching in the temple, 'You know me, and you know where I am from. I have not come on my own. But the one who sent me is true, and you do not know him. I know him, because I am from him, and he sent me'" (vv. 28–29).

This in mind, is it conceivable that the Evangelist would tie up loose ends in the Gospel—including supplying a fresh resurrection story that details the post-

---

[41] The "Father" is mentioned 121 times in John's Gospel, including four times in the Jerusalem resurrection narratives (20:17 [3]; 20:21); the "Son" is mentioned 37 times, including once in the Jerusalem resurrection narrative (20:31). The Son is said to be sent by the Father many times in the Gospel, including in 20:21. Is "Father" always a synonym for God in the Gospel of John? If it is, does it qualify as "inclusive language"? These questions are not easy to answer. Many of the most intriguing feminist studies of John's Gospel accept the "God-as-Father" motif only when "patriarchal understandings of power and relationship" are challenged. See D. A. Lee, "The Symbol of Divine Fatherhood," in *God the Father in the Gospel of John* (ed. A. Reinhartz; *Semeia* 85; Atlanta: SBL, 1999), 181. Lee speaks with such eloquence on this subject that it is worth excerpting a larger quotation from her article: "The Johannine understanding of divine fatherhood thus involves a two-way movement. On the one hand, God's fatherhood, symbolically portrayed in the Father-Son relationship, is an outward movement of giving away power, surrendering selfhood as autonomous and self-sufficient. On the other hand, divine fatherhood draws others into the filial relationship between God and Jesus, so that the Father-Son language becomes the fundamental icon of God's relations with the world....divine fatherhood is not merely the reflection of human experience, but rather challenges, at the deepest level, human projections of authority and sovereignty,...." (p. 81). R. Bauckham, "Monotheism," 164, argues that "the terms 'Father' and 'Son' entail each other. The Father is called Father only because Jesus is his Son, and Jesus is called Son only because he is the Son of his divine Father. So to say that Jesus and the Father are one is to say that the unique divine identity comprises the relationship in which the Father is who he is only in relation to the Son and the Son is who he is only in relation to the Father." See also the discussion on inclusiveness in Father-Son language in M. M. Thompson, *The God of the Gospel of John*, p. 71.

Easter relationship between Jesus and his chief disciples—without employing this highly-charged Father-Son language? It seems to me unlikely. As far as the Evangelist is concerned, as the Father sends Jesus, so Jesus sends the disciples (17:18; 20:21; cf. 13:20; 17:21).[42] This theme is central to John 20, which contains the Gospel's "first" ending, but not John 21, which contains the "supplemental" ending.[43] The only reasonable explanation for why this language—a literary hallmark of the Evangelist—is omitted in John 21 is, in my opinion, that a new individual is writing.[44]

The focus on the post-Easter situation of the disciples requires that this individual, the Redactor, present a new kind of σημεῖον, one which does not point to Jesus' relationship to the Father but to the church.[45] This σημεῖον—the

---

[42] See the discussion in Haenchen, *John 2*, 229.

[43] Some will perhaps argue that the missionary theme in John 21 (esp. v. 11) is a continuation of the theme in 20:21-23, and that Jesus' action of "sending out" the disciples for missionary work mirrors the way he is sent out by the Father. A. Reinhartz, "'And the Word Was Begotten': Divine Epignesis in the Gospel of John," in *God the Father in the Gospel of John* (ed. A. Reinhartz; Semeia 85; Atlanta: SBL, 1999), 97, says that with "this spiritual rebirth, the disciples inherit the abilities that Jesus had, namely, the ability to forgive or retain the sins of others (20:23; cf. 5:14), just as Jesus acquired the abilities of the father to judge and to give life. They will do the works that Jesus does and even greater works than these (14:12). The relationship that the father and son enjoyed will now be entered into by the disciples, 'that they may all be one. As you, Father, are in me and I am in you, may they also be in us, so that the world may believe that you have sent me' (17:21)."

[44] Perhaps the author eliminates Father-Son language because the unity of Father and Son is by now taken for granted in the community? Perhaps the Redactor is a woman, uncomfortable with Father-Son language? Perhaps the focus has moved so distinctly from *Father-Son* to *Jesus-Church* that Father-Son language is jettisoned as being potentially distracting? One can only guess. But, at the very least, the omission of Father-Son language suggests a new author with a new literary focus.

[45] Defined most simply, the σημεῖα that Jesus performs in the Gospel are "designed to elicit faith, as this concluding statement of purpose in 20:30–31 indicates." Waetjen, *Gospel of the Beloved Disciple*, 425. Ridderbos, *Gospel of John*, expands this definition slightly in saying that "the word 'signs' refers not only to certain miraculous acts but to any event in which Jesus' divine glory is manifest (cf. 2:11). In that sense we can understand that the word 'signs' is used here [John 20:30–31] as a summarizing characterization of Jesus' self-revelation." Ridderbos is thus able to include the activities of the risen Jesus as falling under the rubric of σημεῖα, a view to which I subscribe. So M. D. Hooker, *Endings*, 75. Schnackenburg, *St. John*, 1.520, on the other hand, insists that "the apparitions of the risen Lord can hardly be taken as 'signs.' They are no longer part of Jesus' self-revelation to the world but have an entirely different character. They are Christophanies before the disciples...." Haenchen, *John 2*, 212, argues that the Evangelist's "predecessor" understood σημεῖα to be miracles or "proofs that Jesus was the son of God," but that the Evangelist expanded this term to mean "pointers." He also says that these σημεῖα usually *point* to the unity of Father and Son and that they allow readers

last of the new themes / images we encounter in John 21—is the miraculous catch of fish, examined closely in the following chapter of this study.[46] (The fact that Peter is given a role in this event—hauling the net ashore without incurring a tear and thus spilling cargo—conveys the Redactor's belief that Peter is a proficient steward when acting in obedience to Jesus.)[47]

Conclusion

Nowhere in John 20 does the Evangelist intimate that, in the rush to get the Gospel to press, difficult editorial decisions had to be made that resulted in the omission of vital material. Not every tradition about Jesus has been included, the Evangelist says, but enough have been so that the community will "come to believe that Jesus is the Messiah, the Son of God, and that through believing you may have life[48] in his name" (20:31). The last item the Evangelist chooses to cover is Thomas' confession in the house in Jerusalem. Jesus' final statement, "Blessed are those who have not seen and yet have come to believe" (20:29), is a fitting conclusion to a Gospel whose dominant motif has been *believing* (1:7, 50; 3:12; 4:21, 28; 5:38; 6:30; 8:24; 9:18; 11:27; 14:11; 17:20; 19:35). Although Thomas has the luxury of visually inspecting Jesus to establish his faith, others will not be so fortunate, and so the Evangelist elects to close the Gospel with the lesson that the Johannine community must learn to subsist on a new kind of faith, one based not on visual examination of the risen Christ but on personal witness.

---

of the Gospel to "see the relation of man to God and of human possibilities vis-à-vis God in an entirely different light" (p. 212). For the idea that a σημεῖα-source was a major source from which the Evangelist drew in composing the Fourth Gospel, see especially Bultmann, *Gospel of John*, 697–99; and Fortna, *The Fourth Gospel and its Predecessor*, 201–04. Two of the most vocal opponents of the σημεῖα-source remain E. Ruckstuhl and B. Noack. Ruckstuhl, *literarische Einheit, passim*, argues for the literary unity of the Fourth Gospel. Noack, *Zur johanneischen Tradition, Beiträge zur Kritiken an der literarkritischen Analyse des vierten Evangeliums* (Copenhagen: Rosenkilde og Bagger, 1954), 9–40, maintains that the Fourth Evangelist draws on oral traditions rather than a written σημεῖα-source.

[46] See R. T. Fortna, *The Gospel of Signs: A Reconstruction of the Narrative Source Underlying the Fourth Gospel* (SNTSMS 11; Cambridge: Cambridge University Press, 1970): 86–88. For more on the unique character of the sign in John 21, see Smalley, "Sign in John XXI," 275–88; and Beasley-Murray, *John*, 396.

[47] "The Lord has by a 'sign' illustrated the blessing which rests on work done in obedience to His command. He has refreshed His friends with sustenance which is, in part, the product of their own labour." W. Temple, *Readings in St. John's Gospel* (London: MacMillan & Co., 1959), 405.

[48] ℵ C* D L Ψ 69 124 33 788 read "eternal life" (ζωὴν αἰώνιον).

Then comes John 21, replete with visual sightings of Jesus. Given the closing message of John 20, the supplemental chapter is, in a strictly theological sense, anticlimactic. While the addition of the "second ending" and changes in vocabulary, setting, and characters all add to the impression that someone other than the Evangelist is responsible for John 21, the real evidence for a new author comes in the introduction of new themes, the most significant of which is the death of BD.[49] The new material is time-sensitive; it does not reflect an ideological shift but a shift in the circumstances of the community.[50] A dramatic event has transpired that makes supplementing the Gospel necessary. Out of respect for the Evangelist—or perhaps the "original" edition of the Gospel itself—the Redactor sacrifices fluid storytelling in order to preserve the Gospel's original ending. The transition from Jerusalem to Galilee and the contraction of Jesus' inner circle of disciples from twelve to seven is not explained. Instead, the Redactor immediately attends to the business of addressing the crisis precipitated by the death of BD.

Calling upon Jesus and Peter, characters we had not expected to hear from again, the Redactor exhorts the community to celebrate BD's contribution to the Gospel and not grieve over his death. It is BD's witness that is imperishable, not the individual. Peter's death is a major theme of the chapter as well, and, as is true with BD, death does not obscure his significance. He served Jesus' flock as shepherd during his lifetime, and, in his death, he stands as an example of one who sacrifices everything to follow obediently after Jesus. One of the last messages of the chapter—communicated through the acts of Peter and BD—is that martyrdom and lifelong witness are both praiseworthy activities in the Christian profession.[51]

---

[49] Because there is no extant version of the Fourth Gospel that lacks chapter 21, any suggestion that the final chapter was an extremely late addition must meet with suspicion. In fact, as we have seen, more than a few scholars argue that John 21 is part of the original plan of the Gospel and that the scholarly practice of attributing stylistic and thematic irregularities to a new compositional hand avoids the true challenge of locating the continuities that bridge the various sections of the Gospel. See especially Minear, "Original Functions of John 21," 85–98; and Ellis, "The Authority of John 21," 17–25. While I agree that several themes are carried over from John 1–20 to John 21, I maintain that the Redactor does this to establish continuity with the Evangelist's work, and that more striking than the thematic similarities between John 1–20 and John 21 are the dramatic differences.

[50] The text of 21:24, οἴδαμεν ὅτι ἀληθὴς αὐτοῦ ἡ μαρτυρία ἐστίν, suggests some sort of collaborative effort behind the writing of the supplemental chapter. The parenthetical remark of 19:35, which makes essentially the same point as 21:24, may also have been inserted at this time.

[51] In graphic fashion—and determined to tag BD as both witness and martyr—B. W. Bacon, "The Motivation of John 21:15–25," *JBL* 50 (1931): 72, describes Peter's martyrdom as "red witness" and BD's perpetual witness as "white martyrdom."

CHAPTER 7

THE FISHING EXPEDITION AND THE MIRACULOUS CATCH OF FISH

INTRODUCTION: PETER IN JOHN 21:1–11

The supplemental chapter to the Fourth Gospel explicates and celebrates the ecclesial roles of both Peter and BD, assigning an official[1] capacity to both, but, as we will see, does not describe the attitude of the Johannine church toward Apostolic Christians, as is often maintained by commentators. BD is hailed in John 21 as the witness behind the Gospel; Peter is described as a missionary, pastor, and martyr. Their attributes and achievements are complementary. Representing the Johannine community in vv. 21–22, Peter is instructed by Jesus not to fret about BD's death but focus instead on the business of following Jesus. The passage is meant to alleviate the community's concerns about a possible delay in the Parousia and so rekindle its faith. Although the Redactor places his own literary stamp on the chapter, introducing many new themes and eschewing the previously ubiquitous Father-Son language in order to focus on the relationship between Jesus and the church, he follows the example of the Evangelist in describing Peter and BD as possessing together the attributes of the ideal Johannine disciple.

In this chapter I examine Peter's actions in 21:1–11, the first "half" of the supplemental chapter, which includes the fishing expedition on the Sea of Tiberias (vv. 1–4) and the miraculous catch of fish (vv. 5–11). Chapter eight focuses on the conclusion of John 21, which incorporates Peter's threefold profession of love, his receipt of pastoral authority, and his final act of "following" Jesus.

DISASTER AT SEA: 21:1–3

^{1}After these things Jesus showed himself again to the disciples by the Sea of Tiberias; and he showed himself in this way. ^{2}Gathered there together were Simon Peter, Thomas called the Twin, Nathanael of Cana in Galilee, the sons of Zebedee, and two others of his disciples. ^{3}Simon Peter said to them, "I am going fishing." They said to him, "We will go

---

[1] Schnackenburg, *St. John*, 3.343, speaks specifically of Peter being invested with a pastoral "office" (see chapter 8). I will argue that BD's witness should also be construed as an "official" ministry.

with you." They went out and got into the boat, but that night they caught nothing. (¹Μετὰ ταῦτα ἐφανέρωσεν ἑαυτὸν πάλιν ὁ Ἰησοῦς τοῖς μαθηταῖς ἐπὶ τῆς θαλάσσης τῆς Τιβεριάδος· ἐφανέρωσεν δὲ οὕτως. ²ἦσαν ὁμοῦ Σίμων Πέτρος καὶ Θωμᾶς ὁ λεγόμενος Δίδυμος καὶ Ναθαναὴλ ὁ ἀπὸ Κανὰ τῆς Γαλιλαίας καὶ οἱ τοῦ Ζεβεδαίου καὶ ἄλλοι ἐκ τῶν μαθητῶν αὐτοῦ δύο. ³λέγει αὐτοῖς Σίμων Πέτρος· ὑπάγω ἁλιεύειν. λέγουσιν αὐτῷ· ἐρχόμεθα καὶ ἡμεῖς σὺν σοί. ἐξῆλθον καὶ ἐνέβησαν εἰς τὸ πλοῖον, καὶ ἐν ἐκείνῃ τῇ νυκτὶ ἐπίασαν οὐδέν.)

Simon Peter[2] is one of seven disciples who assemble in Galilee some time after the resurrection appearances in Jerusalem. No explanation is given for why this core group of disciples shrinks from twelve to seven in the time it takes to travel from Jerusalem to Galilee. The Redactor implies that this new, smaller group—led by Peter and BD—is the progenitor of the Johannine church.[3] In v. 2 the Redactor suggests that Peter is the leader of the disciples by listing his name first (cf. 6:68; 13:6, 9; 20:2–7) and by describing the other six as gathering "with Simon Peter" (ὁμοῦ Σίμων Πέτρος, v. 2).[4] When in v. 3 Peter makes the simple announcement, "I am going fishing," the others immediately agree to join him, and readers receive a further indication of his authority. Whatever other activities these six disciples might be involved in in Galilee, they are not so pressing that they must pause to deliberate the value of accompanying Peter. In accepting his invitation to go fishing, they appear to acknowledge him as the leader of the expedition.[5]

As was discussed in the previous chapter, two of the fishermen—the sons of Zebedee—are introduced for the first time in the Gospel in 21:2. They are, in a sense, Galilean stowaways, having been transplanted into John 21 as part of the Synoptic or pre-Synoptic Galilee-based fishing scene upon which the Redactor builds.[6] Unlike in the Synoptic Gospels, they are not given anything to do or say: they do not mend nets (Mark 1:19; Matt 4:21) or receive invitations to witness resuscitations (Mark 5:37; Luke 8:51) or request prominent seats in

---

[2] Peter is referred to as "Simon Peter" on fourteen occasions in John's Gospel. In the Synoptic Gospels he is described this way only twice (Matt 16:16; Luke 5:8).

[3] Chennattu, *Johannine Discipleship*, 167, is right to describe this group of seven as "the founding members of the community."

[4] "Das zeigt schon in den ersten Sätzen an, dass Petrus in der Erzählung eine zentrale Rolle spielen wird." Van Tilborg, *Johannesevangelium*, 310. So Schneiders, *Written that You May Believe*, 204.

[5] Simon, *Petrus und der Lieblingsjünger*, 172, calls Peter "der Initiator des Fischfangs." He says, "er gibt nicht nur die Anregung, er setzt sie auch in die Tat um, und die anderen Jünger erklären in v. 3 ausdrücklich, ihm zu folgen." Van Tilborg, *Johannesevangelium*, 307, calls Peter the disciples' "Vormann."

[6] See chapter 6.

God's kingdom (Mark 10:35–37; cf. Matt 20:20). In fact, they do not tell us anything about the Redactor's theology of discipleship.

Two other disciples, Nathanael and Thomas Didymus, are similarly silent throughout the pericope, but they *do* hold meaning for John's audience, having established themselves as important characters in the Gospel. Nathanael, one of the first to express faith in Jesus (he hails him as the "Son of God" in the opening call narrative; 1:49) and Thomas, the very last disciple to come to faith in him (he confesses the risen Jesus as "my Lord and my God"; 20:28) represent the faith journey of the Johannine Christian, which begins in accepting the call to discipleship and reaches its zenith in confessing Jesus as God. In describing Nathanael as "Nathanael from Cana," the Redactor reminds us of the location of the first σημεῖον performed by Jesus (2:1–11). Just as Jesus filled water pots with wine in Cana of Galilee, so he will fill nets with fish on the Sea of Tiberias in Galilee in 21:5–6, and thus we have an *inclusio* focused on God's providence.[7] Two additional disciples join Peter on the voyage, but their names are not given. In 21:7 we learn that one of them is BD, for he surfaces in dramatic fashion as the boat's lookout. About the seventh fisherman we learn nothing more.[8]

Peter's decision to go fishing does not appear to the reader to be a hasty one. The phrase he uses to announce the venture, ὑπάγω ἁλιεύειν, is an infinitive of purpose, which is rare in John's Gospel but which, when it does occur, describes decisions made with great resolve (cf. 4:7 and 14:2).[9] The Greek word for "boat," πλοῖον, appears in v. 3 with the definite article, suggesting that Peter has picked a rendezvous spot near a familiar vessel. Were πλοῖον to appear without the definite article, one could perhaps make a case that the group's decision to go fishing is an impromptu or desperate act (i.e., they see a boat and, lacking other options, climb in to go fishing). As it is, there is a subtle implication that the disciples have met at a predetermined location and that Peter has fishing in mind.[10] There is, however, little to recommend the

---

[7] See the discussion in M. Franzmann and M. Klinger, "The Call Stories of John 1 and John 21," *SVTQ* 36 (1992): 7–16. As we have seen, the Evangelist does not anticipate the addition of the Redactor, and so the inclusio is the product of the editorial expansion.

[8] This final disciple may represent the Evangelist or perhaps the implied reader, or it may be that the Redactor is following the Evangelist's pattern of having disciples following Jesus in pairs (cf. 1:35–40, 45; 13:23–25; 18:15–16; 20:2–10; cf. also 8:17 and 11:1–20).

[9] Brown, *John*, 2.1068, notes that infinitives of purpose are more typical of the Gospels of Matthew and Luke. Barrett, *St. John*, 579, underscores the similarities between this verse and the fragmentary verse in the *Gospel of Peter*, 60: "And I, Simon Peter, and Andrew my brother, we took our fishing nets and went off to sea, and with us was Levi the son of Alphaeus, whom the Lord...."

[10] Beasley-Murray, *John*, 399, is, in my opinion, right to reject the argument of Brown (*John*, 2.1096) that the expedition is an act of "desperation."

suggestion of Barrett that Peter's words are meant to "be seen to have a double meaning and refer to the apostolic mission of catching men."[11] At this point in the story—prior to the reunion with Jesus—these seven individuals are the ones in need of "catching" (evangelism). Their pretensions of self-sufficiency have supplanted the missionary mandate of 20:21–23. Or, to put it differently, it is dinner they are concerned with, not promulgating the Christ faith. Not until Jesus appears and teaches the disciples how to fish (or, perhaps more accurately, what to fish *for*) and invests Peter with the responsibility of safely delivering the catch does "fishing" become a clear missionary metaphor.

As was discussed in the previous chapter of this study, the decision to go fishing and the resulting empty catch represent a startling turn of events compared with 20:21–23, where the disciples were literally bombarded with responsibility and good fortune, having received from Jesus (1) a commission to go into the world (20:21); (2) the gift of the Holy Spirit (20:22); and (3) the authority to forgive sins (20:23). One does not immediately think of the Sea of Tiberias as the best place to seek and forgive sinners, just as one finds it difficult to imagine how seven individuals empowered by the Holy Spirit could fail to catch any fish. Jesus' promise to send (ἀποστέλλω) them into the world to forgive sins has been converted into an opportunity to return home and fish for dinner in the district where the ministry began (1:40–44), a mundane task at which they fail.[12]

As is frequently the case in chapters 1–20, darkness enters the story in John 21 as a symbol for powerlessness, ignorance, or despair (21:3; cf. 1:5; 3:19; 6:17; 8:12; 11:10; 12:46; and 13:30). Peter's seemingly sound decision to set off on a nighttime fishing expedition—"sound" because night is a good time to catch fish and because a nighttime catch increases the odds of getting the fish to market before incurring spoilage—is foiled by the oppressive Johannine night.[13] Not only does the darkness represent the absence of Jesus, it reveals the

---

[11] See Barrett, *St. John*, 579.

[12] After noting that the risen Jesus has demonstrated an ability to "disappear for a whole week" at a time in between resurrection appearances (20:25–26), C. L. Blomberg, *The Historical Reliability of John's Gospel: Issues and Commentary* (Downer's Grove, Illinois: InterVarsity, 2001), 274, suggests that Peter and the others are simply making good use of their time as they wait for their next encounter with Jesus. So F. F. Bruce, *The Gospel of John* (Basingstoke: Pickering & Inglis; Grand Rapids: Eerdmans, 1983), 399. But it is difficult to believe that seven fishermen making good use of their time (and empowered by the Holy Spirit!) would be unable to catch a single fish over the course of one night. What is more believable is that the Redactor has affixed to the Gospel a new resurrection story in which the disciples have not yet been empowered by the Spirit and/or in which their misfortune on the lake represents a period of despair suffered by the Johannine community in the wake of BD's death.

[13] See B. Milne, *The Message of John* (Downer's Grove, Illinois: InterVarsity, 1993), 310.

THE MIRACULOUS CATCH OF FISH   147

inadequacies of self-reliance. For all Peter's experience—and, we assume, knowledge about the habits of fish and fishmongers—the decision to fish at night backfires. The expedition sets out in one kind of darkness and ends up in another. Peter's six associates are unable to offer him any assistance because they are equally guilty of embarking on the wrong kind of fishing mission, one concerned with food rather than evangelism. The reader familiar with 11:10 ("If anyone walks in the night, he stumbles, because the light is not with him") and 15:5 ("apart from me you can do nothing") may suspect that the fishing trip was doomed from the start, undertaken outside the presence of Jesus / the light. Indeed, the disciples' decision to go fishing in the aftermath of the resurrection mocks the notion of Jesus as the true sustenance (cf. 6:27, 55).[14]

More than a few Johannine commentators assume that the fishing boat in John 21 is a symbol for the church, but this is probably not the case.[15] The activity replete with missionary themes in John 21 (esp. vv. 6–11) is not boating but *fishing*. It is not until the disciples step on dry land that they experience a reunion with Jesus. To put it another way, fellowship with Jesus does not commence until the disciples disembark. If Johannine fellowship is to be understood as the gathering of believers in the presence of Christ (cf. 6:67–71; 10:16; 11:52; 13:1–11; 20:19–28), the boat is an inadequate symbol for the church.[16]

A Change in Fortune: 21:4–6

⁴Just after daybreak, Jesus stood on the beach; but the disciples did not know that it was Jesus. ⁵Jesus said to them, "Children, you have no fish, have you?" They answered him, "No." ⁶He said to them, "Cast the net to the right side of the boat, and you will find some." So they cast it, and now they were not able to haul it in because there were so many fish. (⁴πρωΐας δὲ ἤδη γενομένης ἔστη Ἰησοῦς εἰς τὸν αἰγιαλόν, οὐ μέντοι ᾔδεισαν οἱ μαθηταὶ ὅτι Ἰησοῦς ἐστιν. ⁵λέγει οὖν αὐτοῖς [ὁ]

---

[14] Koester, *Symbolism in the Fourth Gospel*, 168, correctly points out that the darkness in John 21, while oppressive, "does not carry the sense of sin or evil found elsewhere in John."

[15] See the discussion in Crosby, *"Do you Love me?"* 188. This is not to deny that the "boat" eventually came to be a symbol for the church in early Christianity or that it (perhaps) plays this role in John 6:17–21, in which the disciples' attempt to take Jesus into their storm-tossed boat is a communal action designed to ensure a safe voyage. On the boat as symbol for the church in John 6, see Brodie, *Gospel According to John*, 277.

[16] Jesus' words to the Samaritan woman in 4:21, "Woman, believe me, the hour is coming when you will worship the Father neither on this mountain nor in Jerusalem," underscore the community's belief that worship is a spiritual practice to be carried out "in spirit and truth" (ἐν πνεύματι καὶ ἀληθείᾳ) and not within the confines of a specific place.

Ἰησοῦς· παιδία, μή τι προσφάγιον ἔχετε; ἀπεκρίθησαν αὐτῷ· οὔ. ⁶ὁ δὲ εἶπεν αὐτοῖς· βάλετε εἰς τὰ δεξιὰ μέρη τοῦ πλοίου τὸ δίκτυον, καὶ εὑρήσετε. ἔβαλον οὖν, καὶ οὐκέτι αὐτὸ ἑλκύσαι ἴσχυον ἀπὸ τοῦ πλήθους τῶν ἰχθύων.)

The appearance on the beach of the risen Christ, described as the "light of the world" in 8:12 and 9:5–6, is accompanied appropriately enough by the rising of the sun.[17] The disciples do not immediately recognize him, which is sometimes adduced by scholars as evidence that John 21 was not originally attached to the Gospel, since, it is argued, disciples already familiar with the risen Jesus' outward appearance (20:19–29) would not now fail to recognize him. But it is something of a stock scene in the NT for individuals to encounter difficulty in discerning the identity of the risen Christ (cf. Luke 24:31; John 20:14, 20), and there is therefore no need to posit their failure to recognize Jesus as evidence of redactional activity.

Jesus calls out to the disciples in 21:5: "Children, you haven't caught any fish, have you?" (παιδία, μή τι προσφάγιον ἔχετε;). From the negative particle μή we immediately suspect he knows the truth of the matter.[18] When they admit that they have thus far failed, he commands them to cast the net on the right (δεξιός) side of the boat, where their luck will change. Bernard's suggestion that Jesus picks one side of the boat for fishing in order to free up the other side for Peter's dramatic leap overboard (21:7) is ingenious but not convincing.[19] Brown and Barrett independently mull over the idea that δεξιός means "fortunate," meaning the right side of the boat is the auspicious side, but they eventually reject this idea in favor of the idea that Jesus gives the disciples a specific command about where to fish so that, in following it, they will demonstrate that obedience to Jesus reaps rewards.[20] This seems to me the correct interpretation. L. Morris and J. C. Laney suggest that a person standing on the shore would be in a better position to judge the position of a school of fish relative to a boat than

---

[17] Πρωΐας appears elsewhere in the NT only in Matt 27:1, where it means "morning." A related word, πρωϊνός, appears in Rev 2:28 and 22:16 and describes Jesus as the "morning star."

[18] Malina and Rohrbaugh, *Social-Science Commentary*, 113, suggest that "children" (παιδία) in v. 5 is short for "children of God," as in John 1:12 and 1 John 3:1. But I think it more likely that παιδία is used as a filial diminutive, as in 13:33 (τεκνία, ἔτι μικρὸν μεθ' ὑμῶν εἰμι). So Ridderbos, *Gospel of John*, 660.

[19] See Bernard, *St. John*, 2.696.

[20] Brown, *John*, 2.1071; Barrett, *St. John*, 580. See also R. Kysar, *John* (ACNT; Minneapolis: Augsburg, 1986), 313–14. In Matt 25:33–34, Jesus' right side is the auspicious side, for it is there that the elect "sheep" are gathered; the "goats" gather ignominiously on his left. Augustine (*Homilies on John's Gospel*, 122.7) maintains that fish caught on the right side of the boat represent people worthy of eternal life. See the discussion in Edwards, *John*, 203.

would the boat's occupants, and therefore submit the idea that Jesus' knowledge about the shoal is a natural phenomenon, gleaned with a sharp eye.[21] The simplest explanation, of course, is that the Johannine Jesus possesses supernatural knowledge![22]

However the fish are detected, the net is cast in the correct place and the resultant haul is so great that the disciples cannot pull the fish aboard. The magnitude of the miracle is thus emphasized, with the message being that God's providence is secured through Jesus (cf. 4:32–34; 6:11–14; 6:27, 48). The story "symbolizes the effective authorization and promise of the Risen One to fulfil the missionary mandate that he has given to his disciples."[23]

PETER AND THE BELOVED DISCIPLE TAKE CENTER STAGE: 21:7–8

⁷That disciple whom Jesus loved said to Peter, "It is the Lord!" When Simon Peter heard that it was the Lord, he put on some clothes, for he was naked, and jumped into the sea. ⁸But the other disciples came in the boat, dragging the net full of fish, for they were not far from the land, only about a hundred yards off. (⁷λέγει οὖν ὁ μαθητὴς ἐκεῖνος ὃν ἠγάπα ὁ Ἰησοῦς τῷ Πέτρῳ· ὁ κύριός ἐστιν. Σίμων οὖν Πέτρος ἀκούσας ὅτι ὁ κύριός ἐστιν τὸν ἐπενδύτην διεζώσατο, ἦν γὰρ γυμνός, καὶ ἔβαλεν ἑαυτὸν εἰς τὴν θάλασσαν, ⁸οἱ δὲ ἄλλοι μαθηταὶ τῷ πλοιαρίῳ ἦλθον, οὐ γὰρ ἦσαν μακρὰν ἀπὸ τῆς γῆς ἀλλὰ ὡς ἀπὸ πηχῶν διακοσίων, σύροντες τὸ δίκτυον τῶν ἰχθύων.)

Of all the verses in John's Gospel, 21:7 is the one that best showcases the positive attributes of BD while simultaneously lauding the achievements of Peter. The faith-enriched perceptual powers of BD allow him to discern the figure of Jesus on the shore—or perhaps recognize the catch of fish as a sign pointing to Jesus. It has been said, and I think correctly, that his great confessional cry, "It is the Lord!"[24] (v. 7), "encapsulates not only the surprise and the wonder but also the relief of the disciples on recognising Jesus as risen

---

[21] See L. Morris, *Gospel According to John* (rev. ed.; NICNT; Grand Rapids: Eerdmans, 1995), 762; and J. C. Laney, *John* (Moody Gospel Commentary; Chicago: Moody, 1992), 375.

[22] This is the most popular argument today and was also popular with the church fathers. One church father who disagrees with this theory is Augustine, who maintains that the fish caught on the right side of the boat represent people worthy of eternal life. (*Homilies* 122:7). See the discussion in Edwards, *John*, 203.

[23] Ridderbos, *Gospel of John*, 660. So Hooker, *Endings*, 77: "Like the saying in Mark 1.17, we may assume that this is to be interpreted as a command to evangelize."

[24] D ὁ κύριός ἐστιν ἡμῶν.

from the dead, *and recognising him as Lord*" (emphasis in original).[25] And yet BD delivers this confessional cry specifically to Peter.[26] His flash of faith has opened the door for Peter to act. Peter is so stirred by the news that he quickly covers himself and leaps into the sea to swim to Jesus.[27] "The author apparently wants to show how much the observation of the beloved disciple affected Peter and how ardently Peter longed to be with Jesus."[28] M. D. Hooker agrees that Peter's enthusiasm, by now a familiar characteristic, is on display here: "Impulsive as ever, it is Peter who jumps into the sea to go to Jesus (v. 7), just as he had rushed first into the tomb (20.6)."[29] R. M. Chennattu sums up the contributions and attributes of both disciples this way:

> [A]s with the empty tomb (20:8), it is the Beloved Disciple who recognizes the presence of Jesus among the disciples. The impetuous character of Peter is evident in his response of casting himself into the sea (21:7; see also Matt 14:28–32). In other words, by this narrative, the contemplative perception and receptivity of the Beloved Disciple (20:8; 21:7) and the impetuosity of Peter are reconfirmed (20:6; 21:7). God continues to manifest himself to the world, but the recognition and deep appreciation of the divine presence and action in human history is one of the challenges faced by the new covenant community.[30]

---

[25] Redford, *Bad, Mad or God?*, 296. Hooker, *Endings*, 76, with many others, suggests that it is BD's intimacy with Jesus that makes recognition of him possible. R. A. Culpepper, "The Plot of John's Story of Jesus," in *Gospel Interpretation: Narrative-Critical & Social-Scientific Approaches* (ed. J. D. Kingsbury; Harrisburg, Penn.: Trinity Press International, 1997), 198, says that "[c]haracteristically, it is the Beloved Disciple who recognizes the risen Lord first."

[26] Haenchen, *John 2*, 223, does not believe BD shares his discovery with the other fishermen: "In chapter 21, he shares his conviction with Peter: 'It is the Lord,' but he remains glued to the spot and does not seem to have communicated his conviction to the other disciples."

[27] Simon, *Petrus und der Lieblingsjünger*, 173, notes that BD's statement to Peter—which is the only conversation they engage in (one-sided or otherwise)—has "a spontaneous, emphatic effect" (*eine spontane, emphatische Wirkung*) on Peter, inciting the leap. T. Thatcher, "Jesus, Judas, and Peter: Character by Contrast in the Fourth Gospel," *BibSac* 153 (1996): 446, says of the scene that Peter throws "himself into the sea in a fit of exuberance."

[28] Haenchen, *John 2*, 223.

[29] Hooker, *Endings*, 76. After stating that BD is "again a step ahead of Peter" in being the first to spot Jesus on the shore, Ridderbos, *Gospel of John*, 660, describes Peter's emotional mindset in a manner similar to Hooker's: "Peter reacts immediately, in a way that is no less characteristic for him."

[30] Chennattu, *Johannine Discipleship*, 170.

T. Söding argues that Peter's motive for leaping overboard is simple: "Er wirft sich in den See, um als erster bei Jesus zu sein."[31] Bultmann is another who suggests that Peter leaps overboard to get to Jesus quickly, and adds that Peter chooses swimming instead of sailing because he knows that the boat is burdened with fish and its journey will therefore be slow.[32] Because one cannot easily get inside the mind of a literary construct, however, it is perhaps more accurate to say that the Redactor conveys the impression that Peter's leap is both purposeful and zealous, and that his goal is to "reach Jesus as soon as possible."[33]

It is interesting that, just before Peter leaps, he takes a moment to wrap his outer garments around himself (ἐπενδύτην διεζώσατο), covering up his nakedness or perhaps his thin undergarments.[34] A variety of symbolic interpretations has been put forward throughout the centuries to explain the behavior of dressing before swimming. One of the more common holds that the "nakedness" Peter hastens to cover is the nakedness of the unresolved shame he feels for having denied Jesus (discussed below).[35] In my opinion, the oldest explanation is still the most compelling: Peter deems it inappropriate to meet the risen Lord while naked or scantily clad and therefore throws on an extra covering—or, at the very least, "tucks in" the undergarment he already wears.[36]

---

[31] T. Söding, "Erscheinung, Vergebung und Sendung (Joh 21)," in *Resurrection in the New Testament* (ed. R. Bieringer, V. Koperski, and B. Lataire; BETL 165; Leuven: Leuven University Press, 2002), 223. The propriety of the leap is discussed below.

[32] Bultmann, *Gospel of John*, 702.

[33] Ibid., 702. So Schenke, *Johannesevangelium*, 111.

[34] I agree with de Boor, *Evangelium des Johannes*, 255, that Peter is probably not completely naked but dressed in "leichte Bekleidung," as befitting difficult work carried out in chilly conditions. So Moloney, *John*, 553.

[35] H. Thyen, "Entwicklungen," 263–64. So S. Agourides, "The Purpose of John 21," in *Studies in the History and Text of the New Testament: in Honor of K. W. Clark* (eds. B. Daniels and M. Suggs; Salt Lake City: University of Utah, 1967), 128. According to Stibbe, *John*, 211, the shame Peter feels as he leaps overboard is a hauntingly familiar sensation: "there is clearly a root of toxic shame in Peter's life even before his rejection of Jesus in the courtyard of Annas." Stibbe continues: "If Peter had no shame, then, like Jesus in John 13:3–5, he would be able to stand naked before others. However, unlike Adam and Eve before the fall, Peter is unable to be naked and unafraid." To say that Stibbe reads a great deal into the text is to understate the case.

[36] Brown, *John*, 2.1072, translates ἐπενδύτην διεζώσατο as "tucked in his outer garments," which fits with the idea that a fisherman who had just worked through the cool of the night would not be naked. Barrett, *John*, 2.580, points out the religious considerations of covering up before engaging in social interactions, noting that "to offer greeting (שאל שלום) was a religious act and could not be performed without clothing." Gee, "Why Did Peter Spring into the Sea?," 480, is one of the many scholars who believe what Peter hastens to cover is his shame, but he goes a step farther than most in saying that this "covering" is a necessary preparation for Peter's new life, which will begin as

Contextually, such behavior makes sense, for the Jewish aversion to nakedness is well documented in early literature (Gen 3:7; 10–11; *Jub.* 3:21–22, 30–31; 7:8–10; 1QS 7:12–14; *t. Ber.* 2:14), and it is the case that certain Gentiles at this time expressed embarrassment about public nudity as well (see Juvenal *Sat.* 1.71; Plutarch *R. Q.* 40; *Mor.* 274A; Diogenes Laertius 2.73).[37]

Regrettably, it is quite common for commentators to view Peter's leap overboard with cynicism. When the cynicism is mild, Peter is described as well-meaning but buffoonish, plunging into the sea with much drama but without much sense, not pausing to consider that sailing might be a more efficient way of covering one hundred yards of water.[38] According to this argument, his zeal is more reckless than admirable, and his leap is meant to remind readers of his impetuous attack on the six hundred Romans in the garden (18:10–11) and his request to have Jesus wash his head and hands as well as his feet (13:4–9). When the cynicism is severe, Peter is described as a pathetic coward who leaps into the water to swim *away* from Jesus, haunted by the shame of denying him (18:17–27).

D. H. Gee—whose antipathy for the Johannine Peter is rarely matched in modern scholarship—maintains that Peter commits four specific shameful acts in this pericope. First, he leaps into the water to swim away from Jesus; second, he "skulks" in the water while the others sail to Jesus; third, he continues "skulking" while the others rendezvous with Jesus and gather around the charcoal fire; and fourth, he agrees to fetch the full net of fish not out of love for Jesus but to postpone the inevitable shaming "confrontation with the Lord."[39]

---

soon as he evades Jesus. But would a lost tunic not be the least of Peter's troubles in such a situation?

[37] See Keener, *Gospel of John*, 2.1229 n. 29. See also Rev 16:15: "See, I am coming like a thief! Blessed is the one who stays awake and is clothed, not going about naked and exposed to shame." Nothing suggests that the Redactor knows the Markan anecdote of the naked young man fleeing the scene of Jesus' arrest in Gethsemane (Mark 14:52)—a scene sometimes thought to have post-resurrectional roots—but it is interesting that in the Markan story the reaction of a man stripped naked is to flee from Jesus and in John's Gospel the reaction of a naked man confronted by Jesus is to clothe himself.

[38] See Maynard, "Role of Peter," 531–48. Van Tilborg, *Johannesevangelium*, 310, argues that Peter, in his haste to reach Jesus, forgets to bring the net ashore, leaving the important missionary task to the other fishermen: "Das Verhalten der anderen Jünger dient als Kontrast. Sie kommen mit dem Boot und ziehen das Netz [21,8]. Es braucht aus Menschen, die das notwendige Tagewerk zu einem guten Ende bringen." But such an argument fails to obscure the textual fact that Peter alone is presented as steward of the catch (v. 11).

[39] Gee, "Why did Peter Spring into the Sea?," 481–89. Goulder, *St. Paul versus St. Peter*, 22, believes that Peter's miscues and stumbles in the Gospel are the result of one or more anti-Petrine writer(s) engaging in "character assassination." He also argues that Peter is characterized more positively in Matthew's Gospel than John's Gospel because "Matthew was a Petrine" (p. 188). I have argued that one of the drawbacks of identifying

Although there is nothing in the text to substantiate any of these claims, it must be said in Gee's defense that he is not alone in his belief that Peter jumps into the water to swim away from Jesus.[40]

When we look at the Greek of 21:8a, however (οἱ δὲ ἄλλοι μαθηταὶ τῷ πλοιαρίῳ ἦλθον), what becomes clear is that the verse is constructed to show Peter coming to Jesus by one route (swimming) while the others come to him by another route (sailing). There is not even a faint implication in the text that he swims *away* from Jesus. If the Redactor were interested in describing some sort of escape attempt, would he bother to repeat the detail about the other six disciples being in the boat? It seems unlikely. The reader already knows where they are. Their position in the boat is highlighted in 21:8 to differentiate their mode of travel from Peter's.[41] That Peter swims *to* Jesus and not *away* from him is confirmed in v. 11 when he obeys an order from Jesus to return to the water and retrieve the net. To believe that his first act upon hearing BD's confessional cry is to swim *away* from Jesus is also to believe that subsequent to that maneuver he changes his mind and swims back toward Jesus, but that the Redactor lets the change in course (and thinking) go unreported.

As mentioned, 21:7 casts both Peter and BD in a very positive light, describing them as two disciples who, as a team, coordinate and expedite the encounter with Jesus. But the verse also shows that neither disciple by himself embodies perfect discipleship. The faith of BD is impressive, as is Peter's zeal, yet Peter does not have sufficient faith to recognize Jesus on the shore, and BD does not have sufficient zeal to join him in a leap overboard, expediting the reunion with Jesus. As in all the other scenes in which they appear, they model the finer points of Johannine discipleship through their combined actions. The reader is meant to discover that the ideal Johannine Christian—again, understood to be an amalgam of Peter and BD—must have both faith and zeal.

John's Gospel as "anti-Petrine" is that it encourages theories of ecclesial development in which the Johannine and Apostolic churches are seen to have suffered through a period of estrangement. In fact, we have no idea how those churches felt about one another. The theory of Charlesworth, *Beloved Disciple*, 391, that "Peter obviously represents the West" and the Beloved Disciple "certainly symbolizes the East" perpetuates this mistaken idea that the Fourth Gospel presents Johannine and Apostolic Christianity as ideologically and geographically distinct entities.

[40] See the discussion in Perkins, *Peter*, 99. C. R. Koester, *Symbolism in the Fourth Gospel*, 137, makes this observation: "It is also striking that the text does not actually say that Peter swam to Jesus, but that he 'cast himself into the sea'; and elsewhere in scripture, that which is 'cast into the sea' is usually marked for destruction—something that was also true of Peter."

[41] Simon, *Petrus und der Lieblingsjünger*, 173, agrees, but asserts somewhat casually that the disciples "obviously" (*offensichtlich*) get to the beach ahead of Peter. Considering that they must drag behind them a net too heavy to haul aboard ship, is it wise to infer this?

To put it another way, believers must be able to perceive Jesus in the most desperate of situations and be willing to put in the work necessary to follow him. One is hard pressed to find another verse in the Gospel that so efficiently reminds the reader that Johannine discipleship consists of both believing (cf. 1:7; 3:18; 4:21, 42; 6:29; 9:38; 10:38; 12:11; 17:30) *and* following (cf. 1:38–43; 6:2; 10:4–5; 27; 12:26; 13:36–37; 20:6; 21:19–22).[42]

MISSIONARY WORK: 21:9–11

⁹When they had gone ashore, they saw a charcoal fire there, with fish on it, and bread. ¹⁰ Jesus said to them, "Bring some of the fish that you have just caught." ¹¹ So Simon Peter went aboard and hauled the net ashore, full of large fish, a hundred fifty-three of them; and though there were so many, the net was not torn. (⁹ὡς οὖν ἀπέβησαν εἰς τὴν γῆν βλέπουσιν ἀνθρακιὰν κειμένην καὶ ὀψάριον ἐπικείμενον καὶ ἄρτον. ¹⁰λέγει αὐτοῖς ὁ Ἰησοῦς· ἐνέγκατε ἀπὸ τῶν ὀψαρίων ὧν ἐπιάσατε νῦν.¹¹ ἀνέβη οὖν Σίμων Πέτρος καὶ εἵλκυσεν τὸ δίκτυον εἰς τὴν γῆν μεστὸν ἰχθύων μεγάλων ἑκατὸν πεντήκοντα τριῶν· καὶ τοσούτων ὄντων οὐκ ἐσχίσθη τὸ δίκτυον.)

When the disciples finally make land (v. 9), they discover Jesus cooking fish on a charcoal fire. He has some bread as well. Despite the fact that he has breakfast prepared, he commands the disciples to "bring some of the fish that you have caught" (v. 10). The redundancy here may be accidental, brought about by the combining of different traditions (i.e., miracle catch narrative [cf. Luke 5:1–11] and post-Easter breakfast narrative [cf. Luke 24:30, 42–43]), or it may be strategic, designed to show that Jesus provides sustenance in a variety of ways. Or it may be that there is only an illusion of redundancy here, and that two distinct images are being provided, one in which Jesus provides fish for the group (i.e., sustenance for the church) and one in which the disciples submit to the task of increasing the size of his congregation.

It is worth noting that Peter is the only one of the disciples who responds to Jesus' command to bring the fish to land, even though the command is issued to the group as a whole (λέγει αὐτοῖς ὁ Ἰησοῦς, v. 10). The positive nature of his response is not obscured by zeal or impetuousness, as some would argue is the case in 21:7. He is vividly depicted as climbing aboard (ἀναβαίνω) the boat to draw (ἕλκω) the net to shore, which he then manages not to tear (v. 11). The verb

---

[42] Busse, *Johannesevangelium*, 265, suggests that Jesus has been waiting for Peter to "follow" him for some time: "Petrus hat ihm, wenn er Hals über kopf bekleidet ins Wasser springt – was mit Blick auf 13,9b ja auch bewußt ironisch erzählt wird – mit diesen Begleitumständen, wenn auch verspätet, endlich signalisiert, was Jesus längst von ihm erwartet hatte."

ἕλκω is well suited in the Fourth Gospel for describing missionary work. In fact, other than in this instance, it is used only to describe people being "drawn" to Jesus (here and 12:32) or to the Father (6:44). The message is plain enough: Peter draws people to Jesus just as Jesus draws them to the Father.[43]

When the Redactor writes of a δίκτυον (vv. 8, 11), he is referring to a large casting net that was typically deployed by fishermen when fishing among shoals. Unlike smaller seine pole-nets used by individual fishermen, δίκτυα were delicate and prone to ripping (hence the believability of the Synoptic scene in which James and John are busy mending [καταρτίζω] nets when called by Jesus [Mark 1:19; Matt 4:21]).[44] Hauling a full δίκτυον to shore without incurring a tear would have been recognized by John's audience as an impressive feat.

Paradoxically, what the disciples had been unable to do as a group—haul to shore a heavy net—Peter accomplishes by himself. The scene makes little sense unless the catch represents something other than aquatic fish, for the sheer weight of a load of actual fish would not be easier for Peter to handle alone than for the seven disciples to transport as a team. Most scholars conclude that Peter's ability to retrieve the large catch without damaging the net symbolizes his talent for bringing people to Christ. "The fact that Peter has a prominent role in this portrayal of salvation indicates that, while providence is universal, it works in a special way through Peter. And that, in turn, implies a special role and responsibility for the church."[45] If Peter's hauling of the net represents his proclivity for missionary work,[46] then his ability to perform the chore without losing any of the contents brings to mind 17:12 and the theme of *perfect shepherding*. It is in that verse that Jesus says to the Father, "While I was with them, I protected them in your name that you have given me. I guarded them, and not one of them was lost except the one destined to be lost, so that the

---

[43] Brown, *John*, 2.1097; Chennattu, *Johannine Discipleship*, 172.

[44] For detailed information on first-century fishing during the time of Jesus, see M. Nun, "The Sea of Galilee and its Fishermen in the New Testament," (Ein Gev, Israel: Kibbutz Ein Gev, 1989). Cited 15 January 2004. Online: http://www.ubfellowship.org/archive/j_arc/fishing2.htm.

[45] Brodie, *Gospel According to John*, 586. A similar interpretation is offered by Hooker, *Endings*, 75: "Jesus commissions his disciples to make still more disciples, and he entrusts Peter the task of caring for them."

[46] Schnackenburg, *St. John*, 3.365–66, is rare in not detecting missionary images in 21:11. For the idea that drawing the net ashore does symbolize missionary work—sometimes understood to incorporate apostolic preaching—see especially Bultmann, *Gospel of John*, 709; Brown, *John*, 2.1098; E. Ruckstuhl, "Zur Aussage und Botschaft von Johannes 21," in *Die Kirche des Anfangs* (ed. R. Schnackenburg, J. Ernst, and J. Wanke; Freiburg: Herder, 1978), 345–48; Wilckens, *Evangelium nach Johannes*, 324; and A. Shaw, "Image and Symbol in John 21," *ET* 86 (1975): 311.

scripture might be fulfilled" (cf. 18:9). Like Jesus, Peter does not lose any of the charges entrusted to him.

In attempting to explain why the Redactor bothers to record the specific size of the catch ("153 large fish"), commentators have come up with a number of interesting theories. Augustine (*Tr. Ev. John.* 122.8) describes 153 as a perfect triangular number, comprising the numbers from 1 to 17. Cyril of Alexandria maintains that the number is the sum of 100 (the fullness of the Gentiles) plus 50 (the remnant of Israel) plus 3 (the Trinity).[47] Evagrius Ponticus (345–399 C.E.) considers 100 to represent the square, 28 the triangle, and 25 the circle.[48] Among modern scholars, B. Witherington claims that ancient zoologists counted 153 species of fish in the world, which would mean that the portrayal of Peter handling a catch of that size conveys his ability to attract the widest possible variety of people to the church.[49] A. Guilding finds a tie-in between John 21:11 and 1 Kgs 5:1–18, in which a combined force of 153,000 people build Solomon's Temple.[50] Sanders and Mastin suggest that the author uses *gematria* (the substitution of numbers for Hebrew letters to conceal meanings) to arrive at a number representing "the full total of the catholic and apostolic Church."[51]

A simpler—but, I fear, less convincing—explanation for why the specific number "153" is given is that it is not a symbolic number but that the author or one of his sources remembered such a tally from a historical catch of fish. R. Bauckham is one who believes the memory of a real catch of fish informs the verse. He counsels against removing the catch from its Johannine, post-Easter origin and seeing it as a transposition of a miracle story set during Jesus' earthly ministry (cf. Luke 5:1–11), as is sometimes done. Bauckham contends that

---

[47] Discussed in Brodie, *John*, 586.

[48] Cited in Grün, *Jesus: Tür zum Leben*, 148.

[49] See the discussion in Witherington, *John's Wisdom*, 355.

[50] A. Guilding, *The Fourth Gospel and Jewish Worship: A Study of St. John's Gospel to the Ancient Jewish Lectionary System* (Oxford: Clarendon, 1960), 226ff.

[51] J. N. Sanders and B. A. Mastin, *A Commentary on the Gospel According to St. John* (HNTC; New York: Harper & Brothers, 1957), 447–48. Other scholars have employed Gematria to reach all sorts of conclusions about the catch. One of the more interesting describes 153 as the combined numeric equivalent of the letters in *En-egedi* and *En-Eglaim*, the two points of land from which people "spread their nets" and catch "a great many kinds of fish" in Ezekiel's vision (Ezek 47:10). On this interpretation see also C. K. Barrett, *St. John*, 581–82; and P. Trudinger, "The 153 Fishes: A Response and a Further Suggestion," *ET* 102 (1990–91): 11–12. Other inventive theories involving Gematria can be found in J. A. Emerton, "The Hundred and Fifty-Three Fishes in John 21," *JTS* 9 (1958): 86–89; R. M. Grant, "One Hundred Fifty-three Large Fishes," *HTR* 42 (1949): 273–75; and N. J. McEleney, "153 Great Fishes—Gematriachal Atbash," *Bib* 58 (1977) 411–17.

"153" comes from the memory of BD himself.[52] R. E. Brown, who is generally cautious about ascribing historicity to miracle stories, also maintains that "authentic eye-witness" informs the tradition. If symbolism were the Redactor's goal, Brown argues, the Evangelist would use a "more obviously symbolic number."[53] H. E. Edwards maintains that Peter, an experienced fisherman, counted the fish himself as a prelude to dividing the profits of the catch among his colleagues evenly.[54] If the preceding analysis in this chapter is correct, however, and Peter's catch is a metaphorical representation of his missionary capability, then the number "153" has a specific but now-lost symbolic meaning.

In contrast to Luke's miraculous catch of fish pericope (5:1–11), in which the nets are described as so full they "were beginning to break" (διερρήσσετο), the Johannine Redactor emphasizes that the net remains un-torn (οὐκ ἐσχίσθη, 21:11).[55] The image brings to mind an earlier theme and theological symbol in the Gospel: unity. Just as Jesus' garment is described as being "without seam" (ἄραφος, 19:23), representing the solidarity of Father and Son at the hour of his

---

[52] See R. Bauckham, "The Audience of the Fourth Gospel," in *Jesus in Johannine Tradition* (ed. R. T. Fortna and T. Thatcher; Louisville: Westminster John Knox, 2001), 111.

[53] Brown, *John*, 2.1076.

[54] H. E. Edwards, *The Disciple Who Wrote these Things: A New Inquiry into the Origins and Historical Value of the Gospel according to St. John* (London: J. Clarke, 1953), 180.

[55] This chapter originally contained a lengthy excursus examining the relationship between Luke's miraculous catch of fish pericope (Luke 5:1–11) and John 21:1–11. Unfortunately, it proved somewhat distracting to a narrative study of Peter in John's Gospel. Because I have mentioned similarities between John 21 and Luke 5 several times in this discussion, however, I feel compelled to state my belief that Luke's fishing story and John 21:1–11 build on a common tradition, and that neither is literarily dependent on the other. I also believe that in the pre-Gospel tradition Peter meets the risen Jesus on the Sea of Galilee and is assigned missionary and / or pastoral responsibilities, conveyed through the metaphor of netting fish, and that Luke changed this into a miracle story set during the *earthly* ministry of Jesus, describing Jesus as the deliverer of God's providence. For detailed discussions of the literary relationship (or lack thereof) between John 21:1–11 and Luke 5:1–11, see especially Neirynck, "John 21," 321–36; A. Shaw, "The Breakfast by the Shore and the Mary Magdalene Encounter as Eucharistic Narratives," *JTS* 25 (1974): 12–26; J. A. Bailey, *The Traditions Common to the Gospels of Luke and John* (NovTSup 7; Leiden: Brill, 1963), 85–100; R. Pesch, *Der reiche Fischfang: Luke 5:1–11 / Jo 21:1–14* (KBANT; Düsseldorf: Patmos, 1969); R. T. Fortna, "Diachronic / Synchronic: Reading John 21 and Luke 5," in *John and the Synoptics* (ed. A. Denaux; BETL 101; Leuven: Leuven University Press, 1992), 387–99; Fitzmyer, *The Gospel According to Luke*, 1.561; Kessler, *Peter as the First Witness*, 45–48; and Goulder, *Luke–A New Paradigm*, 316–28.

glorification (cf. 2:4; 7:30; 8:20; 12:23),[56] so the un-torn fishing net describes the unity of Jesus and those who seek his fellowship in the church. As the fisherman who handles the net without incurring a tear, Peter is portrayed as a missionary without peer. Whereas Luke 5:1–11 emphasizes the sheer magnitude of the miracle, focusing exclusively on divine providence, the Johannine Redactor emphasizes not only the magnitude of the miracle but also the pristine manner in which the catch is netted and brought to Jesus, providing a missionary theme as well as a providential one.[57]

Conclusion

We have seen that Peter engages in three different activities in 21:1–11, all of which demonstrate his initiative and two of which testify to his loyalty to Jesus. His first action is to lead the other six disciples on a fishing expedition in Galilee (vv. 2–4). His bold statement in v. 3, "I am going fishing," does not signal desperation so much as preparation—albeit preparation to engage in the thoroughly non-evangelical task of finding supper![58] His announcement is a thinly-veiled invitation to the others to join him. As a fisherman, Peter understands that he cannot pilot a vessel and haul on board a δίκτυον unassisted. (Ironically, of course, he *does* haul in the net without help, but this is an unexpected windfall of the encounter with Christ.) In the second instance, Peter leaps into the sea to swim to Jesus. The leap takes place only after BD gives up the Lord's coordinates, as it were, announcing Jesus' presence to Peter and Peter alone. Peter's leap is not a leap of faith but of jubilation. His third action is to haul ashore single-handedly the miraculous catch of fish, demonstrating via metaphor his missionary skills.

---

[56] See W. F. Howard, *The Fourth Gospel in Recent Criticism and Interpretation* (2nd ed.; London: Epworth Press, 1935), 202. Scholars are divided on the question of whether the garment is a priestly symbol (cf. Ex 39:27; 36:35 LXX). If it *is*, the insinuation is probably that Jesus dies as both king (19:14, 19) and priest. See Smith, *John*, 357–58. Josephus (*Ant.* 3.161) describes the high priest's garment (also χιτών) as "one long vestment so woven as to have an aperture for the neck."

[57] Marxsen, *Resurrection of Jesus*, 159, suggests that what the historical Peter saw on the Sea of Tiberias in the days or weeks following the crucifixion was not the risen Jesus but *the light!* Marxsen speculates that Peter, during a fishing trip that took place after his return to Galilee from Jerusalem, had a revelation "that Jesus was sending him forth. This is described with the help of the story of the miraculous draught."

[58] There is no reason to accept the suggestion of Stibbe, *John*, 211, that Peter is in a state of "denial" as he fishes, and that, having "failed Jesus so obviously in 18:15–27, he now seeks to suppress and even obliterate the shame in his life by reverting to 'life before Christ', to fishing." Peter's thoughts are not revealed to us to the extent that we can engage in such highly-detailed psychological profiling.

I have argued throughout this study that the concomitant actions of Peter and BD are cooperative and not competitive, and that many scholars are predisposed to ignore or downplay this fact, often because they are guided by the sweeping belief that Peter and BD represent different factions of the early church. But nowhere in the Gospel is the cooperation of these individuals more evident than in 21:7.[59] Here the dissimilar actions of Peter (a zealous leap) and BD (a confessional cry) coalesce to bring about a meeting with the risen Christ. Unlike earlier resurrection appearances in the Gospel in which it takes only one word (20:16) or a couple of words (20:19) from Jesus to make his identity known, here it takes a full-fledged miracle, and even in this case the only disciple with sufficient sensitivity to Jesus to make the connection between miracle and miracle worker is the ethereal BD, who "materializes" in the boat at about the same time Jesus appears on the shore. Without BD's faith, Peter would not know where to jump, when to jump, or whether to jump. Conversely, without Peter's leap, the voyage might end as a sightseeing expedition. The positive contributions of the two cannot be disentangled.[60]

All the disciples (including BD) follow Peter's lead in establishing physical contact with Jesus, although all but Peter choose to sail and not swim the remaining one hundred yards to shore, dragging the heavy net of fish. Lest these six be seen as the true stewards of the catch, Peter is described in v. 11 as the only disciple who obeys Jesus' command to "bring some of the fish" from the boat to the shore. He manages to draw (ἕλκω) the net to shore without incurring a tear or losing any of the fish, which is reminiscent of Jesus drawing (ἕλκω) people to himself (12:32). By coincidence or design, Peter's action in 21:11 fulfils the prophecy made about him by Jesus in Luke 5:10: "From now on you will be catching people."[61]

Although the Redactor may be tacitly acknowledging Peter's ecumenical missionary credentials in describing him bringing such a massive catch of fish to Jesus, he does not describe him as the representative of the Apostolic church. Peter does not act on behalf of—or in concert with—the Twelve. In fact, the Twelve are never mentioned by the Redactor. As in other places in the Gospel, Peter is portrayed as a hero of the *Johannine* community, commanding a boat whose crew contains uniquely Johannine characters (BD and Nathanael) and reuniting with Jesus with the help of the quintessentially Johannine BD.

---

[59] Contra Goulder, *St. Paul versus St. Peter*, 22, who steadfastly maintains that in John 21, as in other parts of the Gospel, BD "is in every way a hero, and he constantly puts Peter in the shade."

[60] I agree with Hartman, "Text-Centered Exegesis of John 21," 37, that "BD is obviously presented as the reliable warranter behind the whole gospel. He is no leader like Peter, and there is no antagonism between the two."

[61] There is no true symmetry between John 21:11 and Mark 1:17 or Matt 4:19, for in those Synoptic scenes Jesus' words are directed to multiple disciples.

Peter's adventures in the Gospel do not end with this deed of hauling the net ashore. In a fireside conversation with Jesus (21:15–17), the event to which we next turn, he is asked to profess his love for Jesus three times and is given the task of shepherding Jesus' flock. He is also informed that he will die by crucifixion. S. S. Smalley is correct to point out that Jesus "confronts Peter at every stage in the narrative, upsetting his equilibrium, and challenging him to make decisions and take new action."[62]

---

[62] Smalley, "The Sign in John 21," 283.

CHAPTER 8

SHEPHERD AND MARTYR

INTRODUCTION: PETER IN JOHN 21:15–25

Five of the seven disciples who participate in the fishing expedition (Nathanael, Thomas Didymus, the sons of Zebedee and the unnamed disciple) are not mentioned in the second half of the supplemental chapter (John 21:15–25), which leaves only Peter and BD to interact with the risen Jesus. Instead of focusing on Peter's ability to draw (ἕλκω) a wide variety of individuals to Jesus, the Redactor now focuses on the care Peter provides for those brought to Jesus.[1] Peter will feed / tend (βόσκω / ποιμαίνω) Jesus' lambs and sheep (ἀρνία / πρόβατα) not as the Good Shepherd but as the *new shepherd*.

When in vv. 21–23 he is instructed by Jesus to shift his attention away from the fate of BD (implied in v. 23) and toward participation in the ongoing life of Jesus, he is functioning as a surrogate for the Johannine community, whose faith has apparently slipped in the wake of BD's death. In what is probably the highest compliment paid to Peter and BD in the Gospel, both individuals are described as following (ἀκολουθέω) Jesus and serving as role models of faithful discipleship even after having died (vv. 18–23).[2] Peter is revered as the community's great missionary, pastor and martyr; BD is hailed as the authenticator of the traditions behind the community's Gospel (v. 24; cf. 19:35). The Redactor does not explicitly describe these modes of service as official ecclesial capacities in the Johannine church, but, as we will see, this is to be inferred.

QUESTIONS AND ANSWERS: 21:15–17

[15]When they had finished breakfast, Jesus said to Simon Peter, "Simon son of John, do you love me more than these?" He said to him, "Yes, Lord; you know that I love you." Jesus said to him, "Feed my lambs." [16] A second time he said to him, "Simon son of John, do you love me?" He said to him, "Yes, Lord; you know that I love you." Jesus said to him, "Tend my sheep." [17] He said to him the third time, "Simon son of John, do you love me?" Peter felt hurt because he said to him the third time, "Do you love me?" And he said to him, "Lord, you know

---

[1] Brown, *John*, 2.1097.

[2] Peter's death, referred to allusively in 13:36, takes place prior to the death of BD, perhaps during the Neronian persecutions in Rome. See chapter 6.

everything; you know that I love you." Jesus said to him, "Feed my sheep." (¹⁵"Ότε οὖν ἠρίστησαν λέγει τῷ Σίμωνι Πέτρῳ ὁ Ἰησοῦς· Σίμων Ἰωάννου, ἀγαπᾷς με πλέον τούτων; λέγει αὐτῷ· ναὶ κύριε, σὺ οἶδας ὅτι φιλῶ σε. λέγει αὐτῷ· βόσκε τὰ ἀρνία μου. ¹⁶λέγει αὐτῷ πάλιν δεύτερον· Σίμων Ἰωάννου, ἀγαπᾷς με; λέγει αὐτῷ· ναὶ κύριε, σὺ οἶδας ὅτι φιλῶ σε. λέγει αὐτῷ· ποίμαινε τὰ πρόβατά μου. ¹⁷λέγει αὐτῷ τὸ τρίτον· Σίμων Ἰωάννου, φιλεῖς με; ἐλυπήθη ὁ Πέτρος ὅτι εἶπεν αὐτῷ τὸ τρίτον· φιλεῖς με; καὶ λέγει αὐτῷ· κύριε, πάντα σὺ οἶδας, σὺ γινώσκεις ὅτι φιλῶ σε. λέγει αὐτῷ [ὁ Ἰησοῦς]· βόσκε τὰ πρόβατά μου.)

The focus on Peter intensifies after the fellowship meal on the beach (vv. 12-14), although we do not know how much time transpires between the meal and Peter's conversation with Jesus because the phrase ὅτε οὖν—although a common Johannine temporal connective—links contiguous events in the Gospel as often as it links events separated by indeterminate periods of time.[3] What the phrase announces most clearly is a change in *theme*: whereas before breakfast the focus was on reunification with Jesus and missionary work, now the focus shifts to ministry and witness.

As in John 1:42, Jesus addresses Peter as "Simon son of John" (21:15). Whereas the Greek in 1:42 is Σίμων ὁ υἱὸς Ἰωάννου, here it is simply Σίμων Ἰωάννου (cf. 21:16–17).[4] The shorter appellation may be an economical abbreviation or it may reflect the literary preference of the Redactor. Just as Jesus referred to Peter with the patronymic "Simon son of John" when he first enlisted him as a disciple in Galilee, now, once more in Galilee, he again refers to him by this name. The suggestion of R. E. Brown that Jesus addresses Peter with the "patronymic used when they first met" in order to treat him "less familiarly" and so test their friendship in the wake of the denials is difficult to accept,[5] as is the theory of R. H. Lightfoot that Peter's grief in 21:17 is due to Jesus' refusal to address him with his "Christian name."[6] In point of fact, Jesus

---

[3] The phrase ὅτε οὖν links contiguous events in 13:12; 19:6, 8, and 30. In 2:22; 4:45; 6:24; and 13:31 it joins scenes separated by indeterminate periods.

[4] This is the reading of B ℵ* C D L W. The variant Σίμων Ἰωνᾶ, which appears in A K C^c M N U S 157 and 1424, is probably meant to harmonize Matt 16:17: μακάριος εἶ, Σίμων Βαριωνᾶ. For the idea that John 21:15–17; 1:42; and 6:68–69 are fragments of a tradition known also to Matthew, see chapter 2 of this study.

[5] Brown, *John*, 2.1102. Ridderbos, *Gospel of John*, 665, says something similar: "It seems that Jesus wants to make Peter feel that, before going further with him, he must first make a fresh beginning with him."

[6] Lightfoot, *St. John's Gospel*, 340. Another who believes Jesus uses the patronymic to chastise Peter is Watty, "Significance of Anonymity," 211: "Peter is 'un-named' by reverting to the identity of 'Son of John' of no greater consequence than his brother Andrew or the sons of Zebedee." Hooker, *Endings*, 78, makes a similar argument when

never addresses Peter by his first name in the Gospel, and therefore the omission of the name in 21:15–17 cannot be interpreted as a snub.[7] Jesus uses the patronymic Σίμων Ἰωάννου here because this passage, like 1:40–42, is a call narrative: Peter's natural-born identity, defined in part by his paternal line of descent, is being transformed. He is being called from one mode of existence to another. The major difference between the two narratives is that in this new one the stakes are higher: for Peter, committing fully to Jesus will mean caring for others in Jesus' absence and, ultimately, surrendering his own life.

In 21:15 Jesus makes the first of three inquiries into the nature of Peter's love for him, saying: "Simon, son of John, do you love me more than these?" (Σίμων Ἰωάννου, ἀγαπᾷς με πλέον τούτων;).[8] Only in this first inquiry does he include the mysterious qualifying phrase, πλέον τούτων, and scholars have long pondered how best to translate the words. Coupled with a genitive of comparison, πλέον should normally be taken to mean "more than," as in Acts 15:28.[9] But Jesus leaves the referent ambiguous.[10] He is clearly asking Peter for something beyond an informal declaration of love, but he does not make it clear what it is Peter's love is supposed to surpass.

Generally speaking, Johannine commentators translate the phrase in one of three ways, and each translation puts a slightly different spin on the conversation. According to the first interpretation, Jesus employs the phrase πλέον τούτων to find out if Peter loves him more than he loves *these implements and fruits of the fishing trade* (i.e., the net, boat, and fish).[11] Peter has, with considerable help from Jesus, shown an ability to use the net and the boat to positive effect (21:6–11), and—if the Synoptic Gospels are any guide (cf. Mark 1:16; Matt 4:18; Luke 5:1–11)—the net and boat were the tools of his trade before he met Jesus. Jesus might therefore be asking Peter if he is willing to sever his connections with the fishing trade in order to pursue an evangelical career. The problem with this interpretation, however, is that it sets the activity of fishing in opposition to the activity of loving Jesus, which makes little sense in light of the fact that "fishing" in John 21, beginning in v. 6, is a metaphor for

---

she notes that Jesus avoids using the terms "Peter" or "Cephas" because Peter has proven through his denials that he is not "rock-like." More persuasive is the idea of de Boor, *Evangelium des Johannes*, 2.260, that Jesus does not refer to Peter by his "official name" (*Amtsnamen*) because he is interested in ascertaining the love of Peter the man, or his "innermost attitude" (*innerste Stellung*) toward Jesus.

[7] In the canonical Gospels, Jesus addresses Peter as "Peter" only in Luke 22:34.

[8] με πλεῖον πάντων W.

[9] In the Synoptic Gospels when the root adjective πολύς is modified to form a genitive of comparison, it usually appears as πλεῖον or πλειών (e.g., Mark 12:43; Matt 5:20; 6:25; 26:53; Luke 11:31; 12:23).

[10] For more on πλέον τούτων, see BDAG, s.v., 849.

[11] Bernard, *St. John*, 705; Keener, *Gospel of John*, 1236.

missionary activity. The net and boat do not compete with Jesus for Peter's affection but equip him to serve Jesus.

According to the second interpretation, Jesus asks Peter if he loves him more than he loves *these fellow disciples*.[12] But because Peter in the previous scene leapt over the rails of the boat to swim to Jesus—leaving the other disciples to fend for themselves—this, too, seems an unsatisfactory interpretation. The other disciples do not compete with Jesus for Peter's love. (In other parts of the Gospel, too, Peter breaks ranks with his fellow disciples to offer Jesus what he considers to be specialized care. See 13:4-8 and 18:10-11.)

According to the third and most common interpretation, Jesus employs the phrase πλέον τούτων to ask Peter if he loves him more than *these other disciples love him*. Here τούτων is the subject of the implied verb ἀγαπάω.[13] But this interpretation also has problems, chief of which is that it casts Jesus in the rather clinical role of statistician. He appears on the shore of the Sea of Tiberias with great drama and also with a stubborn inclination to compare the faiths of the disciples. While the practice of quantifying faith in potential or part-time followers of Jesus is not foreign to John's Gospel (cf. 3:5-12; 6:51-70; 9:1-41), it seems incongruous in a scene in which Jesus is reunited with his disciples and they are depicted as the seeds of the new faith community. J. H. Bernard does well to observe that "comparisons of this kind, between the love which this or that disciple displays or entertains, seem out of place on the lips of Jesus."[14]

Pressed to choose among these three interpretations, I would probably choose the third, but only because it is the least unsatisfactory. What the Redactor is *really* doing here, I think, is supplying a referent he means to remain ambiguous. Neither Peter nor the implied reader is supposed to know what, exactly, πλέον τούτων signifies. No matter how Peter elects to translate the words, his answer must be that his love for Jesus is unsurpassed and unsurpassable. To his credit, Peter seems to understand that it is something of a trick question. Unlike modern commentators who spill much ink struggling to translate πλέον τούτων, Peter ignores the phrase, responding to the first part of Jesus' question only (i.e., "Do you love me?"). He says to Jesus, "Yes, Lord; you know that I love you," attempting to reveal the unbounded nature of his love for Jesus by emphasizing the love's transparency.

With a few small changes (discussed below), this same dialogue repeats itself in verses 16 and 17. The upshot is that Peter has a chance to profess his love for Jesus three times, mitigating the damage of the threefold denial and,

---

[12] Moloney, *John*, 559; A. M. Hunter, *The Gospel According to John* (CBC; Cambridge: Cambridge University Press, 1965), 196; Witherington, *John's Wisdom*, 356.

[13] See, for example, Hartman, "An Attempt at a Text-Centered Exegesis of John 21," 34; Wengst, *Johannesevangelium*, 2.319; Barrett, *St. John*, 584; Brown, *John*, 2.1104.

[14] Bernard, *St. John*, 704.

more importantly, I would say, qualifying himself to perform the three pastoral duties he will shortly be assigned.

Of interest to some is the fact that Jesus employs the verb ἀγαπάω in vv. 15–16 to ask Peter if he loves him but that Peter uses the verb φιλέω to affirm his love. Some scholars believe the Redactor understands there to be a clear distinction between the verbs, with ἀγαπάω representing spiritual or noble love and φιλέω representing the love of friendship, and that Jesus is therefore requesting a type of love that Peter is unable or unwilling to give.[15] According to this interpretation, the author of the chapter, adopting the (supposedly) anti-Petrine bias of the Evangelist, subtly chastises Peter for once more failing to serve Jesus in the manner Jesus requests. A related interpretation finds Peter and Jesus engaging in a typical "two-level Johannine dialogue," similar to what takes place in 3:1–20 and 4:7–26. Like Nicodemus in John 3 and the Samaritan woman in John 4, Peter blithely engages Jesus in conversation without fully grasping the topic. Twice Jesus asks for one kind of love, twice Peter promises to deliver another.[16] The scene would be comical but for the dullness it reveals in Peter.

Either one of these interpretations might be viable if the dialogue ended at v. 16, but it does not. It ends at v. 17, and here Jesus and Peter are both content to use the verb φιλέω.[17] The result is that the conversation closes with Peter professing a love for Jesus that is precisely equivalent to the kind of love Jesus requests.[18] If the Redactor were interested in describing Peter as one incapable of supplying the proper sort of love to Jesus, would he switch verbs in such a manner, allowing Jesus' request for love and Peter's profession of love to align? It is doubtful. It is also doubtful that this conversation is a true Johannine two-level dialogue, for in such dialogues misunderstandings between Jesus and his dialogue partner are not resolved by Jesus adopting his conversation partner's more mundane vocabulary or viewpoint. The Johannine Jesus constantly challenges his hearer to understand him *on his own terms* (in addition to 3:1–10

---

[15] See L. D. George, *Reading the Tapestry: A Literary-Rhetorical Analysis of the Johannine Resurrection Narrative: John 20–21* (Studies in Biblical Literature 14; New York: Peter Lang, 2000), 134–35; and K. L. McKay, "Style and Significance in the Language of John 21:15-17," *NovT* 27 (1985): 321. McKay argues that ἀγαπάω and φιλέω are more than synonyms but does not believe ἀγαπάω had developed connotations of noble love as early as the late first century. He argues instead that John 21 shows ἀγαπάω "in process of acquiring its Christian flavour" (p. 321).

[16] Maynard, "Role of Peter," 542, sees Peter's inability to give the type of love Jesus requires as perpetuating the Gospel's anti-Petrine bias. Grün, *Jesus: Tür zum Leben*, 150, argues that Peter desires to offer Jesus the more "vibrant" or "booming" (*lauterer*) love Jesus requests, but can only muster the "love of friendship" (*Freundesliebe*).

[17] ἀγαπᾷς W.

[18] *Contra* Howard-Brook, *Becoming Children of God*, 477, who maintains that "finding Peter incapable at this moment of *agapē*, Jesus settles for *phileō*."

and 4:7–26, see 10:6 and 12:16). If Jesus' purpose in vv. 15–17 was to draw out increasingly involved professions of love from Peter, we would expect Peter to be the one switching verbs, not Jesus. Taking into consideration the additional fact that ἀγαπάω and φιλέω are used interchangeably in the Gospel—describing both the Father's love for Jesus (ἀγαπάω in 3:35 and 10:17; φιλέω in 5:20) and Jesus' love for BD (BD is ὃν ἠγάπα on most occasions but ὃν ἐφίλει in 20:2)—it becomes all the more clear that the terms are synonyms, and that in each of the three verses of our pericope Peter promises a love equal to what Jesus requires.[19] T. Wiarda correctly concludes that "[i]f Peter is singled out for questioning it is because he has expressed his love more emphatically than the others, not because his love is less adequate."[20]

In v. 15, the command from Jesus to Peter, "feed my lambs" (βόσκε τὰ ἀρνία μου), is conditional: only because Peter has professed his unsurpassable love for Jesus is he qualified to serve as the shepherd of Jesus' flock.[21] To this point in the Gospel, "lamb" has been a term reserved for Jesus (1:29, 36).[22] As the Redactor takes over from the Evangelist, however, "lambs" becomes a collective term that refers to the newest members of Jesus' flock, the initiates to the Christ faith.[23] With the same delicacy he exhibited in hauling the fish/novitiates to Jesus, Peter will nourish them as they seek a place in Jesus' congregation (see below). The verb βόσκω is used in the Synoptic Gospels only

---

[19] I therefore agree with Brown, *John*, 2.1102, that the alternation of ἀγαπάω and φιλέω is "a meaningless stylistic peculiarity."

[20] Wiarda, *Peter in the Gospels*, 112.

[21] βόσκε τὰ πρόβατα μου C* D. Few would quarrel with the statement of Porsch, *Johannesevangelium*, 222, that "die besondere Stellung des Petrus innerhalb des Jüngerkreises gehört zur ältesten urchristlichen Überlieferung."

[22] The reference to Jesus-as-lamb is explicit in 1:29, when Jesus enters the narrative as "the Lamb (ὁ ἀμνός) of God who takes away the sin of the world." It is implicit in 19:14, when Jesus dies a sacrificial death at the moment the paschal lambs are being slaughtered.

[23] I agree with Brodie, *Gospel according to John*, 590, that "lambs" is a synonym for novitiates in 21:15–16 and that "sheep" stands for seasoned believers. (So Theophylact [Aquinas, *Catena Aurea*, 624].) Brodie's subsequent argument that "lambs" in v. 17 no longer refers to initiates but to senescent Johannine Christians undergoing a second childhood (p. 590) is less convincing. D. Rensberger, *Johannine Faith*, 144, argues that all members of the Johannine community are in a sense lambs, for the "community's mission is, like that of Jesus, the lamb of God, to 'take away the sin of the world,' to draw people from darkness into light (1:29; 12:46)." Depending on where one is in the Gospel, Jesus' "flock" is alternately depicted as being composed of the Twelve (6:67–71; 20:24), the "seven" (21:2ff), or some equally intimate group of devoted followers (cf. 11:1–39; 20:1–10). Certain passages in John (10:3–5, 14–15) suggest that the Johannine community understood itself to be the nucleus of Jesus' extended flock. Still other passages (esp. 10:16 but also 4:23–41; 7:35; and 12:20) indicate that they considered extra-community outreach to be an important activity for increasing the size of the flock.

to describe the feeding of swine (Mark 5:11; Matt 8:30; Luke 8:32; 15:15), but in the LXX it often refers to the feeding of sheep or lambs (e.g., Gen 29:7; 37:12; Isa 5:17; 65:25). In Ezek 34:14, βόσκω describes the administration of spiritual sustenance, as it does in our passage, with God's scattered elect (πρόβατα) receiving the promise that they will be brought to feed in the rich pastures of Israel.

In 21:16 the vocabulary changes slightly. Jesus tells Peter to "tend my sheep" rather than "feed my lambs." Peter's role is still a pastoral one, but with augmented responsibilities. Lambs require nourishment above all else, which is why Peter's initial pastoral task in v. 15 is feeding those who newly reside in Jesus, hence the implementation of the Greek βόσκω (cf. Mark 5:11; Matt 8:30; Luke 8:32; 15:15). As the lambs grow into sheep, however—or, to continue with the analogy, as initiates mature into second generation Christians—they become more nimble and independent, requiring oversight and shepherding as well as feeding. Thus βόσκω gives way in v. 16 to ποιμαίνω, a multifaceted verb that describes a variety of pastoral chores (cf. esp. Luke 17:7; 1 Cor 9:7; 1 Pet 5:2).[24] The probable implication is that Peter's initial responsibility is to attract new converts to the Christ faith and see to their immediate needs, but that his ultimate job will be to promote the spiritual welfare of the entire community (cf. Acts 20:28; 1 Pet 5:3; 1 Tim 3:1–7; on ποιμαίνω see also septuagintal Mic 7:14; Ps 77:71; Ezek 34:10).

Before releasing Peter from the conversation, Jesus asks him a third time if he loves him. The question clearly upsets Peter. Unlike in other scenes in the Gospel in which we must infer Peter's mood or thoughts from his actions, here the Redactor tells us plainly that "Peter felt hurt (ἐλυπήθη) because he said to him the third time, 'Do you love me?'" As in other places in the NT, λυπέω denotes grief or agitation (cf. Mark 4:19; Matt 26:37; Rom 14:15; Eph 4:30).[25] Peter's faith has not been questioned, nor has he been reminded explicitly of his denials, yet his reaction is one of sorrow. The simplest interpretation is that his grief arises because he believes his professions of love are not being taken seriously.[26] His strategy is a simple one: he returns to the practice of describing

---

[24] *Contra* McKay, "Style and Significance," 332, who considers the verbs to be interchangeable.

[25] De Boor, *Evangelium des Johannes*, 262, notes that Jesus refuses to spare Peter pain here because it is a "healing, cleansing pain" (*heilsamer, reinigender Schmerz*), which, when faced, will allow Peter to move beyond the memory of the denials and prove his love.

[26] In psychologizing Peter, Haenchen, *John 2*, 226, suggests that as Jesus requests new assurances of love from Peter, he "rescinds his commission on each occasion." Hooker, *Endings*, 78, makes a similar observation: "Each time, Jesus addresses Peter as 'Simon'; by his threefold denial he has shown that he is not yet rock-like, so the name 'Cephas' (i.e. 'Peter', 142) is inappropriate." Ridderbos, *Gospel of John*, 665, paints a rather gloomy picture of the conversation, describing the scene as though Peter were on trial:

his love in terms of its transparency, perhaps believing, as Waetjen suggests, that it "is only Jesus' knowledge of Simon Peter that will authenticate the quality and degree of the love he bears toward Jesus."[27] He puts these words to Jesus: "Lord, you know (σὺ οἶδας) everything (πάντα); you know (σὺ γινώσκεις) that I love you" (21:17). The alternation of οἶδα and γινώσκω is probably not important here, as the alternation of ἀγαπάω and φιλέω was not, but the indefinite adjective πάντα certainly draws our attention. As one of the disciples who was present for the Last Discourse, Peter knows now that Jesus knows "everything" (πάντα, 16:30). If Jesus knows everything, he must know that Peter loves him. So, to ensure that his third profession of love will be taken seriously by Jesus, Peter employs this logic and reminds Jesus that he already knows the answer to his question, part of the "everything" in his knowledge bank.

The strategy pays off. Jesus gives one more instruction to Peter, "feed my sheep" (βόσκε τὰ πρόβατά μου, v. 17), and then drops the subject. The result is that "Jesus attests—again three times and in the presence of the other disciples as in 13:38—his full confidence in Peter as future shepherd of his church."[28] It is worth noting that the Redactor in constructing v. 17 borrows pastoral vocabulary from each of the two preceding verses, βόσκω from v. 15 and πρόβατα from v. 16. The maneuver seems designed to delineate further Peter's responsibilities. He now stands invested with three pastoral duties: feeding Jesus' lambs, watching over his sheep, and feeding those sheep.[29]

Is there an implication that Peter's pastoral task is to nourish his many charges with the word of God as they are able digest it (cf. 1 Cor 3:1–2; Heb 5:12–14), fostering faith in both novitiates and seasoned believers?[30] It would seem so. Waetjen certainly thinks this is the case, and offers the following analysis: "there must be a distinction between ἀρνία and πρόβατα. 'Lambs,' therefore, is a valid rendering of ἀρνία and may symbolically refer to new

---

"Peter's affirmative answer is without hesitation and appeals to Jesus' knowledge of him. The appeal does not have the sense of 'Why ask me? You know me, don't you?' Jesus' knowledge is, rather, the last thing on which Peter can base an appeal before Jesus. His own actions have witnessed against him, and 'more than these' seems to mock him more than justify him. All that is left to Peter is, 'You know that I love you,' an appeal to Jesus' knowledge of him as one of his own (10:14; cf. Luke. 22:32)."

[27] Waetjen, *Beloved Disciple*, 14.

[28] Ridderbos, *Gospel of John*, 666.

[29] See A. J. Simonis, *Die Hirtenrede im Johannes-Evangelium: Versuch einer Analyse von Johannes 10.1-18 nach Entstehung, Hintergrund und Inhalt* (Rome: Päpstliche Bibelinstitut, 1967), 63.

[30] We are not given the specifics of his pastoral duties. Does Peter preach? Administer the Eucharist? Provide administrative support? The book of Acts portrays him primarily as a preacher (1:16–22; 2:14–40; 4:8–12; 10:34–44; 11:5–17, etc.), and many of the scholars we have heard from (e.g., Bultmann, Brown, Wilckens, and Shaw) assume this is the primary task to which shepherding refers in John 21.

Christians or a young age group, perhaps analogous to the 'little children,' the τεκνία and παιδία of 1 John 2–3. Accordingly, Simon is entrusted with the feeding and safe-keeping of those represented by Jesus' lambs."[31] Because John's Gospel maintains that Christ himself is the food of true believers (esp. 6:51–58), the Redactor is careful to say that Peter's role is to administer rather than provide food. It is not explicitly said that would-be disciples *must* go through Peter to get to Jesus, or that he is an essential intermediary, but it is clear he heads a pastoral ministry that is geared to aid congregants in their faith journey.[32]

Is there also an implication that Jesus—in accepting the threefold profession of love—forgives Peter the sin of the threefold denial? This is a more difficult question to answer. The Redactor does not explicitly describe Jesus forgiving Peter's sins, nor does he go back into the body of the Gospel and excise the scene of Peter's denials. Unlike the Synoptists, however, the Johannine Redactor *does* allow Peter an opportunity to square things with Jesus, as it were, for one aspect of the threefold profession of love is that it serves as a symmetrical response to the threefold denial.[33] This should not be construed as Peter's *rehabilitation*, however, as is done in most Johannine commentaries and monographs.[34] Peter is not restored to health in John 21, nor does he need to be; he has functioned throughout the Gospel as a determined follower and authentic disciple of Jesus, propelled by a steady mixture of zeal and impetuousness. His

---

[31] Waetjen, *Beloved Disciple*, 13.

[32] This is an important point. Jesus does not seem to be establishing here an Apostolic succession with Peter as the original chief officer. However, since he earlier invested *all* his closest disciples with the power to evangelize and forgive sins (20:21–23), a process he imagines continuing well into the future (esp. 14:26; 15:16; 17:18), it may be that we are to imagine Peter in 21:15–17 as the leader of an ecclesial institution that is charged with spreading faith in Jesus as the one sent by God with the words of spirit and life (6:57, 63, 68–69).

[33] See Wengst, *Johannesevangelium*, 2.321. Whether or not one ultimately concludes that Peter atones for the sin of denying Jesus or just repairs some of the damage, one thing that can be confidently inferred from the text is that he does not *die* in his sin. The fate of such people is, according to Jesus, to be unable to go (ὑπάγω) where Jesus goes (8:21). Yet Peter's final act in the Gospel is following Jesus (21:20–22). Additionally, Peter's martyrdom is said to "glorify God" (21:19), not normally the fate of sinners. Ultimately, it is perhaps not important to quantify the precise extent of Peter's recovery in vv. 15-17, for the overall message of the pericope is that confessing one's love for Jesus improves the quality of one's discipleship, no matter how far one has fallen in the Lord's eyes. A. Reinhartz, *Befriending the Beloved Disciple*, 60, says essentially this same thing, although more eloquently: "the compliant reader will learn that there is room in the Johannine vision for human imperfection."

[34] This is not hyperbole. It is the rare article or monograph that does not use the word "rehabilitation" when describing Peter's change in fortunes in John 21. See the discussion in chapter 6.

ultimate loyalty to Jesus was predicted by Jesus himself in 13:36—even before the denials were predicted—and therefore members of the Johannine community already know that his story ends well.[35] Although the three professions of love do allow him to mitigate some of the damage of the three denials, they function primarily as warrants for the three pastoral responsibilities he receives: feeding lambs, tending sheep, and feeding sheep.[36] I concur with Ridderbos that "Jesus has sought not so much Peter's triple retraction of his denial, and even less to embarrass him again before the other disciples; it is rather what awaits Peter in the future that prompts Jesus to reinforce his ties with him as never before."[37]

As mentioned in chapter 6 of this study, the practice of seeing John 21 as Peter's "rehabilitation" has had the unfortunate effect in Johannine scholarship of creating (or reinforcing) the idea that there was an epochal moment in the life of the community when it sought solidarity with the Petrine church and/or acknowledged Peter's rising ecclesial significance.[38] "The community's affirmation of its tradition vis-à-vis opponents was perhaps part of its move toward clearer unity with other communities under the leadership of Peter."[39] Haenchen argues that the threefold profession of love "rehabilitates" Peter so he can serve credibly as "leader of the Jerusalem community, which was orphaned by Jesus' death."[40] Many similar opinions are cited in the survey of literature in the introduction to this study.

---

[35] Although I argue that John 21 did not belong to the original edition of the Gospel, I think it is fair to assume that its original readers would have been familiar with chapters 1–20. As I have stressed, John 21 was not written to modify the Christology of the community or address an expanding congregation, but to mollify the community in the wake of BD's death.

[36] Haenchen, *John 2*, 226, says that "the threefold denial of Peter at an earlier time corresponds to a threefold vow taken now and to a commission thrice repeated." See also Cullmann, *Peter*, 204–06. Bultmann, *Gospel of John*, 712, is one of only a handful of scholars who believes the threefold love profession "provides no hint of a relation to the account of the denial."

[37] Ridderbos, *Gospel According to John*, 667.

[38] U. C. von Wahlde, "Community in Conflict: The History and Social Context of the Johannine Community," in *Gospel Interpretation: Narrative-Critical & Social-Scientific Approaches* (ed. J. D. Kingsbury; Harrisburg, Penn.: Trinity Press International, 1997), 227.

[39] Ibid.

[40] Haenchen, *John 2*, 226. Haenchen maintains that Peter in the commissioning scene is *not* "acknowledged as the bishop of Rome." At the same time, however, he has this to say about 21:15–17: "We have here a composition that is carefully weighed and that in this form, which is thought through in detail, it is entirely comparable with Matt 16:17f.: it is a commission and authorization in which Peter is entrusted with the highest task in Christendom." Although Hooker, *Endings*, 77–78, focuses on the internal dynamic of the Johannine church, she finds implicit in 21:15–17 a subordination of Peter vis-à-vis BD: "The final scene in this chapter, like the first, is primarily a commissioning: Peter is

But if such a moment of outreach to Apostolic Christians ever took place—whether stimulated by persecution, internal turmoil, or some other divisive activity—there remains no trace of it in John 21 or any other part of the Gospel. The Redactor is probably aware of Peter's ecumenical appeal—hence the description of Peter "netting" an extremely large number of fish / initiates—but he insists on portraying him as one of the inspirational founding members of the *Johannine* church, as does the Evangelist.[41] Schneiders puts it this way:

> Especially in light of the remainder of chapter 21, it seems clear that the evangelist (or the redactor) intends to clarify for the post-resurrection community the relationship between the two constitutive activities of the church: contemplation, through which revelation is received, and ministry, through which it is mediated. The Beloved Disciple, who rested on the bosom of Jesus (13:23 and 21:20) is the Fourth Gospel's paradigmatic embodiment of contemplative openness to the revelation of Jesus, just as the word made flesh who dwelt in the bosom of God was the incarnation of God's self-revelation to the world (see 1:1, 18).[42]

The result of the short conversation between Jesus and Peter is that Peter is invested with a "special pastoral ministry."[43] Bultmann asserts that "the commission is not given to Peter in terms of mission, as in the later Easter

---

commissioned to tend Jesus' lambs. But he first needs to be forgiven. Here is perhaps one explanation as to why a redactor might have thought it necessary to continue the story for so far Peter, who denied that he was a disciple, has not been restored; now he is called again to follow Jesus, and to continue his work."

[41] As was discussed in the previous chapter, Peter represents the Twelve in only one scene in the body of the Gospel (6:68–69) and never in the supplementary chapter, and thus it is inappropriate to describe him as representative of Apostolic Christianity. He is usually paired with BD (a uniquely Johannine character), and it is through their combined exploits that Johannine faith and praxis is modeled. Peter's confession incorporates an implicit promise of loyalty to Jesus, which is not the case with his Synoptic confessions, but which would have had great significance for Johannine Christians, for whom persecution and expulsion from the synagogue was a distinct possibility. Peter speaks for the Johannine community in inquiring into the fate of BD (13:23–25) and he commands a boat whose crew is one-third Johannine (BD and Nathanael). He is not described as one who is "sent out," but is one who believes in, follows, and loves Jesus—attributes prized by Johannine Christians. He is rewarded with the care of Jesus' sheep, a post reminiscent of that held by the Good Shepherd (cf. 10:11). Whether one is looking at pericopae penned by the Evangelist or the Redactor, Peter is presented as an inspirational founding member of the Johannine church.

[42] Schneiders, *Written that You May Believe*, 204–05.

[43] Ibid., 40. Porsch, *Johannesevangelium*, 223, refers to the office as "das Hirtenamt." See also F. J. Moloney, *Glory Not Dishonor*, 187; and H. J. Flowers, "The Calling of Peter and the Restoration of Peter," *AThR* 19 (1922): 234–99.

stories Matt. 28:19; Luke 24:47f.; Acts 1:7f., and as John. 20:21 also represents it; it is a commission for leadership of the community, as in Matt 16:17–19."[44] Unlike the ecclesial office promised to Peter in Matthew, however, the office assigned to him in John 21 is for his immediate occupation.[45] As S. K. Ray notes, "on the shore of Galilee, the 'future tense' is made 'present active,' and Peter is commissioned and appointed as the shepherd of God's flock."[46]

Peter's Fate Foretold: 21:18–19

[18]Very truly, I tell you, when you were younger, you used to fasten your own belt and go wherever you wished. But when you grow old, you will stretch out your hands, and someone else will fasten a belt around you and take you where you do not wish to go." [19](He said this to indicate the kind of death by which he would glorify God.) After this he said to him, "Follow me." ([18]ἀμὴν ἀμὴν λέγω σοι, ὅτε ἦς νεώτερος, ἐζώννυες σεαυτὸν καὶ περιεπάτεις ὅπου ἤθελες· ὅταν δὲ γηράσῃς, ἐκτενεῖς τὰς χεῖράς σου, καὶ ἄλλος σε ζώσει καὶ οἴσει ὅπου οὐ θέλεις. [19]τοῦτο δὲ εἶπεν σημαίνων ποίῳ θανάτῳ δοξάσει τὸν θεόν. καὶ τοῦτο εἰπὼν λέγει αὐτῷ· ἀκολούθει μοι.)

The phrase ἀμὴν ἀμὴν λέγω σοι appears five times in John's Gospel, although nowhere else in the NT. Most recently in the Gospel it was used by Jesus to call Peter's attention to his upcoming betrayal (13:38). Now Jesus uses it to inform Peter of his upcoming martyrdom. The verses do not form a true inclusio, but Jesus certainly treats the topics of Peter's betrayal and loyalty with equal solemnity.

The reference to Peter fastening his own belt and going about wherever he wished when he was young is thought by some to be a reference to his impetuousness, but it probably serves the simpler purpose of explaining his arrest as the first stage in his loss of freedom. The belt he once used for the

---

[44] Bultmann, *Gospel of John*, 713. In Bultmann's opinion, Peter fades quickly from the limelight, for the "authority of the office" he receives becomes important for the Johannine community only after his death, when it is assumed by BD.

[45] The post promised to Peter in Matthew's Gospel is necessarily a future post, as it is promised during the earthly ministry of Jesus when there is as yet no need for a church or church officers. In chapter 2 of this study I outline my belief that John builds on Matt 16:16–19 in reporting Peter's name change, confession, and his investiture of ecclesial authority. Whereas in Matthew's Gospel the events are described as happening at a single moment in time (16:16–19), John spreads them out throughout the pre- and post-Easter phases of the story (1:42; 6:68–69; 21:11, 15–17, 18–22).

[46] Ray, *St. John's Gospel*, 393. See also J. R. Michaels, "Catholic Christology in the Catholic Epistles," in *Contours of Christology in the New Testament* (ed. R. N Longenecker; Grand Rapids: Eerdmans, 2005), 279.

casual purpose of fastening his garments will be, at the end of his life, replaced by a belt that either fastens him to the cross (Tertullian, *Scorpiace* 15.3)[47] or, what is more likely, binds him between the time of his arrest and execution. On the off chance that readers fail to recognize the image of Peter stretching out his hands and being led by another (ἄλλος)[48] to a place he does not wish to go as a description of his arrest and crucifixion, the Redactor includes a parenthetical remark that makes this clear: "He (Jesus) said this to indicate the kind of death by which he would glorify God" (v. 19). Readers are not supposed to know simply that Peter was martyred but that he was martyred in a particular way, by crucifixion, the manner of Jesus' death.[49] The *new shepherd* and the Good Shepherd lay down their lives for the flock in the same way.[50]

---

[47] Quoted in W. A. Jurgens, trans., *The Faith of the Early Fathers* (3 vols.; Collegeville, Minn.: Liturgical Press, 1970), 1.152.

[48] ἄλλος (v. 18) is replaced by ἄλλοι in ℵ* C^c D* W f^1 565 and 33, creating an image of a large arresting party taking hold of Peter, which may have been designed to magnify the importance of the event and also the disciple. Howard-Brook, *Becoming Children of God*, 479, wonders if ἄλλος means the *Romans* or if it means *God*, "whose will Peter will never completely accept." He suggests that the reader is not meant to know the answer and that "the text leaves this crucial question open, allowing the Johannine community to continue pondering the character of the one whom Jesus has commissioned as their shepherd" (p. 479). For Howard-Brook, Peter represents the Apostolic church, and he maintains that one of the functions of the pericope is to express the Johannine community's "ambivalence about the apostolic churches" (p. 478). In my opinion, Peter represents Johannine Christianity to the same extent BD does.

[49] It was widely assumed in the ancient world that Peter died by crucifixion. In addition to Tertullian, the event is specifically reported by Eusebius (*Eccl. Hist.* 2.25). Clement of Rome (*1 Clement* 5.4) acknowledges that Peter (and Paul) suffered martyrdom. The details Clement provides that Peter "suffered many toils," "gave testimony," and went "to the place of glory that was his due" are reminiscent of John 21:18–19 and may come from the Fourth Gospel or a closely related tradition. The description of a person "stretching out hands" was used by many ancient writers as shorthand for the Roman practice of crucifixion. See *Epistle of Barnabas* 12.2 (on Isa 35:2) and 12.4 (on Ex 17:2); Justin (1 *Apol* 35); Cyprian (*Test.* II, 20); Epictetus 3.26.22; Seneca (*Ad Marciam de consolatione* 20.3) and Dionysius of Halicarnassus (*Antiquities romanae* 7.69). In the *Acts of Peter* 37.8, the apostle is crucified upside down. Cullmann, *Peter*, 87, argues that the activities of "stretching out the hands" and being "girded" are unmistakable references to crucifixion, as does Gnilka, *Johannesevangelium*, 159–60; and Wengst, *Johannesevangelium*, 321. Bultmann, *John*, 714, maintains that readers of the Gospel are left with no option but to see martyrdom as the manner of Peter's death, for "it is precisely to the martyr that the possibility of glorifying God through death is given." Koester, *Symbolism in the Fourth Gospel*, 137, boldly argues that Peter "'girded' himself in the boat before going to Jesus, and Jesus' words suggest that this would eventually mean being 'girded' before being taken to his execution." However, I am not persuaded that Peter's "girding" in 21:7 signifies anything other than a desire to avoid impropriety. For the idea that "stretching out [one's] hands" means something other than crucifixion

In John's Gospel, laying down (τίθημι) one's life (ψυχή) is a voluntary act of self-sacrifice, and it is therefore not a coincidence that both Jesus and Peter use these words when expressing their willingness to die on behalf of another (Jesus in 10:11–15; Peter in 13:37). Peter's death, unlike Jesus', is not a redemptive act, of course; he dies in service to Jesus whereas Jesus dies in service to the Father and for the sake of humankind. And it is never said of the Johannine Jesus during the Passion that death is a place to which he does "not wish to go."[51] (Peter's "imitation" of Jesus goes only so far!) Although Peter does not wish to die, nothing in the text suggests that he resists either his captors or his fate. In fact, when viewed together with 13:36–37 (in which Peter announces his intention to give his life for Jesus) and 20:10 (in which he all but throws himself on the weapons of the enemy to defend Jesus), the language of 21:18–19 strongly suggests that he voluntarily gives himself over to the opposition. Although martyrdom is described here as a form of witness that glorifies God, the text does not suggest that martyrdom is the end to which all Johannine Christians should aspire.[52] As we will learn in our exegesis of vv. 20–

---

in John 21, see especially Bultmann, *Gospel of John*, 713 n. 7; and Porsch, *Johannes-Evangelium*, 224.

[50] Busse, *Johannesevangelium*, 267, reminds us that "[d]ie Funktion des Hirten wird Petrus mit allen Konsequentzen, die Jesus in Kap. 10 schon für sich reklamiert hatten, übernehmen müssen."

[51] Gnilka, *Johannesevangelium*, 159, correctly identifies the place Peter fears to go as "das Grab," as opposed to the place of execution.

[52] Within a few years of the writing of John's Gospel, martyrdom was a fate to which some Christians were going with morbid glee. Writing to the church at Rome around 110 C.E., Ignatius failed to conceal his excitement as he prepared to die a martyr's death: "Allow me to be eaten by the beasts, which are my way of reaching to God. I am God's wheat, and I am to be ground by the teeth of wild beasts, so that I may become the pure bread of Christ." *The Martyrdom of St. Polycarp,* written in the middle of the second century (c. 155), openly celebrates martyrs: "[Christ] we worship as the Son of God; but the martyrs we love as disciples and imitators of the Lord; and rightly so, because of their unsurpassable devotion to their own King and Teacher." The apocryphal *Acts of Peter* (36–41) describes the apostle dying with utmost serenity, exhorting onlookers to faith even as he hangs upside down on the cross. See the discussion in M. Pesthy, "Cross and Death in the Apocryphal Acts of the Apostles," in *The Apocryphal Acts of Peter: Magic, Miracles and Gnosticism* (ed. J. D. Bremmer; Leuven: Peeters, 1998), 123–24. But while John 15:20 expects that martyrdom will be the final act of witness of some of the community's most faithful, it does not champion that form of death. Likewise, 1 John 3:16, often thought to be a product of the community responsible for John's Gospel, seeks to cultivate in the believer a *willingness* to die for a fellow believer, but it does not advocate martyrdom.

25, a life of faithful witness to Jesus is also considered an acceptable path of discipleship.[53]

After Jesus spells out in graphic detail the specifics of Peter's death, he tells him to "follow me" (v. 19). As was suggested earlier, this may be the Redactor's take on the Synoptic theme of *taking up the cross and following* (Matt 10:38; 16:24; Mark 8:34; Luke 9:23; 14:27).[54] If it is not, the Redactor inadvertently provides a stunning parallel to that Synoptic image! What Peter had been eager to do since the Last Supper—follow Jesus with such fervor that he ends up laying down his life for him—he accomplishes in his old age.[55] Although this death has already transpired by the time the Redactor writes, the Redactor treats it as a future event by which Peter *will glorify* (δοξάσει) God.[56]

AN ALTERNATIVE FORM OF WITNESS: 21:20–25

[20]Peter turned and saw the disciple whom Jesus loved following them; he was the one who had reclined next to Jesus at the supper and had said, "Lord, who is it that is going to betray you?" [21]When Peter saw him, he said to Jesus, "Lord, what about him?" [22]Jesus said to him, "If it is my will that he remain until I come, what is that to you? Follow me!" [23]So the rumor spread in the community that this disciple would not die. Yet Jesus did not say to him that he would not die, but, "If it is my will that he remain until I come, what is that to you?" ([20]Ἐπιστραφεὶς ὁ Πέτρος βλέπει τὸν μαθητὴν ὃν ἠγάπα ὁ Ἰησοῦς ἀκολουθοῦντα, ὃς καὶ ἀνέπεσεν ἐν τῷ δείπνῳ ἐπὶ τὸ στῆθος αὐτοῦ καὶ εἶπεν· κύριε, τίς ἐστιν ὁ παραδιδούς σε; [21]τοῦτον οὖν ἰδὼν ὁ Πέτρος λέγει τῷ Ἰησοῦ· κύριε, οὗτος δὲ τί; [22]λέγει αὐτῷ ὁ Ἰησοῦς· ἐὰν αὐτὸν θέλω μένειν ἕως ἔρχομαι, τί πρὸς σέ; σύ μοι ἀκολούθει. [23]ἐξῆλθεν οὖν οὗτος ὁ λόγος εἰς τοὺς ἀδελφοὺς ὅτι ὁ μαθητὴς ἐκεῖνος οὐκ ἀποθνῄσκει· οὐκ εἶπεν δὲ αὐτῷ ὁ Ἰησοῦς ὅτι οὐκ ἀποθνῄσκει ἀλλ᾽ ἐὰν αὐτὸν θέλω μένειν ἕως ἔρχομαι[, τί πρὸς σέ];)

---

[53] Grün, *Jesus: Tür zum Leben*, 152, is probably right to conclude that the text seeks to instil in all Christians one common goal: "Gott in unserem Leben und Sterben zu verherrlichen."

[54] This theory is particularly attractive if the reason Peter must "stretch out his hands" is because he needs to take hold of and carry the *patibulum* (the crossbar from which crucified persons were suspended).

[55] See van Tilborg, *Johannes-Evangelium*, 314.

[56] 1 Pet 4:16 similarly identifies the endurance of persecution as a way of glorifying God. Other passages in the NT suggest that believers may glorify God by confessing Christ (2 Cor 9:13), by performing honorable deeds (1 Pet 2:12), or by abstaining from bodily pleasures (1 Cor 6:20).

At first glance, 21:20 stands out as a rather awkward transitional verse, albeit an important one. "The editors who join this discussion, rather clumsily, to the preceding scene are obviously very interested in it."[57] Peter, finally following Jesus in the manner Jesus requires, something he has been attempting to do since first meeting Jesus, abruptly pivots in his tracks in order to monitor the activity of BD, who is trailing along behind them. Although the Redactor did not pause in 21:7 to remind us of BD's intimate connection to Jesus, he does so now, identifying the disciple who trails behind them as the one who leaned on Jesus' breast at the Last Supper and who vocalized Peter's question about the identity of the traitor.[58]

As he is looking back at BD, Peter says to Jesus, "Lord, what about him?" It is an open-ended question; Peter expects that Jesus will know what he means, just as the Redactor seems to expect that the reader will. What Peter seems to be saying is just this: *Lord, I am destined for execution; what will be his fate?*

Jesus responds by telling Peter not to concern himself with BD's fate. If it is Jesus' will that BD survives until his return, what concern is that of Peter's? Although Peter is already in the process of following Jesus, Jesus ends the conversation by putting to him a second time the command to "follow," steering him irrevocably toward obedient discipleship.

The fact that Peter must "turn around" (ἐπιστρέφω) to look back at BD in v. 21 reveals that he is walking ahead of him, possibly in step with Jesus.[59] Nothing suggests that Peter exits the story ahead of BD because he is superior to him. Rather, he is known to have died before him.[60] We can infer that BD has also died prior to the writing of John 21, albeit much more recently than Peter, because the Redactor works assiduously in v. 23b to correct the false "rumor" (λόγος) that BD is going to survive until Jesus' second coming. He does this by

---

[57] Schnackenburg, *St. John*, 3.367.

[58] It is a standard Johannine mechanism to define a character's credentials or personality traits by reminding the reader of the character's past accomplishments (cf. 3:26; 12:6; 18:14).

[59] Ἐπιστραφείς is an aorist passive participle and intransitive verb, which describes Peter "turning around" or "turning back" to monitor the behavior of BD. This in mind, most English versions of the NT correctly translate BD's act of *following* in v. 20a (ἀκολουθοῦντα) as "following them," meaning Jesus and Peter, with "them" being added as a necessary expansion of the text.

[60] Peter the historical figure is generally believed to have died in Rome during the Neronian persecutions (ca. 64–67 C.E.), although alternate locations and times are occasionally proposed. (See note 49 for patristic assumptions concerning his death.) For an informed look at some of the more exotic legends surrounding the historical character's death, see J. Bolyki, "'Head Downwards': The Cross of Peter in the Lights of the Apocryphal Acts, of the New Testament and of the Society-Transforming Claim of Early Christianity," in *The Apocryphal Acts of Peter: Magic, Miracles and Gnosticism* (ed. J. N. Bremmer; Leuven: Peeters, 1998), 111–22.

repeating Jesus' words and tacking on the disclaimer that the words did not, when originally issued, *promise* BD immunity from death: "Yet Jesus did not say to him that he would not die, but, 'If it is my will that he remain until I come, what is that to you?'" The parenthetical remark only makes sense if BD has died. If he is still alive at the time of the writing, it would not make sense to correct a "rumor" about his longevity.

Some scholars who believe that Peter is consistently portrayed negatively in the Gospel describe vv. 21–22 as depicting him as a jealous rather than zealous disciple. On the verge of making a dramatic exit from the Gospel—finally following successfully the one he has confessed as the Holy One of God—he cannot resist the urge to look over his shoulder and scrutinize a final time the activity of his long-time rival. Even as he marches off to death, the theory goes, he is conscious of the "one-upmanship" of BD.[61] This is a misperception. We have learned that Peter and BD are not rivals but colleagues, embodying different virtues in their attempts to follow and bear witness to Jesus, cooperating when possible. Studies that portray them as competitors usually focus on individual pericopae to the exclusion of the larger story. Peter does not speak for himself here, voicing some petty jealousy, nor does he express a loving curiosity about the fate of this fellow disciple. He speaks for a community that is contemplating the death of its other inspirational founder, BD.

It is precisely because Jesus recognizes Peter's representational role that his response is so harsh: "If it is my will that he remain until I come, what is that to you? Follow me!" Peter has long since died and needs no counseling about how

---

[61] "One-upmanship" is a term employed by R. E. Brown throughout his writings (see esp. *Community of the Beloved Disciple*, 84–87) to refer to the uneven relationship between Peter and BD—understood by Brown to be the representatives of Petrine and Johannine Christianity—although it should be said that Brown is one of many who believe that Peter's image undergoes a perceptible upgrade by the Redactor. Wilckens, *Evangelium nach Johannes*, 329, hears "irritation" in Peter's voice in 21:21 and describes Peter wondering aloud why this person is still keeping pace with him when there has been a reversal (*Umgekehrte*) in their relationship. According to Wilckens, although BD earlier enjoyed "trust" and "intimacy" with Jesus, he should, in Peter's mind, now fall under Peter's "pastoral purview" (*Hirtendienst*). Goulder, *St. Paul versus St. Peter*, 22, translates Jesus' statement to Peter this way: "Mind your own business, Peter." This is not in itself a gross mistranslation of the text, but it does portray Peter as an annoyance to Jesus, which is fully consistent with Goulder's belief that Peter is the "stumbling hero" of the Petrine churches while BD is the true hero of the Gospel (p. 188). Agourides, "The Purpose of John 21," 127–32, sees in vv. 20–23 an attempt by the author to reduce some of the authority recently invested in Peter by the churches of Asia. Söding, "Erscheinung," 230, finds in v. 22 a message to Peter and not the Johannine community. The message is that he must resign himself to the fact that it is God's will that he suffer martyrdom but that a similar fate (*Geschick*) does not await BD.

to serve Jesus. The Johannine community, on the other hand, *does* require redirection; the Redactor seeks to make sure that they do not wallow in grief or anxiety over BD's death and thereby neglect the task of promoting faith in Christ as the one sent from God (cf. 6:29, 40, 57; 7:18; 9:4; 11:42).[62] He refers to this post-Easter community in v. 23 as οἱ ἀδελφοί, as the Evangelist does in John 20:17 (cf. also Luke 22:32; Acts 2:37; 6:3, Rom 16:1; 1 Cor 1:10; Gal 1:2).[63] Μένειν should be understood to refer to *physical survival*, as in 1 Cor 15:6.[64] So if the rumor that BD would cheat death and supply the community with perpetual witness was laid to rest when he was, which v. 23b strongly implies, we can imagine that his death would have adversely affected the community, even raising concerns about a delayed Parousia. Indeed, D. M. Smith speculates that the death of BD was the major event that caused the Johannine community to rethink its assumptions about the "resurrection of the dead or a cataclysmic upheaval or end of world history."[65] R. E. Brown hypothesizes that the Johannine community's answer to "the void left by the death of the Beloved Disciple, the witness par excellence, is that the Paraclete who bore witness through and in him remains with all believers (14:17; 15:26–27)."[66] J. H. Charlesworth suggests that in order "[t]o forestall massive disenchantment and defection from the Community it was necessary to shore up the Johannine tradition."[67] G. H. C. MacGregor concludes that "[t]he stress laid upon the Parousia or 'coming back' of Christ as a definite personal event distinguishes the Redactor from the Evangelist...."[68]

Whether or not one is guided by any of these images, the parenthetical comment of v. 23b—which is really an exposition of 23a—is brilliantly conceived: Jesus reminds the community that he is still very much in control, that BD's fate is his own concern, and that the duty of the community is to follow him (Jesus) as Peter has done.[69] The community already knows that the

---

[62] Sensitive to the commonalities in faith crises faced by all Christian communities (but particularly the marginalized), A. Reinhartz, *Befriending the Beloved Disciple*, 129, makes the following observation: "Although these various issues related to community development and crisis are expressed in peculiarly Johannine terms, they are familiar to contemporary communities, large and small, which continue to struggle with the negotiation of power and continuity."

[63] Interestingly, in 1 Pet 5:9 it is *Peter* who directs community elders to care for the "brother- and sisterhood of believers" (ἀδελφότης).

[64] See Bernard, *St. John*, 711.

[65] D. M. Smith, *The Theology of the Gospel of John* (Cambridge: Cambridge University Press, 1995), 150.

[66] Brown, *John*, 2.1122.

[67] Charlesworth, *Beloved Disciple*, 44–45.

[68] MacGregor, *Gospel of John*, 376.

[69] I disagree with Hooker, *Endings*, 78–79, that in this section of the pericope Peter is being negatively compared to BD. She says, "Peter's task is to tend the sheep (vv. 15, 16,

reward of believing is eternal life (cf. 3:15–16, 36; 5:24; 6:27–30; 10:28 etc.), so there is much to be hopeful about. The final two verses of the appended Gospel (vv. 24–25) explain that what *is* imperishable about BD is his witness. Because he was an intimate companion of Jesus during his earthly ministry and passed down with diligence reports of Jesus' deeds (v. 24; cf. 19:35), his authority to verify the traditions in the Gospel, unlike the disciple himself, lacks an expiry date.

The Redactor closes his contribution to the Gospel in the same way the Evangelist closed chapter 20, stating that not all of Jesus' deeds are recorded. Unlike the Evangelist, however, who assigns a theological motive to his editing (i.e., he leaves out a certain amount of "Jesus material" from the Gospel so that faith will begin to grow from testimony rather than σημεῖα), the Redactor says that recording all of Jesus' deeds would be a feat beyond his abilities. Indeed, if all of Jesus' deeds were to be recorded, he says, "I suppose that the world itself could not contain the books that would be written" (21:25).[70]

CONCLUSION

With good reason, John 21 is widely considered to be the chapter of the Gospel in which Peter fares best. Although a few scholars harbor suspicions about the virtue of his activities, finding, for example, irrational exuberance in his leap over the boat rail in v. 7 and inadequately-expressed devotion in vv. 15-17, most agree that Peter is presented positively, and that he finally manages to serve Jesus in the way Jesus desires. Many see his turnaround as so dramatic

---

17), and he can do this only if he is prepared to follow Jesus (v. 19)—the very thing that the beloved disciple is already doing, without any special prompting. Following Jesus will mean, for Peter, that he will die as a martyr; like Jesus, he will glorify God by his death. What the beloved disciple will be called on to do is not Peter's concern." One reason this argument fails to persuade is that Peter represents the Johannine community here, which is so caught up in the grieving process over BD's death that it has stopped channelling its full energies into following Jesus. A second reason is that BD's speciality is not *following* but *meditative faith*, or, as Schneiders eloquently describes it, "contemplative openness to the revelation of God" (see above). It is usually *Peter's* lead that BD follows (13:23–25; 20:6–8; 21:20).

[70] Nothing suggests that Johann ben Zakkai borrows from the Gospel of John when writing about the boundless wisdom of his own teacher in the Babylonian Talmud (*Sopherim* 16.8), but one finds in that work an echo of John 21:25 nonetheless: "If all the heavens were sheets of paper, and all the trees were pens for writing, and all the seas were ink, that would not suffice to write down the wisdom that I have received from my teachers; and yet I have taken no more from the wisdom of the sages than a fly does when it dips into the sea and bears away a tiny drop." Quotation taken from Hooker, *Endings*, 80–81. A similar theme appears in Philo, *De Posteritate Caini* 43: "...nor, indeed, could even the whole world, both land and sea, contain his riches if he were inclined to display them...."

that they describe John 21 (esp. vv. 15–17) as his "rehabilitation." This does not simply mean that he is restored in Jesus' eyes as one who would rather follow than deny him, a fact that seems plain enough, but that he receives something akin to a spiritual makeover, proving himself to be so adept at missionary work and expressing love for Jesus that he is invested with pastoral responsibilities that would have been far beyond the ability of the character from chapters 1–20 to receive.

As has been pointed out, many scholars see John 21 as conciliatory toward the Apostolic church; more than a few suggest that Peter's popularity had become so great at the end of the first century that it was no longer feasible for the Johannine community to minimize his achievements and depict him as the spiritual inferior of BD. Upgrading his image was a political move undertaken to improve relations with the Apostolic churches.[71]

While I agree that Peter is depicted positively in John 21 and that he garners a host of ecclesial responsibilities that are (at best) vaguely alluded to by the Evangelist,[72] I have argued that this positive portrayal is consistent with what occurs in John 1–20. Both Evangelist and Redactor describe Peter as an exemplary Johannine disciple or "Christian," who confesses Jesus, believes in him, and tries his best to follow him. His missteps underscore his humanity and the difficulties inherent in the task of following Jesus. He appears as the *ideal* Johannine Christian when his attributes are combined with those of BD, for only in scenes in which the two disciples appear together is the community presented with a paradigm of discipleship that incorporates faith *and* praxis.

Within the context of John 21, vv. 15–17 take up where v. 11 left off. Peter is assigned pastoral responsibilities to go with his missionary responsibilities. The pastoral responsibilities may be seen as comprising a pastoral "office," although the office is not said to be hereditary.[73] Schnackenburg explains why "office" is appropriately descriptive of Peter's function:

> [T]he Father entrusted the sheep to Jesus his Son so that they belong to the Son exactly as to the Father (cf. 10:3f, 14; 17:9f) and without

---

[71] In addition to the many works of Brown already cited, see also *The Churches the Apostles Left Behind* (New York: Paulist, 1984), 93 n. 138. I feel compelled at this point to report that one curious and unhappy result of this study is that Raymond Brown, the scholar who has most influenced me and for whom I have profound respect, has come under frequent criticism for his theories concerning Peter's role in the Fourth Gospel. Were the subject of this dissertation anything other than "Peter in the Gospel of John," I am confident that I would frequently be marshalling Brown's opinions to buttress my own.

[72] It is likely that his naming in 1:42 reflects the foundational role he came to play in the early church. Also, 13:36–37 almost certainly refers to his martyrdom.

[73] So Becker, *Evangelium nach Johannes*, 2.646ff.; and Kragerud, *Lieblingsjünger*, 59–66.

giving up his proprietary right, the risen one entrusts them on returning to the Father, to Peter for safe-keeping. Precisely in order to protect these persons as belonging to him, Jesus imposes a pastoral duty upon Peter. On account of this commission which ultimately comes from the Father, and the authorization included within it, Peter's ministry can be designated also as an office and, in relation to Jesus, as an earthly representation, so long as the special character of this spiritual pastoral which differs from human offices with their legal structures, is not left out of consideration.[74]

Three times Peter is asked if he loves Jesus, three times he responds affirmatively. The idea that Peter's answers are initially inadequate and that Jesus must draw him to ever-higher understandings of love (ἀγαπάω instead of φιλέω) in order for his professions to gain value appears ill-conceived when we consider that (1) the verbs are used interchangeably throughout the Gospel to describe Jesus' love for the Father and BD, and (2) Peter and Jesus both settle on φιλέω in v. 17. That said, the vocabulary Peter employs is ultimately less important than the number of professions he makes. The three professions serve to atone for the three denials (18:17, 25, 27) and, more importantly, qualify him for his three pastoral duties.[75]

21:18-19 reveals that Peter's fate, like that of Jesus, is to die by crucifixion. Like the Good Shepherd (10:11, 15), the *new shepherd* lays down his life for others. Martyrdom is presented as an authentic form of witness but not the only one. In fact, such high value seems to have been attached to the witness of BD during his lifetime that his death created anxiety in the community. I agree with Brown, Charlesworth, Smith, and the many other scholars who claim that BD's death prompted the Redactor to restore the community's belief in the inevitability of the Parousia. And, in a sense, what the Redactor is saying in v. 23 is that BD *is* immortal. His body may have suffered corruption, but his witness endures.

The animadversion delivered by Jesus to Peter in v. 22, "What is that to you…follow me!", is a warning to the community to finish its grieving and focus on matters of faith. The last image in the Gospel is a very hopeful one: Peter and BD are shown following Jesus, their deaths having failed to exclude them from participating in his ongoing life. As Talbert notes, "Peter and the beloved disciple stand side by side in John 21 (as in 13:23–25; 18:15–16; 20:2–10), each with his own specific ministry and destiny. If evangelistic outreach

---

[74] Schnackenburg, *St. John*, 3.365.

[75] "The threefold profession of love and commitment on the part of Peter therefore reinforces the idea that Peter's unconditional love for Jesus is the foundation and source of his mission as the shepherd of the new covenant community." Chennattu, *Johannine Discipleship*, 178.

belongs to the disciples as a whole, pastoral care of the flock is given to Peter and the role of prophetic witness to the beloved disciple...."[76]

One particularly interesting fact about John 21 is that Peter is described as *one who loves Jesus* while BD is described *one who is loved by Jesus*. This is further evidence that we are to think of the two disciples as composite halves of the ideal Johannine Christian.

---

[76] Talbert, *Reading John*, 263.

CHAPTER 9

CONCLUSION

INTRODUCTION: HOW TO VIEW PETER?

This study has argued that Peter is portrayed very positively in the Gospel of John. Not only does he carry out activities fundamental to Johannine discipleship during the earthly ministry of Jesus, chief of which are *believing* in Jesus (John 6:69), *following* him (1:42; 6:68; 18:15–16; 20:2–10), and publicly *confessing* him (6:68–69), he demonstrates missionary skills (21:11) and is invested with pastoral responsibilities by the risen Jesus (21:15–17). Throughout the Gospel he often teams up with BD (13:23–25; 18:15–16; 20:2–10; 21:20–23) to follow and express devotion to Jesus, and it is especially through the two's combined exploits that members of the Johannine community learn the necessity of incorporating faith and praxis in discipleship.

Whereas BD achieves distinction in the Gospel for being a recipient of Jesus' love and for possessing an unimpeachable, if rather meditative, faith, thereby showing the reader what a loving relationship with Jesus *looks* like, Peter demonstrates how discipleship is *crafted*. The process, as we have seen, is not always smooth. As Peter experiments with different approaches to discipleship, he is, to employ a colloquialism, all over the map. He challenges (13:6–8) and then obeys Jesus (13:9; 21:11, 19–22); attacks Jesus' opponents (18:10) and then warms himself in their company (18:18–27); fails to enter the courtyard of the high priest (18:15–16) and then successfully enters the empty tomb (20:6–9); fishes without success (21:2-4) and then fishes with great success (21:6–11); issues a threefold denial of Jesus (18:17–27) and then a threefold profession of love (21:15–17); and makes empty promises to follow Jesus (13:37; cf. 18:17–27) before following him so closely that it costs him his life (21:18–19). Despite several spectacular missteps—at least two of which owe to an overwhelming but misplaced desire to "follow" Jesus by shielding him from danger and degradation (13:4–8 and 18:10–11)—he manages to model a number of positive traits, including courage, zeal, loyalty, love, resourcefulness, and determination. I have described him as an "authentic" disciple because he is sincere in his efforts to follow Jesus and because he assembles his program of faith on the run, sometimes recklessly, often to his own embarrassment, yet always with zest and never according to a pre-conceived program. He speaks for the faithful and helps root out the faithless, ministering to Jesus' flock and dying in service to his "Lord."

The idea that Peter comes off well in the Fourth Gospel is, as we have seen, not widely held in Johannine scholarship. Most scholars are convinced that Peter has a relatively "low" Christology (which prevents him from seeing certain truths about Jesus and causes him to be careless in his devotion), that he is a subordinate of BD (said by the scholarly majority to be the Gospel's sole model of sustainable faith), and that he is the representative of the Apostolic church (a less enlightened ecclesial body than the Johannine community). Some commentators attempt to reconstruct the early history of the Johannine church in part by analyzing the improvement Peter's fortunes show between John 1-20 and John 21. Simply put, Peter's "rehabilitation" in John 21 is believed to mark such a significant departure from his portrayal in earlier parts of the Gospel that commentators see behind it an attempt by the Johannine church to align itself with—or, at the very least, gain the favor of—the Apostolic church.

By summarizing briefly the ways these three basic tenets of the conventional wisdom about the Johannine Peter are defective, I will delineate for a final time Peter's major accomplishments in the Gospel.

Peter's Christology

Many renowned Johannine scholars (including Bultmann, Hoskyns, Brown, Culpepper and Perkins) believe that the Christological title Peter assigns to Jesus, "Holy One of God" (ὁ ἅγιος τοῦ θεοῦ; 6:69), summarizes Peter's own understanding of Jesus but is not particularly descriptive of the Johannine Jesus himself. The appellation, they argue, does not unpack Johannine Christology as fully as other confessions in the Gospel, especially those of Thomas (20:28) and Martha (11:27). After all that Jesus accomplishes during his first year in Peter's company, Peter assigns him a title that (1) speaks more to his divinely-sanctioned authority than to his filial relationship to the Father, (2) says nothing about his preexistence, and (3) is used of mere mortals in the Old Testament (Jdgs 13:7; Ps 106:16; cf. also Gk. *Apoc. Ezra* 5:10). Peter's problem, according to many, is that he does not comprehend the deepest truths about Jesus. To borrow from the terminology of Cullmann, he is on the outside of the "Johannine Circle" looking in.[1] He speaks courageously, confessing Jesus at a time when the crowds are "grumbling" and growing hostile, but his testimony is not inspired by the Spirit and not reflective of his behavior toward Jesus.[2]

There are two major problems with analyzing Peter's Christology in this way.[3] First, it gives too much attention to the title Peter applies to Jesus and not

---

[1] Cullmann, *Peter*, 15, 94.

[2] See Culpepper, *John the Son of Zebedee*, 62–84.

[3] More can be discovered about Peter's Christology than what is found in his confession, of course. Much of this study examines his actions in the Gospel and

enough to the pledge of loyalty he makes, which, given the context (the collapse of Jesus' ministry), is the most important aspect of the confession. Second, it improperly characterizes "Holy One of God" as betraying a "low" Christology, or at least a "lower" Christology than one would expect to find in one of Jesus' chief disciples.

Let me take issue with the second point first. In the context of the Bread of Life Discourse, the Christological appellation "Holy One of God" is *not* an inadequate description of Jesus but correctly affirms Jesus' status as one who is "set apart" (i.e., made holy) by God and who is prepared to deliver revelation ("the words of eternal life"). Peter confesses that he and the Twelve "have come to believe" (πεπιστεύκαμεν) and "have come to know" (ἐγνώκαμεν) that Jesus has been made holy and that he has the words of eternal life. Although Peter's confession begins with a seemingly simple rhetorical question, "Lord, to whom else can we go?" this is in fact a bold pledge of loyalty. The Twelve have choices about whom they follow, Peter intimates, but Jesus is the only *sensible* choice. Because Jesus has the "words of eternal life," remaining with him is not only an attractive possibility, it is a life-giving pursuit. Far from demonstrating a "low" Christology, Peter describes Jesus as Jesus describes himself in the Bread of Life Discourse—the event that immediately precedes Peter's confession— which is as one sent by God (6:57) with the words of "spirit and life" (6:63).[4] His confession fits the dualism of the Gospel, for Peter identifies Jesus as God's Holy One, sent with spirit and life, over and against Judas, in whom the devil comes to dwell, and also over and against the world, which is described in the immediate aftermath of the Bread of Life Discourse as both other and evil (7:7).

We have seen that many scholars captivated by the idea that the Fourth Gospel disparages Peter's Christology do not merely compare his confession to the confessions of other Johannine characters to reveal its inadequacies but attempt to show that it pales in comparison to his own confession in the Synoptic Gospels. In the Synoptic Gospels, Peter identifies Jesus as the "Christ" (Mark 8:29; Matt 16:16; Luke 9:20) and/or the "Son of [the living] God" (Matt 16:16). But comparing the confessional language Peter uses in John's Gospel versus the Synoptic Gospels is terribly misleading if one does not also compare the contexts in which the confessions are made. In the Synoptic Gospels, Peter's confession is a decisive turning point because it testifies to Jesus' messianic

---

determines that neither his accomplishments nor his missteps can be traced to a weak Christology.

[4] See the discussion in chapter 2. Particularly helpful is the observation of Schnackenburg, *St. John*, 2.76, that the word *holy* "expresses the closest possible intimacy with God, a participation in God's deepest and most essential being." Thompson, *God of the Gospel of John*, 124, also offers a constructive analysis: "the agency figures that prove most illuminating in interpreting the Gospel's Christology, particularly with respect to how God is made known, are those figures that unite agent (Jesus) and sender (God) most closely."

status and sets the stage for Jesus to begin teaching about his upcoming suffering, death, and resurrection. In John's Gospel, his confession is also a turning point but because it establishes the loyalty of the Twelve and keeps the ministry from losing critical mass. As I emphasized in chapter 2 of this study, what Jesus needs most in the aftermath of the Bread of Life Discourse is not a(nother) Christological title but a pledge of loyalty. He does not ask the Twelve, "Who do you say that I am?" as in the Synoptic Gospels (Mark 8:29; Matt 16:15; Luke 9:20), but "Do you also wish to go away?" At that point in the story, the Christology of the Twelve is less important than their loyalty.

By putting such a heavy emphasis on the title Peter awards to Jesus, scholars undervalue the sublime timing of the confession and the importance of his pledge of loyalty. Delivered at a time when Jesus' ministry is hemorrhaging supporters, Peter's pledge establishes the Twelve as the temporary nucleus of Jesus' new ministry.[5] Recognizing that Jesus is true sustenance, Peter and the Twelve are not offended as the other disciples are by his words about his body and blood being food and drink, but understand the Bread of Life Discourse to be an invitation to participate in his ongoing life. Only after Jesus hears Peter's confession and recognizes that the emigration crisis has abated does he turn his attention to the one "devil" (διάβολός) that still confronts the ministry (6:70). Unlike in Mark (8:33) and Matthew (16:23), the devil / adversary identified in the immediate wake of Peter's confession is not Peter but Judas, which I have suggested is an early sign of the Gospel's favorable attitude to Peter.

Peter and the Beloved Disciple

Just as it is a mistake to saddle Peter with a low Christology, it is a mistake to identify him as the subordinate of BD. Yet this is done with such regularity by capable scholars (e.g., Brown, Culpepper, Gee, Goulder, Droge, Perkins, O'Grady, Watty, Brock, Byrne, and many others) that one would think the Evangelist explicitly assigns him this role! At the Last Supper (when Peter relies on BD to pass along a question to Jesus; 13:23–25), in the courtyard of the high priest (when he relies on BD to whisper a word of introduction to the female gatekeeper; 18:15–16), and during the race to the empty tomb (when he comes in second to BD and fails to see the discarded σουδάριον as a sign pointing to the resurrection; 20:2–10), scholars see Peter as having less faith and less sensitivity to Jesus than BD. Peter's behavior is, in part, seen to reflect his low Christology:

---

[5] There is no hint that the Evangelist assigns to the Twelve any kind of *eschatological* importance, seeing them as the faithful remnant that will bear witness to the reconstitution of Israel. If anything, he describes Peter, BD, and Mary Magdalene as the nucleus of the post-Easter faith community. In the Redactor's mind, the "seven" who gather in Galilee constitute the earliest incarnation of the Johannine church. Either way, Peter is at the center of the group.

he does not follow Jesus in the manner of a *true* Johannine disciple (i.e., BD) because he does not understand the deepest truths about Jesus' person and nature. Some scholars make him out to be an out-and-out "bumbler."[6] If he is not refusing foot-washings that allow him a share in Jesus' life, he is chopping off ears to demonstrate his rugged love for Jesus, and so on. These three scenes are not the only ones in the Gospel in which Peter's unique brand of discipleship comes under attack, but they are the ones most commonly cited as evidence of his spiritual inferiority to BD, and as such they deserve a closer look.

In 13:23–25, the "middle" scene of the trio of Last Supper vignettes in which Peter figures, many scholars see him as a hapless figure who needs help from BD to forward a question to Jesus about the identity of the traitor. In our exegesis of the scene, however, we discovered Peter to be loyal and perceptive figure who *thinks* to raise the question in the first place. Even as the other disciples react to news of impending treachery in the ministry by staring blankly at one another, "uncertain of whom he (Jesus) was speaking," Peter launches an investigation into the identity of the traitor. BD contributes positively to the scene by passing along Peter's question to Jesus, revealing himself to be an intimate associate of Jesus, but he does not upstage Peter. If I am right in believing that πυθέσθαι functions in 13:24 as an infinitival imperative, Peter does not beckon to BD so much as he *signals* him to put the question to Jesus. Far from being BD's subordinate, Peter directs BD's activities.

BD, despite his close proximity to Jesus at the Last Supper, does not take advantage of his position to put the question to Jesus himself. As in 20:6–8, he waits for Peter to act before proceeding. This does not mean that Peter is portrayed as BD's superior, however. The Evangelist designs the scene to show these two important disciples cooperating to expedite the departure of Judas, although the two set out with the simple goal of identifying the traitor. Although BD is introduced to the reader in this pericope primarily as an intimate associate of Jesus, leaning upon his bosom (κόλπος) in the same manner that Jesus resides in the κόλπος of the Father (1:18), he is also introduced as a close associate of Peter. It is this *cooperative* dynamic that readers are meant to take notice of and discover resurfacing in subsequent scenes, not a competitive dynamic so often detected by scholars.

In chapter four of this study I sought to refute the argument that the scene at the courtyard of the high priest (18:15–16) is designed to show Peter as, once again, a hapless figure, cut off from Jesus and, unlike BD, lacking ties to the religious elite. In reality these two verses belong to a larger scene (18:15–27) that highlights Peter's fearfulness but also his intense affection for Jesus. Peter meets far more resistance in attempting to enter the courtyard of the high priest in John's Gospel than he does in any of the other canonical Gospels (cf. Mark

---

[6] "Bumbler" is the specific term applied by R. F. Collins (see introduction), but, as we have seen, many scholars employ similarly derogatory language.

14:53–72; Matt 26:57–75; Luke 22:54–62). Although John hews remarkably close to Synoptic tradition in interspersing the scenes of Jesus' trial / hearing with Peter's denials, he departs from that tradition to emphasize the frequent manner in which Peter encounters obstacles. Unique to the Fourth Gospel are scenes in which Peter is detained at the gate until his credentials can be checked (18:16), interrogated by the gatekeeper (18:17), and confronted by a relative of the man maimed in the garden (18:26–27).

Explicit in the latter scene and implicit in the first two is the idea that Peter has proven himself to be such a close supporter of Jesus that he warrants special observation and harassment from Jesus' enemies. Although BD disappears at the precise moment that Peter could use him most (which is bizarre, frankly, given that he earlier went out of his way to help gain Peter entry), it is reasonable to conclude that the scene portrays both disciples as fervent followers of Jesus. BD earns Peter passage into the courtyard, relying on his connection to the religious elite; Peter penetrates deeply enough to be recognized as a supporter of Jesus. While Peter clearly fails Jesus in denying him three times, he is depicted as taking seriously Jesus' teaching that the vitality of one's faith proves itself through one's willingness to "follow" him (ἀκολουθέω; 18:15; cf. also 1:43; 10:27; 12:26; 13:36; and 21:19–22).

The race to the empty tomb (20:2–10) is the scene in the Gospel in which Peter is most often accused by scholars of being slower of foot and slower on the uptake than BD. But, as I have argued, it is no more helpful to see Peter as the loser of the race *to* the tomb than it is to see him as the winner of the race *into* the tomb. Although both descriptions are accurate in principle, both give credence to the idea that the two are rivals and not collaborators. A more progressive exegetical approach, I feel, is one that detects the Johannine virtues of faith and devotion propelling Peter and BD past one another at various stages in the race, testifying to their shared determination to discover the location of Jesus' body. It *is* a race in the sense that both are running quickly; it is *not* a race in the sense that one must be declared "winner" and the other "loser."

Once inside the tomb, BD sees the neatly-discarded σουδάριον (facecloth) and experiences a flash of post-resurrectional belief, which is a credit to his faith and/or intuitive powers (cf. also 21:7). The revelation does not upstage or denigrate Peter, however. Implicit in the narrative is the fact that BD's faith is incipient or temporary. Like Peter, he does not yet understand the scripture that "he (Jesus) must rise from the dead" (20:9), and so is unable to build on his discovery. We discussed at length the fact that BD is not described as sharing news of the resurrection with Peter or with the mother of Jesus, with whom he now resides (cf. 19:26–27). Because true Johannine faith is faith proclaimed (cf. 1:19; 4:39; 20:21–23; 21:24–25), BD's faith can at best be classified as incipient. Not until 21:7—when he sees the risen Jesus on the lakeshore and proclaims him to Peter—does he demonstrate a mature faith in the resurrection.[7]

In all three of these scenes, then—the investigation of the traitor, the entry into the high priest's courtyard, and the exploration of the empty tomb—Peter and BD comprise together the paradigmatic Johannine Christian, one who treats faith not as a static commodity but as something that gains relevance through proclamation. If BD's specialty, for lack of a better term, is *faithful perception*, which allows him to discern the presence or power of the Lord in the midst of darkness and despair (20:8; 21:7),[8] Peter's is *faithful praxis*. He wields a sword with as much zeal as a fishing net, publicly confesses Jesus as the revealer of God's word, serves as the spokesman and leader of Jesus' disciples (before the resurrection [6:68–69] and after [21:4, 11]), ministers to Jesus' "sheep," and suffers martyrdom. While BD is often said to be loved *by* Jesus, Peter three times professes his love *for* Jesus. This fact is rarely (if ever) mentioned by scholars who insist that the Gospel portrays Peter and BD more as competitors than as colleagues.

Among the books of the NT, James (2:26) is obviously the most famous for reporting that "faith apart from works is dead" (ἡ πίστις χωρὶς ἔργων νεκρά ἐστιν), but this is an implicit message of the Fourth Gospel as well, conveyed by

---

[7] Without impugning the faith of BD, I have attempted to show that his faith is not challenged in the same manner as Peter's. It would be an exaggeration to say that it exists in a vacuum, wholly removed from danger and controversy, but it goes untested in both the denial scene (18:17–27) and the scene of Jesus' arrest (18:1–12), episodes in which Jesus' fiercest opponents gather and condemn him and/or his closest supporters. If the Evangelist wants us to believe that BD is present in those scenes—and nothing suggests that BD has the power to dematerialize in the face of adversity—why does he not counsel Peter against violence in the garden or rush to his defense in the courtyard of the high priest? The answer may be that vocalization is not his strong suit. He speaks only six words in the Gospel. We know he has conversations with Jesus (or at least one conversation: 13:24–25), but we do not know what he says, which is not the case with Peter, Nicodemus, the Samaritan woman, Andrew, Thomas, Nathanael, Martha, Mary, Pilate, the man born blind, and other important characters in the Gospel. In my opinion, both the Evangelist and the Redactor are reluctant to place BD in a conversation with Jesus because this would compromise his characterization as a meditative and perceptive disciple. The Johannine Jesus always gets the better of his earthly associates in conversation, redirecting their questions and even their confessions until they are (often unconsciously) explicating his relationship to the Father (cf. 3:1–9; 4:5–26; 9:2–32). BD is never put in a position in which his faith is susceptible to analysis or refinement. The only things that we, the readers, are explicitly told about him are that he is loved by Jesus and that his faithful testimony authenticates the Gospel. These are impressive credentials, to be sure, but they must not blind us to the fact that BD appears as a paradigmatic follower of Jesus only when he is teamed with Peter.

[8] According to Haenchen, *John 2*, 234, BD "is the guarantee of the right doctrine promulgated by this gospel."

Peter and BD. In return for modeling faith and praxis, the mainstays of the Christian profession, Peter and BD are invested with ecclesial responsibilities. Peter is the missionary, pastor, and notable martyr of the Johannine church; BD is its perpetual witness, validating traditions in the Gospel (19:35; 21:24). Peter's ministry may rightly be considered an "office," for authority is personally vested in him by Jesus. BD's witness can be considered an office as well, for the warrant that assigns it legitimacy is Jesus' love.

PETER AND THE APOSTOLIC CHURCH

In accepting that Peter and BD represent together the complete Johannine Christian, we are forced to abandon the third tenet of the conventional wisdom about Peter in the Gospel of John, which is that Peter represents Apostolic or Petrine Christianity.[9] Unlike in the Synoptic Gospels, Peter is not consistently described in John's Gospel as the spokesman for the Twelve. The Evangelist portrays him in this role only once, and the Redactor never does. Peter's habit is to associate with smaller groups, whether composed of five (1:35–51), seven (21:2–25), or—in the many scenes in which he is paired with BD—two individuals. Whether or not the Evangelist and the Redactor give us the precise sizes of these groups to downplay the image of Peter as representative of the Twelve is hard to say, but what can safely be said is that Peter exemplifies positive traits of *Johannine Christianity*. He is revered as the inspirational co-founder of the Johannine community, present during the entire earthly ministry of Jesus and at the inception of the post-Easter, Johannine "church" (21:2ff.).[10]

Nowhere is his Johannine pedigree more obvious than in John 21, the Gospel "supplement" that seeks to allay fears of a delayed Parousia and differentiates the roles of Peter and BD. Although the chapter is largely devoted to ecclesial issues, the Twelve are never mentioned. If, as many believe, a goal of the chapter is to upgrade Peter's image and extend the hand of friendship to the Apostolic church,[11] why is the image of the Twelve not updated and upgraded as well? Why is it not made clear that the group Peter speaks for in John 6 is acknowledged by the Johannine community to have a representative function in the *post-Easter* church? As it is, the Twelve are given an active role in the Gospel only once, and this is during the earthly ministry of Jesus (6:67–

---

[9] See especially Brown, *Community of the Beloved Disciple*, 71–91, who maintains that the Evangelist ranks post-Easter communities according to their Christologies.

[10] Given my position that Peter represents Johannine Christianity and not Apostolic Christianity—an institutional outgrowth of the work of the Twelve—it is a strange coincidence that I have identified twelve major Petrine episodes in the Gospel (1:40–42; 6:68–69; 13:4–10, 23–25, 36–38; 18:10–11; 15–16, 25–27; 20:2–10; 21:1–11, 15–17, 18–22)!

[11] See the second section of the introduction and *passim*.

69).[12] After the resurrection, they are said to be a group to which Thomas belongs (20:24), but they are not described explicitly as engaging in evangelical work. Recognizing this, E. Haenchen makes the following observation:

> When the risen Jesus comes to the disciples and pours out the spirit on them, the twelve are not mentioned, but 'the disciples' are. That is no accident. The saying of Jesus: "As the Father sent me, so I send you" makes all the disciples into apostles…What is expressed by the doctrine of the priesthood of all believers is very strongly emphasized in this passage: there is a *successio apostolica*, but all believers belong to that succession.[13]

Haenchen does not deny Peter's leadership role. In his exegesis of the fishing story (21:2–11), he repeats this contention that the absence of the Twelve in John 21 is almost to be expected, given their low profile in chapters 1–20, but adds that John 21 "is really only a story about Peter (and according to v. 14, also about the beloved disciple)."[14]

Indeed, the Redactor describes Peter not as the leader of the Twelve but as leader of *seven* individuals, two of whom are characters unique to John's Gospel (Nathanael and BD). Peter alone demonstrates a proclivity for missionary work and is invested with pastoral responsibilities. The Fourth Gospel does not seem to espouse the belief that Christians need mediators to develop a vibrant relationship with Christ (cf. 3:15–16, 36; 5:24; 6:35; 6:47; 11:26, etc.), but it strongly suggests that pastoral guidance, particularly from Peter, makes the spiritual journey more fruitful.

When Peter is viewed in this positive light, two implications (or recommendations) for future research take shape. First, Johannine commentators should dispense with the idea that Peter represents Apostolic, Petrine, Judean, fleshly, Roman or any other kind of Christianity apart from *Johannine Christianity*. If, as I have argued, Peter's flaws owe more to unrestrained zeal than an inability to grasp the doctrine of Jesus' preexistence, and if he describes Jesus in 6:68–69 almost exactly as Jesus describes himself in 6:35–47, how can it be that he represents a less enlightened strain of Christianity than Johannine Christianity? If Peter is BD's equal and not his subordinate, how can the two disciples represent different congregations? Finally, if Peter is the leader of a group of seven disciples that collectively represent the embryonic Johannine church, how can he be the leader of a rival group of Apostolic Christians?

---

[12] Thomas is said to belong to the Twelve in 20:24, but whether the group accomplishes anything in an active sense here (e.g. assembles in the house in Jerusalem for fellowship or some other faith-based activity) is not clear.

[13] Haenchen, *John 2*, 216.

[14] Ibid., 222.

In point of fact we have no idea *what* the Evangelist or the Redactor thinks about Apostolic Christianity—or if they think about it at all! The word "apostle" is never used in the Gospel, let alone the term "Apostolic Church." We know that Jesus has "other sheep" that do not belong to the Johannine "fold" (αὐλή; 10:1ff.), but we do not know who they are. They are certainly not the Twelve, who briefly comprise the entire flock in 6:67–69, and neither are they "the Seven," who appear as the progenitors of the Johannine church in John 21. Peter is a member of each of these groups and should be considered an inspirational founder of the Johannine church and exemplary disciple, as opposed to a charismatic interloper whose stock mysteriously appreciated among Johannine Christians somewhere near the end of the first century and inspired a scribe to upgrade Peter's characterization in the community's Gospel.

The second (related) idea deserving of reconsideration is that John 21 is in large part a "rehabilitation" of Peter that gives us a window into a phase in the development of the Johannine church when external threat or internal chaos was so pronounced that the community sought refuge in ecumenical outreach.[15] While John 21:15–17 does afford Peter a threefold profession of love that allows him to mitigate some of the damage of the threefold denial, the primary function of the threefold profession is to qualify Peter for his three pastoral duties.[16] As Ridderbos notes, verses 15–17 do not look backward but forward: Peter's threefold profession of love "prompts Jesus to reinforce his ties with him as never before."[17] Peter is not portrayed so negatively in chapters 1–20 that he requires "rehabilitation" in chapter 21. The ecclesial post of "shepherd" is formally assigned to him for the first time in John 21, but the reader suspects that he has been in training for the position since 6:68–69, a composition of the Evangelist.

The real purpose of John 21 is not to rehabilitate Peter but to address the death of BD, an event that rattled the community to such an extent that two iconic characters, Peter and Jesus, had to be recalled and given roles in a dialog to put the event into perspective. The setting for their dialog is a previously unknown or unused Galilean resurrection story set on the Sea of Tiberias (cf. Luke 5:1–11). Serving as the community surrogate, Peter asks Jesus about the ramifications of BD's death. The query is simple: "Lord, what about him?" Jesus gives him a paraenetical answer, which is, in essence, just this: *Don't worry about him! Keep your focus on me!* (21:19, 22). As if sensing that Jesus'

---

[15] Brock, *Mary Magdalene*, 52, refers to John 21 as the Gospel's "conciliatory Johannine appendix."

[16] A. J. Simonis, *Die Hirtenrede im Johannes-Evangelium: Versuch einer Analyse von Johannes 10.1–18 nach Entstehung, Hintergrund und Inhalt* (Rome: Päpstliches Bibelinstitut, 1967), 235, is right to observe that Peter's three specific responsibilities comprise one prodigious pastoral task: "das Leben der Schafe zu erhalten."

[17] Ridderbos, *Gospel of John*, 667.

answer will not satisfy every member of the community concerned about BD's death, the Redactor includes his own assessment of the situation, which is entirely positive: BD *is* immortal! His body may have suffered corruption, but his witness continues to authenticate the Gospel, which is itself the enduring good news that the Father has sent the Son (5:23; 10:36) and that those who believe in the Son will not perish but inherit eternal life (3:16).

Concluding Thoughts

Although I have argued that criticisms of Peter in the Gospel of John are greatly overdone, I do not pretend that Peter is portrayed everywhere in the Gospel in a glowing light. In fact, in between confessing Jesus in John 6 and making a threefold profession of love for him in John 21, Peter experiences, to put it mildly, one dreadful night. On the eve of Jesus' execution, he rejects Jesus' offer to wash his feet (13:6–9), cuts off the ear of the servant of the high priest (18:10–11), and denies Jesus three times (18:17, 25–27).[18] Although BD enjoys an easy intimacy with Jesus, Peter does not, but attempts to cultivate an intimacy with Jesus that is conditional. Simply put, he seeks to shield Jesus from adversity and degradation in order to keep him alive and available for fellowship.

Given these errors, it is in some senses surprising that Jesus never strips Peter of his leadership role, perhaps instilling in Andrew the power to "net" novitiates or investing pastoral leadership of the Johannine community in BD, Thomas, Nathanael or Mary Magdalene. But he does not. The Johannine Jesus does not describe Peter as a "stumbling block," as the Matthean Jesus does (Matt 16:23), nor does he address him as Σατανα, as happens in both Mark (8:33) and Matthew (16:23). Indeed, the Johannine Jesus finds Peter to be an individual rather amenable to realignment. It does not prove a difficult task for Jesus to alert Peter to his errors and set him once more on the proper path of discipleship (13:9; 18:11–15; 21:15–17, 19–22).

---

[18] The Gospel rarely affords us a peek inside Peter's mind (but see 21:17, in which he is described as "grieved"), but it is not unreasonable to suppose that Peter finds such cognitive dissonance in the image of the *Holy One of God* engaging in a footwashing ritual or being arrested by the opposition that he reacts precipitously to curtail those events. That does not excuse his behavior; in both scenes he is chastised by Jesus. It does help explain it, however. Chrysostom has this to say about Peter's denials: "Therefore did Divine Providence permit Peter first to fall, in order that he might be less severe to sinners from the remembrance of his own fall. Peter, the teacher and master of the whole world, sinned, and obtained pardon, that judges might thereafter have that rule to go by in dispensing pardon. For this reason I suppose the priesthood was not given to Angels; because, being without sin themselves, they would punish sinners without pity." *Serm. De Petro et Elia*, in Aquinas, *Catena Aurea*, 4:554.

Three days after the denials, Mary Magdalene still recognizes Peter as the leader of the disciples, approaching him first with her report about the disappearance of Jesus' body (20:1–2), a scene constructed by the Evangelist. Peter is again depicted as the leader of the disciples in 21:3–7, verses penned by the Redactor, when he arranges the Galilean fishing expedition. The transition from John 20 to John 21 is not seamless, but Peter's leadership role remains a constant. Famously, he is the first one off the boat when Jesus is spotted on the shore in John 21:7; he is so excited at the prospect of making contact with Jesus that he refuses to sit patiently with the rest of the disciples and let the wind or currents carry him the remaining one hundred yards to shore. When Jesus commands the disciples as a group to bring some of the miraculously-caught fish for breakfast, it is Peter alone who goes back into the water and "draws" (ἕλκω) ashore the fish, demonstrating his unique capacity for missionary work. As we have seen, this same verb ἕλκω is used in 12:32 to describe the risen Jesus "drawing" all people to himself, and so the missionary undertones of John 21 are unmistakable.

Back on dry land, Peter is invested with pastoral responsibility in the "breakfast on the beach" pericope in which he professes his love for Jesus three times (21:15–17). J. Vanier employs what he terms "meditative prose" to describe the maturity Peter has attained by the time the Fourth Gospel draws to a close:

> *Peter has been confirmed as the shepherd*
> *who will feed and tend the flock of Jesus,*
> *who is the Good and Wonderful Perfect Shepherd.*
> *His role is to lead people to Jesus*
> *so that they may dwell in Jesus, and Jesus in them,*
> *and so that they may become beloved disciples*
> *inspired and guided directly by Jesus and by the Holy Spirit.*
> *Peter's role is humble but necessary.*
> *He is called to be a sign and a source of unity for the Flock.*
> *The Church on earth needs a shepherd and shepherds,*
> *To help each one be faithful to their call..*[19]

Although Peter speaks for the Twelve when he confesses Jesus and pledges him allegiance in 6:68–69, readers may get the sense that his own faith undergoes the most profound development in the Gospel. He is introduced in the call narrative (1:35–51) as one who is *brought* (ἤγαγεν) to Jesus. Unlike Andrew, he is not busy honing his discipleship skills by following John the

---

[19] Vanier, *Mystery of Jesus*, 356.

Baptist when Jesus arrives, but is far enough removed from the action that Andrew must go and "find" (εὑρίσκω) him to tell him about Jesus. Upon meeting Jesus, Peter does not confess him as the "lamb of God," as John the Baptist does, or the "Messiah," as Andrew does, or "the one whom Moses wrote about," as Philip does, or the "the Son of God," as Nathanael does. Even when Jesus greets Peter and predicts his name change from Σίμων to Κηφᾶς, Peter has nothing to say. As was noted at the beginning of this study, it is not a propitious start.

By the time the Bread of Life Discourse comes to an end, however—which is perhaps a year later in the storyworld timeline—Peter has, through the process of following Jesus, come to "know" and "believe" enough about him to be able to speak for the other disciples and confess him as the "Holy One of God" who has the "words of eternal life." By pledging loyalty to Jesus, Peter makes certain that the fellowship will retain a critical mass of support. In subsequent scenes, he initiates the process of identifying the traitor in Jesus' closest circle of supporters, engages in a public act of defense of Jesus that is passionate enough to draw the attention of the opposition, serves as the shepherd of Jesus' flock, and dies a martyr's death, glorifying God. He is understood to be such a quintessentially Johannine character that he serves as the community surrogate in the important scene in which Jesus offers counsel to the community about how to cope with BD's death. It is, to put it simply, a remarkable turnaround, and shows the manner in which faith accrues in one who leaves behind one life to begin a new one centered in Christ.

BIBLIOGRAPHY

Abogunrin, S. O. "The Three Variant Accounts of Peter's Call: A Critical and Theological Examination of the Texts." *New Testament Studies* 31 (1985): 587–602.

Agourides, S. "The Purpose of John 21." Pages 127–32 in *Studies in the History and Text of the New Testament—in Honor of K. W. Clark*. Edited by B. L. Daniels and M. J. Suggs. Salt Lake City: University of Utah, 1967.

Aland, K. "Neuetestamentliche Papyri II." *New Testament Studies* 12 (1966): 176–85.

Allies, T. W. *St. Peter: His Name and Office*. London: Richardson and Son, 1852.

Anderson, P. N. "The Having-Sent-Me Father: Aspects of Agency, Encounter, and Irony in the Johannine Father-Son Relationship." Pages 33–57 in *God the Father in the Gospel of John*. Edited by A. Reinhartz. *Semeia* 85. Atlanta: Society of Biblical Literature, 1999.

Aquinas, T. *Catena Aurea: A Commentary on the Four Gospels*. Trans. J. H. Newman. 4 vols. London: Saint Austin Press, 1997.

Ashton, J. *Understanding the Fourth Gospel*. Oxford: Oxford University Press, 1991.

Bacon, B. W. *The Fourth Gospel in Research and Debate*. New Haven: Yale University Press, 1918.

———. "The Motivation of John 21:15–25." *Journal of Biblical Literature* 50 (1931): 71–80.

Bailey, J. A. *The Traditions Common to the Gospels of Luke and John*. Supplements to Novum Testamentum 7. Leiden: Brill, 1963.

Barnett, P. *Jesus and the Rise of Early Christianity: A History of New Testament Times*. Downer's Grove, Illinois: InterVarsity, 1999.

Barrett, C. K. *Church, Ministry and Sacraments in the New Testament*. Carlisle: Paternoster, 1983.

———. *The Gospel of John and Judaism*. London: SPCK, 1975.

———. *The Gospel According to St. John: An Introduction with Commentary and Notes on the Greek Text*. 2nd ed. Cambridge: SPCK, 1978.

Bauckham, R. "The Audience of the Fourth Gospel." Pages 101–14 in *Jesus in Johannine Tradition*. Edited by R. T. Fortna and T. Thatcher. Louisville: Westminster John Knox, 2001.

———. "The Beloved Disciple as Ideal Author." Pages 46–68 in *The Johannine Writings*. Edited by S. E. Porter and C. A. Evans. Sheffield: Sheffield Academic Press, 46–68.

———. "Monotheism and Christology in the Gospel of John." Pages 148–66 in *Contours of Christology in the New Testament*. Cambridge, England: Eerdmans, 2005.

Beasley-Murray, G. R. *John*. 2nd ed. WBC. Nashville: Thomas Nelson, 1999.

Becker, J. *Das Evangelium nach Johannes: Kapitel 1–10*. ÖTK 4. Gütersloh: Verlagshaus Mohn, 1991.

Bernard, J. H. *The Gospel According to St. John*. 2 vols. ICC. Edinburgh: T & T Clark, 1928.

Bezobrazov, S. "John 21." *New Testament Studies* 3 (1956–57): 132–36.

Billerbeck, P. *Kommentar zum Neuen Testament aus Talmud und Midrash*. 8th ed. Munich: C. H. Beck, 1983.

Blomberg, C. L. *The Historical Reliability of John's Gospel: Issues and Commentary*. Downer's Grove, Illinois: InterVarsity, 2001.

———. "John and Jesus." Pages 209–226 in *The Face of New Testament Studies: A Survey of Recent Research*. Edited by S. McKnight and G. R. Osborne. Grand Rapids: Baker Academic, 2004.

de Boer, M. C. *Johannine Perspectives on the Death of Jesus*. Kampen: Kok Pharos, 1996.

Boismard, M. –E. *Du Baptême à Cana: Jean 1.19–2.11*. Paris: Cerf, 1956.

Bolyki, J. "'Head Downwards': The Cross of Peter in the Lights of the Apocryphal Acts, of the New Testament and of the Society-Transforming Claim of Early Christianity." Pages 111–22 in *The Apocryphal Acts of Peter: Magic, Miracles and Gnosticism*. Edited by J. N. Bremmer. Leuven: Peeters, 1998.

de Boor, W. *Evangelium des Johannes*. 2 vols. Wuppertaler Studienbibel. Wuppertal: R. Brockhaus Verlag, 1970.

Borgen, P. D. *Bread from Heaven: An Exegetical Study of the Concept of Man in the Gospel of John and Writings of Philo*. Leiden: Brill, 1965.

Boring, M. E., and F. B. Craddock, eds. *The People's New Testament Commentary*. Louisville: Westminster John Knox, 2004.

Breck, J. "John 21: Appendix, Epilogue or Conclusion?" *St. Vladimir's Theological Quarterly* 36 (1992): 27–49.

Brock, A. G. *Mary Magdalene, the First Apostle: The Struggle for Authority*. Harvard Theological Studies 51. Cambridge, Mass: Harvard University Press, 2003.

Brodie, T. L. *The Gospel According to John: A Literary and Theological Commentary*. Oxford: Oxford University Press, 1993.

Brown, R. E. *The Churches the Apostles Left Behind*. New York: Paulist, 1984.

———. *The Community of the Beloved Disciple: The Life, Loves, and Hates of an Individual Church in New Testament Times.* New York: Paulist, 1979.

———. *The Gospel according to John.* 2 vols. AB. London: Doubleday, 1966, 1970.

———. *The Gospel and Epistles of John: A Concise Commentary.* Collegeville: Liturgical Press, 1988.

Brown, R. E., K. P. Donfried, and J. Reumann, eds. *Peter in the New Testament.* New York: Paulist, 1973.

Bruce, F. F. *The Gospel of John.* Grand Rapids: Eerdmans, 1983.

———. *The Hard Sayings of Jesus.* London: Hodder and Stoughton, 1983.

Bultmann, R. *The Gospel of John: A Commentary.* Translated by G. R. Beasley-Murray. Oxford: Blackwell, 1971.

———. *Synoptic Tradition.* Oxford: Blackwell, 1972.

———. *Theology of the New Testament.* Translated by K. Grobel. 2 vols. London: Bloomsbury, 1955.

Burge, G. M. *The Anointed Community: The Holy Spirit in the Johannine Tradition.* Grand Rapids: Eerdmans, 1987.

Burnett, P. *Jesus & the Rise of Early Christianity.* Downer's Grove, Illinois: InterVarsity, 1999.

Busse, U. "Die 'Hellenen' Joh 12:20ff. und der sogennante 'Anhang' Joh 21." Pages 3.2083–2100 in *The Four Gospels.* Edited by F. van Segbroeck, C. M. Tuckett, J. Verheyden, and G. van Belle. 3 vols. Bibliotheca ephemeridum theologicarum lovaniensium 100. Leuven: Leuven University Press, 1992.

———. *Das Johannesevangelium: Bildlichkeit, Diskurs und Ritual.* Bibliotheca ephemeridum theologicarum lovaniensium 162. Leuven: Leuven University Press, 2002.

Byrne, B. "The Faith of the Beloved Disciple and the Community in John 20." Pages 31-45 in *The Johannine Writings.* Edited by S. E. Porter and C. A. Evans. Sheffield: Sheffield University Press, 1995.

Calvin, J., *Calvin's New Testament Commentaries: John 1–10.* Translated by T. H. L. Parker. Grand Rapids: Eerdmans, 1995.

Charlesworth, J. H. *The Beloved Disciple: Whose Witness Validates the Gospel of John?* Valley Forge, Penn. Trinity Press International, 1984.

Chennattu, R. M. *Johannine Discipleship as a Covenant Relationship.* Peabody: Hendrickson, 2006.

Collins, R. F. "From John to the Beloved Disciple: An Essay on Johannine Characters." Pages 200–11 in *Gospel Interpretation: Narrative-Critical and Social-Scientific Approaches.* Edited by J. D. Kingsbury. Harrisburg, Penn.: Trinity Press International, 1997.

Coloe, M. L. "Welcome into the Household of God: The Foot Washing in John 13." *Catholic Biblical Quarterly* 66 (2004): 400–15.

Conway, C. "Gender Matters in John." Pages 79–103 in *A Feminist Companion to John*. Edited by A.-J. Levine. 2 vols. Cleveland: Pilgrim, 2003.

Conzelmann, H. *An Outline of the Theology of the New Testament*. Translated by J. Bowden. London: SCM, 1969.

Countryman, L. W. *The Mystical Way in the Fourth Gospel: Crossing Over into God*. Rev. ed. Harrisburg, Penn.: Trinity Press International, 1994.

Craig, W. L. "The Disciples' Inspection of the Empty Tomb: Lk 24:12–24; Jn 20.2–10." Pages 614–19 in *John and the Synoptics*. Edited by A. Denaux. Bibliotheca ephemeridum theologicarum lovaniensium 101. Leuven: Leuven University Press, 1992.

———. "The Empty Tomb of Jesus." *New Testament Studies* 31 (1985): 53.

Crosby, M. H. *"Do You Love Me?" Jesus Questions the Church*. Maryknoll: Orbis, 2000.

Crossan, J. D. *The Cross that Spoke: The Origins of the Passion Narrative*. San Francisco: Harper and Row, 1988.

Cullmann, O. *The Christology of the New Testament*. Translated by S. C. Guthrie and C. A. M. Hall. London: SCM, 1959.

———. *The Johannine Circle: Its Place in Judaism, among the Disciples of Jesus and in Early Christianity*. Translated by J. Bowden. New Testament Library. London: SCM, 1976.

———. *Peter: Disciple, Apostle, Martyr*. Translated by F. V. Filson. London: SCM, 1953.

Culpepper, R. A. *Anatomy of the Fourth Gospel: A Study in Literary Design*. Friendship First New Testament 1. Philadelphia: Fortress, 1983.

———. *The Gospel and Letters of John*. Interpreting Biblical Texts. Nashville: Abingdon, 1998.

———. "The Johannine *Hypodeigma*: A Reading of John 13." *Semeia* 53 (1991): 133–52.

———. *John the Son of Zebedee: The Life of a Legend*. Columbia, South Carolina: University of South Carolina Press, 1994.

———. "The Plot of John's Story of Jesus." Pages 188–99 in *Gospel Interpretation: Narrative-Critical & Social-Scientific Approaches*. Edited by J. D. Kingsbury. Harrisburg, Penn.: Trinity Press International, 1997.

Daube, D. "Three Notes Having to Do with Johanan ben Zaccai." *Journal of Theological Studies* 11 (1960): 53–62.

Dauer, A. *Die Passiongeschichte im Johannesevangelium: Eine Traditionsgeschichtliche und theologische Untersuchung zu Joh 18:1-19, 30*. Studien zum Alten und Neuen Testaments 30. Munich: Kösel-Verlag, 1972.

———. "Zur Authentizität von Lk 24,12." *Ephemerides theologicae lovanienses* 70 (1994): 294–318.
Davies, M. *Rhetoric and Reference in the Fourth Gospel*. Journal for the Study of the New Testament: Supplement Series 69. Sheffield: Sheffield Academic Press, 1992.
Davies, W. D., and D. C. Allison. *A Critical and Exegetical Commentary on the Gospel According to Saint Matthew*. 3 Vols. International Critical Commentary. Edinburgh: T & T Clark, 1988.
Dewey, A. J. "The Eyewitness of History: Visionary Consciousness in the Fourth Gospel." Pages 59–70 in *Jesus in Johannine Tradition*. Edited by R. T. Fortna and T. Thatcher. Louisville: Westminster John Knox, 2001.
Dodd, C. H. *Historical Tradition in the Fourth Gospel*. Cambridge: Cambridge University Press, 1963.
———. *The Interpretation of the Fourth Gospel*. Cambridge: Cambridge University Press, 1953.
Domeris, W. R. "The Confession of Peter according to John 6:69." *Tyndale Bulletin* 44 (1993): 155–67.
Donahue, J. R. "Are You Christ?" *The Trial Narrative in the Gospel of Mark* Society of Biblical Literature Dissertation Series 10. Missoula, Mont.: Scholar's Press, 1973.
Drewermann, E. *Das Johannes-Evangelium: Bilder einer neuen Welt, Erster Teil: Joh 1-10*. Düsseldorf: Patmos, 2003.
Droge, A. J. "The Status of Peter in the Fourth Gospel." *Journal of Biblical Literature* 109 (1990): 307–11.
Dschulnigg, P. *Petrus im Neuen Testament*. Stuttgart: Verlag Katholisches Bibelwerk, 1996.
Dunn, J. D. G. "John VI—A Eucharistic Discourse?" *New Testament Studies* 17 (1971): 328–38.
———. "The Washing of Disciples' Feet in John 13:1–20." *Zeitschrift für die neutestamentliche Wissenschaft und die Kunde der älteren Kirche* 61 (1970): 11–16.
Edwards, H. E. *The Disciple Who Wrote These Things: A New Inquiry into the Origins and Historical Value of the Gospel according to St. John*. London: J. Clarke, 1953.
Edwards, M. *John*. Blackwell Bible Commentaries. Oxford: Blackwell, 2004.
Ehrman, B. D. *The Orthodox Corruption of Scripture: The Effect of Early Christological Controversies on the Text of the New Testament*. Oxford: Oxford University Press, 1993.
Ellis, P. "The Authenticity of John 21." *St. Vladimir's Theological Quarterly* 36 (1992): 17–25.
Emerton, J. A. "The Hundred and Fifty-Three Fishes in John 21." *Journal of Theological Studies* 9 (1958): 86–89.

Eshbach, W. M. "Another Look at John 13:1–20." *Brethren Life and Thought* 14 (1969): 117–25.

Evans, C. A. "'Peter Warming Himself': The Problem of an Editorial 'Seam.'" *Journal of Biblical Literature* 101 (1982): 245–49.

Ferreira, J. *Johannine Ecclesiology*. Journal for the Study of the New Testament: Supplement Series 160. Sheffield: Sheffield Academic Press, 1998.

Filson, F. V. "Who was the Beloved Disciple?" *Journal of Biblical Literature* 68 (1949): 83–88.

Fitzmyer, J. A. "Aramaic Kepha and Peter's Name in the New Testament." Pages 121–32 in *Text and Interpretation: Studies in the New Testament Presented to Matthew Black*. Edited by E. Best and R. McWilson. Cambridge: Cambridge University Press, 1979.

———. *The Gospel According to Luke*. 2 vols. Anchor Bible. New York: Doubleday, 1981, 1985.

Flowers, H. J. "The Calling of Peter and the Restoration of Peter." *Anglican Theological Review* 19 (1922): 234-99.

Fortna, R. T. "Diachronic / Synchronic: Reading Jn 21 and Luke 5." Pages 387–99 in *John and the Synoptics*. Edited by A. Denaux. Bibliotheca ephemeridum theologicarum lovaniensium 101. Leuven: Leuven University Press, 1992.

———. *The Fourth Gospel and Its Predecessor: From Narrative Sources to Present Gospel*. Edinburgh: T & T Clark, 1989.

———. *The Gospel of Signs: A Reconstruction of the Narrative Source Underlying the Fourth Gospel*. Society for New Testament Studies Monograph Series 11. Cambridge: Cambridge University Press, 1970.

———. "Jesus and Peter at the High Priest's House: A Test Case for the Question of the Relation between Mark's and John's Gospels." *New Testament Studies* 24 (1978): 371–83.

Fouard, L. C. *Saint John and the Close of the Apostolic Age*. London: Longmans, Green and Co., 1906.

Franzmann, M., and M. Klinger. "The Call Stories of John 1 and John 21." *St. Vladimir's Theological Quarterly* 36 (1992) 7–15.

Gardner-Smith, P. "St. John's Knowledge of Matthew." *Journal of Theological Studies* 4 (1953): 35.

Garland, D. E. "John 18–19: Life through Jesus' Death." *Review & Expositor* 85 (1988): 485–89.

Gee, D. H. "Why Did Peter Spring into the Sea? [John 21:7]." *Journal of Theological Studies* 40 (1989): 481–89.

George, L. D. *Reading the Tapestry: A Literary-Rhetorical Analysis of the Johannine Resurrection Narrative: John 20–21*. Studies in Biblical Literature 14. New York: Peter Lang, 2000.

Glombitza, O. "Petrus—Der Freund Jesu: Überlegungen zu Joh 21:15 ff." *Novum Testamentum* 6 (1963): 277–85.
Gnilka, J. *Johannesevangelium*. Edited by J. Gnilka and R. Schnackenburg. Neue Echter Bibel. Würzburg: Echter Verlag, 1983.
Goguel, M. "Juifs et Romains dans l'histoire de la Passion." *Revue de l'histoire ecclésiastique* 62 (1910): 165–82, 295–322.
Goulder, M. D. *Luke: A New Paradigm*. Journal for the Study of the New Testament: Supplement Series 20. Sheffield: Sheffield Academic Press, 1989.
———. "John 1:1–2:12." Pages 201–22 in *John and the Synoptics*. Bibliotheca ephemeridum theologicarum lovaniensium 101. Leuven: Leuven University Press, 1992.
———. *St. Paul vs. St Peter: A Tale of Two Visions*. Louisville: Westminster John Knox, 1994.
Grant, M. *Saint Peter: A Biography*. New York: Scribner, 1995.
Grant, R. M. "One Hundred Fifty-three Large Fishes" *Harvard Theological Review* 42 (1949): 273–75.
Green, J. B. "Death of Jesus." Pages 146–63 in *Dictionary of Jesus and the Gospels*. Edited by J. B. Green and S. McKnight. Downer's Grove, Illinois: InterVaristy, 1992.
Grün, A. *Jesus: Tür zum Leben*. Stuttgart: Kreuz Verlag, 2002.
Grünenfelder, R., and B. L. Grünenfelder. *Erde und Licht: Mit dem Johannesevangelium auf den Spuren unserer Lebenswünsche*. Stuttgart: Verlag Katholisches Bibelwerk, 2004.
Guilding, A. *The Fourth Gospel and Jewish Worship: A Study of St. John's Gospel to the Ancient Jewish Lectionary System*. Oxford: Clarendon, 1960.
Gunn, D. M. "Narrative Criticism." Pages 171–95 in *To Each Its Own Meaning: An Introduction to Biblical Criticisms and Their Application*. Edited by S. L. McKenzie and S. R. Haynes. Louisville: Westminster John Knox, 1993.
Haenchen, E. *John 1: A Commentary on the Gospel of John Chapters 1–6*. Translated by R. W. Funk. Philadelphia: Fortress, 1984.
———. *John 2: A Commentary on the Gospel of John Chapters 7–21*. Translated by R. W. Funk. Philadelphia: Fortress, 1984.
Hahn, F. "Das Glaubenverständnis im Johannesevangelium." Pages 51–69 in *Glaube und Eschatologie*. Edited by E. Grässer and O. Merk. Tübingen: Mohr [Siebeck], 1985.
Hartman, L. "An Attempt at Text-Centered Exegesis of John 21." *Studia theologica* 38 (1984): 29–45.
Hawkin, D. J. "The Function of the Beloved Disciple Motif in the Johannine Redaction." *Laval Théologique et Philosophique* 33 (1977): 135–50.

Hooker, M. D. *Endings: Invitations to Discipleship.* Peabody, Mass.: Hendrickson, 2003.
Hoskyns, E. C. *The Fourth Gospel.* London: Faber & Faber, 1947.
———. *The Riddle of the New Testament.* London: Faber & Faber, 1947.
Howard, W. F. *The Fourth Gospel in Recent Criticism and Interpretation.* 2nd ed. London: Epworth, 1935.
Howard-Brook, W. *Becoming Children of God: John's Gospel and Radical Discipleship.* Maryknoll: Orbis, 1999.
Hultgren, A. J. "The Foot-washing (Jn 13:1–11) as Symbol of Eschatological Hospitality." *New Testament Studies* 28 (1982): 539–46.
Hunter, A. M. *The Gospel according to John.* Cambridge Bible Commentary. Cambridge, England: Cambridge University Press, 1965.
Inbody, T. L. *The Many Faces of Christology.* Nashville: Abingdon, 2002.
Jeffrey, P. "Do You Mind if I Wash Your Feet? Jn 13 as Pattern for Ecumenism." *Pacific Journal of Theology* 3 (1990): 17–22.
Jeremias, J. *The Eucharistic Words of Jesus.* Translated by N. Perrin. London: SCM, 1966.
Jones, L. P. *The Symbol of Water in the Gospel of John.* Journal for the Study of the New Testament: Supplement Series 145. Sheffield: Sheffield Academic Press, 1997.
de Jonge, M. "The Radical Eschatology of the Fourth Gospel and the Eschatology of the Synoptics." Pages 481–87 in *John and the Synoptics.* Edited by A. Deneaux. Bibliotheca ephemeridum theologicarum lovaniensium 101. Leuven: Leuven University Press, 1992.
———. *Jesus: Stranger from Heaven and Son of God.* Translated by J. E. Steely. Missoula, Mont.: Scholar's Press, 1977.
Jurgens, W. A., ed. *The Faith of the Early Fathers.* 3 vols. Collegeville: Liturgical Press, 1970.
Käsemann, E. *The Testament of Jesus.* Translated by G. Krodel. Philadelphia: Fortress, 1968.
———. "Zum johanneischen Verfasserproblem." *Zeitschrift für Theologie und Kirche* 48 (1951): 292–311.
Keener, C. S. *The Gospel of John: A Commentary.* 2 vols. Peabody, Mass: Hendrickson, 2003.
Kessler, W. T. *Peter as the First Witness of the Risen Lord: An Historical and Theological Investigation.* Rome: Gregorianum, 1998.
Koester, C. R. *Symbolism in the Fourth Gospel: Meaning, Mystery, Community.* 2nd ed. Minneapolis: Fortress, 2003.
Köstenberger, A. J. *Encountering John: The Gospel in Historical, Literary, and Theological Perspective.* Grand Rapids: Baker Academic, 1999.

———. *John*. BECT. Grand Rapids: Baker Academic, 2004.
Kragerud, A. *Der Lieblingsjünger im Johannesevangelium: Ein exegetischer Versuch*. Hamburg: Grosshaus Wegner, 1959.
Kümmel, W. G. *Introduction to the New Testament*. London: SCM, 1965.
Kysar, J. *John*. Augsburg Commentaries on the New Testament. Minneapolis: Augsburg, 1986.
Kysar, R. *John's Story of Jesus*. Philadelphia: Fortress, 1984.
Lake, K. "Simon, Cephas, Peter." *Harvard Theological Review* 14 (1921): 95–97.
Laney, J. C. *John*. Moody Gospel Commentary. Chicago: Moody, 1992.
Lapham, F. *Peter: The Myth, the Man and the Writings: A Study of Early Petrine Text and Tradition*. Journal for the Study of the New Testament: Supplement Series 239; Sheffield: Sheffield Academic Press, 2003.
Lee, D. A. "Partnership in Easter Faith: The Role of Mary Magdalene and Thomas in John 20." *Journal for the Study of the New Testament* 58 (1995): 37–49.
———. "The Symbol of Divine Fatherhood." Pages 177–87 in *God the Father in the Gospel of John*. Edited by A. Reinhartz. *Semeia* 85. Atlanta: Society of Biblical Literature, 1999.
———. *The Symbolic Narratives of the Fourth Gospel: The Interplay of Form and Meaning*. Journal for the Study of the New Testament: Supplement Series 95. Sheffield: JSOT Press, 1994.
Lightfoot, R. H. *St. John's Gospel: A Commentary*. Oxford: Oxford University Press, 1966.
Lindars, B. *Gospel of John*. New Century Bible. London: Oliphants, 1972.
———. *John*. Sheffield: JSOT Press, 1990.
———. "John." Pages 29–108 in *The Johannine Literature*. Edited by B. Lindars, R. B. Edwards and J. M. Court. Sheffield: Sheffield Academic Press, 2000.
Livius, T. *St. Peter, Bishop of Rome: The Roman Episcopate of the Prince of the Apostles*. London: Burns & Oates, 1888.
Loisy, A. *Le quatrième Évangile*. Paris: Alphonse Picard et Fils, 1903.
Lowe, J. *Saint Peter*. Oxford: Oxford University Press, 1956.
Maccini, R. G. *Her Testimony is True: Women as Witnesses according to John*. Journal for the Study of the New Testament: Supplement Series 125. Sheffield: Sheffield Academic Press, 1996.
MacGregor, G. H. C. *The Gospel of John*. Moffatt New Testament Commentary. London: Hodder and Stoughton, 1928.
MacRae, G. W. *Invitation to John: A Commentary on the Gospel of John with Complete Text from the Jerusalem Bible*. Garden City, New York: Image Books, 1978.
Madsen, N. P. *John*. Nashville: Abingdon, 1988.

Malina, B. J., and R. L. Rohrbaugh. *Social-Science Commentary on the Gospel of John*. Minneapolis: Fortress, 1998.
Martyn, J. L. *The Gospel of John in Christian History: Essays for Interpreters* New York: Paulist, 1978.
———. *History and Theology in the Fourth Gospel*. 3rd ed. Nashville: Abingdon, 2003.
Marxsen, W. *The Resurrection of Jesus of Nazareth*. Philadelphia: Fortress, 1970.
Matera, F. J. "John 20:1-18." *Interpretation* 43 (1989): 402–06.
Maynard, A. H. "The Role of Peter in the Fourth Gospel." *New Testament Studies* 30 (1984): 531–48.
McEleney, N. J. "Peter's Denials: How Many? To Whom?" *Catholic Biblical Quarterly* 52 (1990): 467–72.
———. "153 Great Fishes: Gematriarchal Atbash." *Biblica* 58 (1977): 411–17.
McKay, K. L. "Style and Significance in the Language of John 21:15–17." *Novum Testamentum* 27 (1985): 319–33.
McPolin, J. *John*. Dublin: Veritas, 1979.
Menken, M. J. J. "Interpretation of the Old Testament and the Resurrection of Jesus in John's Gospel." Pages 189–205 in *Resurrection in the New Testament*. Edited by R. Bieringer, V. Koperski and B. Lataire. Bibliotheca ephemeridum theologicarum lovaniensium 165. Leuven: Leuven University Press, 189–205.
———. *Old Testament Quotations in the Fourth Gospel: Studies in Textual Form*. Contributions to Biblical Exegesis and Theology 15. Kampen: Kok Pharos, 1996.
Metzger, B. M. *A Textual Commentary of the New Testament*. 2nd ed. Stuttgart: Deutsche Bibelgesellschaft, 1994.
Meyer, A. *Kommt und seht: Mystagogie im Johannesevangelium ausgehend von Joh 1,35-51*. Würzburg: Echter Verlag, 2005.
Michaels, J. R. "Catholic Christology in the Catholic Epistles." Pages 268–91 in *Contours of Christology in the New Testament*. Edited by R. N. Longenecker. Grand Rapids: Eerdmans, 2005.
———. *John*. New International Biblical Commentary on the New Testament. Peabody, Mass.: Paternoster, 1989.
Milne, B. *The Message of John*. Downer's Grove, Illinois: InterVarsity, 1993.
Minear, P. S. "The Beloved Disciple in the Gospel of John: Some Clues and Conjectures." Pages 85–98 in *The Composition of John's Gospel: Selected Studies from Novum Testamentum*. Edited by D. A. Orton. Leiden: Brill, 1999.

———. "The Original Functions of John 21." *Journal of Biblical Literature* 102 (1983): 85–98.
Moloney, F. J. *Glory Not Dishonor: Reading John 13–21*. Minneapolis: Fortress 1998.
———. *The Gospel of John*. Sacra pagina 4. Collegeville: Liturgical Press, 1998.
Morris, L. *Gospel according to John*. Rev. ed. New International Commentary on the New Testament. Grand Rapids: Eerdmans, 1995.
Motyer, S. "The Fourth Gospel and the Salvation of Israel." Pages 83–100 in *Anti-Judaism and the Fourth Gospel*. Edited by R. Bieringer, D. Pollefeyt, and F. Vandercasteele-Vanneuville Louisville: Westminster John Knox, 2001.
Nau, A. J. *Peter in Matthew: Discipleship, Diplomacy, and Dispraise*. Collegeville: Liturgical Press, 1992.
Neirynck, F. "The Anonymous Disciple in John 1." *Ephemerides theologicae lovanienses* 66 (1990): 5–37.
———. "John 21." *New Testament Studies* 36 (1990): 321–36.
———. "John and the Synoptics 1975–1990." Pages 3–62 in *John and the Synoptics*. Edited by A. Denaux. Bibliotheca ephemeridum theologicarum lovaniensium 101. Leuven: Leuven University Press, 1992.
———. "John and the Synoptics in Recent Commentaries," *Ephemerides theologicae lovanienses* 74 (1998): 386–97.
———. "Note on Mt 28:9-10." *Ephemerides theologicae lovanienses* 71 (1995): 161–65.
———. "Once More Luke 24:12." Pages 549–71 in *Evangelica III*. Bibliotheca ephemeridum theologicarum lovaniensium 150; Leuven: Leuven University Press, 2001.
———. "The 'Other' Disciple in Jn 18,15–16." *Ephemerides theologicae lovanienses* 51 (1975): 113–141.
Neusner, J. *The Midrash: A New Translation*. New Haven: Yale University Press, 1988.
Noack, B. *Zur johanneischen Tradition, Beiträge zur Kritiken an der literkritischen Analyse des vierten Evangeliums*. Copenhagen: Rosenkilde og Bagger, 1954.
Nun, M. "The Sea of Galilee and its Fishermen in the New Testament." Ein Gev, Israel: Kibbutz Ein Gev, 1989. Cited 15 January 2004. Online: http://www.ubfellowship.org/archive/j_arc/fishing2.htm.
O'Collins, G., and D. Kendall. "Mary Magdalene as Major Witness to Jesus' Resurrection." *Theological Studies* 48 (1987): 631–46.
O'Grady, J. F. *According to John: The Witness of the Beloved Disciple*. New York: Paulist, 1999.

———. "The Role of the Beloved Disciple." *Biblical Theology Bulletin* 9 (1979): 58–65.

Pamment, M. "The Fourth Gospel's Beloved Disciple." *Expository Times* 94. (1983): 363–67.

Perkins, P. *The Gospel According to John.* Chicago: Franciscan Herald Press, 1978.

———. "John." Pages 942–85 in the *New Jerome Biblical Commentary.* Edited by R. E. Brown et al. Englewood Cliffs, 1990.

———. *Peter: Apostle for the Whole Church.* Columbia: University of South Carolina Press, 1994.

Pesch, R. "The Position and Significance of Peter in the Church of the New Testament: A Survey of Current Research." *Concilium* 4 (1971): 21–35.

———. *Der reiche Fischfang: Luke 5:1–11 / Jo 21:1–14.* Kommentare und Beiträge zum Alten und Neuen Testament. Dusseldorf: Patmos, 1969.

Pesthy, M. "Cross and Death in the Apocryphal Acts of the Apostles." Pages 123–33 in *The Apocryphal Acts of Peter: Magic, Miracles and Gnosticism.* Edited by J. D. Bremmer. Leuven: Peeters, 1998.

Phillips, G. A. "'This is a Hard Saying: Who Can Be Listener to It?': Creating a Reader in John 6." Pages 23–56 in *Narrative Discourse in Structural Exegesis: John 6 and 1 Thessalonians.* Edited by Daniel Patte. *Semeia* 26. Chico, Calif.: Scholar's Press, 1983.

Porsch, F. *Johannesevangelium.* Stuttgarter Kleiner Kommentar—Neues Testament 4. Stuttgart: Verlag Katholisches Bibelwerk, 2001.

Quast, K. *Peter and the Beloved Disciple: Figures for a Community in Crisis.* Journal for the Study of the New Testament: Supplement Series 32; Sheffield: JSOT Press, 1989.

Ray, S. K. *St. John's Gospel: A Bible Study Guide and Commentary for Individuals and Groups.* San Francisco: Ignatius, 2002.

Redford, J. *Bad, Mad or God? Proving the Divinity of Christ from St. John's Gospel.* London: St. Paul's, 2004.

Reinhartz, A. "'And the Word Was Begotten': Divine Epigenesis in the Gospel of John." Pages 83–103 in *God the Father in the Gospel of John.* Edited by A. Reinhartz. *Semeia* 85. Atlanta: Society of Biblical Literature, 1999.

———. *Befriending the Beloved Disciple.* New York: Continuum, 2001.

Reiser, W. E. "The Case of the Tidy Tomb: The Place of the Napkins of John 11:44 and 20:7." *Heythrop Journal* 14 (1973): 47–57.

Rensberger, D. *Johannine Faith and Liberating Community.* Philadelphia: Westminster Press, 1988.

Ridderbos, H. N. *The Gospel According to John: A Theological Commentary*. Translated by J. Vriend. Grand Rapids: Eerdmans, 1997.
Riddle, D. W. "The Cephas-Peter Problem and a Possible Solution." *Journal of Biblical Literature* 59 (1940): 169–180.
Ringe, S. H. *Wisdom's Friends: Community and Christology in the Fourth Gospel*. Louisville: Westminster John Knox, 1999.
Robinson, J. A. T. *The Priority of John*. London: SCM, 1985.
Rowland, C. *Christian Origins: An Account of the Setting and Character of the Most Important Messianic Sect of Judaism*. London: SPCK, 1985.
Ruckstuhl, E. *Die literarische Einheit des Johannesevangeliums: Der gegenwärtige Stand der einschlägigen Forschungen*. Göttingen: Vandenhoeck & Ruprecht, 1987.
———. "Zur Aussage und Botschaft von Johannes 21." Pages 279–308 in *Die Kirche des Anfangs*. Edited by R. Schnackenburg, J. Ernst, and J. Wanke. Freiburg: Herder, 1978.
Sabbe, M. "The Footwashing in John 13 and Its Relation to the Synoptic Gospels." *Ephemerides theologicae lovanienses* 58 (1982): 279–308.
Sanders, J. N., and B. A. Mastin. *A Commentary on the Gospel according to St. John*. Harper's New Testament Commentaries. New York: Harper & Brothers, 1957.
Schenke, L. *Johannes*. Düsseldorf: Patmos, 1998.
———. *Das Johannesevangelium*. Stuttgart: Kohlhammer, 1992.
Schlatter, A. *Der Evangelist Johannes*. 2nd ed. Stuttgart: Calwer, 1948.
Schnackenburg, R. "Der Jünger, den Jesus liebte." Pages 2.97–2.117 in *Evangelisch-Katholischer Kommentar zum Neuen Testament: Vorarbeiten*. 2 vols. Zürich-Neukirchen: Benziger Verlag Zürich, 1970.
———. *The Church in the New Testament*. London: Burns and Oates, 1974.
———. *The Gospel according to St. John*. 3 vols. New York: Crossroad, 1990.
Schneiders, S. M. "The Foot Washing (John 13:1–20): An Experiment in Hermeneutics." *Catholic Biblical Quarterly* 43 (1981): 76–92.
———. *Written That You May Believe: Encountering Jesus in the Fourth Gospel*. New York: Crossroad, 1999.
Schnelle, U. *The History and Theology of the New Testament Writings*. Translated by M. E. Boring. Minneapolis: Fortress, 1998.
Scholtissek, K. "The Johannine Gospel in Recent Research." Pages 444–72 in *The Face of New Testament Studies: A Survey of Recent Research*. Edited by S. McKnight and G. R. Osborne. Grand Rapids: Baker Academic, 2004.
Schüssler Fiorenza, E. *In Memory of Her: A Feminist Theological Reconstruction of Christian Origins*. New York: Crossroad, 1983.
Segovia, F. F. "The Final Farewell of Jesus: A Reading of John 20:30–21:25." *Semeia* 53 (1991): 167–90.

———. "The Journey(s) of the Word of God: A Reading of the Plot of the Fourth Gospel." *Semeia* 53 (1991): 23–54.
Shaw, A. "The Breakfast by the Shore and the Mary Magdalene Encounter as Eucharistic Narratives." *JTS* 25 (1974): 12–26.
———. "Image and Symbol in John 21." *Expository Times* 86 (1975): 311.
Simoens, Y. *La gloire d'aimer: Structures, stylistiques et interprétatives dans le discourse de la Céne: Jn 13–17*. Analecta biblica 90. Rome: Biblical Institute Press, 1981.
Simon, L. *Petrus und der Lieblingsjünger im Johannesevangelium: Amt und Autorität*. Frankfurt: Peter Lang, 1994.
Simonis, A. J. *Die Hirtenrede im Johannes-Evangelium: Versuch einer Analyse von Johannes 10.1-18 nach Entstehung, Hintergrund und Inhalt*. Rome: Päpstliches Bibelinstitut, 1967.
Sinclair, S. G. *The Road and the Truth: The Editing of John's Gospel*. Vallejo, Calif.: BIBAL Press, 1994.
Smalley, S. S. "The Sign in John 21." *New Testament Studies* 20 (1974): 275–88.
Smith, D. M. *Johannine Christianity*. Edinburgh: T & T Clark, 1984.
———. *John*. Abingdon New Testament Commentaries. Nashville: Abingdon, 1999.
———. *John Among the Gospels*. 2nd ed. Columbia: University of South Carolina Press, 2001.
———. *The Theology of the Gospel of John*. Cambridge: Cambridge University Press, 1995.
Snyder, G. F. "John 13:16 and the Anti-Petrinism of the Johannine Tradition." *Biblical Research* 16 (1971): 5–15.
Söding, T. "Erscheinung, Vergebung und Sendung (Joh 21)." Pages 207–32 in *Resurrection in the New Testament*. Edited by R. Bieringer, V. Koperski, and B. Lataire. Bibliotheca ephemeridum theologicarum lovaniensium 165. Leuven: Leuven University Press, 2002.
Spicq, C. "Priestly Virtues in the New Testament." Pages 187–209 in *Sacraments in Scripture*. Edited by T. Worden. London: Geoffrey Chapman, 1966.
Staley, J. L. "What Can a Postmodern Approach to the Fourth Gospel Add?" Pages 47–57 in *Jesus in Johannine Tradition*. Edited by R. T. Fortna and T. Thatcher. Louisville: Westminster John Knox, 2001.
Stanton, G. *The Gospels and Jesus*. 2nd ed. Oxford: Oxford University Press, 2002.
Stauffer, E. *New Testament Theology*. Translated by J. Marsh. New York: Macmillan, 1955.
Stibbe, M. W. G. *John*. London: T & T Clark, 1996.

———. *John's Gospel*. London: Routledge, 1994.
Strecker, G. *Theology of the New Testament*. Louisville: Westminster John Knox, 2000.
Talbert, C. H. *Reading John: A Literary and Theological Commentary on the Fourth Gospel and the Johannine Epistles*. New York: Crossroad, 1988.
Temple, W. *Readings in St. John's Gospel*. London: MacMillan & Co., 1959.
Thatcher, T. "Jesus, Judas, and Peter: Character by Contrast in the Fourth Gospel." *BibSac* 153 (1996): 435–48.
Thomas, J. C. *Footwashing in the Johannine Community*. Journal for the Study of the New Testament: Supplement Series 61. Sheffield: Sheffield Academic Press, 1991.
———. "Jesus Washes the Disciples' Feet." *Living Pulpit* 9 (2000): 28–29.
Thompson, M. M. *The God of the Gospel of John*. Grand Rapids: Eerdmans, 2001.
Thyen, H. "Entwicklungen innerhalb der johanneischen Theologie und Kirche im Spiegel von Joh. 21 und den Lieblingsjüngertexte des Evangeliums." Pages 259–99 in *L'Évangile de Jean: Sources, rédactions, théologie*. Edited by M. de Jonge. Bibliotheca ephemeridum theologicarum lovaniensium 44. Leuven: Leuven University Press, 1977.
———. "Johannes und die Synoptiker: Auf der Suche nach einem neuen Paradigma zur Beschreibung ihrer Beziehungen anhand von Beobachtungen an Passions- und Ostererzählungen." Pages 81–107 in *John and the Synoptics*. Edited by A. Denaux. Bibliotheca ephemeridum theologicarum lovaniensium 101. Leuven: Leuven University Press, 1992.
Titus, E. L. *The Message of the Fourth Gospel*. New York: Abingdon, 1957.
Trilling, W. "Zum Petrusamt im Neuen Testament, Traditiongeschichtliche Überlegungen anhand von Mätthaus, 1 Petrus und Johannes." Pages 111–40 in *Studien zur Jesusüberlieferung*. Stuttgart: Katholisches Bibelwerk, 1988.
Trudinger, P. "The 153 Fishes: A Response and a Further Suggestion." *Expository Times* 102 (1990-91): 11–12.
Underhill, F. *Saint Peter*. London: Centenary Press, 1937.
Vanier, J. *Drawn into the Mystery of Jesus through the Gospel of John*. London: Darton, Longman and Todd, 2004.
van Tilborg, S. *Das Johannes-Evangelium: Ein Kommentar für die Praxis*. Stuttgart: Verlag Katholisches Bibelwerk, 2005.
von Wahlde, U. C. "Community in Conflict: The History and Social Context of the Johannine Community." Pages 222–33 in *Gospel Interpretation: Narrative-Critical & Social-Scientific Approaches*. Edited by J. D. Kingsbury. Harrisburg, Penn.: Trinity Press International, 1997.

Vorster, W. S. "The Growth and Making of John 21." Pages 2208–21 in *The Four Gospels*. Edited by F. van Segbroeck, C. M. Tuckett, J. Verheyden, and G. van Belle. Bibliotheca ephemeridum theologicarum lovaniensium 100. Leuven: Leuven University Press, 1992.

Waetjen, H. C. *The Gospel of the Beloved Disciple: A Work in Two Editions*. London: T & T Clark, 2005.

Watty, W. W. "The Significance of Anonymity in the Fourth Gospel." *Expository Times* 90 (1979): 209–212.

Webster, J. S. *Ingesting Jesus: Eating and Drinking in the Gospel of John*. Academia Biblica 6. Atlanta: Society of Biblical Literature, 2003.

Wengst, K. *Das Johannesevanglium*. 2 vols. Stuttgart: Kohlhammer, 2001.

Westcott, B. F. *The Gospel according to St. John*. Grand Rapids: Eerdmans, 1975.

Westcott, B. F. and J. F. A. Hort. *The New Testament in the Original Greek*. 2nd ed. London: Macmillan, 1896.

Wiarda, T. *Peter in the Gospels: Pattern, Personality and Relationship*. Tübingen: Mohr Siebeck, 2000.

Wilckens, U. *Das Evangelium nach Johannes*. Das Neue Testament Deutsch 4. Göttingen: Vanderhoeck & Ruprecht, 2000.

Witherington, B. *John's Wisdom: A Commentary on the Fourth Gospel*. Louisville: Westminster John Knox, 1995.

Wrede, W. *Vorträge und Studien*. Tübingen: Mohr [Siebeck], 1907.

INDEX OF SCRIPTURE

HEBREW BIBLE

Genesis
3:7	151
3:10–11	151
9:4	40
17:5	35
17:15	35
26:8	114
29:7	167
32:28	35
37:12	167
41:8	70

Exodus
3:14	84
34:33–35	116
36:35	157
39:27	157

Leviticus
3:17	40
17:14	40
17:26	40

Judges
5:28	114
13:4	66
13:7	45, 184,

2 Samuel
4:6	94

1 Kings
5:1–18	156
6:4	114

1 Chronicles
15:9	114

Psalms
77:71	167
106:16	45, 184
118:22	50

Proverbs
7:6	114
9:5	41

Isaiah
8:1–4	61
42:17	41
45:5–7	84
48:12	84
49:23	60
50:5	41
51:17	167
62:2-12	35
65:25	167

Jeremiah
13:1–11	61

Ezekiel
12.1–7	61
34:10	167
34:14	167

Daniel
2:46	84
7:13–15	70
8:18	84

Micah
7:14	167

Nahum
1:3	60

NEW TESTAMENT

Matthew

4:18	163
4:18–22	133
4:19	159
4:21	155
5:1–7:29	54
5:12	54
5:20	163
6:25	163
6:28–30	82
8:30	167
10:1–4	23, 42
10:2–5	26, 57
10:3	133
10:14	60
10:38	174
14:3–12	54
14:5	54
14:27	84
14:28–29	68
14:28–30	89
14:28–31	26, 55, 57
16:5–12	53
16:13–20	39
16:15	186
16:16	29, 46, 144, 185
16:16–19	5, 24, 34, 37, 53, 172
16:17	53, 170
16:18	53
16:21–23	58
16:22	65, 66, 102
16:23	39, 48, 50, 69, 87, 186, 193
16:24	138, 174
16:35	66
17: 1–5	26, 57
17:4	68
17:24–27	26, 57
18:21	26, 57
19:27	26, 44, 57
19:28	23
20:20	145
22:5	82
23:29–34	54
23:37	54
24:51	67
26:6–13	60
26:22	70
26:26–29	59
26:35	65
26:36	82
26:36–46	26
26:37	167
26:37–39	82
26:39	81
26:40–43	83
26:49	84
26:52	90
26:52–53	85
26:53	163
26:57–58	90, 98
26:57–75	188
26:58	92
26:69	94, 99
26:69–75	77, 81
26:73	99–100
26:74	100
26:75	100
27:1	148
27:32	138
27:64	115
28:1	108
28:2–7	107
28:9	108
28:13–15	115
28:16–20	54
28:19	172

Mark

1:16	163
1:16–20	133
1:17	159
1:19	144, 155
1:24	44, 46
3:1–19	26
3:14	42
3:14–15	23

INDICES 215

Mark, continued

3:16–19	57
3:17	36
3:18	133
4:19	167
5:11	167
5:37	26, 57, 144
6:7	42
6:11	60
8:14	53
8:27–30	24, 39,
8:29	29, 46, 185, 186
8:31–33	58
8:32	25, 102
8:33	39, 48, 50, 69, 186
8:34	138, 175
9:2–6	26, 57
9:5	68
10:28	26, 44, 57
10:35–37	145
11:11	42
13:16	82
14:3–9	60
14:19	70
14:22–25	59
14:29–30	89
14:30	77
14:31	65, 66
14:32	82
14:32–42	26
14:33–36	82
14:36	81
14:37–40	83
14:45	84
14:47	85
14:52	152
14:53	98, 99
14:53–65	90
14:53–72	188
14:54	92
14:62	84
14:66	94
14:66–72	77
14:67	99
14:70	100
14:71	101
14:72	99, 100
15:21	138
15:40	92
16:1–2	108
16:5–7	107
16:7	108

Luke

1:13	65
1:15	66
2:44	92
4:34	44, 46
5:1–11	5, 105, 133, 154, 156–158, 163, 192
5:8	26, 57, 84, 144
6:14–16	26, 57
6:15	133
7:36–50	60, 77
8:32	167
8:51	26, 57, 144
9:1–2	23, 42
9:5	60
9:18–21	24, 39
9:20	29, 46, 185, 186
9:23	138, 175
9:28–33	26, 57
9:33	68
10:11	60
11:31	163
12:23	163
12:46	67
14:27	175
15:15	167
15:25	82
17:7	82, 167
18:28	26, 57
19:4	110
22:15–20	59
22:30	23
22:31–34	77
22:32	168, 178
22:33	25

22:34	163	1:34	31, 119
22:39	82	1:35	48
22:39–46	26	1:35–39	30
22:41–42	82	1:35–40	28, 31, 32, 38, 145
22:45	83		
22:47–48	84	1:35–51	23, 25, 29, 47, 50, 190, 194
22:50	86		
22:50–51	85	1:36	166
22:54	92, 93	1:37	48
22:54–62	188	1:37–38	111
22:54–71	90	1:37–40	3
22:55	98, 99	1:38	31, 134
22:56	99	1:38–39	34
22:56–62	77	1:38–43	154
22:59	100	1:39	31, 33, 38, 48
22:62	81, 100	1:40	30
23:26	138	1:40–41	94
23:49	92	1:40–42	5, 33, 37, 163, 190
24:1	108		
24:1–3	108	1:40–44	146
24:4–7	107	1:41	4, 29, 34, 39, 48, 120
24:10	108		
24:12	68, 105, 108, 115	1:41–42	29, 31, 50, 106,
24:30	154	1:42	3, 30, 35, 48, 93, 162, 172, 180, 183
24:34	108		
24:42–43	154		
24:47	172	1:43	97, 188
		1:45	29, 39, 120, 134, 145
John			
1:1	171	1:46	29
1:5	146	1:48–49	134
1:7	3, 124, 141, 154	1:49	39
1:10–11	83	1:49–50	49
1:12	42, 75, 148	1:50	119, 141
1:18	28, 71, 72, 171, 187	1:50–51	38
		2:1	134
1:19	188	2:11	3, 134
1:22–24	5, 84	2:17	120
1:26	30	2:18	84
1:27	5	2:19–22	117
1:29	30, 166	2:22	65, 120, 162
1:29–36	29	2:24	30
1:31	34, 134	3:1–9	98, 165, 189
1:32	5	3:1–20	165
1:33	119	3:2	83

John, continued

3:3–11	77	5:1	132
3:4–9	68	5:2–10	7
3:5	5	5:4–47	43
3:5–12	164	5:6	30
3:12	141	5:10	84
3:14	138	5:10–18	54
3:15–16	179, 191	5:14	132, 140
3:16	3, 193	5:15	106
3:18	3, 38, 154	5:19	74
3:19	146	5:20	70, 166
3:21	134	5:21	62
3:24	5	5:23	193
3:25	38	5:24	179, 191
3:26	176	5:28	5
3:30	31	5:30	87, 102
3:35	70, 166	5:36	74
3:36	179, 191	5:38	3, 41, 141
4:2	5	6:1	132, 134
4:5–26	189	6:2	3, 97, 154
4:7	145	6:4	57
4:7–26	165, 166	6:5–7	135
4:7–29	33	6:5–9	32,
4:9	63	6:6	38
4:9–15	68	6:6–18	135
4:9–26	27	6:8	30
4:18	30	6:11	59
4:19–26	49	6:11–14	149
4:20–23	49	6:13	84
4:21	141, 147, 154	6:15	41
4:22	58	6:17	83, 146
4:23–41	166	6:17–21	147
4:25	34, 38	6:20	84
4:26		6:21	154
4:28	141	6:24	54, 162
4:29	106, 120	6:27	147, 149
4:32–34	149	6:27–30	179
4:38	135	6:29	178
4:39	124, 188	6:30	84, 130, 141
4:39–42	3, 33	6:31–35	41
4:42	51, 100, 101, 154	6:35	191
4:45	162	6:35–47	191
4:46	134	6:35–66	47
4:48	130	6:36	41, 130
		6:38	45
		6:39	5, 88

6:40	3, 178	7:14–20	54
6:41	40	7:18	178
6:44	5, 48, 155	7:28–29	139
6:47	191	7:33	69
6:48	149	7:35	75, 166
6:51–58	5, 9, 41, 169	7:39	65, 120
6:51–70	164	7:45	35
6:52	41	7:52	62
6:53–58	40, 59	7:53–8:11	5
6:54	5, 41	8:12	98, 146, 148
6:57	45, 178, 185	8:13	84
6:59	55	8:14	69
6:60	24, 41, 47, 48, 84	8:17	32, 145
		8:21	69, 75, 84, 169
6:60–66	11	8:22	75
6:63	43, 45, 185	8:22–59	57
6:64	30, 50	8:24	3, 141
6:65	14, 48, 54	8:28	74, 102, 138
6:66	24, 41, 48, 54, 55	8:28–29	87, 102
		8:31	33
6:66–70	10	8:45	43
6:66–71	23, 39	8:56	65
6:67	24, 42, 48, 84	9:1–38	33, 49, 119, 120
6:67–69	97, 192	9:1–41	164
6:67–71	133, 166	9:2–32	189
6:68	19, 30, 43, 45, 144, 183	9:3	134
		9:4	98, 178
6:68–69	3, 4, 5, 14, 18, 30, 33, 37, 38, 42, 50, 64, 70, 88–89, 90, 93, 97, 100, 162, 171, 172, 190, 191, 192, 194	9:5–6	148
		9:17–38	49
		9:18	134, 141
		9:18–10:33	57
		9:22	40
		9:22–38	11
		9:38	43, 100, 101, 124, 154
6:68–71	92		
6:69	30, 46, 48, 63, 69	10:1	192
		10:1–14	90
6:70	46, 48, 67, 70, 79	10:1–15	138
		10:1–18	13
6:70–71	42	10:3	97, 180
7:1	132	10:3–5	166,
7:1–35	57	10:4	3, 51
7:3–5	11	10:4–5	97, 154
7:7	46, 185	10:6	166
7:8	84	10:7	97

INDICES

John, continued

10:9	97
10:11	87, 88, 89, 102
10:11–15	174, 181
10:11–19	62
10:12–13	95
10:14	168, 180
10:14–15	166
10:15	38, 74, 89
10:16	16, 147
10:17	7, 86, 89, 166
10:18	74
10:19–21	120
10:25	43
10:27	3, 51, 97, 135, 154, 188
10:28	88, 179
10:30	72
10:36	45, 72
10:38	3, 28, 42, 50, 74, 154
10:41–42	120
11:1–20	145
11:1–39	166
11:2	5, 67
11:7–8	58
11:8–36	57
11:10	98, 146, 147
11:16	3, 133, 134
11:21–40	118
11:21–45	27
11:25	38, 43
11:26	191
11:27	44, 100, 101, 141, 184
11:27–40	49
11:33	70
11:42	178
11:44	84
11:44–45	116
11:47–53	58
11:48	101
11:52	75, 147
11:55	58
12:1	57
12:2–3	27
12:4	67
12:6	176
12:11	154
12:16	65, 120, 166
12:20	166
12:21–22	32
12:22	30
12:26	3, 97, 154, 188
12:27	70, 74, 84, 86
12:32	117, 138, 155, 159, 194
12:42	101, 124
12:42–43	11
12:46	146, 166
12:48	5, 40
13:1	11, 31, 58, 60, 84
13:1–11	61, 92, 147
13:2	60, 69
13:3–5	151
13:4	62
13:4–5	134
13:4–8	183
13:4–9	102, 152, 164
13:4–10	1, 4, 90, 190
13:4–11	9, 72
13:5–6	9
13:6	11, 63, 64, 65, 144
13:6–7	87, 102
13:6–8	58, 63, 183
13:6–9	57, 193
13:6–10	3, 7, 13, 19
13:6–11	62
13:7	65, 132
13:8	2, 65, 67
13:9	89, 115, 144, 183, 193
13:10	69
13:10–20	68
13:11	69, 84
13:12	162
13:20	135, 140

13:21	84	14:10	28, 33
13:21–25	71	14:11	42, 141
13:21–26	69	14:12	140
13:21–30	92	14:15	75
13:22	131	14:16	38
13:23	28, 32, 58, 72, 170	14:16–17	135
		14:17	178
13:23–25	2, 4, 7, 22, 27, 38, 50, 58, 64, 69, 86, 88, 89, 96, 97, 102, 113, 124, 125, 145, 171, 179, 181, 183, 186–187, 190	14:18	136
		14:21–24	75
		14:22	3, 11, 88
		14:25–26	65, 120
		14:26	38, 135, 169
		14:31	74, 75
		14:36	86
13:23–26	9, 10, 79	15:1	74
13:24	4, 135, 187	15:5	147
13:24–25	91, 189	15:9	75
13:24–26	124	15:10	33
13:25	3, 71	15:12–17	61
13:26–28	74	15:13	89, 102
13:27	69	15:16	169
13:30	83, 146	15:20	38
13:31	162	15:26	135
13:33	76, 148	15:26–27	120, 178
13:33–38	74	15:28	163
13:34	61, 74	16:1–4	84
13:36	3, 77, 87, 97, 102, 138, 170, 188	16:2	88, 101
		16:4–33	83
13:36–37	86, 135, 137, 154, 174, 180	16:5	5, 77
		16:7	135
13:36–38	4, 7, 50, 64, 72, 77, 79, 89, 127, 190	16:7–15	120
		16:13	65
		16:17–19	172
13:37	3, 36, 68, 72, 89, 102, 174	16:32	38, 72, 88, 93, 101
		17:7–8	44
13:38	84, 97, 100, 101, 102, 134, 168, 172	17:9	180
		17:11	72
14:1–17	120	17:12	88, 138, 155
14:1–31	83	17:17–19	135
14:2	145	17:18	135, 140, 169
14:2–3	33	17:19	45
14:5	3, 11, 88	17:20	38, 124, 141
14:6	72	17:21	140
14:8	3, 11	17:26	75
14:8–9	88		

John, continued

17:30	154	18:19–24	98
18:1–2	82	18:20	58
18:1–9	82	18:22	90
18:1–11	101, 103	18:24	5
18:1–12	189	18:25	90, 98
18:1–27	90	18:25–27	25, 90, 98, 101, 158, 190, 193
18:2–3	83	18:26	82, 100
18:3	87, 92	18:26–27	188
18:3–11	67	18:28	83
18:4	58, 84	18:32	5
18:5–8	90, 97	18:36	14, 15, 87
18:6	89	19:6	162
18:7–8	84	19:8	162
18:8	88	19:12	41
18:9	5, 88	19:12–15	58
18:10	2, 67, 68, 73, 85, 115, 183	19:13	35
		19:14	132, 158
18:10–11	3, 7, 15, 64, 66, 79, 84, 152, 164, 183, 190, 193	19:19	158
		19:23	157
		19:25	11, 27, 103, 130
		19:26	19, 73, 74
18:11	2, 74, 81, 87	19:26–27	3, 27, 95, 96, 124, 188
18:11–15	193		
18:13	35, 90	19:27	121
18:13–14	5	19:30	69, 162
18:14	176	19:34	5, 9
18:15	90, 95, 188	19:35	28, 31, 120, 124, 137, 141, 161, 179, 190
18:15–16	2, 3, 4, 7, 10, 22, 27, 28, 38, 92, 102, 105, 110, 113, 124, 134, 135, 145, 181, 183, 186, 187, 190		
		19:40	117
		19:41	82
		19:42	132
		20:1	105, 130, 132
18:15–17	101	20:1–2	107, 194
18:15–27	2, 17, 95, 99, 116, 187	20:1–10	38, 166
		20:2	19, 88, 92, 125, 166
18:16	188		
18:17	2, 91, 188, 193	20:2–4	22
18:17–18	98	20:2–7	144
18:17–25	77	20:2–9	91, 103
18:17–27	4, 7, 13, 73, 152, 181, 183, 189	20:2–10	2, 10, 90, 92, 96, 97, 105, 109, 181, 183, 186, 188, 190
18:18	98		
18:18–24	90		

20:2–20	28	21:1–11	143, 157, 190
20:3–4	68	21:1–14	7, 107
20:3–5	110	21:1–25	25
20:3–10	3, 4, 17, 27, 108	21:2	73, 144
		21:2–4	88, 98, 125
20:4	110	21:2–11	109, 190
20:4–10	135	21:2–25	190
20:5	114, 117	21:3	83, 146
20:5–8	74	21:3–4	133
20:6	3, 68, 154	21:3–7	194
20:6–8	22, 179, 187	21:4	3, 98, 189
20:6–10	94, 115	21:4–6	147
20:8	19, 117, 118, 189	21:5	42, 145, 148
20:9	65, 105	21:6–11	163
20:10	174	21:7	3, 4, 7, 10, 22, 28, 38, 50, 55, 62, 64, 66, 71, 73, 89, 93, 96, 97, 106, 113, 115, 119, 125, 145, 148, 149, 153, 159, 176, 188, 189, 194
20:11	107, 157		
20:14	116, 134, 148		
20:14–17	106, 130		
20:14–18	108		
20:15	82		
20:15–18	107, 108		
20:16	159		
20:16–18	130, 134	21:7–8	91, 103, 149–150
20:17	107, 139, 178	21:8	153
20:19	132, 159	21:9–11	154
20:19–23	130	21:11	3, 4, 7, 12, 38, 50, 88, 113, 138, 172, 180, 183
20:19–28	147, 148		
20:20	148		
20:20–23	136	21:14	62
20:21	136, 139, 140, 172	21:15	163
20:21–23	140, 146, 169, 188	21:15–16	166
20:21–24	132	21:15–17	3, 4, 7, 9, 48, 75, 106, 111, 113, 138, 159, 162, 163, 169, 172, 180, 183, 190, 192, 193, 194
20:24	12, 23, 42, 133, 134, 166, 190, 191		
20:25	65, 130		
20:25–26	146		
20:25–29	119, 130, 132		
20:28	44	21:15–19	4, 12, 38, 53, 72, 90
20:28–29	49, 129, 136		
20:29	43, 129	21:15–25	161
20:30	120, 130	21:16	165, 167
20:30–31	140–141	21:17	68, 165, 168, 180, 193
20:31	120		
21:1–4	7	21:18	62, 77
21:2	133	21:18–19	3, 12, 36, 50,

John, continued

21:18–29	67, 69, 76, 79, 89, 127, 173, 181, 183
21:18–22	7, 14, 43, 113, 172, 190
21:18–23	9, 13, 161
21:19	28, 169, 192
21:19–22	97, 124, 154, 183, 188, 192, 193
21:20	73, 171, 176, 179
21:20–22	3, 6, 169
21:20–23	3, 4, 11, 28, 136, 177, 183
21:20–25	175
21:21	136, 176
21:21–22	177
21:21–25	27
21:22	28
21:22–23	38, 136
21:23	161, 176, 178
21:24	3, 28, 31, 137, 137, 190
21:24–25	188
21:25	129, 130, 179

Acts

1:7	172
1:16–22	168
1:19	92
2:14	92
2:14–40	168
2:37	178
4:8–12	168
4:10	92
4:16	92
4:25–28	83
7:45	93
9:8	93
9:37	69
9:42	92
10:11	116
10:34–44	168
11:5–17	168
13:38	92
13:51	60
19:17	92
20:28	167
22:16	59
28:22	92
28:28	92

Romans

1:19	92
14:15	167
16:1	178

1 Corinthians

1:10	178
3:1–2	168
6:11	59
6:20	175
9:7	167
15:5	108
15:6	178
15:51	137

2 Corinthians

9:13	175

Galatians

1:2	178

Ephesians

4:30	167
5:26	59

Philippians

2:7	60

1 Thessalonians

4:15	137

1 Timothy

3:1–7	67

Hebrews

5:12–14	168

10:22   59

James
2:26   189

1 Peter
2:12   175
4:16   175
5:2   167
5:3   167
5:9   178

1 John
2:1   75
2:12   75
2:22   100
2:28   75
3:1   148
3:7   75
3:11   61
3:16   61, 89, 174
3:18   75
4:4   75
4:7–12   61
5:21   75

2 John
1:5   61

Revelation
1:17   84
2:28   148
16:15   152
18:10–17   92
21:8   67
22:16   148
22:19   67

www.ingramcontent.com/pod-product-compliance
Lightning Source LLC
Chambersburg PA
CBHW021808220426
43662CB00006B/225